D0190823

INSIDE THE
CAMPAIGN FINANCE
BATTLE

INSIDE THE

CAMPAIGN FINANCE
BATTLE

*Court Testimony
on the New Reforms*

Anthony Corrado, Thomas E. Mann,
and Trevor Potter

Editors

BROOKINGS INSTITUTION PRESS
Washington, D.C.

ABOUT BROOKINGS

The Brookings Institution is a private nonprofit organization devoted to research, education, and publication on important issues of domestic and foreign policy. Its principal purpose is to bring knowledge to bear on current and emerging policy problems. The Institution maintains a position of neutrality on issues of public policy. Interpretations or conclusions in Brookings publications should be understood to be solely those of the authors.

Library of Congress Cataloging-in-Publication data available
ISBN 0-8157-1583-8

9 8 7 6 5 4 3 2 1

The paper used in this publication meets minimum requirements of the American National Standard for Information Sciences—Permanence of Paper for Printed Library Materials: ANSI Z39.48-1992.

Typeset in Adobe Garamond

Composition by Cynthia Stock
Silver Spring, Maryland

Printed by R. R. Donnelley
Harrisonburg, Virginia

Contents

Editors' Note   ix
Introduction   1

PART I
Political Parties

ANALYSES OF ACADEMIC EXPERTS

The Rise of Soft Money ▪ Thomas E. Mann   17
Parties versus Interest Groups ▪ Sidney M. Milkis   40
Why Soft Money Has Not Strengthened Parties ▪   49
   Jonathan S. Krasno and Frank Sorauf
Why Soft Money Has Strengthened Parties ▪ Raymond J. La Raja   69
The Need for Federal Regulation of State Party Activity ▪   97
   Donald Green

POLITICIANS AND PARTY OFFICIALS

A Senate Democrat's Perspective ▪ David Boren   116
A Senate Republican's Perspective ▪ Alan K. Simpson   119
Mobilizing Voters: The Coordinated Campaign ▪ Gail Stoltz   122
State Party Activity and the BCRA ▪ Kathleen Bowler   125
State Party Activity under the Levin Amendment ▪ Mark Brewer 137
Role of Federal Officials in State Party Fund-Raising ▪   143
   Mitch McConnell

PART II
Issue Advocacy

SCHOLARLY ANALYSES

Party and Interest Group Electioneering in Federal Elections ▪
  David B. Magleby   147
Electioneering Communications in Recent Elections:
  The Case for a New Standard ▪ Kenneth M. Goldstein   175
Issue Advocacy and the Integrity of the Political Process ▪
  Jonathan S. Krasno and Frank Sorauf   189
Rebuttal to the Expert Reports of Kenneth M. Goldstein and
  Jonathan S. Krasno and Frank J. Sorauf ▪ James L. Gibson   201
Rebuttal to Gibson ▪ Jonathan S. Krasno   221

VIEWS OF THE ADVOCATES:
PARTIES, ORGANIZED GROUPS, AND POLITICAL CONSULTANTS

The National Association of Manufacturers' Advertising
  Helps Lobby Congress ▪ Paul R. Huard   237
Why the Chamber of Commerce Runs Issue Ads ▪ R. Bruce Josten   242
How the Reform Act Adversely Affects the Associated Builders
  and Contractors ▪ Edward L. Monroe   246
A Practitioner Looks at How Issue Groups Select and Target
  Federal Candidates ▪ Rocky Pennington   250
How Issue Ads Are Designed to Target Federal Candidates
  without "Express Advocacy" ▪ Douglas L. Bailey   252
A Consultant's View on How Issue Ads Shaped a
  Congressional Election ▪ Terry S. Beckett   254

PART III
Public Opinion and Corruption

EVIDENCE FROM PUBLIC OPINION RESEARCH

Public Attitudes toward Campaign Finance Practice
  and Reform ▪ Robert Y. Shapiro   259
Public Views of Party Soft Money ▪
  Mark Mellman and Richard Wirthlin   266
The Reform Act Will Not Reduce the Appearance of Corruption
  in American Politics ▪ Whitfield Ayres   270
Rebuttal to Ayres ▪ Robert Y. Shapiro   278
Campaign Contributions, the Appearance of Corruption,
  and Trust in Government ▪ David M. Primo   285

Donor Perspectives

Large Contributions Provide Unequal Access ▪ Robert Rozen   297
Corporate America Contributes Soft Money under Pressure ▪
    Gerald Greenwald   300
Large Contributions Are Given to Influence Legislation ▪
    Robert W. Hickmott   302
Elected Officials Often Used to Obtain Large Donations
    for the Parties ▪ Wade Randlett   305
Why I Participate in a Corrupt System ▪ Peter L. Buttenwieser   308
How My Soft-Money Contributions Have Helped Elect
    Good Federal Candidates ▪ Steven T. Kirsch   315

Officeholder Perspectives

How the Senate Was Corrupted by Soft Money ▪ Paul Simon   317
Consequences of Members Soliciting Soft Money ▪
    Warren Rudman   319
A Cosponsor's Perspective: Why I Don't Raise Soft Money
    for the Party ▪ Christopher Shays   322
Congress Is Mired in Corrupt Soft Money ▪ John McCain   324
Parties Support Members Who Fund-Raise ▪ Dale Bumpers   328
Corruption Is Not an Issue in American Politics ▪
    Mitch McConnell   329

Party Chair Perspectives

Parties Undermined by Soft Money ▪ Donald Fowler   330
Parties Weakened by Appearance of Corruption ▪
    William E. Brock   332

An Explanation
of This Volume

The testimony submitted by some of the country's most knowledgeable political scientists and most experienced politicians in the legal challenge to the Bipartisan Campaign Reform Act (McCain-Feingold/Shays-Meehan) constitutes an invaluable body of knowledge about the complexities of campaign finance and the role of money in our political system. Unfortunately, only the relatively few lawyers, political scientists, and other practitioners actually involved in the litigation have seen most of this writing until now.

Our goal with this volume is to make testimony in this historic case available to a more general readership. We three editors have all been deeply involved in researching and analyzing campaign finance issues for a number of years and have been supporters of reform efforts and defenders of the new law. However, we have taken care to ensure that this book selects the best of the material submitted by both sides of the debate: our credibility and success as editors depend on our ability to give the reader a fair, but concise, summary of the political finance questions. Some of those excerpted here are well known to students of political science or observers of national politics, others are less visible political practitioners with particular inside knowledge they have shared in this court case. What these witnesses all have in common is a willingness to provide the court with sound empirical and practical information on political finance and the possible effects of the new legislation.

For reasons of length, we excerpted only portions of the fact and expert witness reports included in this volume. We lightly edited each excerpt for consistency of citation form, grammar, and punctuation. All court filings

in the *McConnell* v. *FEC* lawsuit are available in full on the Campaign
Legal Center's website (www.campaignlegalcenter.org). The institutional
affiliations listed for each academic contributor are provided for identification purposes only and in no way reflect any endorsements of or support for the work underlying these reports.

Producing this volume from a court record of tens of thousands of
pages in only the few months since the record was closed in late 2002 has
been an enormous task. The Campaign Legal Center, a Washington-based
nonprofit associated with the Campaign and Media Program at the University of Utah, served as the organizing entity for this volume. Its work
could not have been accomplished without the heroic efforts of Marianne
Viray, managing director of the Campaign Legal Center, who supervised
each stage of the production of this book. Mark Glaze and Glen Shor,
associate legal counsel of the Legal Center, and Lana Price, associate managing director, also made significant contributions to this work.

We are also grateful for the extraordinary efforts of Janet Walker, managing editor at the Brookings Institution Press, editors Vicky Macintyre
and Tanjam Jacobson, and Larissa Davis, research/web assistant at Brookings, which made possible the expedited publication schedule necessary to
produce this volume in a timely way.

Funding for this volume was provided by The Pew Charitable Trusts
through the Coalition to Promote Civic Dialogue on Campaign Finance
Program at Colby College. The opinions expressed in this book are those
of the editors or the original authors and do not necessarily reflect the view
of The Pew Charitable Trusts or Colby College. Additional funding for
the Campaign Legal Center's participation in this project was provided by
Straight Talk America, Senator John McCain's former political action
committee, which distributed its funds to charities and other organizations in December 2002.

ANTHONY CORRADO
THOMAS MANN
TREVOR POTTER

INSIDE THE
CAMPAIGN FINANCE
BATTLE

Introduction

Congress last year enacted the Bipartisan Campaign Reform Act of 2002, the first major revision of federal campaign finance law in a generation. The sponsors and supporters of this legislation describe the statute as a long overdue and urgently needed package of reforms designed to restore the system of campaign finance envisioned by Congress when it adopted the Federal Election Campaign Act (FECA) in the 1970s. Its purpose, they argue, is to repair egregious tears in the regulatory fabric that rendered utterly ineffective long-standing prohibitions on corporate and union treasury financing of federal elections and disclosure requirements for federal electioneering. The new law thus represents a necessary response to the changes that have taken place since the FECA was established and seeks to preserve the integrity of the political process by safeguarding it from the corruptive influence of unregulated political contributions.

Opponents portray the law as much more ambitious and ominous. In their view, the reform act represents nothing less than a wholesale assault on protected First Amendment speech and rights of political association. They claim that the law's major restrictions would prohibit or discourage many individuals and organized groups from participating in federal elections, which would reduce the amount of information available to the electorate and serve to further protect incumbents, who are already greatly advantaged in the electoral process. Opponents also claim that the law violates fundamental principles of federalism, since it regulates state party committees, as well as some activities between national, state, and local party committees and thus interferes in the operations and associational efforts of party organizations. In short, they argue, the reform act unconstitutionally limits political speech and participation and thereby undermines the vitality of the political process.

Behind these heated arguments, both sides implicitly acknowledge that the campaign finance system has changed dramatically over the past decade. In recent election cycles, national political parties, including the congressional party campaign committees, have become increasingly dependent on the rapidly rising sums of money received in unlimited donations—commonly known as soft money—from corporations, unions, and individuals. Prominent elected officials, including presidents and Senate and House party leaders, have become actively involved in raising these unregulated funds, often soliciting donors who have interests before Congress or federal administrative agencies. State parties have been more involved in activities that affect federal elections, especially activities that channel soft dollars into electioneering efforts designed to influence the outcome of federal races. Moreover, a substantial portion of the soft money raised by national and state party committees is being used to finance the broadcast of "issue advertisements," which are targeted on the constituencies of specific candidates and crafted to influence voter behavior. Interest groups are also turning to issue advertising as a campaign weapon of choice, since these ads can be financed with unregulated funds and are not subject to public disclosure. This option has provided a diverse array of groups and organizations, including tax-exempt organizations and ad hoc political committees, with a means of becoming more involved in federal elections. As a result, the financial system envisioned by the FECA, which primarily consisted of limited and fully disclosed funds principally controlled by candidates, party committees, and political action committees, has been replaced by a much more extensive and opaque system of funding whose participants and flows of money were not anticipated when the post-Watergate regulatory structure was erected.

Proponents and opponents of the reform act took away very different lessons from these developments. Proponents saw the collapse of a regulatory structure designed to limit corruption or the appearance of corruption. They viewed the often unintended consequences of the FECA as a testament to the need for stronger regulations and more effective and vigilant means of enforcement. They also recognized the need to consider possible constitutional challenges and potential opportunities for circumventing regulations when framing reforms. A principal lesson advocates of reform drew from the experience of the FECA was that any new statute produced by Congress should be less susceptible to the types of subterfuge that had undermined the efficacy of previous regulatory efforts. They did not want to pass a new law only to see it quickly succumb to the fate suffered by the FECA. New regulations were thus needed not only to address the immediate problems of soft money and issue advocacy, but also to "head off at the pass" any alternative approaches that might be used to continue these practices by other means.

By contrast, opponents viewed the changes taking place in the campaign finance system as inevitable and constitutionally protected adaptations to earlier, often ill-advised attempts to restrict the flow of money in politics. From their perspective, campaign funding, like water, would always seek its own level, and the efforts to constrain campaign spending had forced large amounts of money into undisclosed and less controllable approaches. Further regulation would simply exacerbate this problem. FECA experience thus suggested the futility of efforts designed to promote more stringent regulation of political spending.

After a fiercely contested and highly divisive seven-year partisan legislative battle, the proponents of reform finally prevailed in Congress. For three successive Congresses, campaign finance legislation was a major issue on the legislative agenda, but each time it was defeated through a filibuster in the Senate. By 1999 it became clear that a majority in both houses favored reform, but proponents lacked the 60 votes needed to defeat a filibuster. A breakthrough was finally achieved in 2002. The Senate initially passed S. 27, known as the McCain-Feingold legislation for its principal sponsors, Republican John McCain of Arizona and Democrat Russell Feingold of Wisconsin, in March 2001 on a 59 to 41 vote. Following a long delay and extensive parliamentary maneuvering, the House responded by passing H.R. 2356, the companion bill known as Shays-Meehan, for its principal sponsors, Republican Christopher Shays of Connecticut and Democrat Martin Meehan of Massachusetts, on February 14, 2002, by a vote of 240 to 189. On March 20, 2002, the Senate approved the House-passed measure by a 60-40 vote, thereby avoiding a conference to reconcile differences between the two bills. Despite expressing "reservations" about the legislation, President George W. Bush signed the reform act into law on March 27, 2002.

The extraordinary legislative odyssey of the Bipartisan Campaign Reform Act of 2002 is a fascinating story with numerous subplots. These relate to the tenacity of the congressional sponsors, the steadfastness of a small group of moderate Republicans who supported reform, a decision by proponents to pursue a scaled-down reform agenda, the availability of new policy-relevant research that helped to define specific regulatory approaches, Senator John McCain's emphasis on reform during his quest for the Republican presidential nomination in 2000, Democratic gains in the Senate later that year, the surprising and consequential efforts by Democratic leaders Tom Daschle and Richard Gephardt to pass the legislation, and an unusual level of pragmatism within the reform community. These factors combined to alter the legislative dynamics in favor of reform. Even so, success ultimately rested on the decision of a few senators who had supported filibusters in the past but declared that they would no longer continue to support such an effort to block reform legislation. With a successful filibuster no longer an option, majority will prevailed, and the bill was finally adopted.

As with many legislative victories, however, congressional passage of the new campaign finance bill was as much the beginning of the journey as the end. The signing of the reform act into law by President Bush marked the successful conclusion of the legislative stage of the fight. It was also the beginning of a monumental effort to frame the factual and legal issues implicated by the act for certain review by the U.S. Supreme Court. This volume highlights certain aspects of this legal battle and insights about modern campaign finance practices that have emerged in its course.

THE LAWSUIT

A normal aspect of public policymaking, particularly with the advent of broader government regulation of public and private sector activity in the twentieth century, is for major legislative enactments to be challenged in court. Since the days of *Marbury* v. *Madison,* judicial review of the nation's laws has been thought fundamental to the peaceful resolution of policy disputes, and to the provision of adequate public notice of what new laws require and forbid. In more recent times, judicial review has served to turn the courts into another arena of legislative or policy conflict. The role of the judiciary as the ultimate arbiter of policy disputes is especially relevant with regard to campaign finance legislation. Since the Supreme Court's seminal explication of basic campaign finance principles in *Buckley* v. *Valeo* in 1976, campaign finance law has been inextricably linked to First Amendment issues. Consequently, campaign finance law inevitably presents hotly contested First Amendment questions, with opposing sides taking starkly different views of the extent to which the regulation of political fund-raising and spending is constitutionally permissible. Given the controversial legal issues, myriad political interests, and massive stakes involved in the movement for meaningful campaign finance reform, the law's framers fully anticipated that the reform act would promptly be challenged in court. In this, they were not disappointed.

It is no exaggeration to say that the reform act was under court review almost from the moment President George W. Bush—without ceremony, without its congressional sponsors, and with only two observers—signed it into law. Senator Mitch McConnell (Republican of Kentucky), one of the leading opponents of the law, announced weeks before the bill was passed by the Senate that he was preparing a complaint against the proposed law. The formal enactment thus sparked a race to the courthouse doors by McConnell and dozens of other plaintiffs, who challenged the constitutionality of virtually every aspect of the act.

Perhaps the best way of understanding the potentially seismic effect of the law on the nation's electoral practices is to consider the unlikely bedfellows who coalesced around the shared goal of seeing the law struck down. For the most part, the plaintiffs in the case replicate the coalition of interests that for decades have fought various incarnations of reform legislation in Congress. They span the political spectrum from the Republican National Committee to the California Democratic Party and range in ideology from the National Rifle Association and major right-to-life groups to the American Civil Liberties Union and the National Voting Rights Institute (the last objecting only to an increase in the individual hard-money contribution limit). By the May 2002 deadline for filing complaints, eighty-four plaintiffs had filed eleven actions with the U.S. District Court for the District of Columbia, the federal trial court with jurisdiction over the statute.

The case also includes an unusually large number of defendants. Because the reform act is a statute enforced by the Federal Election Commission (FEC) and the U.S. Department of Justice, those agencies are the named defendants in the suit. The act's principal congressional sponsors—Senators John McCain, Russell Feingold, Olympia Snowe (Republican of Maine), and James Jeffords (Independent of Vermont), along with Representatives Christopher Shays and Marty Meehan—are "intervenor-defendants" in the suit, with the same legal prerogatives as the named defendants.

The plaintiffs and defendants paint vastly different pictures of the constitutional framework that is appropriate for an analysis of campaign finance legislation and the reform act's placement within that framework. The defendants believe the reform act is an attempt to restore meaning and effect to contribution limitations and spending prohibitions that the Supreme Court had previously declared constitutionally valid mechanisms of preventing corruption and the appearance of corruption. As the plaintiffs see it, this law departs from Supreme Court precedent and violates the First Amendment in regulating activities that, in their view, exclusively or primarily affect state elections and in imposing financing source prohibitions and disclosure requirements with respect to advertisements that do not expressly advocate an election result.

Whether viewed in terms of the constitutional issues involved, the number of participants, or the sheer size of the trial record, this litigation plainly constitutes the most important campaign finance case since the Supreme Court issued its decision in *Buckley* v. *Valeo* more than twenty-five years ago. Its ultimate result will establish anew—and potentially reorder—the way in which federal campaigns are conducted. Although this book will not attempt a narrative account of that litigation, some background discussion of the unique history of the *McConnell* case is helpful in understanding the nature and importance of the materials to follow. Given the importance of the reform act, Congress both anticipated and desired judicial review. Quite aside from the overarching legal issues, the statute raises a long series of practical questions about implementation for the regulated community: candidates, political parties, and interest groups, among others. The legislature therefore thought it essential for these issues to be resolved as quickly as possible to provide proper notice to political actors and to minimize disruption of ensuing election cycles. With these concerns in mind, lawmakers included in the text of the law a number of provisions designed to achieve fast and final review.

First, the law invokes a provision of the procedural rules for federal courts that establishes a process for expediting court review of statutes that, in Congress's judgment, require especially prompt resolution. Under this provision, the U.S. District Court for the District of Columbia—the trial court with jurisdiction over challenges to congressional enactments—seats a special three-judge panel, composed of two district court judges and a presiding circuit court judge, to conduct a trial. Under the federal rules, if this panel's decision on the merits of the law is appealed, the case departs from the normal course of review, bypassing the U.S. Court of Appeals for the District of Columbia altogether and proceeding directly to the U.S. Supreme Court. As a consequence of the legislative branch's constitutional authority to control the High Court's appellate jurisdiction, the justices are obliged to hear the matter.

Second, the statute includes language, highly unusual in a congressional enactment, expressly directing both the three-judge panel and the Supreme Court to "advance on the docket and to expedite to the greatest possible extent the disposition of the action and appeal." The text further requires the Federal Election Commission to expedite its implementation rulemakings. The act itself took effect the day after the elections held on November 5, 2002.

In order to meet the congressional mandate for expedited review, the trial court—consisting of presiding Circuit Court Judge Karen LeCraft Henderson, an appointee of President George H. W. Bush; District Court Judge Colleen Kollar-Kotelly, an appointee of President Bill Clinton; and District Court Judge Richard J. Leon, an appointee of President George W. Bush—took as one of its first steps the consolidation of the eleven separate complaints. That one combined action, now known as *McConnell* v. *FEC*, presents to the panel all issues brought by all plaintiffs in a single case.

The panel resolved an early tactical skirmish between the plaintiffs and defendants by deciding that *McConnell* v. *FEC* would be, in litigation parlance, a "paper trial." In both civil and criminal litigation, a trial court typically hears actual testimony from live witnesses in the courtroom, a most time-consuming process. In the interest of expedition and the need for a complete factual record, however, the panel decided to forgo live witnesses and a traditional courtroom trial in favor of written testimony.

That critical decision provided the reason and raw material for this book. As a consequence of the court's approach, the parties have gathered testimony from the most comprehensive array of citizens on core campaign finance questions since *Buckley* v. *Valeo*. The purpose of this testimony is to provide evidence establishing the factual predicate for the legal arguments advanced by the parties.

This written testimony was provided in two forms: fact witness declarations and expert witness reports. Fact witnesses testify as to their personal knowledge of facts one of the parties asserts; for example, former members of Congress filed declarations describing their own experiences as active participants in the U.S. campaign finance system. Expert witnesses testify as to their informed opinion on practical campaign finance matters within their own area of expertise; hence leading political scientists have testified on the effect of soft money on the political process or on the influence of issue advocacy advertising on the outcomes of federal elections.

The substantial body of fact statements and expert reports produced for this trial constitute a rich portrait of contemporary campaign finance practices, the way in which those practices developed, and the likely implications of the new law for this regime. The purpose of this volume is to make public this body of information about modern American political

practices. These declarations by many of the country's most knowledgeable political scientists, politicians, and campaign practitioners provide a
snapshot of state-of-the-art political practices, and of the range of opinions on the consequences of those practices, both real and potential.

We have attempted to select some of the best material from both sides
of this debate. Some of the selections were written by well-known experts
in political science, observers of national politics, and politicians. Others
were contributed by practitioners with particular inside knowledge they
have testified to in the *McConnell* case. What they have in common is a
willingness to provide the court with practical information on political
finance and their thoughts on the possible effects of the new legislation.

In selecting materials for this volume, we have not emphasized the constitutional issues in the litigation. Those interested in pursuing the constitutional debates can plumb the voluminous briefs submitted by
plaintiffs and defendants, as well as the decision of the three-judge panel
and, ultimately, of the Supreme Court. (These may be found at www.
campaignlegalcenter.org, which also contains the full, unedited text of all
of the testimony excerpted in this book, as well as the expert and fact witness reports not included.) Instead, it is our intention that by drawing on
the factual record produced as part of the litigation, this volume will bring
the reader to a more complete understanding of the various, often competing, views of the nature and effects of today's campaign practices. We
also hope it provides readers with a basis for making their own judgments
about the virtue of those practices and of the desirability and efficacy of
the reform act.

KEY ISSUES

This book is organized around the twin pillars of the reform act: restrictions on party soft money and on issue advocacy. It also examines in detail
the evidence of corruption or the appearance of corruption associated with
soft money and issue advocacy advertising, in light of the Supreme Court's
historic reliance on evidence of corruption to justify campaign finance
regulation.

The act bans the raising of soft money by national parties and federal
officeholders or candidates. It also restricts soft-money spending by state
and local parties on what are defined as "federal election activities." A provision of the act, known as the Levin Amendment, does allow for some
use of limited soft-money donations for selected federal election activities
by state and local parties.

The act also regulates a class of "issue advocacy" broadcast ads, labeled "electioneering communications." Political advertisements that refer to a clearly identified candidate for federal office, are targeted on the constituency of that candidate, and are broadcast within thirty days of a primary or sixty days of a general election must be financed and disclosed in a manner consistent with existing federal election law. The act prohibits corporations and unions from spending treasury funds, directly or indirectly, for such electioneering communications. It also requires that individuals and groups permitted to finance these communications disclose disbursements in excess of $10,000 and the identity of donors of $1,000 or more.

The reform act contains numerous additional provisions. Most notably, it treats coordinated electioneering communications as contributions to and expenditures by a candidate or party, increases the hard-money amounts individuals can contribute to candidates and parties, raises limits on individual and party support of a candidate whose opponent exceeds certain levels of personal campaign spending (known as the Millionaires' Amendment), and prohibits contributions by minors. Each of these provisions, like the ban on soft money and the restrictions on issue advocacy, is subject to constitutional challenge. But most of the debate surrounding the bill's passage has centered on party soft money and issue advocacy and whether they corrupt the political process. Consequently, we have divided the volume into three major sections: political parties, issue advocacy, and public opinion and corruption. The expert and fact witness reports selected and excerpted for this volume provide information about and insights into some of the most important and contentious issues in the campaign finance debate.

POLITICAL PARTIES. Virtually all of the contributors agree that parties play essential roles in American democracy—in aggregating public preferences, organizing teams of candidates and elected officials, and providing a means of democratic accountability. But there is substantial disagreement over whether the rise of soft money and issue advocacy has strengthened or weakened political parties. The disputes center on such questions as whether state parties are independent actors and genuine partners or mere instruments and funding conduits of national parties and federal officeholders; how much soft money has been used for party building and grassroots activities and how much for broadcast advertising on behalf of specific federal candidates; and whether parties dilute the influence of large donors or facilitate their access to policymakers.

Answers to these questions in turn shape assessments of the provisions of the reform act directly affecting party finance and forecasts of how parties will fare in this new regulatory environment. Will national party committees be able to compensate for the abolition of soft money by raising substantial additional amounts of hard money? Will the new restrictions on state parties dealing with federal election activity constrain their efforts on behalf of state and local candidates? Will parties be put at a disadvantage in comparison with interest groups? Will large soft-money donors (corporations, unions, and individuals) find indirect and less accountable ways of financing federal campaign activities?

GROUPS AND ISSUE ADVOCACY. One of the guarantees of the First Amendment, and a fundamental element of American democracy, is "the right of the people peaceably to assemble, and to petition the Government for a redress of grievances." Forming associations, articulating positions on public policy issues, and lobbying elected officials are central to the democratic process. The government's interest in regulating these activities is limited and the constraints are appropriately high. Nonetheless, the Supreme Court has upheld restrictions on corporate and union treasury funding in federal elections. And in *Buckley* v. *Valeo*, the Court upheld source restrictions and disclosure requirements for independent expenditures by groups for communications that expressly advocate the election or defeat of a candidate for federal office.

The explosion in recent years of election-oriented issue advocacy by groups—communications that support or attack candidates without expressly advocating their election or defeat—has engendered heated debates about the need for and legitimacy of regulation of such communications. Are groups using the cover of issue advocacy to campaign for and against candidates with corporate and union funds and without disclosure? Do such communications inevitably advance both lobbying and election interests? Did the Court leave any constitutional space for Congress to define and regulate a category of electioneering communications that goes beyond its express advocacy standard? Will the reform act's requirement that such communications be financed with regulated funds that are publicly disclosed have a chilling effect on speech and diminish the robust debate about issues that enlivens our democracy?

Supporters of the reform act have rested much of their case for the regulation of electioneering communications on a body of new research on television ads sponsored by candidates, parties, and groups. Opponents have challenged the methodological underpinnings of this research. These scholarly debates are represented by the statements of expert witnesses contained in this volume. Additional testimony by advocates—party and group officials and political consultants—provides more grist for the mill.

CORRUPTION. The motivations of proponents of campaign finance reform vary greatly. Some want to reduce the amount of money in politics and to slow the money chase among officeholders and candidates. Others are concerned primarily with increasing the competitiveness of elections by reducing the financial advantage of incumbents and boosting the campaign resources of challengers. Yet others are motivated by a belief that private donations to public officials, especially very large ones, create inevitable conflicts of interest that taint the policymaking process.

The Supreme Court, in *Buckley* v. *Valeo,* identified only one of these motivations—corruption or its appearance—as a compelling constitutional basis for regulating money in federal elections. The Court's conception of corruption went beyond quid pro quo exchanges of campaign contributions for public favors. These transactions, including bribery and extortion, were already proscribed in criminal statutes. Instead, the Court suggested that its conception incorporated the corrupting potential of privileged access and undue influence of donors, and the corrosive effects on the political system of the widespread appearance of such corruption.

It is no surprise, therefore, that supporters of the reform act have tried to demonstrate the corrupting effects of soft money and issue advocacy, while opponents have challenged those assertions and marshaled their own evidence that public beliefs about special interest influence and the corrupting effects of campaign contributions are not linked to soft money and are unlikely to change as a consequence of the reform act. Reports submitted by witnesses for plaintiffs and defendants provide personal testimony and systematic evidence on these points of contention.

CRITERIA FOR INCLUSION

As we have indicated, the materials gathered as part of the "paper trial" of *McConnell* v. *FEC* are voluminous. Only a fraction of these documents could fit within the covers of this volume. Our primary objective—to shed new light on campaign finance practices central to the congressional debate on the reform act and to the litigation challenging its constitutionality—led to several initial decisions. As noted previously, we chose not to include documents that focused primarily on the constitutional arguments.

In one important respect, we faced a limitation set by others. By order of the district court panel overseeing the litigation, a seal of confidentiality was placed on some of the materials gathered in the case, mostly on the plaintiffs' side. While that seal may be lifted at some point, it will come too late to allow us to include several interesting documents in this volume.

With these exceptions, our criteria for selection included whether the documents provided new and interesting information about campaign finance practices; if together they constituted a rough balance of arguments and evidence from plaintiffs and defendants; and if the testimony could be excerpted and edited to fit the confines of this volume. Filings with the Court in most cases have been excerpted only in part, for reasons of length, and lightly edited, where appropriate, for consistency of citation form, punctuation, and grammar. The text of the original filings of *all* the documents included in this volume may be found in full on the Campaign Legal Center's website (www.campaignlegalcenter.org).

Yet even these simple rules were sometimes difficult to follow. Balance was hard to achieve when the documents produced by the two sides reflected in part their different strategies in challenging and defending provisions of the reform act.

For example, the defendants produced voluminous expert testimony on television ads by groups, parties, and candidates, and on the likely impact of the electioneering communications provisions of the reform act. The plaintiffs chose to put forward a single expert witness on this subject, one whose purpose was to challenge the conduct of the research and the findings from it offered by the defendant team. Consequently, our selections of expert testimony in this section are weighted toward the defendants.

Similarly, much of the defendant testimony on the rise of soft money and its use in federal elections was not directly contested by the plaintiffs. Instead, those challenging the soft-money provisions of the new law focused on its alleged overbreadth, particularly its restrictions on state and local parties and the constraints on national party officials in working effectively with them. Our selections reflect these distinctive litigation strategies.

Another example is evident in the section on corruption. While the plaintiffs forcefully challenged with experts of their own the defendant testimony based on public opinion evidence of the appearance of corruption, they generally chose not to offer fact witnesses on corruption that paralleled those of the defendants.

We have done the best we can to compensate for the imbalances in material produced as a result of these litigation strategies. The reader can review the entire body of materials on the Internet and decide how well we have succeeded. In any case, our purpose is not to reargue the constitutional case but to share with a broader public audience the fascinating insights into contemporary campaign finance practices produced as part of this landmark litigation.

PART I
Political Parties

17
ANALYSES OF ACADEMIC EXPERTS

116
POLITICIANS AND PARTY OFFICIALS

The Rise of Soft Money

THOMAS E. MANN

Thomas E. Mann is the W. Averell Harriman Chair and Senior Fellow in Governance Studies at the Brookings Institution. His scholarly work has focused on elections, parties, campaign finance, Congress, and policymaking. He served as an expert witness for the defendants of the new law: the Department of Justice, the Federal Election Commission (FEC), and the primary congressional sponsors of the legislation.

Mann's full report provides a description and analysis of the development of federal campaign finance law and practice leading up to the enactment of the Bipartisan Campaign Reform Act (BCRA). This excerpt begins with a summary of the central features of the regulatory regime defined by the 1974 amendments to the Federal Election Campaign Act (FECA), which included long-standing bans on corporate and union treasury funding of federal campaigns. It then traces how that regime was undermined by the emergence of party soft money and of electioneering under the guise of issue advocacy. Mann attaches particular importance to a series of administrative rulings by the FEC that sanctioned separate federal and nonfederal accounts for national party committees.

The report documents how the soft-money system was transformed in the 1996 election cycle after President Bill Clinton and his political consultant, Dick Morris, decided to mount an ambitious political advertising campaign under the cover of issue advocacy, financed in large part with unregulated party soft-money funds. Republicans and outside interest groups followed suit, leading to an explosion in the demand for soft money and a striking shift in the electoral strategies of interest groups in the 1998 and 2000 elections.

Mann then argues that the collapse of the FECA regime transformed the role of political parties, elected officials, corporations, and unions in the electoral process and created glaring conflicts of interest and a widespread perception of corruption in the policy process.

The rise of television and the increasingly candidate-centered nature of federal election campaigns after World War II led to a substantial increase in campaign costs and growing concerns about political financing. But it was not until the early 1970s that Congress began to wrestle seriously with the shortcomings of the old system and the challenges of the new. The Revenue Act of 1971 created a presidential public financing system funded with an income tax check-off, but its effective date was delayed until the 1976 election. Congress also passed the Federal Election Campaign Act of 1971, which strengthened reporting requirements and repealed existing limits on contributions and expenditures that had proven ineffective. But it retained the ban on corporate and labor union contributions. It also put new limits on the amount candidates could contribute to their own campaigns and on expenditures for media advertising in presidential, Senate, and House elections.[1]

The fund-raising scandals associated with Watergate and the committee to reelect President Richard Nixon—featuring attaché cases stuffed with thousands of dollars, illegal corporate contributions, and conduits to hide the original source of contributions—led Congress to return to the campaign finance drawing board.[2] In 1974 they produced major amendments to FECA, which constituted the most serious and ambitious effort ever to regulate the flow of money in federal elections.

THE FECA REGULATORY REGIME

The 1974 amendments scrapped the 1971 limits on media advertising but replaced them with an elaborate set of limits on contributions and expenditures. The amendments also provided for public financing of presidential elections and created a new agency, the Federal Election Commission, to administer a strengthened disclosure system and to enforce the other provisions of the law. Barely a year after the 1974 amendments to FECA were signed into law, the Supreme Court, in *Buckley* v. *Valeo,* upheld the constitutionality of the contribution limits, the disclosure requirements, and the presidential public financing system. But it struck down the limits on expenditures (by a candidate's campaign, by a candidate with personal funds, or by others spending independently), except for voluntary limits tied to public financing in presidential elections, and narrowed the class of political communications by independent groups subject to disclosure and limits on the source and size of contributions. For the purposes of this report, two sets of provisions are particularly germane: those governing the role of corporations and labor unions, and those governing political parties.

Corporations and Labor Unions

The new regulatory regime included one very familiar element: a ban on corporate and union contributions and expenditures in connection with a federal election. FECA added some enforcement bite to these decades-old prohibitions by also making it unlawful for anyone to accept such contributions. Two exemptions from this ban were included in the law. The first, the press exemption, specified that the term "expenditure" does not include "any news story, commentary, or editorial distributed through the facilities of any broadcasting station, newspaper, magazine or other periodical publication, unless such facilities are owned or controlled by any political party, political committee, or candidate." The second, the internal communications exemption, permits corporations to communicate with their restricted class (that is, stockholders and executive and administrative personnel and their families) and unions to communicate with their members without any limitations. Finally, while continuing the ban on the use of general treasury funds of corporations and unions in connection with a federal election, the new law allowed these organizations to set up political committees as separate segregated funds. These funds, one form of political action committee (PAC), whose administrative and fundraising expenses may be paid for by their parent corporation or union, raise voluntary contributions from their restricted classes and are subject to federal limitations.[3]

The intent of Congress as revealed by these provisions in the 1974 amendments to FECA was to ensure that corporate and labor union treasuries not be tapped to finance general federal election campaign activity. Decades of disappointing experience with earlier bans on corporate and union funding led not to a repeal of such bans but to a more rigorous regulatory strategy to make them enforceable.

Political Parties

The 1974 amendments to FECA treated political party committees as a type of "political committee" that is required to register with the FEC and is subject to federal limitations on amounts and sources of contributions. The latter included a prohibition on donations from corporations and labor unions. But party committees, as part of the official political party structure at the national, state, or local level, were treated differently from other political committees in several respects. Individuals could contribute up to $20,000 per year to national party committees and an additional $5,000 to a state party committee. Party committees could transfer unlimited sums to other party committees, without such transfers being treated as contributions. The national committees of each party could together contribute $17,500 during an election cycle to a candidate for the U.S. Senate. And national and state parties could make limited "coordinated" expenditures on behalf of their federal candidates.

The expenditure amounts varied by office and state population and were indexed to inflation.

With one exception, no reference was made in the law to different types and purposes of party accounts, one subject to the limitations of federal law, the other not. The text of the law includes no mention of "federal" or "nonfederal" accounts, much less "hard" or "soft" money. The sole exception to the law's limitations on contributions to party committees was that donations to building funds of national or state parties were exempt.

GROUNDWORK FOR SOFT MONEY

As soon as these limits on party funding went into effect in the 1976 elections, two sets of concerns—dealing with grassroots activity and the federal system—arose about the interpretation and impact of the law as it applied to political parties. The first—that traditional grassroots party activity was inappropriately and harmfully being subjected to limits on coordinated party spending—led Congress in 1979 to amend FECA. The 1979 revision is widely but inaccurately believed to have created soft money. Instead, soft money resulted from the response of the FEC to a second concern arising out of the federal system: how best to accommodate the fact that party organizations have roles in both federal and nonfederal election activity.

The 1979 Amendments to FECA

One important feature of the 1979 amendments to FECA was designed to allow state and local parties to spend unlimited amounts of funds raised under the act for grassroots campaign materials and activities. Much of the traditional party paraphernalia and volunteer activities were reduced in the 1976 elections on the presumption that FECA required them to be treated as in-kind contributions from the parties to federal candidates and therefore subject to limits. Congress in 1979 narrowly defined three sets of election-related activities by state and local parties that were exempt from the limitations on party contributions to and coordinated spending on behalf of federal candidates. These included grassroots campaign materials (for example, yard signs and bumper stickers), slate cards and sample ballots, and voter registration and get-out-the-vote (GOTV) activities on behalf of the party's presidential ticket. Congress specified that these exempted sets of activities did not include the use of any broadcasting, newspaper, magazine, billboard, direct mail, or other general public communication or political advertising. Moreover, to qualify for these exemptions from limitations on contributions and coordinated spending by parties, funds for these exempt activities had to be raised in compliance with FECA. In other words, the 1979 amendments did not authorize national party committees to accept unlimited contributions or to accept corporate or union treasury funds. They simply expanded the use that state and local parties could make of their federal (hard money) funds.[4]

FEC Rulings on Federal and Nonfederal Funds

An entirely separate set of administrative actions was laying the predicate for national parties to begin raising funds not subject to federal source and amount restrictions. FECA limited party financing of activities conducted in connection with federal elections. But what of state and local elections? Parties clearly have interests in elections for state and local office. Many state campaign finance laws are more permissive than federal law, allowing contributions from corporations and unions and higher or unlimited donations from individuals and PACs. (Some, albeit many fewer, are more restrictive.) To what extent do federal restrictions apply when party activities have an impact on both federal and state and local elections? The FEC began grappling with this question soon after it was established. In a series of advisory opinions, the commission sought to ensure that a portion of state party activities benefiting both federal and nonfederal candidates be paid for with hard money. In Advisory Opinion 1975-21, the commission ruled that a local party committee had to use hard dollars to pay for a part of its administrative expenses and voter registration drives, on the grounds that these functions have an indirect effect on federal elections. It used this opinion in regulations it issued in 1977 governing the allocation of administrative expenses between federal and nonfederal accounts. The allocation was to be made "in proportion to the amount of funds expended on federal and nonfederal elections, or on another reasonable basis"(11 CFR 106.1(e) 1978). The next year the commission took an even tougher position on the use of nonfederal funds for voter registration and GOTV activities by party committees. In response to a request for guidance from the Illinois Republican State Central Committee, the commission in Advisory Opinion 1976-72 approved the allocation of party overhead and administrative costs between federal and nonfederal accounts, based on the proportion of federal to state races being held that year. But it prohibited the use of nonfederal funds to finance such federal election–related activities as voter registration and GOTV: "Even though the Illinois law apparently permits corporate contributions for State elections, corporate/union treasury funds may not be used to fund any portion of a registration or get-out-the-vote drive conducted by a political party" (FEC AO 1976-72).

Less than two years later the commission reversed its position. The Kansas Republican State Committee requested permission to use corporate and union funds, which were legal under Kansas law, to finance a portion of their voter drive that would benefit federal and state candidates. This time the commission agreed, concluding in Advisory Opinion 1978-10 that expenses for voter registration and GOTV should be allocated between federal and nonfederal accounts in the same manner as party administrative costs.

At this point the FEC rulings on party financing had been made in response to state party requests for guidance on how the financing of their traditional activities was affected by the new federal election law. What emerged was that state parties had to maintain both federal and nonfederal accounts and allocate funds from the two accounts in a manner consistent with federal law. Direct assistance to federal candidates must be financed exclusively with federal funds. Comparable assistance to state and local candidates could be funded entirely with nonfederal funds. State party overhead and administrative expenses were to be allocated proportionately between federal and nonfederal accounts. Initially voter registration and GOTV were treated in the same way as aid to candidates—as a federal election activity requiring exclusively federal funds—but then the FEC reversed course and allowed state parties to allocate the costs of voter drives between the two accounts (FEC AD 00-95 2000). Soon national party officials argued that the commission rulings recognizing federal and nonfederal state party roles and financing arrangements should apply to them as well. They contended that national parties assist candidates for federal, state, and local office; that they work with state and local party organizations on a variety of party-building and campaign activities; and that, therefore, they too ought to be able to maintain separate federal and nonfederal accounts, finance their nonfederal election activity with nonfederal funds, and allocate administrative and other expenses for joint federal/nonfederal activities between the two accounts. The commission agreed. In Advisory Opinion 1979-17, it stated that a national party committee could establish a separate account "for the deposit and disbursement of funds designated specifically and exclusively to finance national party activity limited to influencing the nomination or election of candidates for public office other than elective 'federal office'" (FEC AO 1979-17). The commission thereby permitted the national parties to raise corporate and union funds and solicit unlimited donations from individuals "for the exclusive and limited purpose of influencing the nom-ination or election of candidates for nonfederal office" (FEC AO 1979-17).

The Rise of Soft Money

By the end of the 1992 election cycle, students of political parties and campaign finance came to recognize that important elements of party financing of federal elections were at variance with FECA and with the initial rulings of the FEC that allowed the national parties to raise and spend soft money for limited purposes. Congress had sought to keep cor-porate and union money out of federal elections and to limit the size of individual contributions. Both objectives were undermined, however, by the growing role of soft money, which allowed national party officials and federal officeholders to solicit unlimited contributions and steer them in ways that would benefit their federal election campaigns. Initially, the commission approved only the use of nonfederal or soft-money accounts of the national parties "for the exclusive and limited purpose of influenc-ing the nomination or election of candidates for nonfederal office" (FEC AO 1979-17). Yet later the FEC allocation rules allowed much more gen-erous shares of nonfederal or soft money than could be justified by the state and local campaign activity they financed. Only a trickle of soft money was directly contributed to or spent on behalf of state and local candidates. Some soft money helped state party organizations mobilize support for state and local candidates and expand their staffs and activi-ties. But a major share of these "nonfederal" funds raised by national par-ties was spent to influence the outcome of federal elections. Soft money had become primarily a component of federal election financing, not a means of funding state and local election activity.[5]

The 1996 Election Cycle: The Soft-Money System Transformed

The accommodative regulatory environment, the failure to index for infla-tion the FECA limits on contributions to candidates and parties, and competitive pressures in presidential elections combined to increase demand for soft money. Between 1980 and 1992, the parties became more adept at raising nonfederal funds from corporations, unions, and wealthy individuals and directing them toward locations and activities that would advance their presidential and congressional tickets.[6] But no one had yet questioned that there were still limits to what the parties could accomplish with soft money. While soft money was growing in importance, it remained a relatively small part of national party committee budgets.

The increased activity of the national parties during this period was largely accomplished with hard money. The parties adapted well to the new environment of modern campaigning and FECA financing, in important part by becoming repositories of professional expertise and building effective networks linking candidates with donors and consultants.[7] Relatively generous coordinated spending limits gave them license to provide substantial direct assistance in elections, financed by contributions raised under FECA. It was clear that effective campaigning required a large component of candidate-focused communications. And that, everyone assumed, required hard money.

Issue Advocacy

That view changed in the next presidential election cycle, thanks to the audacious move by then President Bill Clinton and his political consultant, Dick Morris, to finance an ambitious political advertising campaign under the guise of "issue advocacy." Starting in the fall of 1995 and continuing through the middle of 1996, Democratic Party committees spent an estimated $34 million on television ads designed to promote Clinton's reelection. While the ads prominently featured the president, none of these costs were charged as coordinated expenditures on behalf of Clinton's campaign. Instead the party paid the entire cost, based on a legal argument never before made: that party communications that did not use explicit words advocating the election or defeat of a federal candidate could be treated like generic party advertising and financed, according to the FEC allocation rules, with a mix of soft and hard money. Such communications were forms of issue advocacy, it was argued, and neither subject to the spending limits that apply to presidential candidates accepting public funding, nor wholly subject to the limits on the source and size of contributions to political parties.[8]

This argument, and the embrace of issue advocacy as a form of electioneering, had its genesis in *Buckley*. In that decision, the Court established an express advocacy test as a way of narrowing the scope of disclosure requirements and contribution limits for independent expenditures in light of a concern that the language crafted by Congress in the 1974 amendments to FECA was unconstitutionally vague and overbroad.[9] The standard was defined by the Court as communications that "in express terms advocate the election or defeat of a clearly identified candidate for federal office." The Court elaborated in a footnote examples of express advocacy, which became known as the "magic words" test.

This express advocacy standard was constructed to determine which communications by individuals and groups independent of any candidate or party would be subject to regulation. The Court did not require express advocacy in candidate and political party ads for their financing to be subject to federal campaign finance laws. *Buckley* stated that spending by candidates and political committees (including parties) is "by definition, campaign-related." Students of campaign finance thought it an extraordinary leap for a presidential candidate, especially one accepting public funding, and a national political party to argue that the express advocacy standard gave them license to craft and broadcast unlimited political ads and to finance them in large part with soft money.[10]

Parties, Issue Advocacy, and Soft Money

The express advocacy standard had little noticeable effect on the conduct and financing of federal campaigns for almost twenty years after it was set by the Court. It took the creativity and bravado of Morris and Clinton and the failure of the FEC to challenge their use of party soft money to finance television ads promoting the president's agenda and accomplishments to open the floodgates.[11] In May of 1996, the Republican National Committee announced a $20 million "issue advocacy" advertising campaign. Its purpose, in the words of the chairman, would be "to show the differences between Dole and Clinton and between Republicans and Democrats on the issues facing our country, so we can engage full-time in one of the most consequential elections in our history."[12] These presidential candidate-specific ads, like the Democratic ones, were targeted on key battleground states and financed with a mix of hard and (mostly) soft money. Both parties were now financing a significant part of the campaigns of their presidential candidates outside of the strictures of FECA and well beyond the bounds of the 1979 FEC ruling that national parties may raise corporate and union funds and solicit unlimited donations from individuals "for the exclusive and limited purpose of influencing the nomination or election of candidates for nonfederal office."

Very quickly the parties began to use the same funding strategy to campaign on behalf of their congressional candidates; outside groups did likewise.[13] For groups, the advantage of electioneering through "issue advocacy" rather than through FECA "independent expenditures" was that the former could be conducted without disclosure and could be financed with soft (that is, unregulated) rather than hard money. This meant that both political parties and groups could solicit contributions from corporations and unions as well as from wealthy individual donors to finance candidate-specific electioneering communications. Moreover, those same corporations and labor unions could tap their own treasuries to run such electioneering communications themselves or through convenient, largely anonymous intermediary organizations. Research on the 1996 election revealed extensive and elaborate efforts by parties, candidates, unions, corporations, and groups to exploit this new issue advocacy loophole to avoid the strictures of federal election law.[14]

This research also suggested some degree of coordination among parties, groups, and candidates in creating and broadcasting these issue advocacy electioneering communications. Published accounts by former White House insiders and the report of the Senate committee that investigated campaign finance practices in the 1996 election contain detailed information about President Clinton's personal role in authorizing the "issue ad" campaign, editing the ads, selecting locations for their broadcast, and raising the funds needed to pay for them.[15] Similar reports have been made of possible coordination between parties and outside groups regarding the strategic use of issue advocacy electioneering communications to shape the outcome of federal elections.[16] The Supreme Court's distinction between independent advocacy and advocacy coordinated with a candidate was critical to its finding that limits on independent expenditures were unconstitutional. Yet as issue advocacy emerged as a tool for electioneering communication in the 1996 election, it threatened to undermine a central feature of FECA: that communications designed to help a candidate but not treated as contributions must be made independent of that candidate.

Demand for Soft Money Intensifies

The increased demand created by this novel interpretation of nonfederal election activity led to more than a threefold increase in national party soft-money activity between 1992 and 1996—from $80 million to $272 million (table 1). Soft money as a share of total national party spending jumped from 16 percent to 30 percent. Both parties and their elected officials worked hard to solicit soft-money donations from corporations, wealthy individuals, and labor unions. During the 1996 election the national party committees received nearly 1,000 contributions from individuals in excess of $20,000 (the annual federal party contribution limit) and approximately 27,000 contributions from federally prohibited sources.[17]

Less than $10 million of the $272 million was contributed directly to state and local candidates in the 1996 cycle, only 3.5 percent of the soft money spent by the parties. The two parties transferred a total of $115

Table 1. *National Political Party Spending, 1976–2000*
Millions of dollars, except as indicated

| | Democrats | | | Republicans | | | Overall spending | | | |
| | Federal (hard) | Non-federal (soft) | Total | Federal (hard) | Non-federal (soft) | Total | Federal (hard) | Nonfederal (soft) | | |
Election								Amount	Percent	Total
1976	19.4	—	19.4	40.1	—	40.1	59.5	—	0	59.5
1980	35.0	4.0	39.0	161.8	15.1	176.9	196.8	19.1	8	215.9
1984	97.4	6.0	103.4	300.8	15.6	316.4	398.2	21.6	5	419.8
1988	121.9	23.0	144.9	257.0	22.0	279.0	378.9	45.0	11	423.9
1992	171.9	32.9	204.8	256.1	47.5	303.6	428.0	80.4	16	508.4
1994	137.8	50.4	188.2	234.7	48.4	283.1	372.5	98.8	21	471.3
1996	214.3	121.8	336.1	408.5	149.7	558.2	622.8	271.5	30	894.3
1998	155.3	93.0	248.3	275.9	127.7	403.6	431.2	220.7	34	651.9
2000	265.8	244.9	510.7	427.0	252.8	679.8	692.8	497.7	42	1,190.5

Sources: Anthony Corrado. *Campaign Finance Reform* (Century Foundation Press, 2000), p. 70; Federal Election Commission, "FEC Reports Increase in Party Fundraising for 2000," May 15, 2001. Figures for 1976 and for nonfederal spending between 1980 and 1988 are estimates. All other figures are provided by the Federal Election Commission.

million in soft money to state party committees, which financed two-thirds of state party soft-money expenditures. The national Democratic Party managed to finance two-thirds of its pro-Clinton "issue ad" television blitz by taking advantage of the more favorable allocation methods available to state parties. They simply transferred the requisite mix of hard and soft dollars to party committees in the states they targeted and had the state committees place the ads. State party soft-money expenditures for political communication/advertising jumped from less than $2 million in 1992 to $65 million in 1996.[18] State parties enjoyed positive spillover effects from this national party campaign strategy, in terms of covering some of their staffing and administrative costs. But there is no doubt that they were used by national party officials as vehicles for implementing their newly developed strategy of federal electioneering under the guise of issue advocacy.[19]

After the 1996 election, the FEC audit division concluded that the party issue advertising campaigns should have been treated as campaign expenses of the two presidential candidates and thereby subject to spending and contribution limits. The commission rejected the finding and unanimously declined to take any punitive action against the parties or their presidential candidates. The commission also rejected the general counsel's recommendation for an enforcement proceeding, based on the conclusion that the party's issue ads were coordinated with the Clinton campaign and therefore constituted illegal campaign contributions and expenditures.[20] What had seemed a daring test (if not outright violation) of the boundaries of federal election law in 1996 had now received the de facto blessing of the Federal Election Commission. There remained few effective constraints on the ability of parties and other political actors to campaign for and against specific candidates for federal office with unlimited amounts of soft money.

THE 1998 AND 2000 ELECTIONS: A REGULATORY REGIME IN DISARRAY

The 1998 midterm election cycle saw the parties focus their soft-money strategy on Senate and House elections. The total amount of soft money spent—$221 million—was less than in 1996 but more than double the previous midterm election. And soft money as a share of total spending by the national parties jumped to 34 percent. The congressional party campaign committees put a premium on raising and spending soft money to advance the election prospects of their candidates. The two Senate campaign committees effectively abandoned formal coordinated expenditures on behalf of their candidates and delegated this financing tool to state parties. The Democratic Senatorial Campaign Committee made $12.3 million in coordinated expenditures in the 1994 midterm elections; that amount dropped to $8,424 in 1998. The National Republican Senatorial Committee spent $10.9 million of hard money in coordination with their candidates in 1994; the comparable amount in 1998 was $36,775. Both national party committees had discovered they could finance campaign activity on behalf of their senatorial candidates with soft money in the form of "issue advocacy." The same pattern, more pronounced with the Democrats than the Republicans, was evident in the House campaign committees.[21]

Given the breakthrough in the use of soft money to fund candidate-focused campaign ads in 1996, the FEC's decision not to pursue this apparent violation of law and regulation, and the emergence of issue advocacy as the campaign weapon of choice in the 1998 congressional elections, it is no surprise that soft-money financing of party campaigning exploded in the 2000 election cycle. Soft-money spending by the national parties reached $498 million, now 42 percent of their total spending.

Raising a half billion dollars in soft money took a major effort by the national parties and elected officials, but they had the advantage of focusing their efforts on large donors. That focus paid substantial dividends: 800 donors (435 corporations, unions, and other organizations and 365 individuals), each contributing a minimum of $120,000, accounted for almost $300 million, or 60 percent, of the soft money raised by the parties.[22] The top 50 soft-money donors each contributed between $955,695 and $5,949,000. Among the many soft-money donors who gave generously to both parties were Global Crossing, Enron, and WorldCom.[23]

The Republican and Democratic National Committees provided the soft and hard money needed to boost the campaigns of their presidential candidates in key battleground states. Electioneering issue ads were a central component of the political strategies of both presidential candidates and were fully integrated into the campaigns.[24] One estimate based on monitoring television ads in the seventy-five largest media markets between June 1 and election day suggests the parties spent $3 on issue advocacy communications in the presidential campaign for every $1 they spent on express advocacy communications.[25] Once again, the transfer of funds to state parties, which then placed the ads, provided the most efficient allocation method.

The House and Senate party campaign committees were especially active in the soft-money arena. Together they spent $219 million in 2000, more than ten times their soft-money activity in 1992. As in 1998, they largely abandoned the hard-money coordinated expenditure route to assisting their candidates and focused their campaign activity on issue advocacy and get-out-the-vote, both of which could be financed with a large portion of soft dollars. For the first time, the two Democratic campaign committees actually raised and spent more unrestricted soft money than regulated hard money.[26] Research monitoring national party campaign activities in the 2000 election cycle confirms a massive increase in party federal electioneering activities—over the air and on the ground—in targeted states and districts and financed largely with soft money.[27]

A total of $280 million in soft money—well over half the amount raised by the six national party committees—was transferred to state parties, along with $135 million in hard money. By contrast, the national parties contributed only $19 million directly to state and local candidates, less than 4 percent of their soft-money spending and 1.6 percent of their total financial activity in 2000.[28]

By the end of the 2000 election cycle, it simply was not credible to argue that soft money was exclusively or even primarily being used for state and local election activity. Nor was it credible to argue that "issue ads" run by national and state parties were anything other than communications intended to influence the outcome of federal elections. The evidence that national parties were raising soft money, not subject to federal limits, and using it by working through state parties to influence federal elections was decisive. The language in *Buckley* that spending by parties is "by definition, campaign-related" was given powerful empirical support. Scholars might differ about how best to change the campaign finance system, but they could not avoid the conclusion that party soft money and electioneering in the guise of issue advocacy had rendered the FECA regime largely ineffectual.

POTENTIAL CORRUPTION OF THE POLICY PROCESS

The developments in campaign finance law and practice reviewed in this report altered the behavior of private groups, political parties, and elected officials in ways that raised serious concerns about potential corruption of the policy process. Those concerns led Congress to enact BCRA, which repairs the tears in the regulatory fabric and in many ways reinstates the campaign finance system in operation after the 1974 FECA amendments and *Buckley*.

Political Parties

Political parties play an indispensable role in democratic societies, aggregating public preferences, organizing teams of candidates and elected officials, and providing a means of democratic accountability. Political scientists have also traditionally valued parties for nurturing volunteer grassroots political participation, fostering broader electoral competition by supporting challengers to incumbents, and diluting the influence of organized interests.

The rise of soft money has led many scholars to question whether these comparative advantages of political parties have been compromised by developments in campaign finance practice.[29] Do parties dilute the influence of large donors or facilitate their access to policymakers? Do parties operate independently of incumbent officeholders, or are they largely instruments of those incumbents? Does soft money support party-building and grassroots activities, or is it used primarily to finance communications about specific federal candidates? Are state parties independent actors in the soft-money era, or are they more agents of national parties and politicians? While no scholarly consensus exists on the answers to these questions, the preponderance of evidence from recent research supports the position that the relationship between party soft money, private interests, and federal candidates and officeholders has created serious concerns about the integrity of the policy process and respect for the rule of law.

Most important, soft money has led the parties to become the avenue by which elected officials and large private donors frequently come together. The national party committees are dominated by elected public officials—the president or presidential candidate in the case of the Republican and Democratic National Committees, the top House and Senate party leaders for the congressional campaign committees.[30] There is no meaningful separation between the national party committees and the public officials who control them. As described above, the congressional party campaign committees have become very large soft-money operations in recent elections. This party fund-raising depends crucially on the active involvement of each party's highest-ranking elected officials. As inducements for large contributions, policymakers grant access and provide opportunities for face-to-face discussions in intimate settings with the party's most prominent public officials. Presidents and congressional party leaders devote a significant amount of their time to raising soft and hard money for their party committees as well as to assisting candidates directly. And top elected officials and their political strategists determine how party resources—including, importantly, soft money—are allocated in presidential and congressional elections.

Parties also provide an instrument for individual politicians to raise and spend funds for their own campaigns that would not otherwise be permissible by law. The final report of the Senate Committee on Governmental Affairs on the *Investigation of Illegal or Improper Activities in Connection with 1996 Federal Election Campaigns* chronicles the extraordinary lengths to which Democratic and Republican elected officials went to raise party soft money for their "issue advocacy" advertising blitzes in the 1996 election cycle. The tactic of choice for many 2000 Senate candidates was the "joint fund-raising committee." These candidate/party committees gave candidates an opportunity to solicit contributions, often from the same donor, for three campaign pots: up to $2,000 for the candidate's campaign committee, an additional amount of up to the maximum of $20,000 for the party committee's hard-money account, and then any additional individual contribution (or donation from a corporation or union) to the party's soft-money account. The latter two could be transferred to the candidate's state party and used for issue advocacy or GOTV activities that would benefit that candidate's campaign.[31]

Since the soft-money–financed campaign activities of the parties must be mixed with some portion of hard dollars, the party committees also work assiduously to raise the requisite matches. Here too congressional party leaders have played a crucial role, by encouraging their colleagues in Congress, especially those representing relatively safe seats, to transfer funds from their personal campaign committees and leadership PACs to candidates in tight races and to party campaign committees. This encouragement has lately taken the form of party fund-raising quotas on members of Congress. Federal election law permits unlimited transfers from members' campaign committees to party committees. In the 2000 election cycle, 15 percent of the hard-money receipts of the House party campaign committees came from member contributions.[32]

National party links to elected officials and large private donors are mirrored in their ties to state parties. Whatever the positive spillover effects on state party-building and voter mobilization, the evidence summarized above supports the conclusion that since the advent of soft money, national parties have used state parties primarily as vehicles for advancing federal election campaign objectives.[33] The state parties have been willing partners with their national counterparts in seizing the opportunities presented by the soft-money system to boost their federal candidates. "The relationship between the national parties and their state parties has never been closer than it is today."[34] From a reform perspective, however, this means that any successful attempt to limit national party soft-money activity must perforce prevent easy evasion through surrogates such as state and local parties.

Some have argued that parties will be weakened by the elimination of soft money and that electoral competition will suffer.[35] It is true that substantially more money is crossing party books and that they have a major presence in battleground states and districts across the country. But the evidence suggests that soft money has created as many or more problems for parties and done little to nurture grassroots participation or electoral competition.[36] In fact, the period in which the party soft-money system exploded has coincided with a decline in competition in congressional elections.[37] I am aware of no evidence supporting the proposition that party soft-money activities counter or reduce the advantages of incumbency. This may be because the two parties—dominated by elected officials consumed with the immediate goal of winning the marginal seat that might determine which party controls the majority—concentrate their "issue advocacy" spending in the same handful of targeted contests rather than looking to the medium or long term by investing in a somewhat larger number of potentially winnable seats.[38] The provision in BCRA increasing limits on hard-money contributions to parties will in any case cushion if not entirely match the absence of soft money.

THE POLICY PROCESS

These new and altered roles in the electoral process for corporations, unions, and political parties raise troubling questions about the integrity of the policy process. Congress banned corporate contributions in federal elections out of concerns that concentrated wealth and the advantages of incorporation could distort and corrupt democratic government. Labor unions were subjected to comparable regulation to neutralize the political benefits that might result from their publicly facilitated organizational strengths. Large and unlimited individual contributions were proscribed by Congress to prevent the buying of access to or special treatment by government officials. Yet each of these pillars of federal election law has been undermined by the rise of the soft-money system and electioneering issue advocacy in U.S. elections. Very large institutional and individual donors have returned to Washington.

No single motivation can possibly explain the behavior of all of these large soft-money donors. Some enjoy being viewed as "players" in their parties; some hope to help one of the parties hold or gain the White House and Congress; some bank on better access, a more sympathetic hearing, or more favorable treatment from federal officials; others give defensively in response to aggressive solicitation by party and elected officials—a cost of doing business in Washington. But since most of the largest soft-money donors had high stakes in decisions made by Washington policymakers, the public has a substantial basis for its concerns about conflicts of interest and corruption of the policy process.[39]

Since the Supreme Court's *Buckley* decision, corruption or the appearance of corruption has been the dominant legal rationale for regulating campaign finance. Scholars have sought to measure whether campaign contributions corrupt the policy process by buying votes in Congress. Most of this research has examined the connections between PAC contributions (a surrogate for interested money) and votes in the House and Senate.[40] There is little statistical evidence that campaign contributions to members of Congress directly affect their roll call decisions. Party, ideology, constituency, mass public opinion, and the president correlate much more with voting behavior in Congress than do PAC contributions. When these variables are less significant, there is evidence that interest group contributions, particularly to junior members of Congress, have influenced roll call votes—for example, on financial services regulation.[41] The targets of influence are less often victories on final roll call votes than assistance, sympathy, or access at some earlier stage of the legislative process.[42]

In any event, this literature is often used to buttress the argument that political contributions do not corrupt the policy process. This is an odd inference, since it is based on studies of contributions that are limited as to source and size for the very purpose of preventing corruption or its appearance. PAC contributions are capped at $5,000 per election, an amount whose real value has shrunk by two-thirds since it was enacted in 1974. Are we to assume that studies of contributions of $50,000 or $500,000 or $5 million from corporations, unions, and individuals would produce the same generally negative findings? What if the route of influence is not through individual members or on roll call votes? What if large soft-money donors give generously to both political parties?

A more sophisticated understanding of the organizational features of Congress and of the multiple forms of political contributions leads one to take seriously the potentially corrupting effects of political contributions. Initial work along these lines suggests a myriad of ways in which groups receive or are denied favors beyond roll call votes.[43] Members can express public support or opposition in various legislative venues, offer amendments, mobilize support, help place items on or off the agenda, speed or delay action, and provide special access to lobbyists. They can also decline each of these requests. Beyond the chamber floor, venues include rules governing floor consideration, party leadership, party caucuses, standing committees and subcommittees, conference committees, and other collections of members inside the House and Senate. Groups may use their campaign contributions in conjunction with their lobbying operations to reinforce or activate rather than convert members. They may also try to curry favor by running helpful electioneering issue advocacy campaigns for or against particular federal candidates. Moreover, in the executive branch, influence can be sought over appointments and access to decisionmaking forums, as seen in recent revelations about the Enron Corporation.

The currency of campaign contributions extends well beyond PAC contributions to members' campaign committees. These include brokered if not bundled individual contributions, contributions to leadership PACs controlled by members, contributions to parties and candidates in targeted races and informally credited to members, soft-money contributions to parties and section 527 committees connected to members, and direct expenditures on "issue ad" campaigns. The ways and means of potential influence (and corruption) are much more diverse than those investigated in the early scholarly research.

The dramatic growth of soft money and the intimate involvement of elected officials in raising and spending that money to influence federal elections makes that potential influence and corruption all the more serious. That potential for abuse is most vividly illustrated by the series of reports issued by the Center for Responsive Politics tracking patterns of soft-money contributions by groups with a strong interest in pending legislation.[44] Prominent examples include the tobacco, telecommunications, and oil and gas industries. In each case millions of dollars in soft-money contributions were made to the national and congressional party committees of both parties as Congress was considering legislation that would significantly affect those industries. These are only several of the most noteworthy examples of a widespread phenomenon: most corporate soft-money donors have a major stake in federal policymaking and many contribute to both major parties.

Seen from this practical vantage point, parties do not dilute the influence of large donors or insulate elected officials from direct connections with those donors; they instead facilitate and broker such connections. The rise of soft money and of electioneering in the guise of issue advocacy has put parties in the unfortunate position of middleman between large private interests seeking public favors and ambitious elected officials aggressively soliciting large political contributions from those private interests. FECA and its legislative predecessors banning corporate and union funding of federal elections were designed to reduce the glaring conflicts of interests that arise when those with high stakes in congressional and regulatory agency actions make large political contributions. That purpose has been undermined by the developments reviewed in this report.

Whatever the mix of motivations, parties, elected officials, and private interests have been linked in a deceitful game—one based upon the transparent lie that soft money is being raised and used for purposes other than influencing federal elections. That game has been characterized by a constant search for funding conduits and rationales that allow political actors to evade the strictures of federal election law. It has exacerbated conflicts of interest among policymakers. It has encouraged politicians to engage in heavy-handed solicitation of large donations. And it has reinforced the unfortunate public perception that public policy decisions are bought and sold in Washington.

CONCLUSION

This review of the development of campaign finance law and practice leads me to conclude that Congress had ample justification for crafting the provisions of BCRA to deal with the problems of party soft money and electioneering communications in the guise of issue advocacy. The weight of scholarly evidence supports the view that the FECA regime was undermined by the emergence of soft money and "issue advocacy," raising serious concerns about potential corruption in the policy process and disrespect for the rule of law. In my view, BCRA is an incremental step to repair these egregious tears in the regulatory fabric. The new law accomplishes this objective by updating existing provisions that limit contributions to political parties and that prohibit corporate and union treasury spending in federal elections to take into account contemporary realities of campaigning.

NOTES

1. Frank J. Sorauf, *Money in American Elections* (Glenview, Ill.: Scott, Foresman, 1988).

2. Ibid.

3. Trevor Potter, "Where Are We Now? The Current State of Campaign Finance Law," in Anthony Corrado, Thomas E. Mann, Daniel R. Ortiz, Trevor Potter, and Frank J. Sorauf, eds., *Campaign Finance Reform: A Sourcebook* (Brookings, 1997).

4. Anthony Corrado, "Party Soft Money," in Corrado and others, *Campaign Finance Reform: A Sourcebook*.

5. Herbert E. Alexander and Anthony Corrado, *Financing the 1992 Election* (Armonk, N.Y.: M. E. Sharpe, 1995); Frank J. Sorauf, *Inside Campaign Finance: Myths and Realities* (Yale University Press, 1992).

6. Alexander and Corrado, *Financing the 1992 Election*.

7. Paul S. Herrnson, *Party Campaigning in the 1980s* (Harvard University Press, 1988).

8. John C. Green, ed., *Financing the 1996 Election* (Armonk, N.Y.: M. E. Sharpe, 1999); Anthony Corrado, *Campaign Finance Reform* (New York: Century Foundation Press, 2000).

9. Trevor Potter, "Issue Advocacy and Express Advocacy," in Corrado and others, *Campaign Finance Reform: A Sourcebook*.

10. Green, *Financing the 1996 Election*; Corrado, *Campaign Finance Reform*; Citizens' Research Foundation, University of Southern California, *New Realities, New Thinking: Report of the Task Force on Campaign Finance Reform* (Los Angeles, 1997); Thomas E. Mann, "The U.S. Campaign Finance System under Strain," in

Henry J. Aaron and Robert D. Reischauer, eds., *Setting National Priorities: The 2000 Election and Beyond* (Brookings, 1999).

11. Corrado, *Campaign Finance Reform.*

12. Ibid.

13. Green, *Financing the 1996 Election*; Corrado, *Campaign Finance Reform.*

14. Annenberg Public Policy Center, *Issue Advocacy Advertising during the 1996 Campaign: A Catalog,* Report Series 16 (Philadelphia, September 1997); Green, *Financing the 1996 Election*; Corrado, *Campaign Finance Reform.*

15. Dick Morris, *Behind the Oval Office: Winning the Presidency in the Nineties,* 1st ed. (Random House, 1997); *Investigation of Illegal or Improper Activities in Connection with the 1996 Federal Election Campaigns,* S. Rept. 105-167, 105 Cong. 2 sess. (GPO, 1998).

16. Corrado, *Campaign Finance Reform.*

17. *AFL-CIO* v. *Federal Election Commission,* 2001.

18. Ray La Raja, "Sources and Uses of Soft Money: What Do We Know?" in Gerald C. Lubenow, ed., *A User's Guide to Campaign Finance Reform* (Lanham, Md.: Rowman & Littlefield, 2001).

19. Green, *Financing the 1996 Election*; Corrado, *Campaign Finance Reform.*

20. Anthony Corrado, "Party Finance in the 2000 Elections: The Federal Role of Soft Money Financing," *Arizona State University Law Journal,* vol. 34 (2002).

21. Federal Election Commission, "FEC Reports on Political Party Activity for 1997–98," press release, Washington, April 9, 1999.

22. David Rogers, "'Soft Money' Study Shows Concentration of Donation by Wealthy Contributors," *Wall Street Journal,* March 16, 2001, Eastern edition, p. A16.

23. Larry Makinson, *The Big Picture: The Money behind the 2000 Elections* (Washington: Center for Responsive Politics, 2001).

24. David B. Magleby, ed., *Financing the 2000 Election* (Brookings, 2002); Corrado, "Party Finance in the 2000 Elections."

25. Craig B. Holman and Luke P. McLoughlin, *Buying Time 2000: Television Advertising in the 2000 Federal Elections* (Brennan Center for Justice, New York University School of Law, 2001).

26. Federal Election Commission, "FEC Reports Increase in Party Fundraising for 2000," press release, Washington, May 15, 2001; Corrado, "Party Finance in the 2000 Elections"; Magleby, *Financing the 2000 Election.*

27. Jonathan Krasno and Kenneth Goldstein, "The Facts about Television Advertising and the McCain-Feingold Bill," *PS: Political Science,* vol. 35 (June 2002), pp. 207–12; Magleby, *Financing the 2000 Election*; David B. Magleby, ed., *The Other Campaign: Soft Money and Issue Advocacy in the 2000 Congressional Elections* (Lanham, Md.: Rowman & Littlefield, 2003); Holman and McLoughlin, *Buying Time 2000.*

28. Federal Election Commission, "FEC Reports Increase in Party Fundraising for 2000."

29. Stanley Kelley Jr., "Political Parties and the Regulation of Campaign Financing" (Princeton University, 2002), available at www.brookings.edu/gs/cf/KelleyDoc.pdf; Frank J. Sorauf and Jonathan S. Krasno, "Political Party Committees and Coordinated Spending," prepared for the Federal Election Commission in *Federal Election Commission (FEC)* v. *Colorado State Republican Party* (1998); Brennan Center for Justice at New York University School of Law, "Scholars Opinion Letter on Shays-Meehan Legislation," letter to Representatives Shays and Meehan, July 9, 2001, available at www.brennancenter.org/programs/downloads/ polisci_letter71001.pdf; Thomas E. Mann, "Political Science and Campaign Finance Reform: Knowledge, Politics, and Policy," paper prepared for Annual Meeting of the American Political Science Association, Boston, August 29–September 1, 2002, available at http://apsaproceedings.cup.org/ Site/papers/000/000001MannThomas.pdf.

30. Daniel M. Shea, *Transforming Democracy: Legislative Campaign Committees and Political Parties* (State University of New York, 1995); Kathryn Dunn Tenpas, *Presidents as Candidates: Inside the White House for the Presidential Campaign* (New York: Garland, 1997); Sorauf and Krasno, "Political Party Committees and Coordinated Spending"; Corrado, *Campaign Finance Reform*; Diana Dwyre and Robin Kolodny, "Throwing Out the Rule Book: Party Financing of the 2000 Elections," in Magleby, *Financing the 2000 Election.*

31. Corrado, "Party Finance in the 2000 Elections."

32. Michael J. Malbin and Anne H. Bedlington, "Members of Congress as Contributors, When Every Race Counts," paper prepared for Annual Meeting of the American Political Science Association, Boston, August 29–September 1, 2002, available at http://apsaproceedings.cup.org/Site/papers/022/022001 MalbinMich.pdf.

33. On spillover effects, see La Raja, "Sources and Uses of Soft Money"; Stephen Ansolabehere and James M. Snyder Jr., "Soft Money, Hard Money, Strong Parties," *Columbia Law Review,* vol. 100 (April 2000), pp. 598–619.

34. Sarah M. Morehouse, "State Parties: Independent Partners: The Money Relationship," paper prepared for Annual Meeting of the American Political Science Association, August 31–September 3, 2000.

35. La Raja, "Sources and Uses of Soft Money."

36. Brennan Center for Justice at New York University School of Law, "New Study Finds That Parties' Voter Mobilization Efforts Are Not Dependent on Soft Money," press release, July 3, 2001, available at www.brennancenter.org/press-center/pressrelease_2001_070301.html; David B. Magleby, ed., *Outside Money: Soft Money and Issue Advocacy in the 1998 Congressional Elections* (Lanham, Md.: Rowman & Littlefield, 2000); Magleby, *The Other Campaign*; Corrado, "Party Finance in the 2000 Elections."

37. Norman J. Ornstein, Thomas E. Mann, and Michael J. Malbin, *Vital Statistics on Congress 2001–2002* (Washington: AEI Press, 2002).

38. Jonathan S. Krasno, "The Electoral Impact of 'Issue Advocacy' in the 1998

and 2000 House Races," in Kenneth Goldstein and Patricia Strach, eds., *The Medium and the Message* (Upper Saddle River, N.J.: Prentice-Hall, forthcoming).

39. David B. Magleby and Kelly D. Patterson, "Trends: Congressional Reform," *Public Opinion Quarterly,* vol. 58 (Autumn 1994), pp. 419–27.

40. Frank J. Sorauf, *Inside Campaign Finance: Myths and Realities* (Yale University Press, 1992); John R. Wright, Interest Groups & Congress: Lobbying, Contributions, and Influence (Boston: Allyn and Bacon, 1996).

41. Thomas Stratmann, "Can Special Interests Buy Congressional Votes? Evidence from Financial Services Legislation," paper prepared for Annual Meeting of the American Political Science Association, Boston, August 29–September 1, 2002, available at http://apsaproceedings.cup.org/Site/papers/022/022023 StratmannT.pdf.

42. Richard Hall and Frank Wayman, "Buying Time: Moneyed Interests and the Mobilization of Bias in Congressional Committees," *American Political Science Review,* vol. 84 (September 1990), pp. 797–820.

43. Ibid.; Richard Hall, *Participation in Congress* (Yale University Press, 1996); Matthew N. Beckmann and Richard L. Hall, "With the Help of Their Friends: Lobbying for (and against) Protectionist Trade Policy," paper prepared for annual meeting of the American Political Science Association, Boston, August 27–September 1, 2002, available at http://apsaproceedings.cup.org/site/papers/022/022020HallRichar.pdf.

44. Jennifer Keen and John Daly, *Beyond the Limits: Soft Money in the 1996 Elections* (Washington: Center for Responsive Politics, 1997), available at http://www.opensecrets.org/pubs/btl/contents.html; Corrado, *Campaign Finance Reform.*

Parties versus Interest Groups

SIDNEY M. MILKIS

Sidney M. Milkis is the James Hart Professor of Politics at the University of Virginia and an expert on political parties and their role in American government. He served as an expert witness for the Republican National Committee, one of the lead plaintiffs in the McConnell *case.*

Milkis's report focused on the historic development and functions of political parties in American politics and his views on the likely effect of the Bipartisan Campaign Reform Act (BCRA) of 2002 on party activity. In this excerpt, he contends that the Federal Election Campaign Act (FECA) strengthened candidate-centered campaigns and interest groups at the expense of political parties. He argues that the growth of soft money and other resources revitalized political parties and strengthened their role as intermediaries between the political system and interest groups. Consequently, instead of corrupting the political process, political parties have made the political system less corrupt and more responsive to the concerns of the electorate. Milkis further argues that the reform act will diminish the national character of party organizations and, like FECA, will strengthen the influence of interest groups in American politics.

Since the dawn of the twentieth century, many factors have threatened the indispensable yet fragile place of parties in American politics, including the growth of the mass media and the development of a mass entertainment industry. But these forces would have been far less debilitating were it not for reforms such as the direct primary, registration laws, and campaign finance reforms. The campaign finance laws of the 1970s—the Federal Election Campaign Act of 1971 and the 1974 amendments that were added to it—further advanced a reform effort to "purify" politics—to eliminate even the "appearance" of corruption. But these initiatives, in fact, enhanced the role of special interests, attenuated the link between representatives and their constituents, and made political life seem less relevant and more remote from the everyday lives of American citizens, thus contributing to the decline of participation in elections.

The campaign finance laws strengthened candidate-centered campaigns and interest groups at the expense of parties. By limiting the amount of money parties could give to candidates, FECA required candidates to raise more money on their own. The success of candidates thus became dependent on their individual abilities to raise money needed for high media visibility and the construction of a personal organization. Moreover, by limiting the amount of money any individual could contribute, FECA reduced the role of large contributors and at the same time gave incentives for the formation of federal political action committees (PACs); FECA also encouraged the creation of unregulated groups that operated entirely outside of the disclosure requirements. Consequently, during the 1970s, the number of PACs exploded.

PACs, organizations formed by interest groups for the primary or sole purpose of giving money to candidates, did not begin with the campaign finance laws. Prior to the 1970s, labor and business organizations, which were prohibited from making direct contributions to federal campaigns, formed political action committees that allowed them to participate in the political process. But PACs multiplied rapidly after the campaign finance laws restricted the role of parties in funding elections; indeed, FECA specifically legitimized PACs by explicitly granting to both corporations and labor unions the right to create, administer, and raise funds for their PACs, and to cover all organizational expenses from corporate and union treasuries. From 1974 to 1982 the number of political action committees organized by business and unions more than quadrupled, increasing from 608 to 2,601. In the next six years, PACs of all types (including those unconnected to business and unions) rose to a total of 4,268 in 1988. There were 4,328 federal PACs as of March 31, 2002.

PACs thus became a rival to political parties in support of candidates but without obligations to govern or to appeal broadly to electorates. Equally important, the growing influence of advocacy groups strengthened pressure group politics: during the 1970s, advocacy groups exercised power by influencing congressional committees, administrative agencies, and courts, advancing policies that were not vetted in elections and the legislative process. Some interest groups did generate large rosters of supporters through direct mail solicitations. But these appeals to the public asked not so much for the citizens' votes, time, energy, and ideas as for contributions to fund campaigns waged by policy experts. Consequently, as the political scientist Hugh Heclo has pointed out, with the reform legacy of the 1970s, American society further "politicized itself" and at the same time "depoliticized government leadership."[1]

This development did not surprise anyone who understood and appreciated the role parties had played historically in providing a vital link between citizens and their government. By the late 1970s, that role, and the unhappy consequences of its serious decline, resulted in efforts of party renewal. The 1979 amendments to the campaign finance laws were designed deliberately with the idea of bringing the parties back into the political process. As Robert Tiernan, chairman of the Federal Election Commission, admitted in testifying on this legislation: "Unfortunately, the FECA has had, or is perceived to have had, some unforeseen effects on party and grass roots political activity. . . . Changes in the [1974] statute are desperately needed to permit state and local party committees flexibility for vigorous campaign activity." Morley Winograd, president of the Association of State Democratic Chairpersons, echoed Tiernan's concerns, confirming the deleterious effect FECA had on political parties. The collaboration between local, state, and national committees had been weakened, in no small part owing to the fear of violating regulations that were difficult to interpret. Local committees, in particular, Winograd reported, were "reluctant to engage in federal-election related activity": "They generally do not have legal and accounting assistance available, and local committees, therefore, have not chosen to run risks of federal regulation." State parties, he continued, "felt frozen out of the 1976 Campaign," thus diminishing "the politics of party, the politics of coalition and accommodation, which is our nation's best defense against the divisiveness of special interest politics."[2]

In response to these concerns, FECA was amended to allow state and local party committees "to purchase without limit, campaign materials used in connection with volunteer activities on behalf of a candidate (such as buttons, bumper stickers, and yard signs)." A similar exemption was created to allow state and local party committees "to engage in certain voter registration and get-out-the-vote activities on behalf of the nominees of such party for President and Vice President."[3] It is my understanding that even before the 1979 amendments, the Republican National Committee had established nonfederal accounts to support state and local candidates and other party-building activities—a traditional role for parties prior to FECA. During the 1980s and 1990s, both Republicans and Democrats made use of nonfederal contributions, pumping new life into some state and local party organizations. As Ray La Raja's declaration (later in part 1 of this volume) shows, Democratic and Republican state party organizations have gotten stronger since 1979, becoming more likely to engage in such critical associational activities as conducting polls, providing campaign training, performing campaign research, and recruiting candidates.

The Republican and Democratic use of nonfederal funds to reinvigorate state and local party organizations has, therefore, buttressed the *national* character of the parties. A. James Reichley, the foremost authority on the history of party organizations, has noted that some national party managers had some initial inclination to couple this growing financial support with even more control of operations. But the constitutional division between the national and state governments provides state and local parties with powers and resources to resist centralized control. "If they have funds," Reichley wrote in 1992, "no matter at what geographical level they are raised, state and local parties will probably soon exert more independence, and in some cases are already doing so."[4]

The enactment of BCRA threatens the reinvigoration of national parties and the revitalization of America's federal democracy. Condemned as "soft money" and viewed as an effort to circumvent campaign finance laws, nonfederal funds have been charged with corrupting or appearing to corrupt the political process. This charge, abetted by expensive campaigns mounted by the Brennan Center for Justice and The Pew Charitable Trusts, has become received wisdom. As Whitfield Ayres shows in part 3 of this volume, however, the public has been largely indifferent to the BCRA. In the midst of the debate on the Hill over this legislation, Americans did not consider "reforming election campaign finance laws" as a high priority for President George W. Bush and Congress. BCRA, in fact, placed dead last on the list of Americans' political concerns, far behind more prepossessing issues as homeland security, the economy, and education. Indeed, even though John McCain made campaign finance reform the centerpiece of his presidential campaign in 2000, the public never considered "soft money" an important election issue. Like many party reforms, the BCRA has support in Congress, the media, and among "public interest" activists but has scarcely touched politics outside of the capital beltway.

Indeed, there is no evidence that "soft money" has corrupted parties or the political process. To the contrary, by strengthening parties, the use of nonfederal funds almost certainly has made the political process less corrupt and more responsive than it otherwise would have been. As political scientists have been arguing since the end of the nineteenth century, when the national government first sought to regulate partisan activity, party organizations help to reduce the amount of government corruption by linking representatives and interest groups to collective organizations with a past and a future. By the very act of supporting political parties, donors and interest groups must defend their political actions and policy positions publicly and in coordination with a large governing coalition. In this way, as Nelson Polsby has argued, party leaders and organizations can "deflect undue demands on the office holder, substitute with money from other sources money that is withheld or threatened to be withheld by importunate interest groups or individual donors, and assure that donations do not greatly distort the programmatic commitments embodied in party policy."[5] Professor La Raja indicates that there is a wide consensus in political science that interest groups' campaign contributions tend to assist powerful incumbents, whereas political parties support challengers and candidates in closely contested campaigns. This difference between party and interest group disbursements supports Polsby's view that party politics pose a protective layer of decisionmakers between candidates and donors.

Indeed, nonfederal money strengthens parties' ability to act as a critical intermediary between government action, on the one hand, and donors and interest groups, on the other. It does so by addressing a critical problem in contemporary American democracy: how to energize party-building activities and encourage citizen participation in an age when centralized decisionmaking and mass media appeals threaten to dominate political life. National party committees use nonfederal accounts in collaboration with state and local party organizations in a way that strengthens the national character of parties—that makes it possible for parties to penetrate every corner of the Union, recruiting candidates, attracting volunteers, and mobilizing voters.

BCRA is thus a remedy for a disease that has been misdiagnosed. More ominously, it will short-circuit the efforts of the past two decades to revitalize political parties and the critical function they play in making American democracy work.

I have been asked by counsel to assume that the BCRA will reduce the collaboration among national, state, and local parties that nonfederal funds have facilitated by, among other things, restricting the ability of the national, state, and local committees of the same party to transfer and "swap" funds and restricting joint fund-raising among the national, state, and local committees. Indeed, the BCRA goes so far as to restrict collaboration among different state parties. For example, state parties are prohibited from engaging in joint fund-raising with other state parties in raising so-called Levin Funds, which are nonfederal funds that state and local parties may raise, in contributions up to $10,000 per donor, so long as state law allows, for certain "federal election activity."

In my opinion, the restrictions on financial collaboration among national, state, and local party committees would diminish the *national* character of party organizations that historically has made them bulwarks of America's federal democracy. The Republican and Democratic National Committees in Washington are not federal parties, but national parties that contribute money and other campaign support to state and local candidates. The BCRA, therefore, would establish federal standards on campaign finance decisions at the state and local level. More generally, national party organizations will no longer provide a powerful link between national, state, and local offices. BCRA will sever the link, rendering parties both more *centralized* (as the national committees will be less able to support party-building activities at the state and local levels) *and* more *fragmented* (as cooperation between national, state, and local parties as well as among the state organizations will be restricted).

As was the case in the 1970s, the BCRA will weaken *party politics* and strengthen *pressure group* politics. Nonfederal funds have served as an important incentive for candidates and interest groups to cooperate with political parties; consequently, these funds have strengthened political parties as intermediary organizations between public officials and special interests. By banning nonfederal funds, the BCRA will encourage interest groups to exert influence directly on candidates and public policy.

The respected journalist Thomas B. Edsall has dubbed the BCRA "PAC Attack II." "Instead of reducing the power wielded by special interest groups in American elections, the [BCRA] reform bill is magnifying that power and making PACs, the *bêtes noires* of Common Cause and other good government groups, key players in finances once again."[6] In fact, the BCRA—and PAC Attack II—may be worse. The new reform legislation treats parties and interest groups unequally: for example, whereas a corporation or labor union can use unregulated funds to engage in issue advocacy, the new reforms will greatly burden political party advocacy. Consequently, political operatives of all ideological persuasions are likely to channel "soft money" to interest groups. Moreover, many political operatives are scrambling to create new organizations in which they can place the "soft money" that had been going to parties. According to Edsall, some of these groups, such as Progress for America, which has raised millions of dollars that it uses to promote President Bush's policy agenda, are being set up as 501(c)(4) organizations, which do not have to reveal the sources of the money raised or the details of how it is spent.[7] The result, Edsall states, will not only be a more fractious political process, but also a less accountable one: "When soft money was channeled through the parties, laws required full disclosure of both contributor and expenditures. But the new vehicles for this money are almost certain to be more secretive, with little or no obligation to reveal their activities."[8]

Indeed, based on my September 20, 2002, interview with Jay Banning, the RNC's director of administration and chief financial officer, it is my understanding that the BCRA prohibits the national committees' use of nonfederal funds for activities that in my opinion help define the national parties as political associations, including: support for state and local candidates; the coordination of activities of state and local party office holders (for example, the RNC supports meetings of, and communication among, Republican state attorneys general); political training and support of candidates, campaign managers, and grass-roots activists; research on issues and policies; the organizational activities of allied groups, such as the Young Republicans; outreach to particular ethnic, racial, and women's groups; public advocacy through media, brochures, and direct mail of party policies; annual meetings and conferences; and internal communications with party members about campaigns and issues through media such as websites, direct regular mail, and direct e-mail. The ability of an organization to communicate with its membership goes directly to its associational role. What's more, the BCRA treats parties and interest groups unequally with respect to this critical associational activity: corporations, labor unions, and other membership organizations may use nonfederal funds to communicate with their executives, administrative personnel, members, and shareholders on any subject, including to urge support for particular candidates or issues.

Advocates of the BCRA claim that since 1996, parties have abused nonfederal funds, employing issue ads for negative advertisements against candidates—oftentimes, without any reference to the political parties, their platforms, or the policies they support. It is important to point out, however, that interest groups have also increased their political advertisements that connect, indeed subordinate, the discussion of issues to electioneering, much of it negative in tone. As an Annenberg Public Policy Center study indicates, the ads of special interest groups represented 68 percent of all spending on issue ads in the 1999–2000 cycle; interest groups spent more than $347 million on these issue advertisements. The names of these groups did little to tell viewers who the sponsors of these messages were; indeed, in some cases they were misleading. For example, the Citizens for Better Medicare, which spent $65 million on television ads, is funded primarily by the pharmaceutical industry. Not only were the funding sources of interest groups ads more misleading than party-sponsored ads, they also tended to be more negative, especially in the early stages of the 2000 campaign.[9]

Whereas the BCRA will prohibit national parties from using nonfederal funds for issue advocacy, interest groups can continue to use nonfederal funds for issue advocacy, albeit with restrictions in the final 30 days before a primary and 60 days before a general election. It is unlikely, then, that the elimination of parties' use of nonfederal funds will reduce issue advertising. Instead, more funds will flow to interest groups that air issue advertising. Moreover, given the importance of the mass media in contemporary politics, restricting the funds that the political parties may use to pay for television and radio ads may very well have a deleterious effect on what deserves to be called party-building activities. Nearly every candidate who runs for office does so as a Democrat or Republican; consequently, it virtually is impossible for parties to completely separate support for candidates, issue advocacy, and party building. To ask parties to do so is to forget Schattschneider's refrain that they are the "only organizations that can win elections." It is ironic that as champions of BCRA criticize parties for muting their partisanship in issue ads, the public has recoiled at the growing partisan combat in Washington, D.C., so much so that parties have sought, with the help of nonfederal funds, to navigate toward somewhat more centrist and bipartisan positions.

Criticism of the parties' use of issue advertising should not lead to the elimination of national parties' nonfederal funds but to greater specification of its uses. Instead of a meat cleaver approach that eliminates soft money, reform could restrict its use to more conventional party building activities. Reformers have claimed that the national parties transfer nonfederal money to state parties for the sole purpose of funding issue ads. There is ample evidence, however, that Democrats and Republicans have used these funds for a number of routine, yet critical associational activities. Research that has focused on the states, rather than presidential elections, for instance, has shown that state parties use nonfederal funds in identifying supporters, mobilizing them, and strengthening the organizations that hold their allegiance.[10] Cast against the history of parties, the use of nonfederal funds serves the same purpose that party pamphlets and patronage foot soldiers played in the nineteenth century. In fact, the use of nonfederal funds for voter mobilization efforts may be one of the few devices left to parties to encourage participation in an age when barely half of the eligible electorate bothers to vote in presidential elections. As Professor La Raja shows, between the 1992 and 2000 elections cycles, spending on voter mobilization by Democratic and Republican state parties increased steadily from $9.6 million to $53.1 million. The BCRA is likely to reduce voter mobilization efforts. According to two MIT political scientists, eliminating nonfederal funds "will starve many grass activities of state and local parties." Eliminating all current "soft-money" expenditures, Stephen Ansolabehere and James Snyder estimate, "would lead to a 2 percent decline in voter turnout—without soft money, approximately 2 million fewer Americans would have gone to the polls in 1996."[11]

NOTES

1. Hugh Heclo, "Issue Networks and the Executive Establishment," in Anthony King, ed., *The New American Political System* (Washington: American Enterprise Institute, 1978), p. 124.

2. *To Amend the Federal Election Campaign Act of 1971, as Amended, and for Other Purposes,* Hearing before the Senate Committee on Rules and Administration, 96 Cong. 1 sess. (GPO, 1980), pp. 8–9, 34.

3. *Federal Election Campaign Act Amendments of 1979,* House Rept. 96-422, 96 Cong. 1 sess. (GPO, 1979), p. 2.

4. A. James Reichley, "Party Politics in a Federal Polity," in John Kenneth White and Jerome M. Miller, eds., *Challenges to Party Government* (Southern Illinois University Press, 1992), p. 60.

5. Declaration of Nelson W. Polsby, *Republican National Committee and Gant Redmon v. Federal Election Commission,* United States District Court for the District of Columbia, June 15, 1999.

6. Thomas B. Edsall and Juliet Eilperin, "PAC Attack II: Why Some Groups are Learning to Love Campaign Finance Reform," *Washington Post,* August 18, 2002.

7. Thomas B. Edsall, "New Ways to Harness Soft Money in Works," *Washington Post,* August 25, 2002.

8. Edsall and Eilperin, "PAC Attack II."

9. Annenberg Public Policy Center, University of Pennsylvania, "Issue Advertising in the1999–2000 Election Cycle," 2001.

10. Ray La Raja and Elizabeth Jarvis-Shean, "Assessing the Impact of a Ban on Soft Money: Party Soft Money Spending in the 2000 Elections," Policy Brief, Institute of Governmental Studies and Citizen's Research Foundation.

11. Stephen Ansolabehere and James M. Snyder Jr., "Soft Money, Hard Money, Strong Parties," *Columbia Law Review,* vol. 100, no. 3 (April 2000), p. 619.

Why Soft Money Has Not Strengthened Parties

Jonathan S. Krasno and Frank Sorauf

Jonathan S. Krasno is a Visiting Fellow at the Institute for Social and Policy Studies at Yale University. Frank Sorauf is a Regents' Emeritus Professor of Political Science at the University of Minnesota. Krasno and Sorauf served as expert witnesses for the defense and are experts on public opinion, political parties, and campaign finance.

In their review of the academic empirical data on political party and interest group activity, Krasno and Sorauf refute the claim that soft money has had a significant effect in building stronger party organizations. They note that trends in voter turnout, levels of party competition, and party identification do not support the thesis that parties have become stronger in recent decades. They describe how the diverse interests of candidates and parties work against the development of broadly based party organizations and argue that parties have focused their soft-money resources on advertising in a relatively small number of races, instead of devoting these funds to the type of activities that might provide a lasting or positive impact on state and local party organizations.

Krasno and Sorauf also argue that the reform act's ban on soft money will not significantly hinder party efforts to mobilize voters and thus depress voter turnout. They present a detailed analysis of party soft-money expenditures to make the case that only a relatively small proportion of soft-money spending is devoted to voter mobilization. Furthermore, they note, the higher contribution limits included in the reform act will provide adequate resources for party building in the future and may actually work to the benefit of state and local party committees.

BUILDING PARTIES WITH SOFT MONEY

There is no need to speculate about the immediate impact of a soft-money ban on parties since there is a long record of soft-money receipts and expenditures dating back a decade and longer.[1] The two national committees and the congressional campaign committees raised nearly $1.2 billion in soft money from 1991 to 2000, including more than $700 million in the 1997–98 and 1999–2000 election cycles.[2] Of this sum, more than $500 million was transferred to state parties during this period, in addition to the $235 million of hard money that the national committees sent to the states.[3] We evaluate the impact of these resources on parties by refer-ring back to the various roles they play in our political system.

To begin, there is no evidence that these financial resources have played any appreciable role in the historic level of party loyalty achieved within Congress over the last decade. Leaders on all sides have gone to great pains to confirm their willingness to steer financial support to party colleagues regardless of their voting records, and there is no reason to doubt them. There is anecdotal evidence of some financial strong-arming in the states as party leaders in legislatures with highly centralized systems like New York's or California's have reputedly used their control of electoral resources to reward and punish legislators according to their support of the leadership. In Congress, however, this has not been the case. This con-clusion does not contradict our earlier argument about the corruptive potential of soft money, for the behaviors in each situation are fundamen-tally different. The use of soft money to enforce party discipline involves leaders using their control of campaign resources as leverage on the entire caucus on a broad swath of roll call votes important to the leaders. Our argument about corruption, on the other hand, involves the donors' use of parties as conduits to route soft money to legislators in return for a wide variety of actions on a relatively narrow set of issues.

At first glance, the effect of soft money on the numbers of Americans voting and on electoral competition seems rather unimpressive. Voter turnout, already low, continued its slow decline in the 1990s with the exception of 2000, when a slightly greater percentage of Americans cast ballots than had four years earlier. Even so, voter turnout at the end of the 1990s was actually slightly lower than it had been at the start.[4] Similarly, electoral competition returned to historically low levels as soft-money receipts rose. This was particularly true for the House of Representatives, the set of elections in which the lack of competition has been of greatest concern and which, because of their large numbers and equally sized dis-tricts, offer analytical advantages. There the number of close contests has declined markedly since 1996 as spending has skyrocketed.[5] Granted, par-ties cannot be held completely responsible for these disappointments, but one of the main arguments for strengthening parties is their ability to stimulate greater turnout and competition.

Our concern here, however, has less to do with byproducts of stronger parties than with the actual strength of these organizations. The $1.2 bil-lion raised and spent over the last decade suggests that today's parties should be more formidable than those in the recent past. Yet there is much reason to doubt that assumption. To begin with, survey data show no real increase in the strength of partisan attachments. The National Election Studies (NES) asks respondents a series of questions about their identification with parties, building from these a seven-point scale that has been the academic measure of partisanship for fifty years. After a decade of lavish spending, however, the percentage of strong partisans, those with the greatest attachment to their party from whose ranks the most active citizens come, has shown virtually no advance.[6] In 1992, 29 percent of respondents identified themselves as strong Democrats or Republicans, compared with 31 percent in 2000.[7] These figures are near the historic low registered over the course of the fifty-year series of NES surveys, and this lack of enthusiasm for parties is echoed in responses to other questions about them that the NES asks.[8] The inference is obvious: whatever party building the $1.2 billion of soft money has funded over the past decade, it has done little or nothing to attract citizens to the party banners.[9]

The most obvious explanation for these results is that parties have been remarkably restrained about proclaiming their virtues and only somewhat less shy about skewering their opponents. The chief way in which parties speak directly to citizens is through television advertisements.[10] Media tracking data from the top seventy-five media markets show that parties were extremely active advertisers in both 1998 and 2000, sponsoring ads that appeared over 310,000 times.[11] But the parties' commercials in these years were distinguished most notably for their failure to mention either party by name. Viewers with sharp eyes might have spotted a disclaimer like "Paid for by the Democratic National Committee" near the end of an ad, but the words "Democrat" or "Republican" appear nowhere else in the vast majority of party ads run during 1998 (85 percent did not mention party) or 2000 (93 percent).[12]

While parties are curiously absent from their own commercials, candidates are nearly ubiquitous; their names were mentioned in 95 percent of ads aired by parties in 1998 and 99 percent in 2000.[13] The clear implication is that parties dedicated their advertising dollars to promoting the fortunes of their candidates, not themselves. Muting their partisanship served the needs of candidates, who in their quest for swing voters were eager to attract support from independents and crossovers. Thus parties mimicked candidates by rarely invoking partisan labels, instead focusing on the characteristics of the candidates. The candidates that parties focused on, moreover, were usually not their own candidates but their opponents'. Party ads mentioned the opposing candidate in 51 percent of spots aired, their own candidate in 17 percent, and both candidates in 32 percent.[14] It is no surprise, then, to discover that most of the spots parties aired were regarded as "attack" advertising by the coders who reviewed these ads.[15] Candidates displayed the opposite pattern, using their commercials to proclaim their virtues. The reason candidates shy away from attack advertising is the fear that it will make them appear mean. The fact that parties are left to do the dirty work of campaigning cannot make them more appealing to the public.

The data on parties' television advertising also illustrate another aspect of party building over the last few elections: its remarkably narrow focus. The top seventy-five media markets serve at least half of households in more than 335 congressional districts. Yet in both 1998 and 2000, more than half of the advertisements that parties sponsored in these markets appeared in just a dozen races.[16] Clearly the parties were concentrating their resources on the contests where they judged their funds might be decisive, but in consequence the vast majority of Americans heard nothing from them about their candidates. There is clearly a tension between building parties everywhere—if their ads could somehow be construed to affect partisanship—and trying to win specific elections. We would not advocate that parties do only the first without regard to the second, but adopting the opposite strategy inevitably limits the amount of party building in which they engage.

Finally, there is the matter of formal party organizations. Here we are confronted with a dizzying array of organizations, from the traditional state and local committees that have been such a large part of the scholarship on American democracy to the newly prominent legislative campaign committees (LCCs) and a variety of caucuses and offshoots affiliated with the parties or their leaders.[17] We focus on the former, the more locally based organizations that are closer to ordinary voters and historically have been the great source of grassroots political activity during campaigns. Indeed, even those political scientists who oppose restrictions on soft money argue mainly that soft money is worth saving for its effect on traditional party organizations.[18] We believe that close examination of the evidence suggests that soft money has had little lasting or positive impact on state and local organizations.

Our opinion is informed by two case studies we undertook for previous litigation, *Colorado II* and *Missouri Republican Party* v. *Lamb*.[19] In both instances, the plaintiffs argued that various restrictions on political parties would cripple their ability to act during and between campaigns. The facts, however, did not support these claims. The executive director of the Colorado Republican Party, for instance, at the time of this litigation was a resident of the Washington, D.C., area hired by the Republican National

Committee (RNC). The Colorado party received most of its funds from the National Republican Senatorial Committee (NRSC), and other money was raised for it, with little involvement by state officials, at events featuring visiting members of Congress and the first Bush administration. Despite this infusion of resources, the party was not able to organize a phone bank for volunteers or print out mailing labels for its own members.[20]

The situation in Missouri, several years later, was nearly identical. Again, the apparatus of the state party proved unwilling or unable to undertake basic tasks such as phone banking or leafleting on its own. In addition, without any state limits on the size of the contributions it received, Missouri's Republican Party relied heavily on large donors: 80 percent of its receipts came from just 36 donors (excluding the national parties) from a total list of contributors numbering approximately 1,000.[21] Like its counterpart in Colorado, the Missouri party's direct involvement in campaigns was limited largely to writing checks. Both committees paid outside vendors to run their phone banks and send their mailings; in addition they sent much larger checks to consultants for advertising. A highly specialized campaign industry allows parties to purchase campaign services, leaving them to raise money and choose from a menu of options. With the variety of paid alternatives available, the parties have fewer incentives to seek out citizen involvement in campaigns beyond their cash. The mass-based party organizations so highly esteemed by scholars seem to have been largely abandoned for a newer version relying on commercial services.

Other scholars echo these concerns. For example, in a recent "cyberforum" on parties for a group of experts invited to comment on the Bipartisan Campaign Reform Act, a number of participants questioned whether soft money has had any lasting effect on parties. One explained: "Soft money does not appear actually to build party infrastructure. . . . Soft money funds the 'coordinated campaign,' but leaves very little behind in terms of permanent assets for the party once the campaign is over."[22] Another participant was blunter: "I would argue that soft money doesn't really make the parties strong; it makes the people who bring soft money to the party strong."[23]

Impressions such as these reflect the extent to which parties have transformed themselves into organizations serving the immediate electoral needs of specific candidates. That was always the purely electoral life of the LCCs, but state and local parties—though also preoccupied by elections—had an enduring organization of their own, and their strength was always measured by their ability to recruit candidates, mobilize activists, organize party legislators, and debate party issues—as well as to manage the assorted tasks of delivering the party vote. All of that meant that they had a complex set of roles and tasks far beyond raising money and serving as conduits for national party funds.

Against this critique of the development of state parties in recent decades are two objections. The first is that a technological revolution has overtaken and transformed the old ways of campaigning. Thus parties have had to adapt or risk irrelevance; a number of our colleagues take the emergence of these "service parties" as signs of parties' inherent vitality and significance.[24] There is no doubting that technological changes have occurred, but they have not rendered obsolete the old-fashioned personal campaigning by candidates and volunteers. Our enthusiasm for volunteerism rather than subcontracted campaigns is not nostalgic; it is pragmatic. Research shows that face-to-face campaigning is vastly more effective in stimulating turnout than the phone banks and direct mail that have replaced it. Even more fundamental, local activists bring energy and talent to the political sphere. They help educate citizens about politics and deepen their involvement in their communities. For parties, when the election is over and TV ads no longer aired, when the phone banks and direct mail vendors are abandoned, activists remain a durable asset that the parties can continue to count on. No one can help but be impressed by the vast amounts of money flowing through parties, but the money has passed through them without leaving behind any lasting benefit.

Other political scientists accept the traditional model of state and local parties but argue that soft money has done them some good.[25] None of these scholars claim that anything more than a small fraction of each dollar raised has been spent to the benefit of state parties. By one estimate the soft money that state parties devoted to "grassroots party building" from 1992 to 1998 amounted to just under $20 million out of their total soft-money expenditures of $520 million during this period.[26] Adding some of the other expenditures to the party-building category—a portion of overhead costs, for example—may bring the totals higher, but they remain a small portion of the soft money they spent. Indeed, these data point to one major reason for the organizational weakness of the state parties: a chronic lack of investment.

CANDIDATES VERSUS PARTIES

That so little building of political parties, at least in a useful and lasting way, has occurred over the last decade does not mean that this trend will continue. Supporters of soft money place great stock in the possibility that the continued availability of vast sums of money will eventually work to the greater benefit of parties, even as they argue that some portion of these moneys are already spent in positive ways.[27] We are far less sanguine about the future, for we believe that party strategies over the last decade, far from being haphazard, are deliberate and well-considered responses to their need and desire to support candidates at all costs. As we noted above, that overwhelming concentration on the promotion of candidates conflicts with the building of parties.

One of the parties' greatest strengths is their breadth: parties encompass diverse constituencies. Democrats and Republicans contest elections in all corners in the country—sometimes with little success for long periods of time—and voters everywhere overwhelmingly identify with one of them. Thus there is some sort of Democratic and Republican party in even the most inhospitable territory. With every presidential election we hear the plaintive appeals of Democrats and Republicans in various locales pleading for their national party to campaign more heavily in their areas. Victory, though seemingly impossible, is often argued to be within reach; moreover, local partisans hope to provide encouragement and resources to the other party candidates on the ballot. Indeed, according to press reports, California Republicans succeeded in convincing the RNC and Bush campaign to divert resources from several states including Florida in the final days of the 2000 campaign to avoid disheartening local partisans by seeming to abandon the state to the Democrats.

From the standpoint of Republicans in California, that decision surely made sense, but for the Bush campaign it might have been disastrous had the race in Florida turned out differently. Of course, other Republicans would also regret any allocation of funds that costs them the presidency. This shared interest in the White House is much less relevant for specific candidates for the House or Senate. Indeed, the competition for party resources among various congressional candidates is fierce, beginning with mandatory pilgrimages to Washington to seek the blessings of legislative campaign committees. Party operatives attempt to weed out the likely candidates from the hopeless so that the parties may invest wisely in those races where its help is most meaningful, a process often called "targeting."[28] But even if we assume that parties (or anyone) possess the prescience to predict which races might be close many months in advance, it is clear that the more parties are able to direct their funds to the small set of races thought to be teetering in either direction, the fewer Americans are affected by their efforts. As we noted earlier, the logic of targeting conflicts with the process of building stronger parties everywhere.

The more fundamental question, however, is why so little of the soft money spent within a state is used to help its party organizations in any meaningful and lasting way. Given their acknowledged goal of targeting a small number of candidates, the answer must involve the perceived needs of those candidates as Election Day approaches. Candidates, unlike parties, have no certain political life following an election loss. All of the resources they can muster are expended in the attempt to win office. Parties that primarily serve candidates follow the same rule. The problem is that developing a grassroots organization—identifying leaders, recruiting volunteers, providing training and creating opportunities to interact and work together—might take years of effort. Candidates would happily accept the help of legions of party workers; they just have no interest in diverting time and money to help build that network, especially if those efforts fully ripen in later elections.[29]

Candidates have no reason to oppose stronger, more traditional party organizations, but they have even less reason to inconvenience themselves by helping build them. Incumbent public officials may have done much of the hard work of raising money for parties before a campaign, and even when they are not directly involved, specific candidates are often invoked in fund-raising appeals by party officials. Furthermore, parties and party organizations are for the vast majority of donors of secondary importance to individual candidates. As a consequence, parties present themselves as allies of candidates, a natural inclination for party leaders who are eager supporters of their tickets. Even if a state or local party official hesitated to help an individual candidate, the financial power wielded by the LCCs in Washington, organizations explicitly controlled by federal officeholders, keeps state and local committees beholden to their wishes. The substantial financial transfers to states and the dependence of many state organizations on the federal committees leaves many of them virtual agents of these committees.

The very notion that candidates and parties have separate interests may be surprising to those accustomed to see parties and candidates bound together by a common purpose. We would agree up to a point. We agree that control of government redounds to the benefit of all party members; few would advocate, for example, wasteful or foolhardy spending. Nonetheless, with respect to campaigns, parties' interests are clearly distinct from those of candidates, even presidential candidates trying to win a nationwide election. Because parties embrace innumerable candidates running for innumerable offices, there is, in effect, a need to be everywhere at once. Because parties are enduring institutions (or hope to be), they stand to benefit from long-term investments that candidates cannot undertake. Because parties seek loyal adherents while candidates welcome voters of all stripes, invoking partisan labels serves parties better than candidates.

What if we are wrong? What if parties were to choose sometime in the future to devote greater dollars to their own needs by trying to attract supporters, polish their public images, and rebuild local organizations? We would applaud these developments, but we doubt that banning soft money would hinder them. Even more noteworthy than the parties' soft-money receipts during the 1990s was the hard-money fund-raising by the national committees alone: $445 million (1991–92), $384 million (1993–94), $638 million (1995–96), $445 million (1997–98), and $705 million (1999–2000). The total of $2.6 billion over these ten years is clearly sufficient to maintain the current, paltry investment in party building or even a much more expansive program. The money is available; parties have lacked the incentive or the control to spend it on themselves.

Nor would a loss of soft money shrink parties to the point of being overshadowed by interest groups. The Federal Election Commission (FEC) reports that all Political Action Committees (PACs) combined raised $2.3 billion from 1991 to 2000 and contributed about $1.1 billion to candidates.[30] Parties more than kept pace with hard money alone, helped by larger contribution limits and their roster of elected officials.[31] But this comparison overlooks the fact that much of the money flowing to parties is interested money, including contributions from PACs. More fundamentally, reducing the comparison between parties and interest groups solely to financial matters misses the crucial aspect of parties' nature, as well as the main advantages that they possess over interest groups. These advantages begin with the tens of millions of Americans who identify with the Democrats or Republicans, and the thousands of officeholders whose names are listed on ballots with their party affiliations. Interest groups—especially once the full array of organizations like 501s and 527s are included—may have more money than parties, but no combination of groups has constituencies outside or inside government that compare with the parties'.

Finally, no one should underestimate the parties' ingenuity and capacity for adaptation, skills they have successfully exercised for more than a century in meeting every change in American electoral politics. Certainly, BCRA's implementation will decrease the amount of money available to state and local party organizations in the short run, but that loss will stimulate them to broaden their base of contributors and raise more hard money. Belt tightening will also force them to use their money more efficiently and effectively; it may even lead to an era in which campaign budgets reflect some rational definition of need. Many parties will also substitute less expensive volunteer efforts for some of the high-priced services currently purchased with soft money. Rebuilding their cadres of activists and returning to a more mass-based form of campaigning would also help increase voter turnout and improve candidate recruitment. But most of all, these steps would reestablish the parties' ties to local electorates and restore one historic line of responsibility for the decisions they make. It would free the state parties from the "dole" and its accompanying interventions and control by national party committees. One may think of the soft-money ban in BCRA as a form of "tough love," an affectionate rebuke likely to help state and local parties more than it hurts them.

VOTER TURNOUT

Voting is, by far, the most common way that people participate in politics.[32] It owes its popularity to the relative convenience of casting a ballot—a task usually requiring an hour or so every two to four years—and to the importance that people attach to it. Even nonvoters overwhelmingly agree that "voting in elections is extremely important in making someone a true American."[33] Scholars place similar importance on voting and often characterize it as a chief means of exercising popular control of government. It is no exaggeration to claim that voting is an essential responsibility of democratic citizenship.

Turnout in the United States

In the comparative perspective, the proportion of eligible citizens who cast ballots in the United States lags far behind the turnout rate in most other industrial democracies. Most of that gap can be ascribed to a variety of legal differences—from registration requirements to the scheduling of elections—that make voting in the United States more difficult than elsewhere.[34] As a result, a better comparison may be historical. Even here, however, today's turnout rates are well below those in past elections. In 1960, for example, 62.8 percent of eligible citizens voted in one of the closest elections in U.S. history; in 2000, just 51.2 percent cast ballots in an even closer contest.[35] This decline is part of a steady trend downward over the last four decades.[36]

The long-term decline in turnout has caused much consternation among policymakers and scholars. For some of these observers, the low levels of voter turnout are an indication of a growing emergency in American politics in which citizens have grown disaffected or bored by their leaders and their government.[37] Others view these claims as overwrought and point to survey results showing that Americans typically report greater faith in their government and interest in campaigns than citizens in other countries. Regardless of how they interpret the decline in voting, there is widespread agreement that turnout rates merit close attention and that higher levels would be desirable. Parties, given their traditional emphasis on mobilizing their voters, could potentially play an important part in halting and reversing the shrinking percentage of Americans who vote.[38]

As a result, one must be concerned about the argument in the debates over BCRA that the ban on soft money would hinder parties' efforts to mobilize voters and thus depress turnout. The Congress attempted to soften the financial blow to parties' mobilization programs by passing the Levin Amendment allowing state and local parties to use limited amounts of soft money to conduct generic voter registration and turnout efforts. This concession will surely help make more funds available in these areas. The more basic issue, however, is whether the broader ban on soft money will hamper parties' ability to boost turnout. The answer reflects our argument about how parties have come to function primarily as purchasers of campaign services in their attempt to aid individual candidates. The data show that parties devote relatively meager amounts of soft money to promoting turnout, and further analysis reveals that they have spent most of this money in ways that minimize even this limited impact.

We begin by citing a scholar on parties' use of soft money, Professor Ray La Raja, also an expert for the plaintiffs in this case. Working with a database of more than 500,000 separate expenditure entries reported to the FEC by federal, state, and local party committees in 1999–2000, Professor La Raja and his co-author divided these items into six categories, including the parties' spending on "mobilization."[39] Spending on mobilization by federal, state, and local party committees summed to $49.6 million in 2000. From 1992 to 1998, state party spending on mobilization slowly grew from $8.6 million to $22.6 million, reaching $41.8 million in 2000.[40]

The question is whether $49.6 million is a lot or a little money. We are inclined toward the latter. In 2000, the parties' spending to promote turnout accounted for 10.4 percent of their $478 million in soft-money expenditures.[41] Granted, it is not realistic to expect that parties could spend all of their soft money on mobilization. Overhead and fund-raising are costly, accounting for 47 percent of their soft-money spending. Traditional grassroots activities like yard signs, bumper stickers, and rallies added up to another 2.6 percent of their expenditures. The remaining amount was spent on "media" (33.4 percent) and "other/unidentified" (6.6 percent).[42] Thus nearly half of all soft money went toward administrative or fund-raising expenses, leaving parties with about fifty cents of every soft-money dollar to spend on a variety of purposes, including mobilization.

Moreover, turning out voters came in a very distant second to spending on media advertising. From our perspective, this allocation and the fact that the parties' media focused so heavily on specific candidates are indicative of a broader trend toward service parties. Just as we argue above that party building is of little importance to candidates in the midst of their campaigns, we conclude here that mobilizing voters was a far lower priority than airing television ads and competing for undecided voters. Whether spending three times more on media than on turnout efforts made good political sense for parties or for candidates they support is an open question. The parties obviously thought so, a decision that severely limited the amount available to spend on mobilizing voters.

Mobilization Expenditures in the 2000 Election

Before dismissing the $49.6 million spent by the parties in 2000 on voter mobilization, it is important to consider the impact of these funds. We attempted to do so by replicating Professor La Raja's coding of mobilization expenditures in the 2000 elections.[43] Using the same FEC data, we identified 28,157 entries totaling $40.4 million in soft money as relating to voter mobilization by searching the parties' descriptions of the purpose of their expenditure for a series of key words or phrases like "absentee" or "election day."[44] We are not able to replicate exactly La Raja's painstaking coding, but we are satisfied that we capture all of the main components of spending that he describes as mobilization and that the resulting data set is reasonably close to his specification.[45] Given the analysis we undertake, they are sufficient for our purposes.

Our inquiry focused on two related questions. The first concerns the actual activities on which party mobilization funds were spent, such as mail, phone banks, or canvassing. The second is whether these expenditures were for services purchased from subcontractors or whether they pay for activities or actions undertaken by the parties themselves. Both questions are inspired by a set of papers by Professors Alan Gerber and Donald Green measuring the impact of different activities on citizen turnout rates. Their studies used an experimental approach in which randomly assigned groups of respondents were exposed to reminders to vote delivered via mail, telephone, or in person. Their conclusions are an emphatic endorsement of the importance of face-to-face appeals. Regardless of the model estimated and the set of controls introduced, Gerber and Green found the impact of canvassing to be many times the effect of phone calls or mail. For example, in a large-scale experiment conducted during an election in New Haven, individuals who had been canvassed turned out to vote at a rate 8.7 percentage points higher than those in the control group.[46] By comparison, the impact of mail and phone calls was minimal, barely distinguishable from zero.[47] The authors have subsequently replicated this finding in a variety of other studies.[48]

We divided turnout expenditures into these and several other categories by again searching for key words or phrases in the description of the purpose of each item. For instance, we listed as canvassing any entry that made reference to "canvass" (includes canvassing and canvasser), "field worker," "literature drop," "poll worker," or "walker." In the end, we identified seven distinct categories of expenditures: canvassing, mail, telephone, media, voter files, administration, and other/unspecified.[49] The results show that parties spent the largest amount of soft money on mail ($14.9 million), telephone ($10.8 million), and voter files ($4 million).[50] Canvassing, the category of greatest interest and greatest impact, lagged well behind with just $1.2 million invested. Most of the money for canvassing was used to pay people to go door to door.[51] As a result, the average soft-money expenditure for canvassing was just $168, compared with an average of $16,100 for each outlay for mail. Entries relating to canvassing account for more than one-fourth of 28,157 cases in the data set, but these cases only account for 3 percent of total spending.

It is possible that some of the $8.4 million in the other/unspecified category should be attributed to canvassing.[52] Unfortunately, descriptions like "voter registration" or "generic get-out-the-vote" make it impossible to determine whether the activity involved was canvassing or telephone or mail or something else. Even if we were to include all payments apparently made to individuals as canvassing, it would add less than $1 million to the total devoted to face-to-face contact.[53] Political parties in several states—led by the Democratic parties in Louisiana, Kentucky, and New Jersey—did devote considerable resources to canvassing, but in other states such expenditures were minimal. Altogether, parties spent twenty times more soft money on phone calls and mail than they spent on canvassing.

The likeliest explanation for the neglect of canvassing is the organizational weakness of parties. Canvassing is not among the services routinely available from the campaign service industry, leaving parties to fend for themselves. But organizing an extensive face-to-face campaign—recruiting workers, providing materials and maps, handling logistics—is a fairly labor-intensive enterprise, whether one uses volunteers or paid labor. This is the case, furthermore, whether the face-to-face persuasion takes place at a front door, the local mall, or a membership meeting. The fact that three state parties named above accounted for the vast majority of spending on canvassing (80 percent) suggests that most other state committees either did not have the capacity to organize a canvassing effort or were unwilling to devote the resources.[54] Gerber and Green speculate that "the long-term decay of civic and political organizations may have reached such a point that our society no longer has the infrastructure to conduct face-to-face canvassing on a large scale."[55]

We tested this hypothesis by examining expenditures of individual parties to determine whether they were for subcontracted services or for activities that the parties performed themselves. The sheer number of separate expenditures in the data set made it impossible to check the recipient of each payment. Instead, we drew a random sample of 250 expenditures and used the optical records maintained by the FEC to determine whether payments were made to a company for services or not:[56] 226 of the items we scrutinized were payments to individuals or for services organized and conducted by the parties, while just 24 were disbursements to subcontractors. But the latter group included virtually all of the largest expenditures in our sample, so that total payments to subcontractors ($340,280) greatly exceeded spending on the parties' own activities ($78,957). This pattern is reflected in the larger dataset as well. The 25 largest soft-money expenditures accounted for over 15 percent of mobilization spending ($6 million). All of these large payments were made to subcontractors, and almost all of them were for direct mail or phone banks. By comparison, there were more than 19,000 separate expenditures of $50 or less that added up to just $550,000 of spending. Judging from the data of our sample, we would surmise that nearly all of these small disbursements involved activities that parties undertook themselves.

In sum, the parties' efforts to mobilize voters in 2000 were much less impressive than they may at first seem. The amount of soft money devoted to turnout efforts was a relatively small portion of the total amount available, and just a third as much as the parties spent on media advertising for their candidates. Even worse, the soft money that the parties did spend on mobilization went overwhelmingly to vendors to pay for phone banks and direct mail. These activities have been promoted as staples of modern campaigning for years, but research shows that they have almost no impact on the likelihood of citizens' voting. Rather, experiments show that old-fashioned, face-to-face appeals are most effective in inspiring people to vote. This sort of canvassing was once the traditional focus of state and local party organizations, but in their dedication to serving candidates they are no longer interested in personal campaigning, and in their disrepair they may not be capable of mobilizing their voters.

There is no law requiring parties to spend wisely. The effectiveness of various strategies is difficult to test, especially during the heat of a campaign, and techniques that may appear to work well in one election can become outmoded later. Rather, we are responding to the concern that banning soft money will cause turnout to decline. We find that allegation to be groundless for the simple reason that the parties have done little to mobilize voters in recent years. The money has been there, but the commitment and the infrastructure necessary to organize an effective mobilization campaign have been missing. The parties have chosen to spend far more money to promote candidates than to turn out their vote, and they have chosen to hire others to send letters and make phone calls rather than organize their own, more personal effort to get people to the polls. There is more than enough hard money available to replace the soft money that parties have spent on mobilization, but it will be up to the parties to find ways to spend it usefully.

NOTES

1. Soft money was "invented" earlier in 1979 from a FEC ruling, but the parties were not required to report until after the 1990 election.

2. These figures do not include the $308 million raised in the 2001–02 cycle as of June 30, 2002 (www.fec.gov/press/20020919partyfund/20020919 partyfund.html). Nor do these figures include soft money raised directly by state parties.

3. Federal Election Commission, *Campaign Finance Reports and Data* (www. fec.gov/finance_reports.html).

4. See *Statistical Abstract of the United States,* 2002 edition. Estimated turnout in presidential elections was 55.1 percent of the voting age population in 1992, 49.1 percent in 1996, and 51.2 percent in 2000.

5. Competitiveness has been measured in a variety of ways both before elections when forecasters attempt to predict which races will be close and after when returns are available. One familiar measure is to count the number of "marginal" districts, races where the incumbent won less than 60 percent of the vote. The number of marginals declined since the use of soft money in House elections from 115 in 1992, 119 in 1994, and 120 in 1996 to 91 in 1998 and 76 in 2000. See Norman J. Ornstein, Thomas E. Mann, and Michael J. Malbin, *Vital Statistics on Congress, 2001–2* (Washington: American Enterprise Institute, 2002).

6. See Angus Campbell, Philip E. Converse, Warren E. Miller, and Donald Stokes, *The American Voter* (University of Chicago Press, 1960; Midway Reprint).

7. National Election Studies (www.umich.edu/~nes/nesguide/taptable/tab2a_1.htm).

8. See National Election Studies (www.umich.edu/~nes/nesguide/taptable/tab2b_1.htm and www.umich.edu/~nes/nesguide/taptable/tab2b_2.htm).

9. It is noteworthy that this time period has been regarded as one in which experts, influenced by parties' success raising funds, have pronounced them resurgent. One of the few scholars to question this conclusion has asked how it is possible for parties to prosper without followers. See John J. Coleman, "Resurgent or Just Busy? Party Organizations in Contemporary America," in John C. Green and Daniel M. Shea, eds., *The State of the Parties: The Changing Role of Parties in American Parties,* 2d ed. (Lanham, Md.: Rowman and Little-field, 1996).

10. For example, see Ray La Raja and Elizabeth Jarvis-Shean, "Assessing the Impact of a Ban on Soft Money: Party Soft Money Spending in the 2000 Elections" (Berkeley, Calif.: Institute of Governmental Studies, 2001) (www.cfinst.org/parties/papers/laraja_softmoney.pdf), showing television advertising was (after expenses) the parties' largest expenditure of soft money. It is a trait that parties share with candidates who have long been noted for their reliance on paid television. Parties, however, cannot count on the same level of free media coverage of their activities that candidates enjoy.

11. See Jonathan Krasno and Kenneth Goldstein, "The Facts about Television Advertising and the McCain-Feingold Bill," *PS: Political Science,* vol. 35 (June 2002), pp. 207–12.

12. Just 15 percent of party ads in 1998 and 7 percent in 2000 mentioned either political party. See ibid.

13. Coders were asked separate questions about both candidates and coded references in the text and/or visuals. For results, see ibid. For information about the coding, see www.polisci.wisc.edu/tvadvertising/Coding%20th%20Ads.htm.

14. Calculated by the authors. The calculation for 2000 makes use of a version of the 2000 data set from May 14, 2002. A later version of these data is provided with the expert report filed by Professor Kenneth Goldstein.

15. The tone of a commercial was coded according to the following question: In your judgment, is the primary purpose of the ad to *promote* a specific candidate ("In his distinguished career, Senator Jones has brought millions of dollars home. We need Senator Jones."), to *attack* a candidate ("In his long years in Washington, Senator Jones has raised your taxes over and over. We can't afford 6 more years of Jones."), or to *contrast* the candidates ("While Senator Jones has been raising your taxes, Representative Smith has been cutting them.")? See Jonathan S. Krasno and Daniel E. Seltz, *Buying Time: Television Advertising in the 1998 Congressional Elections* (New York: Brennan Center, 2000).

16. See Krasno and Goldstein, "The Facts about Television Advertising and the McCain-Feingold Bill."

17. Among the last we would include organizations like the Democratic Leadership Council or Log Cabin Republicans.

18. See, for example, statement by Raymond La Raja, *CFI "Cyber-Forum": How Would McCain-Feingold Affect the Parties?* (www.cfinst.org/parties/mf_responses.html).

19. Frank J. Sorauf and Jonathan S. Krasno, "Political Party Committees and Coordinated Spending," prepared for the Federal Election Commission in *Colorado II*, 1997; Frank J. Sorauf and Jonathan S. Krasno, statement prepared for *Missouri Republican Party* v. *Lamb*, 2000.

20. Sorauf and Krasno, "Political Party Committees and Coordinated Spending," pp. 35–36.

21. Frank J. Sorauf and Jonathan S. Krasno, statement prepared for *Missouri Republican*, 2000.

22. Statement by John C. Green, *CFI "Cyber-Forum": How Would McCain-Feingold Affect the Parties?*

23. Statement by Robin Kolodny, *CFI "Cyber-Forum": How Would McCain-Feingold Affect the Parties?*

24. For example, see David Manafee-Libey, *The Triumph of Campaign-Centered Politics* (New York: Chatham House, 1999).

25. See particularly comments of Raymond La Raja, *CFI "Cyber-Forum": How Would McCain-Feingold Affect the Parties?*

26. Ray La Raja and Karen Pogoda, "Soft Money Spending by State Parties: Where does it really go?" Institute of Governmental Studies and Citizens Research Foundation Working Paper (Berkeley, Calif., 2000), p. 17.

27. For example, see comments of La Raja, *CFI "Cyber-Forum: How Would McCain-Feingold Affect the Parties?"*

28. Parties could always target with their hard money, but their ability to shift resources to favorite candidates was constrained by limits on their direct contributions and coordinated expenditures. One result of these limits is that the NRSC for a time routinely spent the maximum allowed for coordinated expenditures on almost all of its candidates. This pattern contributed to the decision by one candidate in 1988 to sue the committee for additional money it had decided not to use on his race. See Jeff Holyfield, "Riegle Expected to Win Big Over Dunn," Associated Press Political Service, November 8, 1988.

29. It is worth noting that these volunteer efforts offer little or no profit for the campaign industry that provides services to parties and candidates.

30. Ibid.

31. Individuals may give up to $20,000 yearly to parties, $5,000 to PACs under FECA. The BCRA raises the annual limit on contributions to national parties to $25,000.

32. The National Election Studies asks respondents about a variety of activities: registration, voting, along with whether they tried to influence others, attended a political meeting, worked for a party or candidate, wore a button or put a bumper sticker on their car, and gave money to a campaign.

33. Survey item from the 1991 National Election Studies Pilot Study. The full question reads: "Is voting in elections extremely important, very (important), somewhat (important), or not at all (important) in making someone a true American?"

34. Among the legal arrangements increasing turnout rates in several other countries is mandatory voting whereby failure to cast a ballot is punishable by a fine. See David P. Glass, Peverill Squire, and Raymond E. Wolfinger, "Voter Turnout: An International Comparison," *Public Opinion,* vol. 6, 1984, pp. 49–55.

35. Turnout rates in state and local elections are generally much lower when they do not coincide with the presidential ballot.

36. This decline is especially vexing because it has occurred as blacks, always legally eligible to vote, were allowed to exercise the franchise in the South, and registration requirements were being eased throughout the nation. The 26th amendment giving eighteen- to twenty-year-olds the right to vote, on the other hand, depressed turnout rates by adding millions of eligible voters from the age group with the lowest level of turnout.

37. For example, see Walter Dean Burnham, *The Current Crisis in American Politics* (Oxford University Press), 1983.

38. Steven J. Rosenstone and John Mark Hansen, *Mobilization, Participation, and Democracy in America* (Macmillan, 1993).

39. La Raja and Jarvis-Shean, "Assessing the Impact of a Ban on Soft Money," p. 3. Mobilization is defined as "costs of registering and contacting voters through direct mail, telephone banks, canvassing, and voter files." Note that this characterization includes activity that might be more geared to persuading voters than to reminding them to vote.

40. Ibid., pp. 3, 6.

41. Ibid. Direct comparisons are available only for state parties in previous years. State parties' spending on mobilization ranged from 9 to 16 percent of their soft money expenditures during this period. In 2000, state parties devoted the most money to mobilization, $41.8 of the $49.6 million spent by parties at all levels.

42. Ibid. Media refers to cost of television, radio, and print ads, including production costs. Other/unidentified are items whose purpose could not be determined, including consultants.

43. These data were compiled by Krasno with the help of Robert Biersack of the FEC, and further coded by Krasno.

44. The FEC asks filers to describe the purpose of their expenditure in their own words. The result is thousands of different descriptions, largely due to variations in describing the same activity. Following La Raja, we coded descriptions including the following key words or phrases as mobilization expenses, regardless of their timing: "GOTV" (acronym for "get-out-the-vote"), "voter," "absentee," and "Election Day." In addition, we also categorized entries containing the words "phone," "mail," "postage," "slate," "printing," "canvass," or "list" as related to turnout if they were made in the last two weeks of the campaign. The FEC file

includes allocations of federal and nonfederal, or soft, money. In this discussion, we focus on only the latter.

45. One possible explanation for the disparity is our decision to limit certain mobilization expenditures to those occurring in the last two weeks of the campaign. La Raja is not clear about how to treat these items, but by focusing on late phone calls, direct mail, and other outreach programs, we felt certain that we included only those activities whose impact on mobilization is most direct.

46. Alan S. Gerber and Donald P. Green, "The Effects of Canvassing, Telephone Calls and Direct Mail on Voter Turnout: A Field Experiment, *American Political Science Review,* vol. 94 (2000), pp. 653–63.

47. Ibid., p. 659. Phone calls may be more effective if the caller is familiar, such as a college student calling another college student, the sort of circumstance that rarely occurs with the paid phone banks that predominate in campaigns. See Alan S. Gerber and Donald P. Green, "Do Phone Calls Increase Voter Turnout?: A Field Experiment," *Public Opinion Quarterly,* vol. 65 (2001), pp. 75–85.

48. These papers are available at Yale University Institute for Social and Policy Studies, *Voter Mobilization Experiments* (www.yale.edu/isps/publications/voter.html).

49. Mail includes entries with the key words "mail," "postage," or "voter labels"; telephone includes "phone," "call," or "voter id"; media includes "ad," "advertising," "television," "TV," or "radio"; list includes "list," "voter record/abstract/data/disk/history/info/file," "phone match." Administration includes rents, payroll taxes, and a variety of reimbursements. Other/unspecified, the largest category, is dominated by expenditures like "GOTV," "Election Day worker," or "absentee ballot program" that are most likely canvassing, mail or telephone, but cannot be determined. Other/unspecified also includes almost $1 million of spending on consulting unrelated to the other categories.

50. Voter files, a standard tool in modern campaigning, generally provide a list of registered voters in a locale. They may be purchased directly from jurisdictions or from list vendors who frequently add vital information like phone numbers or other contextual data to the file. These lists are particularly useful in guiding direct mail and phone banks so that campaigners may focus their efforts on citizens most like to turn out on Election Day, or, in the case of the recently registered, on those eligible to vote. They are probably of less value to canvassers, who tend to go to all of the doors in a neighborhood, not specific doors.

51. We reached this conclusion by observing the size of the expenditures and noting that the purpose of these expenditures—typified by entries like "Election Day canvasser" or "Poll worker"—appeared to refer to individuals hired. In addition, our analysis of a sample of disbursements described below confirmed that most entries were payments to individuals.

52. The same is true of the $4 million spent on voter lists, although in this case it is likely that these lists served the parties' phone banks and direct mail, not their door walkers.

53. This is accomplished by recoding all entries from the other/unspecified category where soft-money expenditures were less than $200 as canvassing.

54. It is possible that large expenditures for canvassing in several other states may have been overlooked because of different reporting conventions. For example, an activity described as "GOTV canvassing" in Louisiana or New Jersey might have been called "Generic GOTV" elsewhere, making it impossible to determine the activity involved. The total amount of money at stake, however, is relatively small because of the low cost of hiring canvassers. As we note above, the average disbursement for canvassing was $168.

55. Gerber and Green, "The Effects of Canvassing, Telephone Calls and Direct Mail on Voter Turnout," p. 662.

56. Most of these calls were easy to make. Payments to individuals were obviously signs of party activity, as were expenditures for stamps (though large payments may have been made on behalf of direct mail vendors) or for food or catering. We also categorized several large payments to local party organizations as expenditures by the parties themselves, though we could not be sure this money was not passed on to one or more subcontractors.

Why Soft Money Has Strengthened Parties

RAYMOND J. LA RAJA

Raymond J. La Raja is an assistant professor of political science at the University of Massachusetts at Amherst whose research focuses on American political parties, elections, and campaign finance. He served as an expert for the Republican National Committee, a lead plaintiff in the McConnell *case.*

La Raja's report presented an analysis of party organizations and party financial activity to highlight the use of soft money for party-building activities at the national, state, and local party level. In this excerpt, he argues that the relationships among national, state, and local party committees have been strengthened in recent decades because parties have been able to raise sufficient funds to invest in party-building programs at every level. He further notes that party organizations have developed a division of labor among different components of their structure, with national committees taking primary responsibility for administrative functions and fund-raising, while state and local committees concentrate on campaign activities and voter mobilization efforts.

La Raja contends that parties have strong incentives to devote resources to traditional party-building functions as a result of their desire to win elections and construct legislative majorities. Parties have an incentive to support challengers, for example, and thus provide a necessary counterbalance to the proincumbent efforts of interest groups. Most important, he presents detailed analyses of national and state party soft-money expenditures to demonstrate how these funds are used to support party organizations and finance voter education and turnout efforts. He also observes that many soft-money donors are small contributors and that these gifts are unlikely to have a corrupting effect on the political process.

The reform act, La Raja concludes, will reduce the capacities of parties to serve as a moderating vehicle for divisive factional group politics. In his view, the act will advantage interest groups rather than parties and cause money to shift from party committees to organized groups, with particular benefits flowing to those with large memberships.

ACTIVITIES AND IMPORTANCE OF AMERICAN POLITICAL PARTIES

Political parties are essential institutions in democracies. This is a widely accepted premise among political scientists. In the United States, political parties have played a critical role linking citizens to their government locally and nationally. Through efforts to build coalitions of candidates, officeholders, and voters at every level of government, American political parties have been agents of consensus in a society characterized by individualism and diversity of interests. But unlike parties in Europe, American party organizations have not been highly centralized. Instead, political parties at each level have enjoyed considerable autonomy while they work together toward common goals.

American political parties have focused primarily on winning elections rather than pursuing rigidly defined ideological doctrines. While the major parties have articulated different principles and policies over the years, they choose to emphasize issues that allow them to build diverse and decentralized coalitions. Party leaders have continuously adapted the party organization over the years to help them build support among voters for the party and its candidates. In the early days of the Republic, the party's electoral apparatus grew out of the need to mobilize electoral support among an increasingly diverse and large electorate. As the U.S. population expanded, party leaders and activists developed campaign technologies to attract and bring supporters to the polls. The earliest technologies included party-sponsored newspapers, the distribution of party ballots to voters, and "treating" voters to popular forms of entertainment. Technologies have changed through the decades, but the overriding goals remain the same: to attract support for the party and elect its candidates to office.

Strong organizations are important for political parties and American democracy. Party organizations provide an arena for a varied set of party activists and professionals to coalesce behind party candidates. Among the varied set of political actors in American life, the party organization remains uniquely the ongoing operation that serves the interests of more than a single candidate or set of issues. It is the core "node" in a partisan network that extends from elected officials to candidate organizations, party-allied groups, campaign consultants, and ultimately, the voters. As such, these organizations serve an important function in coordinating party messages, supporting campaigns, and building large coalitions.

Parties are an essential institution for promoting political competition, which is a sine qua non of democracy. In a healthy party system, when the party candidates experience defeat at the polls, the party organization assumes responsibility for evaluating the loss, for developing new strategies, and for marshaling resources to win future elections.[1] As the most recognizable organization within an extended party network, an active party committee that coordinates political activities augments accountability in an American electoral system that is highly decentralized among numerous candidate committees and political action committees.

To maintain strong organizations, the parties need to engage in general party building during election and nonelection years. By "party building" I mean efforts to strengthen the capacity of the party organization to perform its traditional functions. These include year-round fund-raising, recruiting and training candidates, researching and crafting campaign themes, identifying and mobilizing voters, and educating the public about policy issues. Party building does not include acting as a financial conduit for individual candidates to funnel money into their campaigns.

Political parties at every level work together toward common goals. While American party committees have considerable autonomy, they rely on each other for information and resources. They are also bound to each other by the success of party candidates at different levels of government office. Martin Van Buren, for example, helped elect Andrew Jackson in 1828 through this important insight. He understood that local candidates benefited from being associated with a popular candidate like Jackson at the top of the ticket. But Jackson needed to get voters to the polls, a task that was ideally suited to local party organizations. The mutual necessities of local and national party figures help establish a thriving party organizational network that generates partisan loyalties in the electorate, economies of scale in campaigns, and the sinews that tie local parties to a national party apparatus.

To participate across federal, state, and local elections, political parties at each level may keep three separate financial accounts: (1) a *federal account,* which includes funds that are raised and spent under the guidelines of the Federal Campaign Election Act (FECA) and its amendments; (2) a *nonfederal account,* which includes funds that are raised and spent under state laws, and which can only be used for state and local elections; and (3) an *allocation account,* which is a hybrid account that includes both federal and nonfederal funds to be used for "party-building" activities that affect party candidates across the ticket. It is my understanding that state parties transfer funds from their nonfederal accounts into the allocation accounts for party-building activities that may affect the entire party ticket, and not just state and local elections. In 1990 the Federal Election Commission (FEC) issued rules that established accounting guidelines to determine how much federal and nonfederal funds could be allocated to particular activities.

Party scholars observe that relationships among local, state, and national organizations have strengthened in the past three decades. They attribute this strengthening to the role of the national parties in providing resources and expertise to their lower levels.[2] The national committees have raised money to spend on building the state and local parties. They do this by transferring funds, particularly nonfederal funds, to the state organizations. National committees also help state and county organizations develop programs to improve party operations and staff professionalism. Both the Republican National Committee (RNC) and Democratic National Committee (DNC) hire personnel in Washington who are chiefly responsible for supporting party affairs in the states, including fund-raising, voter identification, mobilization, and campaign strategies.

This kind of party activity, coordinated by the national committees, is exactly what prominent political scientists hoped for when they issued their landmark report in 1950 to strengthen American political parties.[3] By centralizing fund-raising, merging party efforts at every level, and working closely with candidates, the party committees have tightened the party nucleus, which is a development that encourages greater accountability in the electoral process. National parties have emerged as strong actors during the past three decades because they have been able to raise sufficient funds to invest in party-building programs at every level.

According to John Bibby, a preeminent party scholar who is an especially strong analyst of state political parties,

> Fund transfers from the national organizations to state parties, joint national-state party campaign activities, and national party technical assistance to state affiliates have all resulted in a nationalizing of party campaign efforts and substantially heightened levels of integration between the two strata of party organization. Thanks to assistance provided by the national party committees, many state parties have been strengthened.[4]

Political parties are important agents for recruiting and training candidates. The institution of the direct primary has all but eliminated the ability of political party leaders to handpick their nominees, as they did at the turn of the century. But seeking out and encouraging candidates to run for office remains a vital party function. Professors Gary Moncrief, Peverill Squire, and Malcom Jewell provide examples from Vermont and Alabama where leaders from party organizations that were historically in the minority invested time and resources in local districts seeking candidates to run against the opposition.[5] In V. O. Key Jr.'s classic account of Southern politics, he attributes the transient and demagogic nature of personal political factions in Alabama (as in other Southern states) to the lack of strong

party organizations that could provide "a somewhat orderly and systematic means for the development and grooming of party candidates and a
continuity of personnel that encourages at least a germinal sense of group
responsibility for party action." In the absence of strong parties, Key
argues, Alabama political leaders were "self-appointed and self-anointed
and attract to themselves sub-leaders by favor, chance or demagogic skill."[6]

Parties have a strong incentive to invest in recruiting because they want
to win majorities in the legislature. They are strategic in their efforts
because they look for districts that are winnable and they seek good candidates. Good candidates usually have local name recognition and some
experience in public affairs. They have the best shot at winning. In my survey of state party activity during the 2000 election cycle, fifty-four of
ninety-four major state parties reported that they recruited candidates
often and only three claimed they never performed this function.

Party officials are the most likely source of recruitment contacts for
state legislative candidates. According to Moncrief, Squire, and Jewell, 46
percent of 535 state legislative candidates that were surveyed said officials
in the local party approached and encouraged them to run for office
before they announced their candidacy.[7] About one-third said officials in
the state party organizations approached them. In contrast, only 14 percent were approached by interest groups to run for office. The political
party is the most effective agent of recruitment among the many groups
that engage in electoral politics.

The parties help candidates by training them and their campaign staff.
In my survey, almost half of the parties reported they frequently helped
candidates this way; only twelve of ninety-four parties said they never or
rarely performed this function. Parties also steer donors to candidates,
encourage well-known elected party officials to help the candidate with
shared public appearances, and get voters to polls on Election Day.[8] The
promise or refusal of support from the party organization can make an
important difference in whether a candidate chooses to run for office, particularly in an era of cash-intensive campaigning that requires skillful
application of advanced campaign technologies.

National and state political parties can be an important source of campaign contributions for state-level candidates facing tough races. There is
wide consensus in political science that parties support challengers more
than interest groups, which prefer to contribute to incumbents. The reason for this is rooted in the different incentives of these two groups. Parties desire to win majorities in legislatures so they invest in boosting their
control of offices whenever possible. Most interest groups, in contrast,

seek to build relationships with officeholders as a way of improving access to the legislative process and lobbying their position. In political science, there is strong empirical support for the theory that interest groups allocate resources primarily to pursue the "access" strategy, meaning they give to candidates who are most likely to win office, which is usually the incumbents.[9] Political parties, however, allocate resources for electoral strategies, meaning they contribute money to a party candidate who is in a potentially close election.

Parties give more of their resources to nonincumbents than political action committees (PACs). Interest groups may be reluctant to support challengers because these candidates are generally less likely to win. Supporting challengers also poses the risk of incurring the resentment of the incumbent legislator should he or she get reelected. PACs are much more likely to contribute to incumbents than political parties. In the 2000 elections, three-fourths of PAC contributions to federal candidates went to incumbents, while parties gave 39 percent to incumbents. Parties gave twice as much of their resources to challengers (22 percent) as PACs (11 percent) in federal elections.

National parties make contributions to state-level candidates, including during years when there are no federal races. For example, the RNC contributed roughly $500,000 to the Republican gubernatorial candidate in Virginia in 1999 as well as substantial funds to the Republican gubernatorial candidate in New Jersey.[10] The national parties also contribute money to local legislative candidates. During the 2000 election cycle, the Republicans, for example, allocated 7 percent ($9.5 million) of their nonfederal funds for contributions to state and local candidates. The national committees contributed a combined $19 million to state and local candidates. By helping state and local candidates win office, the national parties advance their policy agenda and public support for this agenda below the federal level. The desire of the national party to associate with state and local party affairs is also part of a long-term strategy to strengthen the party. National party leaders recognize the importance of developing a "farm team" of experienced candidates and elected officials who will eventually run for higher office.

National parties allocate about one-quarter ($136 million) of their nonfederal money to party-based operations affiliated with the headquarters in Washington. Of this amount, $57.8 million (43 percent) went for administration such as paying salaries, benefits, office equipment, and supplies. Another $52.6 million (39 percent) was invested in fund-raising activities. Only $10.3 million (8 percent) was allocated for media and

$8.5 million (6 percent) for voter mobilization and grassroots activity. A division of labor exists among the levels of parties, with the national organizations taking primary responsibility for administrative functions and fund-raising, while state and local parties engage more directly in campaigns and voter mobilization.

National parties assist state parties in raising funds. A common perception is that the national parties transfer nonfederal money to state parties for the sole purpose of funding issue ads. But national party support of state parties goes deeper than this. For example, the national committees provide expertise to state staff in raising money. Both the RNC and DNC sponsor regional fund-raising seminars for staff from state and local parties. The national party staff can be invaluable in showing state party workers how to organize operations for fund-raising and telemarketing. These tasks require considerable experience, which is often lacking in smaller states where staff turnover is high and much of the work is done through volunteers.

National party transfers to state organizations also help with party building. Transfers from national parties are allocated for administration (which includes salaries, benefits, office equipment, and supplies), voter mobilization, and media campaigns. As transfers to the state parties increased, so did spending on state party work. Between the 1992 and 2000 election cycles, spending on voter mobilization increased steadily from $9.6 to $53.1 million.

The most dramatic increase in state party spending was for media activities during presidential election years for issue ads. The emergence of significant amounts of issue advertising by state parties in 1996 is rooted in the deficiencies of a presidential public funding system that is severely out of step with important changes in the electoral season. Presidential primaries are "frontloaded," meaning that a party nominee emerges several months before the national conventions. Under this circumstance, the parties face what political scientists refer to as a "prisoner's dilemma" during the period leading up to the party convention. Both parties can wait several months until their respective conventions, when public funds are released to their presidential candidates for the general election. Alternatively, they can begin to set the issue agenda before the convention. The dilemma is complicated by the number of issue groups that have a strong incentive to shape the political dialogue by broadcasting messages early in the electoral process.

The wide-open period gives an advantage to any political party or interest group that chooses to broadcast issue ads before the conventions. If both parties and interest groups forgo issue ads during this period, then the election will be fought during the few months beginning after the conventions. If one party or major interest group decides to move earlier, it has a compelling advantage to set the policy agenda for the upcoming presidential campaigns. The fear of leaving an advantage to the opponent spurs the parties and interest groups to move first. Issue ads before the convention reflect an effort to capture this policy space rather than relinquish it to opponents and factional interests within either of the parties.

It is my understanding that the Bipartisan Campaign Reform Act (BCRA) does not allow political parties to air issue ads that refer to a federal candidate at any time using nonfederal funds. The BCRA also prohibits interest groups from airing issue ads with nonfederal funds during a blackout period. This does not prevent interest groups from using nonfederal funds early in the election by "frontloading" issue ads to set the policy agenda for presidential and other elections. If the last provision barring interest groups from using nonfederal funds for issue ads during a blackout period does not withstand constitutional scrutiny, the political parties will be at even more of a disadvantage in comparison with interest groups since the latter will have relatively more ability to communicate their messages up through Election Day. Interest groups already dominate issue advertising, as shown later in this report.

While it is apparent that national committees target party building in competitive states, it is also true that every state party receives money from them, even if there are no competitive federal elections in the state. According to Marianne Holt, who led the "Outside Money" project for the 1998 elections sponsored by the Pew Charitable Trusts, the transfer of national party funds for get-out-the-vote (GOTV) drives "has increased the state and local party role as they spend more and more soft money. . . . Such campaign activity has not only strengthened the national party committees but has infused the state parties with a vitality and power not seen in the past two decades."[11]

Political parties use nonfederal money to develop and disseminate political messages. The national parties possess research divisions that focus on message development through the use of polling data and focus groups. In conjunction with the party leadership in government, party operatives craft issue themes that will frame the party's policy and campaign agenda. The national party committees help to coordinate the daily flow of political messages by sending out faxes and e-mails to the parties' elected officials at every level. The state parties also send out similar political information related to state policy issues and campaigns.

Nonfederal money is used to spread the party message. In place of the traditional party newsletter, political parties now commonly use e-mail to spread the word among adherents. Every major state party has a website where voters can get information about candidates and opportunities to serve the party. One of the most important and expensive methods of reaching partisans is through direct mail. The state political parties devote as much as 22 percent of nonfederal funds from their nonfederal accounts for this activity, according to data provided by the Center for Public Integrity. Direct mail is useful because the parties can pursue several goals simultaneously: raise money, explain the party position on issues, and contrast their position with the opposition. Direct mail tends to be targeted toward the party's loyal or likely voters.

Political parties also use broadcast media to spread their political messages. Broadcast media are particularly important in persuading "undecided" voters to side with the party and its candidates. Usually, party-based ads focus on selected issue themes developed before the start of the electoral season. The fact that these ads are sponsored by the national or state parties and used throughout the nation gives them a generic "cookie-cutter" quality.[12] Local candidates sometimes dislike this generic quality, but the similarity of themes provides some policy coherence across party candidates. The theme-focused party ads encourage accountability in elections since voters will be able to know what the party candidates stand for collectively. Even when voters do not recognize the link between party-based ads and party candidates, institutional intermediaries, such as the news media, help make these links for the voter.

At the grassroots level, political parties mobilize volunteers and develop local support for the party and its candidates. The state political parties provide the support infrastructure that allows local volunteers to reach out to voters. They do this by creating detailed voter lists, operating phone banks, developing precinct maps for canvassing, purchasing yard signs and bumper stickers, and handling all the administrative paperwork involved with purchases and filing with the election regulatory agencies in the state and with the Federal Election Commission.

Grassroots efforts at the local level have increased or been maintained since the 1980s. According to a survey of 335 local Republican committees, a greater percentage of these organizations have been getting involved in a variety of grassroots efforts that Congress wanted to spur through its amendments to the FECA in 1979.[13] For example, the percentage of committees distributing posters and lawn signs increased from 62 to 92 percent between 1980 and 1996. The Democratic local committees show similar gains.

The modern party organization relies heavily on outside campaign consultants to do much of its work. By "outsourcing" particular tasks to professionals, the modern party organization has adopted some of the same
administrative strategies as contemporary business firms, governmental
agencies, and not-for-profit organizations. One important aspect of the
relationship between the party organization and its consultants is that the
latter tend to work for only one of the major parties. In fact, many consultants gain political experience working for the party organization early
in their careers. While some casual observers of politics may lament that
politics has been overrun by "hired guns" working for any candidate with
money, more acute observers have remarked that consultants constitute an
extended network of party activists.[14] What may be striking to the histo-
rian of political parties is how much more professional these operations
are than in the days when party precinct captains routinely walked the
local streets, building face-to-face support for the party. Earlier party
organizers, however, relied on the best available technology to suit their
needs. The modern party exploits new technology to achieve the same
goal of spreading the party message and electing its candidates to office.
That is why party workers employ many strategies developed by commercial enterprises to identify and inform citizens: direct mail, surveys, and
telephone calls. Political organizations need to reach large and dispersed
audiences with their political messages, while competing in a broadcast
and print environment saturated with entertainment and commercial
information. For this reason, it is hardly surprising that they avail themselves of the latest communication technology and strategies.

To perform the activities I have mentioned above, political parties need
money. While party historians describe an era when the party organization
relied on armies of volunteers to perform campaign activities, the modern
party relies more on professionals to perform its work. In this they are no
different from other modern organizations, including the many civic
organizations throughout the nation. Increasingly, civic organizations and
interest groups rely on "checkbook" volunteerism to perform their work.[15]
Citizens make contributions to favored organizations where professional
staff execute the work to advance the goals of members.

Political parties rely more on professionals because they seek to reach
out to voters with sophisticated technologies that require special expertise.
These technologies include public polling, direct mail, telemarketing and
broadcast advertising. Similarly, nonparty interest groups, such as
EMILY's List and the National Rifle Association, have come to rely on the
same kind of professionals to reach out to their members.

While party activity at the national and state level has assumed a professional cast, party volunteers remain important at the local level. These volunteers usually participate in the weeks before Election Day. The ebb and flow of volunteers today appears no different than in the past. While conventional historical accounts of political parties suggest that citizens attended party meetings and rallies year-round, recent historical research suggests otherwise. The flow of partisan volunteers into politics was highly seasonal, and a rather small, core group of dedicated activists managed party affairs day to day.[16] Today, the modern party organization is also managed by a core of activists. The emerging strategies they adopt reflect the realities of changing technologies and demographics.

Political parties provide the campaign "hoopla" that has been a staple of American politics. I define "campaign hoopla" as the traditional public display of partisan symbols such as yard signs, banners, and bumper stickers, along with the revelry among partisans in the form of rallies and speeches in public spaces. In the aftermath of the FECA and its amendments, much of this hoopla was depressed because candidates—particularly the presidential candidates—were afraid these displays of partisan ardor might be counted as political contributions that would violate the federal laws.

Some professional campaign practitioners are skeptical of spending money on these kinds of grassroots activity. They see it as "wasted money" that could be spent on getting voters to the polls or on more advertising. But this hoopla is important for generating enthusiasm about political campaigns and building the morale of party activists. An enthusiastic group of party activists are likely to spread the word among friends and neighbors, getting others involved in campaigns. In this way grassroots hoopla may generate network effects that encourage greater awareness about the party message and participation in campaigns among party activists. According to my analysis of the reports filed with the FEC, state political parties spent $11.3 million in the 2000 cycle on party "hoopla." In contrast to the conventional wisdom, this sum reflects an increase over the decade. Between the midterm elections, 1994 and 1998, party spending on hoopla increased from $3.3 to $4 million. The growth during presidential elections has been more prominent: $1 million in 1992, $8.1 million in 1996, and $11.3 million in 2000.

Parties mobilize voters by identifying likely supporters, registering them, and getting them to the polls on Election Day. Since the early days of the Republic, political parties have been important agents of mobilization. In the so-called "heyday" of political parties, the organizations used a variety of techniques to get voters to the polls. They helped immigrants gain citizenship, registered voters, and sponsored popular entertainments at the polling booth. The techniques have changed and parties face stiffer competition to get the attention of voters. Between the 1992 and 2000 election cycles, the combined nonfederal spending by 100 major state parties to mobilize voters increased from $8.6 to $41.8 million. It is difficult to evaluate how this spending affects turnout, and there is vigorous debate among political scientists about factors that affect turnout. According to a two scholars from MIT, the reduction of party nonfederal funds could decrease voter turnout by slightly more than two percentage points, which represents about 2 million voters.[17]

IMPORTANCE OF NONFEDERAL MONEY FOR THE EFFECTIVE OPERATIONS OF POLITICAL PARTIES

Political parties use nonfederal money for issue advertising, including advertising that relates to state and local elections when a candidate is mentioned. Party spending on media activities reflects efforts to win support for the party and its candidates. Broadcast media efforts are targeted usually toward the undecided voters, in contrast to "ground" mobilization strategies—that is, direct mail, telephone calls, and canvassing—that urge partisan loyalists to go to the polls. While most ads occur during the final months of the campaign season, the parties will also spend money outside the campaign season to bolster support for particular party policies, or to challenge the policies of the opposition. The Democrats pursued this strategy in 1995, when the party sponsored ads attacking the Republicans in Congress on the issue of shutting down the government during the budget standoff. The Republicans aired issue ads nationwide during discussions of the balanced budget amendment and welfare reform legislation.

Political parties compete with interest groups when airing political ads. Political parties accounted for a little less than one-third of issue ads in the 2000 cycle, while interest groups accounted for two-thirds, according to a report by the Annenberg Public Policy Center (APPC) at the University of Pennsylvania. The Republican Party spent $83.5 million (16 percent of the total) and the Democratic Party spent $78.4 million (15 percent of the total). One nonparty group, Citizens for Better Medicare, which is funded by the pharmaceutical industry, spent almost as much money on issue ads as either political party.

Overall, the top six nonparty spenders accounted for almost one-fourth of issue ads for the cycle. The APPC reports notes that political party spending may be underrepresented because researchers counted party spending only in the seventy-five largest media markets. These figures, however, closely match my own data on party-based issue ads collected by examining financial reports filed with the FEC. The APPC data on issue ads reveal the breadth of interest group spending that competes with parties to disseminate political messages. Under the BCRA, the percentage of ads sponsored by nonparty groups is likely to rise because national parties, unlike interest groups, will be required to pay for all advertisements with federal money, regardless of when broadcast. State and local parties will have fewer resources to broadcast ads because they can no longer receive nonfederal funds from the national committees.

The rate of growth for interest group advertising is rising faster than for political parties and candidates. According to data compiled by the Brennan Center for the 1998 calendar year, interest groups spent 42 cents for every dollar that the parties spent on advertising (electioneering and issue ads combined). In 2000, interest groups closed this gap considerably by spending 60 cents for every dollar the parties spent. If the national political parties are not able to raise and spend soft money for issue advertising, this gap will diminish even more.

According to the most recent data from the Brennan Center in 2000, interest group advertising that mentions federal candidates was more negative than similar party-based advertising.[18] Almost 70 percent of ads aired by interest groups were "attack" ads, while 45 percent of ads aired by parties were attack ads. Parties also aired more "contrast" ads, which tend to help viewers recognize key differences between the parties' candidates. Under the BCRA, it is conceivable that additional spending by interest groups will result in more negative advertising.

Transfers of nonfederal money from the national committees to the state committees have helped sustain or expand state party activity. The amount of transfers from national organizations to state organizations has increased from $18 million in the 1992 cycle to $279 million in the 2000 cycle. The national committees of the Republican Party provided more than half of nonfederal receipts for its state party affiliates during the 2000 election cycle (adjusted from "swaps" of federal money transferred to national committees). The national committees of the Democratic Party provided 63 percent of state party nonfederal receipts. The conventional wisdom is that all the money went into issue ads that benefited federal candidates. But this is not so. While 44 percent went for media-related disbursements, almost half of nonfederal money paid for party-building activities such as administration and voter mobilization.

My doctoral research suggests that these transfers have enabled the state parties to perform more activities. Supporters of the BCRA have tended to focus on how the transfers to state parties are associated with increased spending on media. While this is certainly true, it should not be forgotten that the state parties use nonfederal money for other kinds of efforts. For example, an increase of one dollar transferred between 1994 and 1998 from national committees of the Democratic Party to a state party resulted in an additional 22 cents of spending on mobilization activities such as voter identification, phone banks, direct mail, canvassing, and various forms of grassroots activity. These estimates have been controlled for changes in the competitiveness of U.S. Senate, U.S. House, and gubernatorial contests in the states between 1994 and 1998. Similarly, a dollar increase in transfers by Republican national parties was associated with an increase of 23 cents on administrative spending and 8 cents for mobilization activities. In 1979, Congress intended to encourage this kind of party-based mobilization and grassroots activity when it amended the Federal Election Campaign Act.

Since 1979, when Congress passed these amendments to strengthen party organizations, parties appear to have gotten stronger. I compare data on political parties collected in 1980 with the data I collected during the 2000 election cycle.[19] On almost every measure for which my survey questions match the 1980 questionnaire, political parties appear to be more active today than in 1980. For example, in 1980 only 44 percent of the Democratic state parties recruited candidates, while in the 2000 cycle, 85 percent performed this activity. Similarly, the size of the organization has increased as measured by the number of employees, the size of budgets during the off-election year, and the existence of permanent party headquarters. The Republicans made solid gains as well, although not as dramatic because they began their party-building efforts in the 1960s under RNC chairman, Roy C. Bliss.[20] While I would not argue that the Democratic Party began its party-building efforts with the rise of nonfederal funds, it seems apparent that nonfederal funds helped it expand party-based operations.

Political parties work closely together through the exchange of nonfederal funds. By transferring funds among party committees, the party organizations increase interdependence and create an efficient use of campaign funds. The parties trade nonfederal dollars for federal dollars to meet specific needs of the campaigns in each state. In states where campaign finance laws permit parties to raise funds in larger increments than allowed under federal laws, these parties may transfer money they raise under "hard" limits of federal laws to states that need federal funds. In return they receive nonfederal dollars. The necessity of trading funds among parties provides opportunities to strengthen the party network across state boundaries and encourage party solidarity.

National and state political parties use nonfederal dollars for nonfederal election activity. According to the Center for Public Integrity, the state party organizations have spent $232 million exclusively from the nonfederal accounts. This money was spent on candidate contributions and party-building activities that included voter registration, direct mail, and various forms of get-out-the-vote strategies; it does not include transfers to other party committees. It should be emphasized that these disbursements are *in addition* to the sums of nonfederal money that the state parties reported to the Federal Election Commission in their *allocation* accounts. Combined party disbursements on mobilization and grassroots in both nonfederal and allocation accounts amounted to $132 million in 2000. While media activities account for 40 percent of nonfederal disbursements, state organizations invested one-quarter of their funds in "ground" mobilization activities.

What Will Be the Effect of the BCRA on Political Parties?

The ban on nonfederal funds to national political parties will likely divert nonfederal money toward interest groups. Political parties compete with interest groups for donations. They also rely on some interest groups to donate money to them. Under the BCRA, donors may not give nonfederal money to the national parties, but they may continue to donate to interest groups or state and local parties in some states. Interest groups will take advantage of the vacuum left by the national committees to raise the nonfederal funds that parties have raised in the past. According to recent articles in the *Washington Post*, interest groups are already positioning themselves to recoup the funds that parties will not receive once the BCRA takes effect. The *Washington Post* reports that lobbyists and activists are already developing strategies to develop "non-party vehicles to take soft money to pay for commercials, voter-mobilization, and other programs" designed to help candidates.[21]

Under the BCRA rules, several types of interest groups may continue to spend nonfederal funds. For example, 527 and 501(c) organizations may use their nonfederal funds to inform and mobilize their members and supporters. Professor David Magleby has shown that outside groups target key races with issue ads and voter mobilization programs. He estimates that 211 interest groups communicated with voters in the seventeen most competitive congressional races during the 2000 cycle.[22] The number of outside groups engaged in issue ads and mobilization is likely to increase under the BCRA.

Professor Emeritus Herbert Alexander, the dean of scholars in the field of campaign finance and former executive director of the Citizens' Research Foundation, concurs with this opinion. He argues that "an examination of some serious problems affecting the electoral system indicates that the problems will remain and probably be exacerbated by the new law." Notably, Professor Alexander believes that "soft-money PACs and unincorporated associations will seek out soft money that formerly went to the parties."[23]

The largest and wealthiest interest groups have viable alternatives for using nonfederal funds in elections if they cannot donate them to the political parties. As my research with Apollonio and that of Malbin and his colleagues suggests, it seems likely that groups that were the largest single nonfederal funds donors to parties, such as labor unions and issue groups with large memberships, should benefit from the new laws because they have various options.[24] These groups will substitute for nonfederal funds donations to parties with direct membership mobilization and additional federal contributions to candidates. Large business organizations may do likewise, although they frequently lack the structural advantages to mobilize voters that membership groups possess. These groups gave to political parties in the past because of party fund-raising requests, and because interest group leaders understood that the party was the most effective coordinator of campaign activity. That is, the parties use resources efficiently across numerous elections. It is likely that membership groups, such as the AFL-CIO or NARAL Pro-Choice America (NARAL), will invest their nonfederal funds in their own campaign operations now that they cannot donate them to the national committees.

Even if the provision imposing a blackout period on interest group issue ads paid for with nonfederal funds is upheld, the national parties remain at a disadvantage compared with interest groups since the latter may continue to defray nonmedia costs, such as administration and voter mobilization, with nonfederal funds. Under the BCRA, the national committees must pay for everything with federal funds. State parties will also suffer since they have come to rely on national party nonfederal funds for party-building activities.

The organizations that gave both federal and nonfederal funds will likely shift additional resources into federal funds contributions and lobbying. Those that are effective at electoral politics will invest additional amounts into campaigns that include member mobilization and issue ads. EMILY's List and the National Rifle Association (NRA) will do particularly well under the provisions of the BCRA. They will be able to bundle contributions from members and channel them to favored candidates. They may also use their nonfederal funds to mobilize members and broadcast issue ads outside the blackout period prior to elections. Some activists are also forming 527 committees that may continue to raise and spend nonfederal funds. For example, the founders of DaschleDemocrats.org claim they are completely independent from Senate Majority Leader Tom Daschle. The committee is headed by several former senators and Clinton administration officials. Even Senator John McCain, a sponsor of the BCRA, acknowledges that groups may get around provisions that attempt to limit the use of nonfederal funds.[25]

The largest nonfederal donors are already giving significant amounts of federal (hard) money. My research with Apollonio on interest group political contributions shows that the median amount of federal money contributed to candidates is greater than $78,000 for groups that give *both* federal money to candidates and nonfederal money to parties (data provided by the Center for Responsive Politics). The median nonfederal donation to political parties for this group of "dual" donors is only $25,000. For groups that give *only* federal money to candidates, the median federal contribution is slightly more than $10,000. These figures indicate that nonfederal donors already dominate the federal money system of political contributions; they will have little trouble adjusting to a system that prohibits nonfederal donations to national party committees.

The number of groups that donate nonfederal money is much larger than the number of groups that give federal contributions, and the vast majority of these nonfederal donors are small donors. In the 1998 election cycle, there were 2,777 federal PACs that made federal funds contributions. In contrast, there were 11,383 entities (corporations, labor unions, tax exempt organizations, and the like) that donated nonfederal money, not including individual donations. One obvious reason there have been more nonfederal donors is that it is easier to make these donations because groups do not need to form a political action committee. Most groups that made nonfederal donations were small, local business organizations such as construction firms, hotels, funeral homes, towing services, dental offices, hardware stores, landscape services, legal offices, accounting firms, and retail food outlets. The donations of these groups that give nonfederal money only are rather small: the median is just $375.[26] While the intended target of the BCRA is the large, wealthy organizations, the new law also prevents smaller entities from participating at the federal level through contributions that could hardly be called "corrupting."

As interest groups increase their spending in elections, political campaigns may lose thematic coherence. Political parties broadcast "cookie-cutter" issue ads that employ selected themes that the parties want to associate with their candidates. If interest groups dominate the airwaves, we are likely to see a set of interests advertised before campaigns that reflect the concerns of a relatively small segment of the citizenry who feel intensely about a particular issue. Professor Kathleen Jamieson's research team at the APPC shows that interest groups already account for two-thirds of the more than $500 million spent on issue ads during the 2000 election cycle. In the APPC report, Professor Jamieson wrote, "Over the last three election cycles, the number of groups sponsoring ads has exploded, and consumers often don't know who these groups are, who funds them, and whom they represent."[27]

Interest group ads lack the accountability that is present when a party sponsors ads. An important difference between advertising by outside groups and political parties is that the former are not linked with the candidate at the ballot box. Therefore outside groups can air ads without facing reprisals from voters, an arrangement that undermines accountability in the campaign process. Professor Magleby, for instance, cites numerous groups in his study with indistinct names such as Foundation for Responsible Government, American Family Voices, Coalition to Make Our Voices Heard, and Committee for Good Common Sense.[28] More of these groups may emerge if nonfederal funds are channeled away from the parties and toward interest groups.

When parties broadcast political ads their candidates are perceived as responsible for these ads, even when these ads are not express advocacy. Evidence for this perception comes from the willingness of candidates to restrain the activities of their parties. In at least two important Senate contests the candidates publicly declared they would request the political parties not to spend nonfederal funds in their races. In the Wisconsin 1998 Senate contest, Senator Russell Feingold requested that the Democratic Party refrain from running issue ads in Wisconsin. The party complied even though it risked losing a very important seat. In the 2000 New York Senate contest, both candidates agreed not to use party nonfederal funds. The candidates were careful to articulate that they could not be held responsible for the advertisements done by outside groups. For example, candidate Hillary Clinton declared: "If we make an agreement to do away with soft money, I assume it will include everything. Now obviously there are groups that we have no direct control over that we will have to ask to abide by whatever agreement you reach."[29] Candidates can credibly deny their association with interest groups, even if these interest groups have had close relationships with the candidate in the past.

The political parties keep each other accountable with their issue ads because they can easily identify the opposing party ads and link them to the party candidate. In his report on nonfederal funds and issue advocacy in the 2000 elections, Professor Maglebly provides some examples of how this works:

> The Republicans successfully challenged DCCC [Democratic Congressional Campaign Committee] ads in Kentucky Six and New Jersey Twelve. The ads were pulled from the air, and the Republican candidates achieved public relations victories against not only the DCCC but also the Democratic candidates. A spokesperson for the Kentucky Sixth Congressional District candidate Scotty Baesler stated that having the ad pulled "hurt us in a significant way. It allowed Fletcher to raise a credibility issue." Interestingly, as the race progressed, the Democratic campaigns were more careful and it was the Republicans who had more controversial ads pulled. Both parties tried to make the opposing candidates take the heat for soft-money ads that went too far.[30]

The example used by Professor Magleby demonstrates that parties and their candidates are jointly punished for becoming too controversial. The traditional head-to-head competition between the party candidates provides the natural mechanism for holding the party organizations accountable.

If party organizations lose their central role as coordinators of electoral activity, interest groups and individual candidates will pursue their campaign goals more independently. Instead of choosing the party as an arena to build and coordinate campaign themes, interest groups, with narrower interests, will increasingly take up the functions that parties leave off. Already, groups like EMILY's List behave increasingly like political parties by using nonfederal funds to identify and train candidates for office and to mobilize voters.[31] In the 2000 elections, the Democratic Congressional Campaign Committee gave EMILY's List $1.3 million in nonfederal funds for help in mobilizing voters.[32] It is likely that EMILY's List will raise these funds on its own in upcoming elections and deploy them to further its organizational goals.

The last set of reforms in 1974 empowered political action committees because parties were severely restricted.[33] The same consequences are likely with the BCRA. Membership PACs, such as EMILY's List, NARAL, and the NRA, should have relatively greater influence in elections now that national committees will forgo resources that are available to interest groups. Keeping track of the activities of outside organizations will be much more difficult than for parties. Professor Magebly's effort to assemble information about interest group activity in elections is notable for the very reason that it is so difficult to find out which groups engage in campaign activity.

I was part of a team in California that visited local broadcast stations, interviewed leaders of local interest groups, and contacted candidates about political campaigns being waged against them. As much as the research team attempted to extend its network of "informers" who knew about campaign activity by outside groups, we had no way of ascertaining the full range of efforts by such groups. For example, while officials from the California AFL-CIO would provide the cost of sending direct mail to members during the presidential primary, they would not provide figures about the cost of telephone banks. Nor would they cite figures about administrative costs to support campaign activity. Regarding issue ads by outside groups, an organization called Republicans for Clean Air ran negative advertisements against John McCain. We could not determine the sponsors of this ad until reporters in Washington discovered that two brothers from Texas, who strongly supported George W. Bush, paid for these advertisements using a post office box in Herndon, Virginia. When I tried to obtain figures from the local ABC affiliate about the cost of airtime they purchased, this office claimed they did not have to turn over these records. This direct personal experience trying to monitor outside electoral activity revealed to me the potential difficulties of identifying the source of interest group campaign activities, including issue ads. By reducing the amount of money that flows through political parties, the BCRA is likely to spark more outside activity that is difficult to track.

Experience in the states illustrates how outside spending may increase if party funds are restricted. Professor Michael Malbin, executive director of the Campaign Finance Institute, coauthored a study of campaign finance in states with ambitious regulatory frameworks.[34] Malbin and Thomas Gais show that efforts to diminish the need for money in politics have not met with success. They point to Wisconsin as an example of a state that made a robust effort to reduce the role of money in politics by limiting contributions to and from the political parties. The result was the formation of "conduit" committees. Others have reported a rise in independent expenditures.[35] The most recent efforts to finance campaigns with "clean money" and reduce political spending in Maine have run aground because outside groups have augmented their spending to influence a few key seats that held the balance of power in the legislature.[36]

The ban on nonfederal funds to national political parties encourages the formation and strengthening of shadow party organizations. Wisconsin's experience with tight restrictions on political parties saw the rise of "conduit" committees to channel money to candidates in competitive races because the parties could no longer perform this function.[37]

The reduction of party influence will spur factional groups within the parties to pursue their own brand of campaigning. For example, the New Democratic Network, which reflects the centrist wing of the Democratic Party, will compete more intensively for funds and political influence against the Progressive Donor Network, which reflects the liberal wing.[38] These two factions should attract the funds that formerly went to the Democratic national committees. They will invest their resources to support candidates who espouse their particular visions of the Democratic Party. Thus, by weakening the national committees in relation to quasi-party groups, the BCRA reduces the parties' capacity to build coalitions during the electoral process and moderate the potential divisiveness of factional group politics.

While the reformers hope that the enactment of the BCRA will diminish the importance of money in politics, research demonstrates that campaign finance laws have a limited impact on the amount of money in elections. In a study of U.S. campaign spending between 1978 and 1998, Stephen Ansolabehere, Alan Gerber, and James Snyder conclude that growth in spending is associated with rises in the gross domestic product (GDP).[39] The authors provide two possible explanations. First, as GDP grows, so does the size of government, which means more groups will seek to influence government activity. The second explanation is that, as personal income rises, giving rises.[40] Political spending, in this scenario, appears to rise like consumer spending for other goods and services when the economy expands. Notably, even in Great Britain, where the government imposes strict spending limits on candidates and television advertising, the amount of political spending corresponds to changes in the GDP. The researchers conclude that "regulation of spending through limits and TV restrictions may be elusive."[41]

The BCRA will make it tougher for political parties to work together on fund-raising and will reduce the level of interaction among levels of party committees. The ban on joint fund-raising for Levin Amendment funds prevents state and local parties from working together to raise money for party-building activities.

The BCRA prohibits party members at the national level from helping state and local parties raise nonfederal money. This prohibition will have negative consequences for state parties, particularly the parties in the small states. According to Beverly Shea, finance director of the RNC, whom I interviewed on September 6, 2002, "Fund-raising in the states is the toughest job of all." She says most party donors are not familiar with the work of state parties. While state parties appear to be doing a better job of fund-raising in recent elections, Shea states that the leaders of many state party organizations are not well positioned to raise money.

State staff turnover is particularly high because state organizations cannot afford to pay salaries commensurate with those of the national organizations and consulting firms. The consequence is that fund-raising can sometimes be a haphazard process. State organizations have not always invested in long-term strategies to develop donor networks, nor have they established professional routines for fund-raising. According to Shea, who also has experience at the state level, the selection of party chairs "appears to drive a wedge between partisan factions within a state to a degree that it does not at the national level, leaving some prospective donors refusing to give to the state party." Fund-raising at the national level draws from a larger and more diverse pool of donors, and the selection of the party chair appears less relevant to prospective donors.

For these reasons, the RNC plays an important supportive role for state party fund-raising by providing ongoing advice, continuity, technical assistance, and transfers of nonfederal money. Now that national committees may no longer raise and transfer nonfederal money, state parties must invest additional resources in fund-raising operations. Raising money costs money.

WOULD LESS RESTRICTIVE ALTERNATIVES HAVE BEEN LESS HARMFUL THAN A UNILATERAL BAN ON NONFEDERAL FUNDS FOR NATIONAL COMMITTEES?

There were many alternatives Congress could have adopted which would have been far less harmful to parties than the ban on national party nonfederal funds, while addressing the major concerns of those who supported BCRA. For example, a cap on nonfederal donations would have done less harm to the political parties than a unilateral ban. The typical nonfederal donation is actually quite low. In a study I did after the 1998 election cycle for the Institute of Governmental Studies and the Citizens' Research Foundation, I found that there were 24,546 nonfederal fund donations to the political parties from individuals and entities. The average donation was only $8,750, and this does not include the many donors who gave in increments of less than $200. More than 90 percent donated less than $25,000. The sum of donations under $25,000 amounted to almost 40 percent of party nonfederal funds. The vast majority of donations come in under $100,000. The sum of donations under $100,000 amounted to just below 80 percent of party nonfederal funds. Based on these numbers, it appears that a cap on nonfederal donations at $100,000 would have addressed any perceived problems with mega-donors, without severely limiting party resources. Parties would have retained a good portion of nonfederal funds from donors under the $100,000 level, while the mega-donors that give more than this amount would have been eliminated. BCRA, with its unilateral ban on nonfederal funds to the national parties, uses a meat cleaver approach, which makes no distinction between small and large donors, and forces the party to lose an important source of funds for party building activity.

Another less restrictive alternative Congress could have adopted was to restrict issue ads paid for with nonfederal funds. The focus of reformers has been to eliminate the issue ads that they believe have generated a huge demand for nonfederal funds. Why could Congress not have simply restricted issue ads paid for with nonfederal funds or imposed a blackout period as the law does for interest groups? I am not an expert on constitutional law, so in noting this possibility, I am assuming here that there would be no serious constitutional problems with preventing the parties from spending nonfederal funds on issue ads.

A ban on nonfederal funds for national political parties may weaken the incentive for parties to invest in long-term party building. With fewer resources, the national committees will be compelled to lay off staff that was assigned to help state parties. State parties benefit from the advice and technical support of the national committee staff when they fund-raise, recruit, and train candidates and develop voter programs. According to RNC Finance Director Beverly Shea, the RNC staff frequently analyze fund-raising operations and offer advice when state leaders ask for consultations.

The national party has absorbed the cost of hiring experts to monitor and advise state level committees. These personnel have been paid for, in part, through nonfederal money.

National committees will save precious federal funds for political contributions and independent spending rather than invest it in building up the state organizations. Drafters of BCRA have assumed that the parties would simply shift their federal funds resources into voter mobilization and forgo broadcast advertising. The national parties, however, may choose to use their hard dollars for independent expenditures and coordinated expenditures rather than invest more money in party-based mobilization campaigns in the states. Party operatives in Washington who are concerned chiefly about candidates at the top of the ticket may prefer to use federal funds on television ads, leaving the mobilization campaigns to outside groups. It would be risky for them not to save federal funds for broadcasting ads at the close of the campaign, especially when interest groups are increasingly active in campaigns. By cutting off nonfederal funds to the national parties, the party's joint mobilization campaigns are jeopardized, particularly in states that lack the resources and expertise to mount these efforts on their own.

Provisions in the BCRA presuppose that state and local committees will be able to raise funds independently to compensate for the nonfederal funds that will no longer come from national committee transfers. The national committees have been an important source of revenue for the state parties for both nonfederal and federal funds. The Democratic committees at the national level transferred almost $170 million in nonfederal funds to the state organizations for the 2000 elections, which accounted for 63 percent of state party nonfederal receipts (when the figures are adjusted for swaps of federal and nonfederal funds between committees). In aggregate, the Republican state organizations were somewhat less reliant overall on their national committees for nonfederal money, receiving 53 percent of their nonfederal funds through national committee transfers.

I am skeptical of the claim by some advocates of the BCRA that parties will move additional resources into voter mobilization and grassroots programs now that they cannot use nonfederal money for issue ads. This claim depends on whether state and local organizations can conduct comprehensive GOTV programs under the new federal requirement that parties use federal funds or a mix of federal funds and Levin Amendment money. Contrary to the intent of the drafters of the BCRA, federal law may actually reduce the amount of resources dedicated to voter mobilization, by taking the central coordinating organizations out of the picture—the national committees—and imposing greater administrative burdens on the local committees. The requirement that local committees raise and spend all their GOTV funds independently and file with the FEC once they surpass a relatively low threshold of federal funds spending is particularly onerous for committees that are run almost entirely by volunteers. In 2000, only 158 local party committees filed reports with the FEC from the many hundreds of active local organizations nationwide. It is not inconceivable that local committees will give up GOTV activity because the administrative burdens are too heavy.

State and local organizations that rely primarily on large donors may find it difficult to meet the requirements of the BCRA and run GOTV and voter registration programs. According to the new federal law, state parties must pay for GOTV with federal funds or a mix of federal funds and Levin Amendment money, *if* there is a federal candidate on the ballot, which is a likely occurrence. That means that state organizations may not use money regulated under state laws that exceeds the source and limit restrictions of the BCRA. There are thirty states that allow unlimited contributions from one or more sources (such as individuals, PACs, unions, corporations); eleven states allow unlimited contributions from any source. As far as I know, there are no empirical studies to assess the reliance of state organizations on contributions that exceed the federal constraints. State organizations also invest more than $14 million in GOTV for state and local races, *in addition* to the $24 million that state parties spend on GOTV for all candidates, including federal, that is reported to the Federal Election Commission. The fact that state organizations spend so much on GOTV should encourage careful scrutiny of the BCRA provisions regulating this important activity.

In short, I think two basic adjustments—a cap on national party nonfederal funds and restrictions on paying for issue ads with nonfederal funds—would have addressed the chief concerns of reformers, without causing undue harm to the political parties. The BCRA's outright ban on national party nonfederal funds will, however, significantly and unnecessarily weaken political parties at all levels.

NOTES

1. Philip Klinkner, *The Losing Parties: Out-Party National Committees, 1956–1993* (Yale University Press, 1994); Paul S. Herrnson, "Party Leadership

and Party Organizational Change," in John C. Green, ed., *Politics, Professionalism, and Power* (New York: Latham, 1994), pp. 186–204.

2. Paul S. Herrnson, *Party Campaigning in the 1980s* (Harvard University Press, 1988); John F. Bibby, *Politics, Parties, and Elections in America*, 5th ed. (Belmont, Calif.: Wadworth, 2003).

3. See the supplement to the *American Political Science Review*, vol. 44.

4. Bibby, *Politics, Parties, and Elections in America*, p. 114.

5. Gary F. Moncrief, Peverill Squire, and Malcolm E. Jewell, *Who Runs for the Legislature?* (Upper Saddle River, N.J.: Prentice-Hall, 2001).

6. V. O. Key Jr., *Southern Politics in State and Nation* (Random House, 1949), p. 46.

7. Moncrief and others, *Who Runs for the Legislature*, p. 43.

8. See ibid.

9. See, for example, Paul S. Herrnson, *Congressional Elections: Campaigning at Home and in Washington*, 3d ed. (Washington: Congressional Quarterly Press, 2000).

10. Hank Shaw, "Warner Collects Support: Dem Has Backers Who Give to GOP," *Free Lance-Star* (Fredericksburg, Va.), July 21, 2001.

11. See David Magleby, ed., *Outside Money: Soft Money and Issue Advocacy in the 1998 Congressional Elections* (Lanham, Md.: Rowman and Littlefield, 2000).

12. Jonathan S. Krasno and Daniel E. Seltz, *Buying Time: Television Advertising in the 1998 Congressional Elections* (New York: Brennan Center, 2000), p. 198.

13. John Frendreis and Alan R. Gitelson, "Local Parties in the 1990s: Spokes in a Candidate-Centered Wheel," in John C. Green and Daniel M. Shea, eds., *The State of the Parties: The Changing Role of Contemporary American Parties*, 3d ed. (Lanham, Md.: Rowman and Littlefield, 1999), pp. 135–53; data cited are from table 9.1, p. 138.

14. Robin Kolodny and Angela Logan, "Political Consultants and the Extension of Party Goals," *PS: Political Science and Politics,* vol. 50 (June 1998), pp. 155–59.

15. See Robert D. Putnam, *Bowling Along: The Collapse and Revival of American Community* (Simon & Schuster, 2000); Sidney Verba, Kay Lehman Schlozman, and Henry E. Brady, *Voice and Equality: Civic Voluntarism in American Politics* (Harvard University Press, 1995).

16. Glenn C. Altschuler and Stuart M. Blumin, *Rude Republic: Americans and Their Politics in the Nineteenth Century* (Princeton University Press, 2000).

17. See Stephen Ansolabehere and James M. Snyder, "Soft Money, Hard Money, Strong Parties," *Columbia Law Review,* vol. 100, no. 3 (2000), p. 617.

18. Craig B. Holman, "The End of Limits on Money in Politics," Brennan Center Report (New York, 2001).

19. For 1980 data, see Cornelius P. Cotter, James L. Gibson, John F. Bibby, and Robert J. Huckshorn, *Party Organizations in American Politics* (University of Pittsburgh Press, 1984).

20. See Herrnson, *Party Campaigning in the 1980s,* and "Party Leadership and Party Organizational Change."

21. Thomas Edsall and Juliet Eilperin, "PAC Attack II: Why Some Groups Are Learning to Love Campaign Finance Reform," *Washington Post,* August 18, 2002.

22. David Magleby, "Election Advocacy: Soft Money and Issue Advocacy in the 2000 Congressional Elections," Center for the Study of Elections and Democracy Report (Brigham Young University, 2001).

23. Herbert E. Alexander, "The Political Process after the Bipartisan Campaign Reform Act of 2002," *Election Law Journal,* vol. 2, no. 1 (2003), pp. 47–54.

24. D. E. Apollonio and Raymond La Raja, "Interest Group Contribution Strategies with Soft Money," paper presented at the annual meeting of the Midwest Political Science Association, April 2002; Michael J. Malbin and others, "New Interest Group Strategies: A Preview of Post McCain-Feingold Politics?" preliminary report on 2000 (Campaign Finance Institute Interest Group Project, 2002).

25. Thomas Edsall, "Lawmakers Embracing 'Stealth PAC' Advantage; Committees Allow Relatively Unregulated Fundraising," *Washington Post,* April 11, 2002.

26. Apollonio and La Raja, "Interest Group Contribution Strategies with Soft Money."

27. Kathleen Hall Jamieson, "Issue Advertising in the 1999–2000 Election Cycle," Annenberg Public Policy Center Report (University of Pennsylvania, 2001), p. 1.

28. Magleby, "Election Advocacy."

29. Randal C. Archibold with Clifford J. Levy, "Lazio Issues New Challenge on Soft Money," *New York Times,* September 21, 2000, p. B1.

30. Magleby, "Election Advocacy."

31. See affidavit of Joe Solmonese, chief of staff of EMILY's List, paras. 4, 25.

32. Thomas Edsall, "EMILY's List Makes a Name for Itself; Pro-Choice Democratic Women's Lobby Is Proving a Powerful Opponent," *Washington Post,* April 21, 2002, p. A5.

33. Frank J. Sorauf, *Inside Campaign Finance* (Yale University Press, 1992).

34. Michael J. Malbin and Thomas L. Gais, *The Day after Reform: Sobering Campaign Finance Lessons from the American States* (Albany, N.Y.: Rockefeller Institute Press, 1998).

35. See also Alan Ehrenhalt, "Political Pawns," *Governing Magazine,* July 2000.

36. Associated Press, "Maine Law Triggers Soft Money Flood," March 21, 2002.

37. See Malbin and Gais, *The Day after Reform.*

38. Franklin Foer, "Will McCain-Feingold Breed Democratic Fratricide?" *New Republic,* June 3, 2002, available from www.nytimes.com/aponline/national/AP-Clean-Elections.html, accessed March 21, 2002.

39. Stephen Ansolabehere, Alan Gerber, and James M. Snyder, "Corruption

and the Growth of Campaign Spending," in Gerald C. Lubenow, ed., *A User's Guide to Campaign Finance Reform* (Lanham, Md.: Rowman and Littlefield, 2001), pp. 25–46.

40. See Verba and others, *Voice and Equality.*

41. See Ansolabehere and others, "Corruption and the Growth of Campaign Spending," p. 43.

The Need for Federal Regulation
of State Party Activity

Donald Green

Donald Green is a professor of political science at Yale University and director of Yale's Institution for Social and Policy Studies. His expertise lies in the areas of political parties, campaign finance, elections, and public opinion. He served as an expert witness for the defense. In addition to his report, Green prepared a rebuttal that responded to the arguments made by witnesses for the plaintiffs. The excerpt presented here includes material from each of these documents.

One of the central issues raised in the McConnell *case concerns the extent of the reform act's regulatory reach and the question of whether the law goes too far in regulating state and local party spending. In this selection, Green defends the reform act's regulation of certain components of state and local party activity by analyzing the overlapping structures and scope of interaction between national, state, and local parties. He explores the effects of state party activity, particularly the effects of voter turnout programs, to demonstrate that state efforts have a significant impact on federal elections. His empirical analyses of the relative importance of various means of voter mobilization—advertising, mail, telephone, and face-to-face contact—suggest that parties have not been spending their funds in ways that are likely to have a significant effect on voter turnout.*

Green contends that regulation of state and local party activity would help reduce the corruptive influence of soft money, and that parties will adapt to the reform act's prohibitions by raising more federally regulated money. Without such regulation, he argues, the reform act's ban on soft money could easily be circumvented by simply channeling funds through state and local committees.

This report's recurrent theme is that parties are highly adaptable strategic actors. Notwithstanding their resistance to laws that restrict their ability to solicit and transfer large donations, parties will quickly adjust to the new incentive system created by the Bipartisan Campaign Reform Act (BCRA), for example, by broadening their base of contributors. But it is the parties' very adaptability that poses a serious danger should the Court strike down the provisions that limit how state parties may finance federal election activity. Political parties are flexible, multitiered organizations that are structured in ways that are designed to win power. Regulations directed at them must take into account the many institutional, social, and ideological interconnections among local, state, and national party organizations, because a narrow regulatory strategy that focuses solely on the national parties would encourage political parties to reorganize their financial activities in ways that circumvent the new restrictions. The BCRA creates a comprehensive regulatory system covering activity that bears directly on the election of federal candidates; if the BCRA is undercut in ways that permit back-door financing of federal campaigns, one can be certain that these loopholes will be exploited.

Although state and national parties are distinct institutions, rarely in American history have state and national political parties been in serious conflict, and even more rarely have state parties seen it in their interests to withdraw their support from the national presidential nominee. This pattern should hardly be surprising, since one of the strands that links local, state, and national partisans is a deep sense of attachment to the political party to which they belong. Although there is often speculation that activists and voters feel a sense of attachment to their state parties that they do not feel toward the national party, survey evidence from the 1950s to the present demonstrates that split party attachments are unusual.[1] Local and state partisans want to see their team win federal office, and with good reason. National and subnational partisans generally share similar ideological and programmatic visions. Even when they disagree, subnational partisans recognize that federal officeholders and the resources they command can be enormously beneficial to state and local parties and candidates.

The links between state and federal parties run deeper than an overlap in personnel and "we-feeling," important though these may be. Indeed, the links run deeper than the informal social ties that state and federal party members often share with their constituents and donors or the string of political connections that former state party leaders accumulate when they ascend to leadership positions in national political parties.[2] The American political system ties the fortunes of state legislators and U.S. House members through the institutional mechanism of redistricting. The most important legislative activity in the electoral lives of U.S. House members takes place during redistricting, a process that is placed in the hands of state legislatures. The chances that a House incumbent will be ousted by unfavorable district boundaries are often greater than the chances of defeat at the hands of the typical challenger. Thus federal legislators who belong to the state majority party have a tremendous incentive to be attuned to the state legislature and the state party leadership.

For example, in early 1999 the Republican National Committee, recognizing that state legislatures in Tennessee and Georgia would soon control redistricting, transferred substantial sums of money to those states' Republican parties in an effort to win the few seats necessary to gain the majority. As Edwin Bender, in a report for the National Institute on Money in State Politics explains:

"In a number of states with legislatures that are controlled by narrow margins, a win or two in the state House or Senate in 2000 could mean the difference between a redistricting committee controlled by Democrats or Republicans, and districts that favor one party over the other. . . . As a result, national party organizations have been flooding the states with campaign donations, both soft money and hard, to influence the redistricting process."[3]

Given the overlapping structure of officeholding in national, state, and local parties and the special incentives for federal officeholders created by redistricting, the regulatory environment created by the BCRA must encompass national, state, and local parties. The importance of primary election challenges to federal officeholders who inhabit districts with lopsided proportions of their fellow partisans coupled with the possibility that federal officeholders or their allies might make a bid for statewide office means that federal officials cannot afford to be out of favor with the political party of their home state.

The scope of the BCRA makes even more sense when one considers the many informal interactions between federal officeholders and state political parties. State parties and federal officeholders, after all, tend to have long-standing political relationships that not infrequently assign an important party fund-raising role to federal officeholders. Federal officeholders and their allies often figure prominently within state parties. State parties and federal officeholders share many of the same campaign donors. State parties have no shortage of favors to ask of federal officeholders on behalf of important donors; federal officeholders in turn have considerable incentives to accede to or anticipate these requests, particularly since many of them aspire to higher office or aim to bequeath their seats to their allies or offspring. To exclude state and local parties from the purview of federal legislation ignores the many points of intersection between national parties and their subnational comrades in arms.

What justification is there for regulating the federal and generic election activity of state parties in the context of federal elections? First, state and local parties play a direct role in the electoral campaigns of federal candidates. The appeals that state and local parties make to voters and funders frequently mention both federal and nonfederal candidates, particularly when presidential candidates or contested U.S. Senate seats are at stake. The reasoning behind this tactic is easy to discern. In addition to the economies achieved when multiple candidates are presented to voters, designers of campaign literature recognize that voters are often more interested in federal races than they are in state legislative races.[4]

What about state and local party communications that make no mention of federal candidates? Because the partisan proclivities of the electorate express themselves toward *both* state and federal candidates, state parties influence federal elections directly even when they mobilize their supporters on behalf of a candidate for state office. Consider, for example, the immense correlation between voting for state and federal offices in California, a state that maintains a database of how each vote on each ballot was cast. Professor Jeffrey B. Lewis of the University of Southern California at Los Angeles assembled these data for the 1992 election using ballots cast in Los Angeles County. That election featured a U.S. Senate contest between Barbara Boxer, the Democratic candidate, and Bruce Herschensohn, the Republican candidate. The individual-level ballot data enable us to say precisely what proportion of voters who cast Democratic or Republican ballots for state legislative office voted for Boxer, who won with a plurality of 48 percent. Those who voted for a Republican state senate candidate were 5.6 times more likely to vote for Herschensohn than Boxer (531,081 versus 95,675); those who voted for a Democratic assembly candidate were 5.9 times more likely to vote for Boxer than Herschensohn (600,373 versus 101,590). No less striking patterns of party voting obtain regardless of which state and federal offices one examines. For example, among the 2,159,164 voters who cast a ballot for a Democratic or Republican state assembly candidate, 86.4 percent cast ballots for the same party when voting for U.S. House candidates.

These findings undercut the argument that voter mobilization activity lies beyond the scope of federal authority because it does not directly involve federal candidates.[5] The evidence from California, as well as from numerous opinion surveys and exit polls that demonstrate the powerful correlation between voting at the state and federal levels, shows quite clearly that a campaign that mobilizes residents of a highly Republican precinct will produce a harvest of votes for Republican candidates for both state and federal offices. A campaign need not mention federal candidates to have a direct effect on voting for such a candidate. That parties recognize this fact is apparent, for example, from the emphasis that the

Democrats place on mobilizing and preventing ballot roll-off among African Americans, whose solidly Democratic voting proclivities make them reliable supporters for officeholders at all levels. [6] As a practical matter, generic campaign activity has a direct effect on federal elections.

When considering the overlap between state and federal elections, it should be remembered that states at their discretion choose whether to hold their elections at the same time as federal elections. New Jersey and Virginia, for example, choose to hold their state elections during odd-numbered years. Against the argument that states are unable to change the timing of their elections is the fact that states in recent decades have changed the timing of their gubernatorial elections, so that they no longer coincide with presidential elections and the "coattails" associated with presidential victories. Indeed, in their complaint the California Democratic and California Republican Parties acknowledge that they exercise this discretion when they point out that California deliberately holds its elections so as to maximize voter turnout while minimizing administrative costs.

Thus it is entirely reasonable that the BCRA prevents national parties from funneling soft money to subnational elections, whether on behalf of state candidates or to pay for voter mobilization or generic campaign activity. These activities have direct implications for the election of federal officials.

The Need for a Comprehensive Regulatory Scheme that Prevents Circumvention

The BCRA contains an integrated set of provisions designed to prevent national, state, and local parties from circumventing fund-raising restrictions. Many of these provisions involve prohibitions on the transfer of funds. For example, national parties are prevented from accepting soft-money transfers from state parties. State parties may not fund federal campaigns, directly or indirectly, using soft money. National parties may not accept soft-money donations even for purposes of supporting state party activity that has no direct bearing on federal offices. Local, state, and national parties are prevented from contributing hard or soft money to certain tax-exempt organizations. In this section, I discuss the rationale for these restrictions.

Before taking up the issue of corruption in the next section, let us imagine the practical consequences of relaxing any or all of these restrictions. If state parties could transfer soft money to the national parties, donors would simply be instructed to direct their soft-money donations to state parties that are not subject to state contribution limits, which would serve as financial intermediaries for the national parties. A similar argument could be made about direct spending by state parties on federal campaigns, which is in some ways analogous to a transfer of funds. If state parties were allowed to spend soft money on federal campaign activity, states like Virginia or Illinois, which impose few restrictions on campaign contributions, would see their state parties become the political equivalent of offshore banks, funneling large sums of money to races around the country as though they were national parties.

The prohibition against national parties transferring soft money to state parties stems from concerns about the corrupting influence of unlimited donations, which I discuss below. Suffice it to say that lifting this prohibition returns us to the path that leads to an ever-widening soft-money loophole. To create a system in which the national parties are banned from raising soft money, except for soft money raised on behalf of their state party allies, inevitably puts pressure on party operatives to construe national party expenditures as transfers to the states. Under the pre-BCRA provisions, the parties demonstrated great ingenuity in moving money around so as to minimize the amount of hard money needed to fund federal election activity. If the BCRA provisions regarding state and local parties were overturned, clever accountants will doubtless figure out ways to place a maximal share of the national parties' overhead and fund-raising costs on the state parties' budget ledgers. This incentive system also puts pressure on the state parties to engage in as much federal election activity as possible so that the national parties can recoup their soft-money investment. It would be no small irony if the BCRA provisions governing national-state party transfers were struck down on the grounds that Congress interfered unduly with state activity, because the resulting regulatory system would feature a dramatic increase in the role of state parties in federal elections. For this reason, when reflecting on issues of federalism it is critically important that one consider not only the current role of state parties in federal election activity but also the probable future role should the regulatory system change in ways not intended by Congress.

The provisions governing state and national party transfers to tax-exempt organizations have a somewhat different character and rationale. The BCRA forbids the state and national parties from making donations—even hard-money contributions—to certain tax-exempt organizations. At first, this provision may seem unnecessary, since presumably hard money has been collected in ways that reduce concerns about corruption.

Why not let the parties make donations using hard money to tax-exempt organizations involved in electoral activity?

When addressing this question, one must bear in mind that parties seek to win elections in order to gain power.[7] From an economic standpoint, it makes no sense for parties to transfer funds in order to assist political campaigns, since they could more efficiently (and with greater control over the end-product) spend directly on political activity. The parties' motive for transferring funds to tax-exempt organizations that are engaged in electoral activity is to gain control of these organizations, because doing so gives parties control over the soft money that tax-exempt organizations are free to raise.[8]

For example, the Republican National Committee is alleged to have controlled the tax-exempt National Policy Forum and other pro-Republican organizations.[9] Correctly surmising that the national parties could easily circumvent the new regulatory regime by creating satellite party organizations in the guise of tax-exempt organizations, which would be free to collect donations of unlimited size, the authors of the BCRA closed this loophole. Parties are prevented both from making these transfers and from setting up placeholder party organizations. These restrictions do not impinge upon the parties' ability to foster interest groups or build political coalitions. Should parties wish to transfer money to political action committees (which themselves must raise only hard money), they remain free to do so under the BCRA.

The ban on hard money transfers to so-called Levin accounts stems from the same concerns that led to a ban on transfers to tax-exempt organizations. If parties could contribute hard money to Levin accounts, they could gain influence over how the account is spent, including the money raised by the less restrictive Levin provisions. The underlying theory behind these BCRA provisions boils down to a simple and persuasive proposition: one should not allow the parties to skirt the soft-money ban by using hard money to take control of soft-money accounts.

The fungibility of campaign expenditures explains why donations to state parties solicited by state party officials for the purpose of conducting voter mobilization drives is a source of federal concern. In what way might they pose a threat of corruption to federal officeholders? Voter mobilization activities are an integral part of electoral campaigns; national parties spend millions on voter mobilization. National parties would be quite grateful to any other entity that engaged in this activity on their behalf, freeing up the national parties to spend their money on other things. From an accounting standpoint, this arrangement would be tantamount to a massive transfer of funds to the national parties. If a donor were intent upon currying favor with federal officeholders and the national parties they inhabit, there would be no better opportunity than making lavish donations to this type of generic campaign activity, were such donations outside the purview of the BCRA. The many informal connections between state and federal politicians and between national and subnational parties make this type of exchange easy to orchestrate.

Just as parties cannot co-opt tax-exempt organizations, they are not allowed under the BCRA to form ersatz party organizations in the guise of "leadership political action committees (PACs)." The BCRA prohibits state and national parties or their leaders from forming associations that raise soft money. Leadership associations not only represent a potential loophole; they constitute precisely the type of fund-raising entity that amplifies the power of those public officials who are best positioned to raise large sums of money and act upon the donors' wishes. Concerns about corruption become especially acute when large donors form close and enduring relationships with officeholders who occupy leadership positions within government.

MONEY AND LAWMAKING

To what extent do campaign contributions influence legislative voting, legislative effort, and access to elected officials? To what extent did the campaign finance system that the BCRA replaced appear corrupt?[10]

In order to ascertain whether campaign contributions affect roll call voting, legislative effort behind the scenes, or access to public officials, political scientists have used a variety of different research approaches. First, they have conducted extended interviews with those who make political contributions. James Herndon's 1982 interviews with business and labor PACs suggest that their contributions to members of Congress are motivated by a desire to gain access to legislators.[11] Second, political scientists have conducted quantitative studies of how members of Congress allocate their time during a typical workweek. Laura Langbein quantifies the link between money and access, finding a statistical relationship between PAC contributions and the ways that members of Congress allocate time during their weekly schedules.[12] Third, they conduct somewhat more qualitative studies of the effort that legislators expended on behalf of legislation before a committee. Richard Hall and Frank Wayman's study of the way that House members shepherd legislation through committees suggests that money may buy not only access but legislative effort.[13]

Although contributions were not related to floor voting on dairy price supports, job training, and energy deregulation, Hall and Wayman find that contributions predict the amount of effort that supporters exerted on these issues during the committee markup process. By far the most common approach involves a statistical analysis of the correlation between roll-call votes and campaign contributions. Here, as Hall and Wayman point out in their review of roll-call voting research, the evidence is quite mixed. On tobacco issues, for example, some analysts find strong statistical relationships between tobacco industry contributions and votes on tobacco regulation, but on the whole it appears that the typical roll-call vote is weakly predicted by Members' financial backing.[14]

The aforementioned studies are suggestive, but they suffer from a basic methodological limitation. Correlations between contributions and legislative behavior cannot disentangle whether contributions reward fealty, create it, or merely reflect ideological affinity between legislators and their financial backers. For that matter, one may imagine scenarios in which contributors show special generosity to their political adversaries in an effort to blunt their opposition. In response to this basic methodological critique, recent research on campaign finance has taken a more dynamic approach, examining how legislators and contributors behave over time. Here, the ideological proclivities of legislators are held constant, and what varies is their capacity to deliver favors to contributors.

One study of this kind is Stacy Gordon's analysis of a series of votes on California's Senate Governmental Organization Committee.[15] Gordon finds that contributions have a stronger effect on those votes that are crucial to the legislative outcome. The implication of this study is that while contributions may influence only a small proportion of legislative balloting, contributions may nonetheless have a significant impact on legislative outcomes. Another dynamic approach is to examine the manner in which interest groups allocate their campaign contributions as the power wielded by legislators changes. Gary Cox and Eric Magar address the question "How much is majority status in the U.S. Congress worth?" by examining the flow of campaign dollars before and after a switch in party control of the House and Senate.[16] Cox and Magar find strong statistical evidence that donors favor the party in power, a clear indication that they see their donations as a means to gain access and influence, as opposed to a mere expression of ideological affinity. This work builds on the previous work of Thomas Romer and James Snyder, who examine how PAC contributions to Members and chairs of congressional committees change as these elected officials switch committees or leadership assignments.[17] Romer and Snyder find powerful evidence that representatives who join the Banking Committee, for example, enjoy a substantial influx of new contributions from banking PACs; the Ways and Means Committee seems to be especially attractive to corporate and trade PACs; and committee leadership positions are always rewarded with an extra dollop of cash.[18] Whether contributors seek access or influence remains unclear from the dynamic relationship between legislative power and donations; there can be no doubt, however, that contributors target their donations to officeholders who are best positioned to reciprocate with valuable favors or to retaliate against them in the event that they do not contribute.

One particularly lurid example of the strategic way in which interest groups target their donations occurs when large donations are made to both parties simultaneously. In such cases, donors seem to throw ideological affinity to the wind, ensuring instead that whichever party wins remains in their debt. For purposes of illustrating this point, let us put aside instances where corporate or union donors give token amounts of money to one party while showering the other with cash (for example, Union Pacific gave $676,858 to GOP committees in 1995–96, while giving Democratic committees just $5,550). Let us also ignore donations made by corporate executives and focus solely on donations made by corporate entities and unions. According to the Federal Election Commission (FEC), the list of lavish donations to both parties is lengthy. One notable example from the 1999–2000 election cycle is Enron's contribution of $607,065 to Democratic Party committees and $688,210 to Republican Party committees, but this pattern is by no means restricted to such celebrated cases. The tactic of two-party donations has become commonplace. During the 1999–2000 reporting cycle, AT&T donated $1,432,469 to the Democrats and $2,197,261 to the Republicans. MGM Mirage, Inc. gave $658,086 to the Democrats and $861,997 to the Republicans. Public spirited though these and many other corporations may be, it strains credulity to think that their evenhanded distribution of shareholders' money to both parties grows out of their desire to foster democratic discourse.

Ironically, the most strident charges of corruption of federal officeholders by party fund-raising come from the parties themselves. In the wake of the Enron collapse at the beginning of 2002, Democrats charged the Bush administration with letting its energy policies be shaped by Enron executives, who were prominent Republican donors. The National Republican Senatorial Committee fired back with a memo entitled "Enron Corporation and Arthur Andersen: The Democratic Connection," which pointed out that the two companies and their employees

donated $4.55 million to the Democratic Party and "affiliated commit-
tees," including forty-eight of fifty Democratic senators. The current scandal is reminiscent of the partisan crossfire that occurred in the wake of
Democratic fund-raising scandals, only here the Republican Party finds
itself on the defensive and mounts a counterattack: "As Democratic officials fraudulently and maliciously attack the Bush administration for
being 'an Enron government,' they ignore the deep, long relationship
between Enron, [its accounting firm] Arthur Andersen and the Democratic Party." Among the traits common to the Republican and Democratic
Parties is their shared belief that the opposition is beholden to special
interest contributors.[19]

MONEY AND PARTY BUILDING

What will become of parties in the wake of the BCRA? Some campaign
professionals who inhabit parties and who are dependent on their fund-
raising success would have us believe that parties cannot survive without
access to unlimited donations. Their protests are hardly surprising, since
campaign professionals have an interest in contending that campaigns
cannot be waged on a large scale without large sums of money. Their
livelihood revolves around the sale of services to parties and campaigns,
services such as the preparation of media advertisements, the design and
distribution of direct mail, the execution and analysis of opinion polls,
and so forth. Naturally, campaign professionals are quick to paint a grim
portrait of what campaigns and democracy would be without their ads,
polls, and four-color mailers.

The history of federal hard-money contributions, however, suggests
that the parties have been quite capable of finding new ways to raise ever-
larger quantities of hard money even under the old contribution limits.
This point has already been made with respect to the national parties,
whose hard-money receipts have increased by hundreds of millions of dollars in the space of one decade.

At the state level, the history of fund-raising belies the notion that contribution limits seriously impair parties' ability to raise money. Measuring
state party fund-raising is complicated by the fact that standardized
reports are available from the FEC regarding only expenditures of alloca-
ble soft money. (Recall that under the pre-BCRA system the parties could
spend soft money for certain joint state/federal election activities so long
as a portion of these expenditures was also paid for with hard money.)
Nevertheless, the trend is quite clear. Soft-money expenditures have risen

markedly over time, even when one focuses attention on federal midterm elections in which the vagaries of presidential campaign strategy are absent. According to the FEC, the state parties spent $80.2 million in allocable soft money in 1993–94; four years later, this figure had risen to $153.2 million. This increase was not confined to states like Illinois or Virginia, which place no limits on contributions to political parties, even from corporations or labor unions. Consider, for example, Connecticut, which prohibits labor and corporate contributions as well as national party transfers and places a $5,000 individual contribution limit on donations to state parties. In 1993–94, the parties spent $1,020,102 in soft money in accordance with state limits; despite some of the most stringent campaign finance laws in the country, this figure had doubled to $2,086,438 by 1997–98. Parties are skilled at raising money and adapt their tactics to the regulatory regime within which they operate.

Adaptation and Party Fund-Raising

The adaptability of parties mentioned by Raymond La Raja and charted in the historical narrative of Sidney Milkis earlier in this volume is central to understanding how the BCRA is likely to shape campaign finance in the years ahead. The parties will not stand still once soft money becomes unavailable to the national party committees. To assume that the dollars that are currently donated as soft money will simply dry up fails to anticipate the actions that parties will take in order to recoup these funds. Underlying the recent attempts by the California Democratic and Republican Parties to demonstrate how the BCRA's provisions will result in a deadweight loss of revenues is the assumption that neither party will do anything to gain a fund-raising advantage over the other, which is absurd. The logic of interparty competition forces parties to innovate and adapt.

I therefore reject the flawed methodology of extrapolating from past contribution patterns as though no adaptation will occur. One can readily envision several compensating trends that will occur once the use of soft money for federal election activities is restricted. Under the provisions of the BCRA, which relaxes the hard-money limits, state and national parties will be encouraged to broaden their financial base of hard-money contributors. The dramatic increase in hard-money fund-raising over the past decade leaves little doubt that this can be achieved. Indeed, the task of cultivating new party supporters will be made easier to the extent that the BCRA allays public cynicism about corruption and party finance. Second, much of the soft money that formerly flowed through the national parties to the states in the form of nonfederal transfers will instead go to the states in the form of Levin contributions. As Professor La Raja points out, the parties now tap an abundance of small soft-money contributors who, under the terms of the BCRA, will still be able to support the parties through Levin funds. And, of course, the BCRA does nothing to restrict soft-money donations to state parties insofar as these funds are used to pay for activities that do not affect federal elections.

SOFT-MONEY FUNDING AND PARTY STRENGTH

Suppose for the sake of argument that state parties were to lose substantial funding as the result of the BCRA. Suppose that the upward trajectory in state party hard-money fund-raising were suddenly halted.[20] Would the lack of money undermine the "strength" or "capacity" of state parties, as Professor La Raja asserts? What evidence suggests that party strength and funding are related? Professor La Raja presents data from a 1997 survey, the methodology of which is not described, to suggest that 335 local Republican committees became more likely to distribute lawn signs between 1980 and 1996, purportedly because of an infusion of soft money.[21] Curiously, however, the data in his report show that these organizations simultaneously became *less* likely to conduct voter registration drives and *less* likely to organize telephone campaigns. Taken as a whole, these trends suggest that the infusion of soft money did not lead to a general increase in voter mobilization activity.

Even if one were to accept the notion that these local parties became more active, the causative role of soft money here is impossible to distinguish from a myriad of other factors, such as the revitalization of party competition in the South, the revival of partisanship in the electorate, the ideological polarization of the parties after the Carter administration, and so forth.[22] Exactly the same criticism can be leveled at the 1980 versus 2000 comparison of state parties that Professor La Raja presents.

Soft money encouraged state parties to shuttle money back and forth to satisfy allocation formulas and to pay for expensive mass media campaigns orchestrated by the national parties. Notice that this top-down integration of what had formerly been a decentralized arrangement of local, state, and national parties has caused them to drift markedly from the idealized notion of a decentralized political party described by Professor Milkis. If decentralized party politics and local government are indeed the "bedrock of American democracy," soft money has contributed to its erosion.

Limiting soft money, far from weakening parties, will make them stronger. Parties will be encouraged to reach out to their supporters for volunteer labor and small donations. To do so, parties will be encouraged to inspire their activists with a policy agenda. The free flow of soft money has meant that parties have little need to inspire support; they can simply purchase all of the labor they require to execute a campaign. Professors La Raja and Milkis support more ideologically robust and accountable parties but fail to recognize that the abundance of soft money reduces the role played by issues.[23]

Soft Money and Its Effects on Voter Mobilization

If belts had to be tightened in the wake of the BCRA, would voter mobilization suffer?[24] Professor La Raja would have us believe that the $41.8 million that the state parties[25] spend on "voter mobilization" would evaporate, causing voter turnout to decline by more than two percentage points.

Putting aside the questionable overarching assumption that soft-money restrictions will reduce the quantity of money that state parties collect, the estimated drop in turnout that he envisions hinges on several subsidiary assumptions. One is the notion that the quantity of money slated for voter mobilization will decline if state party budgets are cut. The parties could well decide to trim the fat from their immense and rapidly growing media budgets and leave voter mobilization activities intact. The second assumption is that voter mobilization activities performed by parties will not be performed by other interest groups, an assumption that runs counter to Professor La Raja's own opinion that these groups "will substitute for non-federal funds donations to parties with direct membership mobilization." The third assumption is that the money spent by "voter mobilization" activities increases voter turnout at the rate of one additional vote for every $15 to $20 spent. This figure is based on the cost-effectiveness of door-to-door canvassing as a means of voter mobilization, as reported in a study by Alan Gerber and Donald Green and since replicated in several other experiments by Donald Green, Alan Gerber, and David Nickerson.[26]

If door-to-door canvassing orchestrated by state parties were widespread, a cut in this segment of their budgets could indeed result in a drop in voter turnout. But face-to-face canvassing operations are in fact quite rare. Indeed, the Krasno and Sorauf report underscores just how rare this type of campaign activity has become. Their detailed inspection of expenditures reveals that, of the $40.4 million that parties spent in direct connection with voter mobilization activity, $14.9 million went to direct mail, $10.8 million to phone banks, $4 million to voter databases. Canvassing accounted for just $1.2 million to $2.2 million, depending on how one chooses to treat activities that could not readily be classified.

If all forms of "voter mobilization" were equally effective, there would be no need to attend to the nuances of how campaigns spend their money. It appears, however, that direct mail and commercial phone banks are much less effective than door-to-door canvassing. My Yale colleagues and I have conducted several large-scale randomized experiments involving partisan and nonpartisan direct mail, and we find that partisan direct mail in particular has negligible effects on voter turnout.[27] For example, in a 1999 state legislative race in New Jersey, turnout was 54.20 percent among the 17,816 registered Democrats and Independents who were sent six pieces of direct mail urging a Democratic vote, as compared with 54.18 percent turnout among a corresponding group of 1,925 voters who received no direct mail.[28] Although we have not studied the effectiveness of partisan phone banks, we have performed two large-scale field experiments involving nonpartisan get-out-the-vote appeals conveyed by commercial phone banks; in neither case did these phone calls increase voter turnout.[29]

The consequences, therefore, of withdrawing $40 million from the "voter mobilization" activities described by Professor La Raja are essentially confined to the consequences of withdrawing $1.2 to $2.2 million in door-to-door canvassing. Given these numbers, a complete halt to face-to-face canvassing would result in a loss of 60,000 to 147,000 voters nationwide, which amounts to at most a 0.08 percentage point decline in turnout amid an electorate of 190,000,000 voting-eligible citizens. And even this modest effect hinges on the dubious assumption that parties will raise significantly less money and cut back their door-to-door canvassing as a consequence of the BCRA, which specifically encourages such activity with its Levin provisions and increased hard-money limits.

Why, then, do parties (and candidates) spend so much more money on direct mail and commercial phone banks than on door-to-door canvassing, if the latter is so much more effective at stimulating voter turnout? The answer is that parties are interested in winning elections, not raising voter turnout per se. The parties judge that the persuasive effects of direct mail and phone calls make them worthwhile, even if they do nothing to increase voter participation.

NOTES

1. On this point, see Donald Green, Bradley Palmquist, and Eric Schickler, *Partisan Hearts and Minds* (Yale University Press, 2002).

2. Two of the many examples that could be adduced include Ann L. Wagner, co-chair of the Republican National Committee (RNC) and chair of the Missouri Republican Party, and Joe Carmichael, vice chair of the Democratic National Committee (DNC) and chair of the Missouri State Democratic Party.

3. Edwin Bender, *States, Redistricting, and Election 2000* (National Institute on Money in State Politics, 2000).

4. The even-year federal elections mandated by the Constitution dominate the political landscape, particularly in presidential election years. By my calculation, the presence of a presidential candidate on the general election ballot raises statewide voter turnout by an average of 17 percentage points over the period 1960–2000. (Voter turnout was calculated as number of voters divided by the size of the voting-age electorate, as measured by *America Votes* and *Statistical Abstract of the United States*.) Thus a sizable fraction of all voters who cast ballots in joint state/federal elections show up precisely because there is a federal candidate on the ballot.

5. This argument rekindles a time-honored tradition of using voter mobilization campaigns as a Trojan horse to open loopholes for partisan campaign spending; the original exemptions for soft money were justified partly on the grounds that get-out-the-vote activity would help strengthen parties. As it happened, only a small fraction of the soft money (or hard money, for that matter) that flowed to state and national parties was spent on voter mobilization activity, even broadly conceived to include direct mail and commercial phone banking. According to the classification system presented by La Raja and Jarvis-Shean, 8.5 percent of national party soft-money expenditures went to "mobilization" and "grassroots." The figures for state and local parties are each 15 percent. See Ray La Raja and Elizabeth Jarvis-Shean, "Assessing the Impact of a Ban on Soft Money: Party Soft Money Spending in the 2000 Elections," unpublished manuscript (Institute of Governmental Studies and Citizens' Research Foundation, 2001), p. 3. Although the details of their classification scheme cannot be discerned from their discussion, it seems likely that they have, if anything, overestimated spending on mobilization, since much of what parties and consultants call "get-out-the-vote" activity is direct mail or phone calls designed to call attention to particular issues or candidates. Such expenditures could fairly be classified along with other forms of mass communications aimed at persuading voters.

6. Roll-off refers to instances in which voters cast ballots for the prominent offices at the top of the ticket but do not cast ballots for lower offices.

7. A similar argument explains why the BCRA's provisions concerning "public communications" by parties, as distinct from communications by independent organizations, are not limited to those communications occurring during the sixty days preceding a federal election. Unlike interest groups, which pursue an issue-based agenda that transcends the election of candidates, parties are primarily and continuously concerned with acquiring power through electoral victory. Parties never engage in public communication without regard to its electoral consequences.

8. In the regulatory environment that preceded the BCRA, the parties seldom received large donations from tax-exempt organizations. National parties had no need to acquire soft money through this indirect route; they could simply raise soft money themselves. National parties, on the other hand, frequently transferred large sums of money to tax-exempt organizations because, unlike state parties, these tax-exempt organizations are not bound by allocation formulas that specify how much hard money must be spent in conjunction with soft-money expenditures.

9. "RNC's Schemes 'Evade Federal Election Laws,'" *Washington Post*, February 10, 1998, p. A6.

10. One may also ask whether the appearance of corruption in fact undermines the legitimacy accorded to democratic institutions by the electorate. Among the few studies to address this question empirically is the cross-national investigation by Mitchell Seligson, who finds that countries with higher levels of corruption (as rated by specialists familiar with the inner workings of these countries) also have electorates that accord less legitimacy to the country's political institutions. Mitchell A. Seligson, "The Impact of Corruption on Regime Legitimacy: A Comparative Study of Four Latin American Countries," *Journal of Politics*, vol. 64 (2002), pp. 408–33.

11. James F. Herndon, "Access, Record, and Competition as Influences on Interest Group Contributions to Congressional Campaigns," *Journal of Politics*, vol. 44 (1982), pp. 996–1019.

12. Laura I. Langbein, "Money and Access: Some Empirical Evidence," *Journal of Politics*, vol. 48 (1986), pp. 1052–62. Note that the size of the PAC contributions at issue in Langbein's research pale in comparison with the immense soft-money contributions that were seen toward the end of the 1990s.

13. Richard L. Hall and Frank W. Wayman, "Buying Time: Moneyed Interests and the Mobilization of Bias in Congressional Committees," *American Political Science Review*, vol. 84 (September 1990), pp. 797–820.

14. Fred Monardi and Stanton A. Glantz, "Are Tobacco Industry Campaign Contributions Influencing State Legislative Behavior?" *American Journal of Public Health*, vol. 88 (1998), pp. 918–23. See also the literature review in Frank J. Sorauf, *Inside Campaign Finance: Myths and Realities* (Yale University Press, 1992), pp. 163–74.

15. Stacy B. Gordon, "All Votes Are Not Created Equal: Campaign Contributions and Critical Votes," *Journal of Politics*, vol. 63 (2001), pp. 249–69.

16. Gary W. Cox and Eric Magar, "How Much Is Majority Status in the U.S. Congress Worth?" *American Political Science Review*, vol. 93 (1999), pp. 299–309.

17. Thomas Romer and James M. Snyder Jr., "An Empirical Investigation of the Dynamics of PAC Contributions," *American Journal of Political Science*, vol. 38 (1994), pp. 745–69.

18. This analysis is confirmed by Dow and others' 1998 statistical analysis of campaign contributions by economic interest groups to members of the California

Assembly, which shows quite clearly that industries (such as agriculture, labor, and finance) target their contributions to members who sit on the committees with jurisdiction over them. Unlike Romer and Snyder in "An Empirical Investigation of the Dynamics of PAC Contributions," however, Dow does not examine the manner in which contributions change as members change committee assignments. See James K. Dow, James W. Endersby, and Charles E. Menifield, "The Industrial Structure of the California State Assembly: Committee Assignments, Economic Interests, and Campaign Contributions," *Public Choice,* vol. 94 (1998), pp. 67–83.

19. These charges are readily found in press releases issued by both parties. In a RNC press release issued on April 29, 2000, Jim Nicholson, then chairman of the RNC, charged that "there are just two reasons Clinton and Gore won't let reasonable legislation become law—first, because they'd rather have the political issue, and second, because they're dependent for campaign contributions on the trial lawyers, and are doing their bidding." In a DNC press release issued on March 28, 2002, Terry McAuliffe stated that "the Energy Secretary rubber-stamps rules and regulations drafted by a Republican energy donor [and that] every day there are more and more disturbing disclosures about the cozy relationship between the administration and Enron and the never-ending favors it dispensed for big donors."

20. According to the Robert Biersack declaration (available at www.campaign-legalcenter.org), hard-money receipts by the state parties rose from $111.2 million in 1991–92 to $180.5 million in 1995–96 to $309.6 million in 2000.

21. See John Frendreis and Alan R. Gitelson, "Local Parties in the 1990s: Spokes in a Candidate-Centered Wheel," in John C. Green and Daniel M. Shea, eds., *The State of the Parties: The Changing Role of Contemporary American Parties,* 3d ed. (Lanham, Md.: Rowman and Littlefield, 1999), pp. 135–53.

22. Green and others, *Partisan Hearts and Minds.*

23. The famous 1950 report that these authors cite with reverence advocates not the mere strengthening or centralization of parties but instead the creation of parties that promote vigorous grassroots participation: "Party membership ought to become a year-round matter, both with constructive activities by members and with mechanisms by which party organizations can absorb the benefits of wider political participation." See Committee on Political Parties of the American Political Science Association, *Toward a More Responsible Two-Party System* (Rinehart, 1950), p. 30. Soft money has proven inimical to this goal for the reasons articulated by Senator Brock, in part 3 of this volume.

24. When assessing the likelihood of this scenario, one should bear in mind the fact that soft-money expenditures on the mass media dwarf soft-money expenditures on voter mobilization. On the dramatic growth of media expenditures in relation to mobilization expenditures, see the La Raja report.

25. Professor La Raja reports the figure of $53.1 million for parties at all levels; see his presentation in this volume.

26. Alan Gerber and Donald Green, "The Effects of Canvassing, Direct Mail, and Telephone Contact on Voter Turnout: A Field Experiment," *American Political Science Review,* vol. 94 (2000), pp. 653–63; Donald Green, Alan S. Gerber, and David Nickerson, "Getting Out the Youth Vote in Local Elections: Results from Six Door-to-Door Canvassing Experiments," May 2002.

27. Gerber and Green, "The Effects of Canvassing, Direct Mail, and Telephone Contact on Voter Turnout"; Donald Green, Alan Gerber, and David Nickerson, "Testing for Publication Bias in Political Science," *Political Analysis,* vol. 9 (2001), pp. 385–92.

28. Green, Gerber, and Nickerson, "Getting Out the Youth Vote in Local Elections."

29. Gerber and Green, "The Effects of Canvassing, Direct Mail, and Telephone Contact on Voter Turnout"; Alan S. Gerber and Donald Green, "Do Phone Calls Increase Voter Turnout? A Field Experiment," *Public Opinion Quarterly*, vol. 65 (2001), pp. 75–85.

A Senate Democrat's Perspective

DAVID BOREN

David Boren was a U.S. senator from Oklahoma from 1979 to 1994. Boren was a fact witness for the defense. He testified as to his experience running for reelection while following a personal policy of refusing political action committee contributions and discussed the impact of soft money on the campaign finance system during his tenure in Congress. In this excerpt, he describes some of the methods parties use to raise soft money and its corruptive effect on the legislative process.

When I left the Senate in 1994, I left with a sense of gratitude for having had the privilege to serve there, but also in a state of great alarm about its future. Congress as an institution is in trouble, and only a change in the way our campaigns are financed can mend the broken trust between the American people and their government.

During my time in the Senate, I was one of a handful of senators who did not take any money from political action committees (PACs). I also tried to minimize the time I spent raising "soft money" for the Democratic Party, and as a result, I received almost no money from the Democratic Party for my campaigns. At the time, the Democratic Senatorial Campaign Committee (DSCC) and other national party organizations kept records, or "tallies," of how much soft money a senator had raised for the party. The DSCC then gave little money to the campaigns of those senators who had not raised adequate party funds. In my view, this practice demonstrates very clearly that soft money is not used purely for "party-building" activities, but that there is at least a working understanding among the party officials and senate candidate that the money will benefit the individual senators' campaigns.

Political parties raise soft money in various ways. One very effective fund-raising tool was the gala dinners and other functions where big donors purchased "tables" with soft-money contributions. Like other senators, I was expected to "sell a table" and attend these functions, and, from time to time, I did. Sometimes, lobbyists called me or other senators, offered to buy a "table" for the corporation they represented and then offered to "make sure the donation goes on your tally." At the fund-raising dinners themselves, donors could often choose which senators they would like to have at their table. They often chose the senator who was a member of the congressional committee that mattered to the particular industry.

In addition to dinners, the Democratic National Committee (DNC), DSCC, and Democratic Congressional Campaign Committee (DCCC) organized a variety of other events for large soft-money donors, such as breakfasts to talk about policy issues. I also occasionally attended these events. While donors did not necessarily lobby us for specific legislative actions at these events, donors would frequently say, "I've been meaning to come by and see you" or "Can your scheduler set up an appointment for someone in my firm?" Each senator knows who the biggest donors to his party are. Donors often prefer to hand their checks to the senator personally, or their lobbyist informs the senator that a large donation was just made. Senators play golf with donors at weekend retreats and attend dinners and briefing sessions together. Through these functions, donors and members of Congress become part of a small village where everyone knows each other and knows who is providing funding to the party. This creates a tremendous hydraulic: it is extremely difficult to decline to see, and perhaps do favors for, someone whom you know personally and who has been generous to you and your party.

As a member of the Senate Finance Committee, I experienced the pressure firsthand. On several occasions when we were debating important tax bills, I needed a police escort to get into the Finance Committee hearing room because so many lobbyists were crowding the halls, trying to get one last chance to make their pitch to each senator. Senators generally knew which lobbyist represented the interests of which large donor. I was often glad that I limited the amount of soft-money fund-raising I did and did not take PAC contributions because it would be extremely difficult not to feel beholden to these donors otherwise. I know from my firsthand experience and from my interactions with other senators that they did feel beholden to large donors.

Everyone becomes a victim of the system. Many members of Congress vie for positions on particular committees such as Finance and Ways and Means in large part because it makes it much easier for them to raise money. They then spend large amounts of their scarce time raising money for their party from businesses that have specific matters pending before their committees. They know exactly why most soft-money donors give: to get access and special influence based on their contributions.

Donors also feel victimized. Now that I've left office, I sometimes hear from large donors that they feel "shaken down": because others are making large donations, they also feel pressure to donate, or no one on Capitol Hill would be willing to see them or support their interests. Individual members of Congress and individual donors cannot unilaterally "disarm" by opting out of the system. The soft-money loophole has created an arms race that cannot stop until appropriate legislation, such as the Bipartisan Campaign Reform Act, is passed to stop it.

A Senate Republican's Perspective

ALAN K. SIMPSON

Alan K. Simpson was a U.S. senator from Wyoming from 1979 to 1997. Simpson was a fact witness for the defense. He testified to the role of soft money in the campaign finance system and the special treatment political parties give to large donors. In this excerpt, he describes how members of the Senate are involved in soft-money fund-raising and the corruptive effect soft money can have on the legislative process.

During my tenure in the U.S. Senate, I became acutely aware of the need for campaign finance reform, particularly with the impact of soft money on the political system. I have seen firsthand how the current campaign financing system prostitutes ideas and ideals, demeans democracy, and debases debates.

The national parties often ask senators to make phone calls to raise soft money and the process is like a boiler-room operation. When I was in the Senate, the Republican leadership would take us off Capitol Hill—usually to the Reagan Center—give us a list of heavy hitters, and tell us to make phone calls to get more money from these donors. Sometimes, the party asked us to solicit soft money for attendance at events that included access to the president; other times major donors were given access to certain lawmakers. The more money one donates, the higher-level players he or she has access to. I did not enjoy making these phone calls and after participating once or twice, I told the party that I would no longer telephone donors.

Although I rarely made phone calls for the party, I agreed to attend and speak at their donor events. Often, donors would give large sums of soft money to attend events with elected officials. Donors were often allowed to choose whom they wanted to sit with at events, provided they gave enough money. Party leaders would inform members at caucus meetings who the big donors were. If the leaders tell you that a certain person or group has donated a large sum to the party and will be at an event Saturday night, you'll be sure to attend and get to know the people behind the donation, especially if you are told that the reason people donated was because they wanted to sit at the same table with you. At these events, it was not uncommon for the donors to mention certain legislation that affected them. Even if some members did not attend these events, they all still knew which donors gave the large donations, as the party publicized who gives what.

The parties often ask members to solicit soft money from individuals who have maxed out to the member's campaign. Donors do not really differentiate between hard and soft money; they often contribute to assist or gain favor with an individual politician. When donors give soft money to the parties, there is sometimes at least an implicit understanding that the money will be used to benefit a certain candidate. Likewise, members know that if they assist the party with fund-raising, be it hard or soft money, the party will later assist their campaign.

There is little practical difference between hard and soft money these days in terms of how the funds are used. Politicians care only that money is available; it doesn't matter where it came from. Although soft money cannot be given directly to federal candidates, everyone knows that it is fairly easy to push the money through our tortured system to benefit specific candidates. I always knew that both the national and state parties would find ways to assist my candidacy with soft money, whether it be staff assistance, polling, get-out-the-vote (GOTV) activities, or buying television advertisements.

Large donors of both hard and soft money receive special treatment. No matter how busy a politician may be during the day, he or she will always make time to see donors who gave large amounts of money. Staffers who work for members know who the big donors are, and those people always get their phone calls returned first and are allowed to see the member when others are not. For example, one longtime contributor might come into my office and say, "Al, I'm really proud of the work you're doing here, and I'm proud to have supported you over the years. I just wanted to let you know that my company has an important issue up before Agency X. We don't want you to do anything; we just want to make you aware." A few months later, that same contributor would come back and say, "We're still waiting for the agency to make a decision. We probably don't need you, and we wouldn't want you to influence the decision, but maybe you could see if the agency would move the issue up on their priority list?" Without hesitation, I would make a call to the secretary of the department in charge of the agency. I would not tell the secretary how to decide the issue, nor would I make any threats; I would simply communicate that my constituent would appreciate a prompt decision. Senators make these types of phone calls all the time.

Too often, members first think of not what is right or what they believe, but how it will affect fund-raising. Who, after all, can seriously contend that a $100,000 donation does not alter the way one thinks about—and quite possibly votes on—an issue? Donations from the tobacco industry to Republicans scuttled tobacco legislation, just as contributions from the trial lawyers to Democrats stopped tort reform. When you don't pay the piper that finances your campaigns, you will never get any more money from that piper. Since money is the mother's milk of politics, you never want to be in that situation.

In addition to the example listed above, I remember specific instances when senators' votes were affected by the fear of losing future donations. One time, Senator Bob Dole and I were seeking votes on an important national issue. More than once, we heard a senator tell us, "I realize it's an issue of great importance, but if I vote for that I won't get any more money. I want to be here for another term. You do want me back here next year, don't you?" These senators know that it's a bad idea to poison the well that nourishes the system.

Soft money also affects legislative priorities. I remember one senator from a state with a large Asian population who came to me with a proposal to ease immigration restrictions on people from Asian countries. This senator told me that the Asians have a lot of money and that they were ready to give it to the Republicans if the party would support immigration reform.

Both during and after my service in the Senate, I have seen that citizens of both parties are as cynical about government as they have ever been because of the corrupting effects of unlimited soft-money donations.

Mobilizing Voters:
The Coordinated Campaign

GAIL STOLTZ

Gail Stoltz has been the political director of the Democratic National Committee (DNC) since 2001. She was a fact witness for the defense and testified on the party's coordinated campaign, voter registration, and voter mobilization efforts in election cycles. This excerpt includes her description of the "coordinated campaigns" that state parties conduct in conjunction with party and candidate committees to turn out Democratic voters.

One of my major functions is overseeing our "coordinated campaign" programs in the various states. A coordinated campaign is a project of the state party to register, identify, and turn out voters on behalf of the entire Democratic ticket, including federal, state, and local candidates. The purpose is to increase turnout of Democratic voters for the benefit of all the party's candidates, whether for state, local, or federal office. Typically, the various state parties draft a coordinated campaign plan, which is then approved by the political staff at the DNC. The DNC's outside political consultants and donors to the coordinated campaign, such as labor unions and other interest groups, also sometimes review the coordinated campaign plan.

State parties often hire campaign consultants, such as direct mail and phone bank specialists, to assist in the coordinated campaign. Direct mail consultants design mailings and then mail them to voters or prepare them for processing by volunteers. Phone bank consultants often organize and hire staff to run phone banks themselves, or they set up phone banks for Democratic Party volunteers. Sometimes the DNC provides recommendations to the state parties about which vendors to use, and sometimes the DNC endeavors to assist the state parties in negotiating contracts with these vendors.

A coordinated campaign is financed with a combination of funds raised by the party itself and funds contributed to the state party by various national party committees, including the DNC; by candidate committees; and, as permitted by and pursuant to applicable state law, by individuals and entities such as labor organizations, corporations, state-registered political committees, and other organizations. These funds are then spent for the operating expenses of the coordinated campaign (staff, rent, and the like) and for the costs of voter contact activities such as literature distributed by volunteers or paid workers, telephone banks, slate cards, and mailings.

Federal, state, and local candidates participate in the design and operation and, in some cases, the funding of the coordinated campaign. Candidates may participate because of their leadership roles in the party within the state or because they are running for office and will thus benefit from the coordinated campaign activities that assist their own campaign and the entire ticket. Sometimes these candidates contribute their own campaign funds from their authorized committees to the coordinated campaign, but more frequently the candidates ask donors to contribute funds directly to the coordinated campaign in both federal and nonfederal funds.

If a participant in the coordinated campaign committee for a state, including the DNC, is responsible for a donation by a donor to the coordinated campaign, that donation is credited against the participant's funding commitment to the coordinated campaign. The DNC sometimes asks donors to give funds directly to state parties as part of an effort to fund fully as many coordinated campaigns as possible. For example, the DNC may ask a donor to contribute to one particular state's coordinated campaign. If the donor agrees, DNC staff normally contact the state party staff to tell them that a donation is coming, and that this donation should be credited toward the DNC's commitment to help fund the coordinated campaign.

Sometimes DNC staff finds it hard to persuade donors to give to coordinated campaigns since they are run by state parties. We then try to convince the donors that it is important to win at all levels of the ticket and remind them that their contribution will help federal as well as state candidates. The candidates who raised money from donors—or had money raised on their behalf—to help complete their coordinated campaign commitment are aware when those donations come in or are made.

The DNC helps develop the coordinated campaign in a state and provides money, advice, and technical assistance. The DNC also helps with recruitment and training of staff and workers. The DNC decides which coordinated campaigns to invest in on the basis of whether there are competitive federal and state elections in that state. For example, the DNC is more likely to contribute more funds to a state that has just received an added congressional seat through redistricting or that has a competitive governor's race or an open U.S. Senate or congressional seat.

The goal of the coordinated campaign is to win "from the top down." In other words, it is designed to help Democratic candidates at all levels of the ticket. Coordinated campaigns are also important for other reasons. For example, state legislature candidates often are the "farm team" for federal candidacies, especially in states with term limits. Also, the ground operations such as voter development and get-out-the-vote activities can be important to the success of federal elections in the state. Also, races for governorships, mayoral offices, and other state and local offices are important because the candidates and officeholders resulting from those races can have significant effect on voter development, and thus on the success of the Democratic ticket, in the pertinent election or future elections.

The DNC's and political director's major focus during presidential election years is the election of the presidential candidate. In such years the DNC provides more resources to coordinated campaigns, in part to secure the election of the presidential candidate. The DNC hopes that the chosen presidential message is good for all Democrats on the ticket. During such years, the DNC coordinates with presidential campaign committees regularly through frequent discussions and meetings between the DNC and campaign staff. DNC and presidential campaign staff are also in daily contact about which message to focus on. This is particularly true once it is clear who the Democratic nominee will be. At that point, the DNC works in tandem with the presidential campaign and the nominees. The DNC and the campaign exchange polling data, see each others' ad scripts, and in the 1996 and 2000 election cycles, used common campaign/media strategists or consultants. For example, during a particular week the presidential campaign may want to emphasize the candidate's views on Social Security. During a morning message call, the DNC, campaign staff, and consultants may discuss this message and work to make sure the coordinated campaigns emphasize this message.

State Party Activity and the BCRA

KATHLEEN BOWLER

Kathleen Bowler has been the executive director of the California Democratic Party (CDP) since 1995. She testified on behalf of two plaintiffs, the California Democratic and Republican parties. Her declaration described the CDP's structure, goals, expenditures, and range of activities. In this excerpt, Bowler summarizes the finances and activities of the CDP and provides a state party official's understanding of how the reform act will affect the operations of state and local party committees. She contends that the reform act will severely limit party fund-raising and associational activities and thus provide a relative advantage to interest groups in the electoral process.

CDP is integrally related to the Democratic National Committee (DNC), which is the governing body of the Democratic Party of the United States. Under its charter, the DNC is made up principally of the state chair and highest ranking officer of the opposite gender from each recognized state Democratic Party, and of 200 additional members apportioned to, and selected by, the state parties, on the basis of a formula taking into account population and Democratic voting strength. Thus, CDP's chair and vice chair are members of the DNC by virtue of their state party offices; and CDP has elected 20 other persons to represent CDP on the DNC. In addition, the chairman of the CDP, Art Torres, has been elected by the DNC, on the recommendation of the DNC chair, to serve on the DNC Executive Committee. The DNC often works with CDP in planning and implementing strategy and operations to elect Democrats to all levels of office and in disseminating the Democratic Party's message. Members of the DNC representing the CDP attend regular meetings of the DNC, as well as training sessions, regional caucuses, and numerous other meetings and events.

CDP has a core staff of approximately twenty-four people during non-election years. Those employees are divided into six divisions: accounting, administrative, finance (which includes fund-raising), political/communications, and research. The party maintains year-round offices in two locations: Sacramento and Los Angeles. The cost of maintaining the offices and staff, apart from the costs of specific activities, is substantial. It includes not only staff costs, but also related expenses such as health and pension benefits and workers' compensation, as well as rent, utilities, legal fees, general liability insurance, printing, office equipment, and similar overhead expenses. Many of these expenses are not directly related to election activity and are typical of any large membership organization. Like other organizations, we hold conferences and meetings, distribute literature that describes the party's goals and principles, respond to member inquiries, and issue press releases.

CDP's regular and ongoing operating expenses, including fund-raising expenses, between 1997 and 2000 ranged between $2.1 million and $3 million. These figures do not include convention costs, which have typically been several hundred thousand dollars annually. As I explain further below, these costs cannot be reduced without significantly impairing the party's ability to perform its core functions.

CDP maintains a federal committee that is registered with the Federal Election Commission (FEC). It is required to comply with the federal contribution limits and reporting requirements, and it has a federal account that is limited to contributions received within the federal limits ($5,000 per contributor per year). In accordance with federal law, this account does not include any contributions from corporations or labor unions.

I have reviewed the federal contribution figures since 1995. The amount of federal money raised through contributions has been relatively constant. For example, we raised $4,316,528 in the 1995–96 cycle; $4,076,870 in the 1997–98 cycle; $4,837,967 in the 1999–2000 cycle; and $3,455,887 in the 2001–02 cycle (as of June 30). These are federal contributions raised directly by CDP; these figures do not include any transfers from other party committees or candidates. These numbers reflect a substantial effort over the years to raise federal money; even with increased efforts, I believe it would be exceedingly difficult to raise substantially more federal money.

CDP is also registered as a political committee, in accordance with California law, and is required to comply with California law as well as federal law with respect to its campaign activities. Its nonfederal campaign activities are subject to direct regulation by the Fair Political Practices Commission, and it regularly files reports of all its receipts and expenditures with the California Secretary of State. California law was changed significantly by the adoption of Proposition 34, a comprehensive campaign finance measure, in November 2000. Under Proposition 34, contributions to candidates by individuals, committees, or entities other than political parties are limited: $3,000 to state legislators, $5,000 to statewide candidates other than governor, and $20,000 to governor. ("Small contributor" committees may give slightly more.) Contributions by political parties to candidates are not limited, although they count toward the voluntary spending limits, if a candidate has accepted such limits. Expenditures made by a political party on behalf of a candidate are also unlimited, but they do not count toward the spending limits. As a practical matter, this means that if the party sends out a mailer endorsing a candidate that costs $2,500, that amount does not count against the candidate's limits, but if the party gives a $2,500 contribution to the same candidate, it will count against those limits. Contributions to political parties for the purpose of making contributions to state candidates are limited to $25,000 per year per contributor; contributions for other purposes (such as administrative and overhead costs, voter registration, generic get-out-the-vote, and support of ballot measures) are not limited. Contributions to the political parties are not limited as to the source (in other words, corporations and unions may contribute).

Consistent with its state and local focus, CDP has always raised more nonfederal money than federal money. These amounts have also been relatively constant over the past four cycles. In the 1995–96 cycle, we raised $12,991,251; in the 1997–98 cycle, we raised $15,957,831; in the 1999–2000 cycle, we raised $15,617,002; for the 2001–02 cycle, we have raised $13,928,496 through June 30. I would expect the final figures for this cycle to be somewhat higher than 1999–2000. Again, this is money raised directly by CDP; these figures do not include any transfers from other party committees. This is money that we have used to fund our state and local activities.

In the past, the party has placed contributions that meet the federal limits as to amount and source into its federal account. Other contributions, representing a substantial majority of the party's income, have been placed in its nonfederal accounts. The federal account pays for direct contributions to federal candidates, as well as expenditures coordinated with a federal candidate as permitted by federal law. It would also be used for independent expenditures in support of a federal candidate (although I am only aware of one such expenditure since 1995). The nonfederal accounts would be used for direct contributions to state or local candidates, as well as coordinated or independent expenditures made on their behalf. There are 120 legislative officers, 8 statewide elected officers, and 4 members of the State Board of Equalization (elected by district). In addition, there are elections for judicial office and local office, and ballot measures at both the state and local level.

One of the party's most significant nonfederal expenses is its direct mail program in support of its endorsed nonfederal candidates and ballot measures. CDP typically spends $7 to $8 million per cycle in nonfederal funds on its mail program in support of its nonfederal candidates. Obviously, the majority of our nonfederal contributions (approximately $13 to $16 million per cycle) go into this program.

The costs of certain activities, which have been construed by the FEC since about 1990 as having an effect on both federal and nonfederal elections, are "allocated" between our federal account and our nonfederal account. Allocation is required for administrative expenses (for example, rent, utilities, salaries), generic voter identification, partisan voter registration and GOTV activities that are not candidate-specific, fund-raising expenses, and communications on behalf of both federal and nonfederal candidates (such as a mailer that mentions both). This allocation is done in accordance with the Federal Election Commission's (FEC) regulations; the precise allocation formula depends on the nature of the activity. For example, administrative expenses and generic party activities have been allocated on the basis of the "ballot composition" formula, which calculates the ratio of federal offices and nonfederal offices expected to be on the general election ballot in that cycle. In the 1999–2000 cycle, which included a presidential race, administrative expenses were to be allocated in the ratio 43 percent federal to 57 percent nonfederal. In this cycle, where the only federal office on the ballot is the congressional race, administrative expenses are to be allocated in the ratio 12.5 percent federal to 87.5 percent nonfederal. Public communications are allocated using a "time and space" formula. For example, the costs of a mailer that endorses one federal candidate and nine nonfederal candidates equally would have to be paid one-tenth from the federal account and nine-tenths from the nonfederal account. Fund-raising expenses are allocated on a "funds-raised" basis. For example, if a fund-raising dinner raises $100,000, and $40,000 is deposited into the federal account and $60,000 into the nonfederal account, then the dinner expenses are paid using 40 percent federal dollars and 60 percent nonfederal. While I do not always agree with the FEC's characterization of a particular activity as having an effect on a federal election, the allocation system has been a fair and understandable method of dealing with activities that may have some effect on a federal election, even if somewhat remote and indirect. It also recognizes the reality that most states combine federal and nonfederal elections, and that certain expenditures may affect both.

Over the years, CDP has received transfers of both federal and nonfederal money from the DNC, the Democratic Congressional Campaign Committee (DCCC), and the Democratic Senatorial Campaign Committee

(DSCC). The majority of these transfers were for issue advocacy, although money has also been transferred for voter registration, get-out-the-vote activities, and even administrative expenses. We are able to raise a substantial amount of money for our nonfederal activities and do not rely on national party transfers for these purposes. Some transfers were not for particular expenses but were "trades" between CDP and the DNC that reflected our different needs in a particular election cycle. For example, in 2000 we had some additional federal money at the end of the year, and the 2001–02 cycle was going to require a lower percentage of federal money for allocated expenditures. The DNC needed federal money but had additional nonfederal money. So, we traded. This is legal and was fully reported on our state and federal campaign reports.

The FEC has determined that issue advocacy is a form of generic party activity and must be allocated between federal and nonfederal money. The allocation ratio for the state parties has been somewhat more favorable than the ratio for national parties. In 2000, CDP's federal portion was 43 percent, while that of the national parties was at least 65 percent. Since federal money is harder to raise and is less available, transferring money to CDP for issue ads allowed CDP to run ads that it otherwise might not have been able to afford and allowed the ad to be run with a lower percentage of federal money. CDP also benefited by having its name on the ad (which gave the party increased visibility for all of its races), and the ads typically featured themes that were popular "Democratic" themes and were designed to motivate voters around those issues (such as health care and Social Security). It is important to note that this was all done legally and only after the FEC had indicated that this was permissible. It is also my view that the "transfer" issue is something of a "red herring" in that it could have been addressed by the FEC or Congress on a very direct basis and cannot be used as a justification for imposing a number of other restrictions on the political parties that have nothing to do with the problems supposedly created by these transfers.

The BCRA's Unreasonably Broad Definition of "Federal Election Activity"

The Bipartisan Campaign Reform Act (BCRA) creates a new term—"federal election activity"—and requires that any activities falling within the scope of that term must be paid for either completely with federal contributions or with a combination of federal contributions and a new form of federally regulated money—"Levin amendment" contributions. Levin contributions are not limited by federal law as to source (they may include corporate or union contributions if permitted under state law), but they are subject to the federal limits as to amount. Under the BCRA, both federal contributions and Levin contributions will be limited to $10,000. This means that state parties such as California will now be required to have at least three accounts: a federal account, a federally limited Levin account, and the state's nonfederal accounts. (In California, the party must maintain separate accounts for candidate-related contributions and expenditures, and for noncandidate-related contributions and expenditures.) The first two of these accounts are federally limited, and only these two accounts may be used to fund "federal election activities" after the BCRA goes into effect.

Under the new definition of "federal election activity," virtually all of CDP's activities in support of its state and local candidates, as well as most of its "generic" party-building activity, will be considered "federal election activity" even though those activities have only a remote or indirect effect on any federal election or, in some cases, no effect at all. As a result, nonfederal money cannot be used at all for these activities. This has the following consequences for our activities.

Even after excluding transfers from other parties and contributions to other organizations, it is clear that the vast majority of CDP's historical activities in support of its candidates and measures and/or to build the party's membership base and promote its ideology may be classified as "federal election activity." This means that those activities can no longer be funded from the nonfederal money we raise in accordance with California law—they will have to be funded either completely with federal funds or a combination of federal funds and Levin amendment funds.

The cost of communicating with voters in California is substantial. It is a geographically large state, with a very large population and several expensive media markets. The cost of television is higher for the party than it is for candidates. If the national parties are prohibited from transferring money to assist with ads, it is unlikely that CDP will be able to afford to do them, although we would like to be able to do them to the same extent as other organizations and without additional limitations on the type of money used. Even if the party limits its communications to mail, in order to compete for attention effectively the mail must have a visual impact and there must be repeated contact. In my experience, an organization cannot reach voters effectively by mail unless it sends at least 12 to 15 pieces in relatively close proximity in terms of time. The average cost of a CDP mail piece has been approximately $0.25–$0.35 (postage alone is at least $0.10 per piece); the average number of mail pieces for a state Senate district is 150,000; the average number for a state assembly district is 90,000. A statewide mail piece, such as a vote-by-mail piece, costs approximately $260,000. None of these pieces mention federal candidates, yet all of these costs will have to be paid with federally limited funds. If CDP's income is limited by the BCRA by the percentages indicated above, CDP will clearly not only not be able to do any television or radio advertisements, its mail program will be reduced below the level of effective communication of its message.

In addition, GOTV efforts other than the mail program will suffer. A ground campaign is very expensive to run. Although CDP recruits volunteers, a significant number of persons must also be paid. I estimate that in the coming election, approximately 50 percent of the GOTV work will have to be done by paid staff. Candidates cannot, for the most part, afford to conduct this kind of campaign; they use the media or mails because these methods are more effective for the money spent. Nor do candidates have the infrastructure set up to conduct this kind of campaign. The parties, through their local organizations, conduct the only real ground campaign. We anticipate supporting at least 30 local offices for the upcoming election. The vast majority of these offices will have paid staff doing at least some training, recruiting, coordinating, and so on. If the parties cannot conduct or support these activities, either from lack of available funds or restrictions imposed on coordinating party activities at more than one level, these activities are likely to simply disappear over time.

Effects of the BCRA on Fund-Raising and Associational Activities

The broad definition of "federal election activity" and the limits on raising money that can be used to fund those activities will be exacerbated by several other provisions of the BCRA. First, the BCRA prohibits national party officers or agents from raising Levin money, as well as nonfederal funds. It also prevents the use of such funds if they have been raised by other party officials, such as County Central Committee officers. CDP and DNC's by-laws provide that the chair and vice chair of CDP are members of the Democratic National Committee by virtue of their office. Similarly, County Central Committee chairs are members of CDP's Executive Committee. Members of the DNC in California, as well as County Central Committee officers, are also often active in party activities at the state level, and the DNC includes a number of state, federal, and local officials and even a CDP staff person. The political parties are designed to have a great deal of "overlap" in their membership and leadership. The provisions of the BCRA, particularly the criminal provisions, will make it difficult, if not impossible, for persons to engage in activities on more than one level (local, state, national) if those activities or communications can subject them to investigation or prosecution for assisting another party committee in raising what are essentially federally regulated funds.

The BCRA restricts transfers of federal money between party committees if that money is to be used in conjunction with Levin money for "federal election activities." This makes no sense. Federal money is, by definition, raised in compliance with all of the federal limitations as to both source and amount. CDP can use its own federal money for "federal election activities" but cannot use any federal money transferred from another party committee. The only apparent explanation for these restrictions is a desire to inhibit intraparty coordination and further inhibit the development of strong parties. Since federal money is difficult to raise and, under the BCRA, will have to be used in large measure for even nonfederal electoral activity, it is unlikely that such funds would be transferred unless one party committee had "surplus" funds and another party committee needed such funds, as in the case of a closely contested seat. In these cases, the parties should have the freedom that other organizations have to make basic organizational decisions about where money is best spent. Even though Levin funds are not subject to all the federal restrictions (although subject to significant restriction), the same is true for the transfer of Levin funds among the state and local parties. Transferring money already raised within certain limits cannot be said to be circumventing such limits. The limits on transfers and the ban on joint fundraising activities between party committees make it clear that the real intent of the Levin limit is to restrict overall spending and weaken the parties by reducing their participation in the election process.

Fundamentally, the BCRA attempts to separate and isolate each level of the party. Currently, the parties at all levels are bound together not only by ideology, but also in the common enterprise of electing candidates up and down the ticket. In various ways, the parties attempt to coordinate their efforts, reach out to their core constituencies, and allocate their collective resources to achieve both electoral goals and ideological goals. In the electoral context, the Democrats have had the coordinated campaign, which has been an effort to bring all the elements of the party together to maximize their resources and the likelihood of electoral success. The coordinated campaign involves representatives of the national, state, and local parties, as well as constituent groups that have historically provided strong grassroots support, coming together to discuss the very real and practical problems of winning campaigns. If these persons have to worry about whether their discussions amount to "soliciting," "receiving," "directing," or "spending" nonfederal money, and whether their communications subject them to criminal prosecution, it will be virtually impossible to engage in the kind of collective planning and decisionmaking that is part and parcel of election campaigns. Moreover, these restrictions are not imposed on other groups participating in the political process—only on the political parties.

CDP has also made certain expenditures that are directly related to its state and local electoral activities that will be prohibited by the BCRA. For example, contributions to organizations described in IRS Code Section 501(c) are prohibited if they engage in federal election activity, including voter registration and GOTV. Most committees that are organized to support or oppose ballot measures in California are organized as 501(c)(4) committees; it is my understanding that this has been required by the IRS. Virtually all of these committees engage in some activity that would be characterized as GOTV. The ban on contributions means not only that CDP cannot contribute directly to a particular ballot measure committee, it also cannot make "in-kind" contributions to such a committee. The CDP by-laws give the party the authority to endorse ballot measures; CDP commonly communicates its endorsement by including it in mail pieces that contain a combination of candidate and ballot measure endorsements. Each of these constitutes an "in-kind" contribution to the benefited committee unless done completely independently of the committee. This ban on contributions to ballot measure committees, whether direct or in-kind, means that CDP will be prohibited from involvement in many of the most significant state controversies—issues such as affirmative action, education of immigrant children, welfare reform, restrictions on union membership, and term limits, all of which have been the subject of ballot measures in recent years.

Other Structural Problems Created by the BCRA

The BCRA severely limits the abilities of state and local parties in one other way: it prohibits a party committee from making an independent expenditure in support of or in opposition to a federal candidate if any other national, state, or local party committee anywhere in the country has made a coordinated expenditure. Conversely, it prohibits a party committee from making a coordinated expenditure in support of or in opposition to a federal candidate if any other national, state, or local party committee anywhere in the country has made an independent expenditure. As a practical matter, I do not have any way of knowing what party committees have made such expenditures without examining the reports of each and every party committee in the country, and even then, because of the lag time between the close of a reporting period and the actual filing date for that period, I might not be aware of a particular coordinated or independent activity that has taken place. As a matter of law, I understand that CDP is entitled to make independent expenditures so long as those expenditures are truly independent and are not coordinated with the candidate. Although CDP can ensure that its independent activities have not been coordinated with a candidate, it has no control over (and usually no knowledge of) the activities of other party committees. Even within California, CDP has no control over (and usually no knowledge of) the activities of the County Central Committees. These committees function independently of CDP.

CONFLICT WITH STATE LAW

The basic principles of the BCRA are at odds with Proposition 34, the California campaign finance law enacted by a vote of the people in November 2000. As stated above, that law combines limits on contributions to candidates with voluntary spending limits. However, the law was specifically designed to allow the political parties to play a greater role in state and local elections and to provide an "insulation" effect between large contributors and candidates. Because the role of the parties in California was viewed as basically a positive one, the limits for contributions to the parties for candidate expenditures were set relatively high ($25,000) and are unlimited for items such as administrative expenses, generic party building, voter registration and GOTV expenses, and ballot measure expenditures. Contributions and expenditures by the party on behalf of its state candidates are not limited, reflecting the view that these expenditures are not harmful. Finally, the spending limits for candidates were specifically set with the intent that political party expenditures would augment the candidates' expenditures and would not count against the candidates' voluntary expenditure limits. In other words, the parties can support their candidates by mail and other means without such expenditures counting against the spending limits. The point was to encourage the parties to actively support their candidates and thereby reduce the candidates' need to raise large campaign treasuries, while allowing the parties and the candidates to cooperate in effectively communicating the candidates' (and the parties') message. The BCRA will adversely affect the party's support for all of its candidates, but particularly its state and local candidates. If all party communications and GOTV activity for state and local candidates becomes "federalized" and can only be financed with federally limited money, the party will simply be unable to afford these activities, and it will not be able to provide the kind of organizational support for its state and local candidates envisioned by Proposition 34. Although nonfederal money can be contributed directly to state and local candidates, such contributions will count against the spending limits, and therefore the overall resources available to the state candidates will be significantly reduced.

ADDITIONAL ISSUES

I understand that various "experts" have asserted either that the parties will simply be forced to raise more federal money (assisted by the new, higher limits) or, to the extent they experience a drop in actual income, will be forced to go back to volunteers and increased grassroots efforts. Both of these assertions are wrong. Over the last twenty years, the party has tried a number of different approaches to raise money within the federal limits. The most successful program has been our telemarketing program. In recent years, our telemarketing program has raised between $800,000 and $2 million. The average contribution is $27.00. The main drawback for this program is that it is very expensive to run. On the average, it costs approximately $0.40–$0.50 for every dollar raised. We have also conducted a joint fund-raising direct mail campaign with the DNC. This will be prohibited under the BCRA; if CDP wished to continue it, it would have to incur the increased costs of doing it "in-house." In reviewing our federal contributions since 1995, I consider it significant that the number of contributions made at the $5,000 level (that is, the number of persons giving the current maximum) was very small, usually accounting for less than 5 percent of the total. The total amount from those contributions has ranged from $170,000 (1999–2000) to $355,000 (1995–96). Since the number of contributions at the $5,000 level is so small, I do not believe that doubling the limit from $5,000 to $10,000 will result in a substantial increase in the amount of federal money contributed.

In my view, the BCRA poses one additional very real risk for the parties—that they will become marginalized in the political process. People become active in political parties, and make contributions to the parties, because the parties play a central role in defining the issues and articulating those issues through their candidates. Although many interest groups are also involved with the parties, the force and role of these groups is moderated in the "give and take" of party politics so that no particular group monopolizes the parties or the selection of candidates. If the issues are instead defined by those interest groups (including the narrower ideological factions within the parties that are free to set themselves up as independent organizations not subject to the restrictions of the BCRA), and if those groups set the agenda for elections, both the candidates and the public will be likely to focus on those groups as they seek to influence the outcome of a particular election. The parties will become underfinanced, ineffective bystanders as other groups drive both issues and candidates.

State Party Activity
under the Levin Amendment

MARK BREWER

Mark Brewer has been chair of the Michigan Democratic Party (MDP) since 1995. He testified on behalf of two plaintiffs, the California Democratic and California Republican parties. In his declaration, Brewer described the Michigan Democratic Party's goals, range of activities, structure, and expenditures. He gave particular attention to the potential effects of the Levin Amendment, a provision in the reform act that permits state and local party committees to raise and spend limited amounts of soft money for voter identification and mobilization efforts. Brewer highlights the complexities of this provision and contends that it will impose substantial accounting and compliance burdens on state and local party organizations.

Although I am familiar with the term "soft money" being used to refer to unlimited contributions from individuals, labor organizations, and corporations, from the perspective of a state party committee, there is no such thing as unregulated "soft money." There are federally regulated contributions and state-regulated contributions. In accordance with Federal Election Commission (FEC) regulations, 11 C.F.R. §102.5, MDP maintains a "federal account" to receive federally regulated contributions and "nonfederal" accounts to receive state-regulated contributions, as described below. State-regulated contributions to state party committees—that is, contributions to the nonfederal accounts—are very frequently mischaracterized as "soft money."

Under Michigan state law, individuals and state-registered political and independent committees may contribute an unlimited amount to the state party's nonfederal accounts, but contributions of treasury funds from labor organizations and corporations are prohibited, except to special accounts for building and maintaining party headquarters, holding certain state conventions and state party meetings, and covering expenditures in connection with ballot initiatives and other expenditures permitted by state law. Under state law, MDP is permitted to contribute up to $68,000 per general election cycle to a candidate for statewide office, $10,000 per general election cycle to a candidate for state senate, and $5,000 per general election cycle to a candidate for state representative. A state party may contribute up to $750,000 per general election cycle to a candidate for governor who has elected to receive public funding. MDP contribution limits for local candidates range from $5,000 to $34,000 per general election cycle. The MDP may make unlimited contributions for state and local ballot questions.

In nonpresidential election years, in which there is not a heavily contested U.S. Senate race, most of the state-regulated funds raised by the MDP are not transferred or raised by national party committees or their officers or agents, or by federal candidates, but by MDP officers and staff and state and local officeholders, candidates, and organizations. For example, in the 1997–98 election cycle, of the total of $7,744,536 raised by MDP, only $1,288,620 was transferred by national party committees, and of this, virtually all was transferred in exchange for federally regulated funds raised by MDP—and not transferred as a net contribution to the state party.

In the 2001–02 election cycle, in which there were very few significantly contested federal elections, virtually all of the significant races were statewide, or state or local. In particular, MDP put most of its energy and resources into the race for governor, in which our party had an excellent chance of recapturing the governorship for the first time in twelve years. In this election cycle to date, MDP, its state and local candidates, and nonfederal committees such as the Democratic Governors Association have raised or contributed virtually all of the state party's funding.

Democratic federal officeholders in Michigan (U.S. senators and members of the U.S. House) help raise federally regulated and state-regulated funds for the MDP through direct solicitation and, more frequently, appearances at fund-raising events. In the most recent election, these federal officeholders helped to raise state-regulated funds for MDP in order to help elect the Democratic nominee for governor of Michigan, and to help elect other candidates to statewide and state office.

In any given election year, MDP's disbursements for advocacy of state and local candidates and of the party's positions on ballot propositions are made without coordination with federal candidates and officeholders. In nonpresidential election years, such as 1998 and 2002, in which there are no or very few significant contests for federal office, MDP's disbursements for voter registration, activities and communications promoting the party, its ideas and positions without mentioning any federal candidate, and for voter registration and get-out-the-vote communications and activity are made without coordination with federal candidates or officeholders.

Together with our finance committee and other state party officers, I play a significant role in raising funds for the MDP, consisting of both federally regulated and state-regulated funds. That task occupies approximately 35 percent of my time. I have never personally solicited or received a contribution to MDP, whether federally regulated or state-regulated, that was made in order to curry the favor or influence of a federal officeholder.

Under the Bipartisan Campaign Reform Act (BCRA) and the FEC's regulations, "federal election activity" is defined to include activities and communications, depending on when and how those activities and communications are carried out, generally promoting the party and its platform without mentioning any federal candidate; voter registration and programs to persuade voters to vote and assist them in voting, again without mentioning any federal candidate; certain administrative expenses of the state party; certain voter identification expenses; and even certain expenditures solely promoting state and local candidates, as explained below.

Under BCRA and the FEC's implementing regulations, such "federal election activity" must be paid for by any state or local party committee, either 100 percent with federally regulated funds or with a combination of federally regulated funds and "Levin amendment" contributions, consisting of contributions allowed by Michigan law, but only up to $10,000 a year from any one donor. Thus in order for MDP (or any local party committee) to spend state-regulated funds of any kind on communications and activities that promote the Democratic Party generally, and/or that aim to turn out voters, even to benefit solely our state and local candidates, and *without mentioning any federal candidate*, MDP is required to use "Levin amendment" funds. A state or local party's solicitation and receipt of such funds, moreover, is subject to at least six additional detailed, complex, federally imposed restrictions and conditions, as follows:

—The state or local party must establish at least three separate sets of accounts, including a federal account, a nonfederal account, and a "Levin" account; or use one account for nonfederal and Levin contributions, provided that the state party demonstrates through a reasonable accounting method approved by the FEC that the party had received sufficient contributions or Levin funds to pay for the applicable share of any "federal election activity."

—Local party committees that are not even "political committees" under the Federal Election Campaign Act (FECA)—and therefore are not otherwise subject to the jurisdiction of the FEC at all—are required, in order to expend any funds on "federal election activity," including activity that advocates the election only of state and local candidates, to establish one or more "Levin accounts" or demonstrate through a reasonable accounting method preapproved by the FEC that the local party has received sufficient funds meeting the other Levin requirements, to make such disbursements for "federal election activity."

—The "Levin" contributions must have been raised solely by the committee that expends or disburses them.

—The state or local party committee must not accept or use any donations or other funds solicited, received, directed, transferred, or spent by or in the name of a national committee of a political party, any officer or agent acting on behalf of a national party committee, or any entity that is directly or indirectly established, financed, maintained, or controlled by such a national party committee.

—The state or local party committee must not accept or use any donations or other funds solicited, received, directed, transferred, or spent by or in the name of a federal candidate or federal officeholder, or an agent of either, or an entity directly or indirectly established, financed, maintained, or controlled by, or acting on behalf of, one or more federal candidates or individuals holding federal office.

—The state or local party must not raise Levin funds by means of any joint fund-raising activity with any other state, district, or local committee of any political party, the agent of such a committee or an entity directly or indirectly established, financed, maintained, or controlled by such a committee.

As a matter of common sense, and as my years of experience in raising funds for the MDP indicate, it will be extraordinarily more difficult to raise both federally regulated funds and Levin funds than it has been, and would be, to raise regular state-regulated funds under Michigan law. For the advocacy of state and local candidates, MDP could receive and spend a contribution from an individual or state-registered committee of an amount well in excess of $10,000, since those contributions to MDP are unlimited under state law. Under BCRA, however, MDP could not spend the portion of such a contribution in excess of $10,000 and could not even spend the first $10,000 unless such portion met the six complex restrictions and conditions set forth above. Thus federal law will clearly restrict and inhibit MDP from spending funds for advocacy of the election of state and local candidates, the expenditure of which funds is expressly permitted and contemplated by Michigan law.

To further illustrate the complexity of complying with BCRA, consider the example of a Michigan Democratic Party volunteer who calls up a voter to determine his or her support for the Democratic Party or its candidates and programs in the 2003–04 election cycle. The costs of the telephone program are to be paid as follows. If the call inquires about the voter's views on a ballot proposition and does not inquire about the likelihood of voting or about views on any candidate, the costs are paid for 36 percent with federally regulated funds and 64 percent with state-regulated funds. If the call asks the voter the likelihood of voting for a specific *state* candidate, with no mention of any federal candidate, and the call is made *after* the date of the earliest filing deadline for the 2004 primary election, then the costs must be paid for 100 percent with federally regulated funds, or 36 percent with federally regulated funds and 64 percent with "Levin amendment" funds consisting of contributions from sources allowed under Michigan law, but only up to $10,000 per donor, only if deposited into a special account, and only if the raising and spending of the contributions meet the six separate, detailed conditions and restrictions set out in BCRA and detailed earlier.

The costs of complying with BCRA will be very substantial. Currently, about 10 percent of MDP's annual budget is spent on compliance with federal election law. Under BCRA, because of the extraordinary record-keeping and reporting requirements imposed by BCRA, I estimate that that percentage will increase by 50 percent and amount to at least 15 percent of the annual budget. The number of full-time equivalent staff positions devoted to compliance will increase from two currently to four under BCRA. The sheer complexity and compliance burden of BCRA will significantly reduce the resources available to MDP to disseminate its message about party policy, issues, and candidates.

Failure to comply with any provision of BCRA is a federal criminal offense, and any such failure involving over $25,000 is a federal felony. The prospect of facing prospective criminal penalties for failing to comply with the morass of ambiguous and complex rules under BCRA will, in my view and experience, clearly discourage and inhibit individuals from serving as state and local party officers, staff, and volunteers.

Because of its substantially overbroad scope, ambiguities, and heavy penalties, BCRA will intimidate, deter, and inhibit Democratic voters and activists from volunteering to become state or local party officers, or volunteers, for a number of reasons and will inhibit the ability of MDP and its local party organizations to communicate its ideas, values, and positions to the voters of Michigan in many ways.

For example, the chair and vice chair of the MDP are, by virtue of these positions, members of the Democratic National Committee (DNC), and I serve on the Rules and Bylaws Committee of the DNC. BCRA prohibits any national party committee "officer or agent acting on behalf of" a national party committee from raising any state-regulated funds. The term "acting on behalf of" is not defined in the FEC's implementing regulations. Am I, as state party chair, prohibited from raising state-regulated funds for MDP? Is the MDP vice chair so prohibited? Are other state party officers (several of whom are also DNC members) also so prohibited? BCRA is unclear and, although the FEC's regulations suggest that the answer is no, the intervening defendants in this case (Senators John McCain and Russell Feingold and Representatives Martin Meehan and Christopher Shays) have threatened to overturn the FEC regulations through action under the Congressional Review Act and/or a lawsuit challenging the regulations as being contrary to the intent of BCRA.

Because BCRA prohibits national party committees from raising, directing, transferring, or spending any state-regulated contributions for MDP, and from transferring or raising any "Levin amendment" funds or even hard money to be used with "Levin amendment" funds, BCRA will drive a wedge between the national party and the state parties whose representatives make up the Democratic National Committee, requiring me as a state party chair—and all of the other MDP officers, and all local party officers—to be careful of every word we utter to any national party officer or employee, manifestly crippling the ability of MDP, and the ninety-nine local party committees in Michigan, to associate and work with national party committees in the pursuit of common ideological, partisan, and electoral goals.

Role of Federal Officials in State Party Fund-Raising

MITCH MCCONNELL

Mitch McConnell is a U.S. senator from the Commonwealth of Kentucky and the Republican Whip. McConnell is the namesake plaintiff in the lawsuit challenging the constitutionality of the Bipartisan Campaign Reform Act (BCRA). He has been a member of the Senate since 1984 and served as chair of the National Republican Senatorial Committee (NRSC) during the 1998 and 2000 election cycles. In his declaration, McConnell states that as a U.S. senator he is actively involved in fund-raising for state parties and candidates. McConnell argues that the reform act will have a deleterious effect on the associational activities between state party organizations and elected officials.

The BCRA will substantially impair my activities (and the activities of those construed to be my agents) with respect to national, state, and local political parties, and state and local candidates.

As a federal officeholder, I will no longer be able to raise money not subject to the BCRA's restrictions (soft money) for the purpose of voter registration, voter identification, get-out-the-vote activities, issue advocacy, building funds, and national support for state and local candidates. I have been involved substantially in raising money for each of these activities in the past and would do so in the future, absent the BCRA.

As a member of the Republican Party, the NRSC, and the State Central Committee of the Republican Party of Kentucky, I could be considered an agent of the Republican National Committee (RNC) and would thus be banned from raising any money for state and local political parties or candidates under the BCRA. Moreover, had the BCRA been in effect during my four years as chairman of the NRSC, I would have been federally prohibited from raising any money for state and local parties or candidates. As set forth above, I have been involved substantially in raising money for state and local political parties and candidates in the past and would do so in the future, absent the BCRA.

The BCRA prohibits federal officeholders from raising any Levin funds for state and local parties to support, among other things, grassroots activity (such as voter registration within 120 days before either the primary or general election, as well as get-out-the-vote efforts). In the past, I have been substantially involved in raising money not subject to the restrictions, prohibitions, and reporting requirements of federal law for the purpose of supporting these grassroots activities. Absent the BCRA, I would do so in the future.

The BCRA specifically permits federal officeholders to raise an unlimited amount of money that is not subject to the limitations, prohibitions, and reporting requirements of federal law, including donations from corporations and unions, for special interest groups that engage in grassroots activity. I have raised such funds in the past for national, state, and local political parties that represent broad coalitions of diverse Americans, as opposed to single-issue, special interest groups, and would do so in the future, absent the BCRA.

The BCRA also prohibits federal officeholders from raising money for any state or local party in excess of $10,000, or from corporate or union sources. The legislatures of a vast majority of the states have enacted laws that permit federal officeholders to raise more than $10,000 from individuals and/or raise funds from corporations or unions for state and local political parties. Absent the BCRA, I would raise such money in the future in compliance with the laws of those states.

The BCRA also prohibits federal officeholders from raising money that is not subject to the limitations, prohibitions, and reporting requirements of federal law for the building fund of the Republican Party of Kentucky, which is particularly ironic in my case, given that the state party has recently named the building after me. I have raised such money in the past and would do so in the future, absent the BCRA.

Although federal officeholders may attend and speak at state party fund-raisers, the BCRA prohibits federal officeholders from soliciting funds for the state party at such events if the funds are not subject to the restrictions and prohibitions of federal law. I have solicited such funds in the past and would do so in the future, absent the BCRA.

As a federal officeholder, I will be limited by the BCRA to raising funds for candidates in the amount of $2,000 or less per election, and the funds may not come from corporations or unions. The legislatures of a vast majority of the states have enacted laws that permit federal officeholders to raise more than $2,000 from individuals and/or raise funds from corporations or unions for state and local political parties. Absent the BCRA, I would raise such money in the future in compliance with the laws of those states.

The BCRA contains a specific exemption that allows federal officeholders to speak at state, local, and district party fund-raising events. No such exemption, however, exists for fund-raising events for state and local candidates. Thus I risk possible civil and criminal action by merely attending a fund-raising event for a gubernatorial or mayoral candidate.

PART II
Issue Advocacy

147
SCHOLARLY ANALYSES

237
VIEWS OF THE ADVOCATES:
PARTIES, ORGANIZED GROUPS,
AND POLITICAL CONSULTANTS

Party and Interest Group Electioneering in Federal Elections

David B. Magleby

David B. Magleby is the dean of the Family, Home and Social Science College at Brigham Young University, director of the Center for the Study of Elections and Democracy, and Distinguished Professor of Political Science. He was an expert witness for the defense and reported on interest group and political party electioneering advocacy research that he and his nationwide team of academic specialists have conducted during the 1998 and 2000 election cycles.

This selection begins with Magleby's discussion of the regulatory and strategic incentives that have encouraged individuals and interest groups to pursue candidate-specific issue advocacy communications, which he takes to mean "electioneering communications," rather than communications that expressly advocate the election or defeat of federal candidates. He then presents examples of the various approaches used by noncandidate groups in recent elections to campaign on behalf of specific candidates without being subject to the disclosure and contributions limits of the Federal Election Campaign Act (FECA).

Magleby summarizes the strategies and techniques used in group election advocacy efforts, including the themes and content of the messages, the ways groups mask their identities, and the methods they employ in targeting their efforts. These tactics, he argues, make it difficult for voters to ascertain the sources of the messages they are receiving. For the most part, he notes, these electioneering efforts are directly related to federal elections rather than legislative lobbying and can have a significant effect on the dynamics and outcome of federal elections, especially in close contests.

Electioneering Advocacy by Groups and Individuals

Interest groups and individuals have multiple means to seek to influence the outcome of a federal election. Many of these strategies fall under the scope of the FECA and Bipartisan Campaign Reform Act (BCRA). However, interest groups, individuals, corporations, and unions have found ways to conduct electioneering and circumvent FECA requirements. Some provisions of BCRA seek to remedy this situation. In this section, I review what the Center for the Study of Elections and Democracy (CSED) case studies have found about election advocacy and genuine issue advocacy in the 1998 and 2000 elections, including five presidential primary elections.

My research also demonstrates that the absence of magic words is not a reliable indication that a message lacks an electioneering purpose. Groups and individuals can very effectively communicate a "vote against" or "vote for" message without using the magic words. Electioneering advocacy— whether broadcast advertisements or direct mail or other forms of advocacy—is clearly focused on defeating or electing a candidate and not primarily focused on an issue. This is demonstrated by the CSED survey research, by the content of the ads, by the fact that these ads are concentrated in competitive races, and by the fact that most ads run in the period shortly before an election.

Why Conduct Electioneering Outside the FECA Framework?

There are four primary reasons to conduct electioneering outside the FECA framework. First, it permits groups and individuals to avoid disclosure. Second, it allows them to avoid contribution limits. Third, it permits some groups (such as corporations and labor unions) to spend from generally prohibited sources. And fourth, it allows greater control of message and activity while still influencing an election.

AVOID DISCLOSURE. The 1996, 1998, and 2000 election cycles all saw examples of groups who sought to avoid accountability for their communications by pursuing an electioneering advertising/election advocacy strategy rather than limiting their activities to independent expenditures or other activities expressly permitted by the FECA. In 1996 a group that masked its identity was Koch Industries, which financed, at least in part, a group acting in several races named Triad. One of the congressional races where Triad was active in 1996 was the Kansas Third Congressional District.[1] In 1998 the AFL-CIO helped pay for ads in the Connecticut Fifth Congressional District race through a group named the Coalition to Make Our Voices Heard. Steven Rosenthal defended campaigning under an obscure name in this case saying, "Frankly we've taken a page out of their book [other interest groups] because in some places it's much more effective to run an ad by the 'Coalition to Make Our Voices Heard' than it is to say paid for by 'the men and women of the AFL-CIO.'"[2] Mr.

Rosenthal accurately captures the reason why groups will continue to hide their identity—it improves the chances of persuading voters. This is more likely to be the case when voters would take less seriously a communication from a group they dislike or distrust.

There are many other examples of groups who sought to mask their identity, usually while trying to persuade voters to vote against one candidate. One of the most active groups in 2000 was Citizens for Better Medicare (CBM). For voters watching or listening to an ad, naming the sponsor group evokes a much more positive impression than does advertising the name of the pharmaceutical industry, a major underwriter of the group.[3] This technique hides the kinds of interests paying for the advertisement. Another group with an unobjectionable name, the Committee for Good Common Sense, aired ads that supported incumbent Jay Dickey in the Arkansas Fourth Congressional District race in 2000.[4]

AVOID SOURCE LIMITATIONS. Federal law has long banned corporations and labor unions from spending treasury funds for campaign communications other than communications to their stockholders, employees, or membership. The ban on using corporate treasury funds for contributions goes back to the Tillman Act of 1907; corporate expenditures in campaigns have been banned since 1947. The ban on union treasury funds goes back to the Smith-Connally Act of 1943, which was later included in the Taft-Hartley Act in 1947. The rationale for the bans is to reduce the threat that these groups will purchase influence over elected officials through large corporate and union expenditures in federal elections, as well as to prevent the boards of these organizations from spending treasury funds in the political arena in ways that may not be representative of the members' or shareholders' views.[5]

The ability of corporations and trade unions to effectively campaign through electioneering advertisements and election advocacy makes a sham of these long-standing federal laws. The data CSED has gathered on television and mail communications clearly demonstrates that these communications are indistinguishable from candidate and party ads in terms of their purpose.

AVOID CONTRIBUTION LIMITS. Another reason to conduct electioneering activities outside the FECA is that groups can raise larger amounts of money in less time. The ability to spend a million dollars or more in a particular U.S. House race, as the AFL-CIO did in 1996, makes contribution limits to candidates and parties seem very low indeed. Even in Senate races

where spending is typically higher, groups like Citizens for Better Medicare, Pharmaceutical Research and Manufacturers of America (PhRMA),
NAACP National Voter Fund, and NARAL Pro-Choice America
(NARAL) were able to far exceed what individuals, political action committees (PACs), or parties could do through hard-money contributions.

Nature and Extent of Electioneering Advocacy

As with PACs and other forms of participation in funding candidates,
there is substantial diversity among those who engage in electioneering
advocacy. CSED found substantial interest group election advertising in
the 1998 elections. More groups ran "issue" ads in 1997–98 than in
1995–96, and the overall amount of money spent on "issue" ads also rose.[6]
And several of the races in our sample had as much campaign activity by
interest groups as by candidates. Interest groups focused their efforts on
the relatively small number of competitive House and Senate elections: in
the twelve House and four Senate races we monitored, 111 interest groups
were active in 1998. These groups ran altogether a minimum of 218 ads
on TV or radio and mounted at least 258 phone banks or direct mail
efforts.[7] Most records show that groups used direct mail from before the
primary election through Election Day, whereas they used phone banks
more in the final month. Television ads aired throughout the election
cycle, but most heavily in the final month and a half of campaigning. In
contrast, genuine issue ads are more likely to run earlier since rates are
cheaper and proximity to an election is less important. Our 1998 data also
show that interest groups produced more direct mail, print, radio ads, and
phone banks than the political parties but that the parties focused more
on television advertisements.[8]

The 2000 presidential primaries provided interest groups an opportunity to influence the choice of both parties' standard bearers. Growing out
of their ground-war strategy of 1998, organized labor and the teachers'
unions mounted a substantial grassroots mobilization for Al Gore, giving
special emphasis to the Iowa caucuses and the New Hampshire primary.[9]
In the primaries, John McCain was a lightning rod for interest group electioneering attacks in New Hampshire and South Carolina by groups critical of his stand on campaign finance reform, his support for fetal tissue
research, and his support of an increased tobacco tax. The attacks in New
Hampshire did not hurt McCain and may have backfired, but in South
Carolina they helped George W. Bush.[10] Some groups generally allied with
one party used the primaries to launch attacks on the leading contender

in the other party, while other groups sat out the primaries and saved their resources for the general election.[11]

The 2000 primaries had perhaps the best-known example of electioneering advertisements during the New York Republican primary. A group calling itself Republicans for Clean Air ran television ads in the New York City and Pennsylvania markets attacking John McCain's environmental record. The ads sparked controversy, partly because no one knew who Republicans for Clean Air were. After three days the actual funders of Republicans for Clean Air came forward. It was a group comprised of two brothers, Sam and Charles Wiley of Texas. Some McCain senior staff believe the ad cost them victory in New York.[12]

Electioneering by interest groups and individuals that is not covered by the FECA includes two general types of communications: first, television and radio advertising, and second, the "ground war," which includes direct mail, telephone, the Internet, newspaper advertising, and personal contact. Only the broadcast advertisements are covered by BCRA.

EXPANDED ACTIVITY. Most groups already involved in electioneering advocacy expanded their involvement in the 2000 general elections. Examples of groups who reported increased activity in 2000 are the AFL-CIO,[13] the Chamber of Commerce,[14] NARAL,[15] and the National Rifle Association (NRA).[16] In the seventeen races we monitored in 2000, at least 237 interest groups (and at least 93 national and state party organizations) communicated with voters.[17] The Annenberg Public Policy Center of the University of Pennsylvania estimates that interest groups spent an estimated $509 million overall in electioneering advocacy and pure issue advocacy in 1999–2000.[18]

Electioneering campaigning in the 2000 general elections showed greater congruence in issue agendas between party committees and candidates and between allied groups and candidates than in 1998.[19] Some Democratic-leaning groups, like the NAACP and EMILY's List, that had been active as interest groups or in funding campaigns through hard-money contributions in 2000 added electioneering advocacy to their activities. On the Republican side, new groups conducting electioneering advocacy included the Republican Majority Issues Committee (RMIC) and business and pharmaceutical interests funded Citizens for Better Medicare and Americans for Job Security.[20]

BROADCAST AND CABLE ELECTIONEERING. Broadcast advertising is the most visible mode of communicating an electioneering message and is also widely believed to be the most effective for reaching a mass audience. There is also little doubt that it is one of the most expensive. In all of the contests we monitored in 1998 and 2000, interest groups used broadcast, including television and radio, to communicate with voters. As our survey data and focus group data from 2000 demonstrate, interest groups effectively communicate an electioneering message without using the magic words of express advocacy.[21] More than four out of five voters said the interest groups' ads "primary objective" or "purpose" was "persuading you to vote for or against a candidate."

Broadcast advertising was an especially important element in all of the competitive races we monitored in 2000, and occasionally campaign ads were even broadcast beyond voting district boundaries. In Senate races, television and radio were also major components of the candidate and outside money campaigns.[22] In our 2000 case studies, we conservatively estimate that $99.7 million was spent on radio and television, including cable television in the seventeen races we monitored.[23] When compared with candidate spending on these same media and in these same races, interest groups spent roughly two-thirds as much as candidates. And political parties exceeded either candidates or interest groups in spending on television and radio.[24] Interest groups and parties also utilize the cheaper and more targeted cable stations. Citizens for Better Medicare made extensive use of cable, spending over $70,000 in the California Twenty-seventh District alone.[25] In the Washington Second District in 2000, the Sierra Club spent about $45,000 on cable television ads.[26] Candidates also turned to cable, especially in races like the California Twenty-seventh. Democratic challenger Adam Schiff purchased a total of 21,072 units of airtime from Charter Communications, the Twenty-Seventh District's cable television company, for nearly $600,000. James Rogan, Schiff's opponent, went even further, purchasing 54,080 units from Charter Communications at a cost of over $1 million. These purchases included seventeen different ads from Rogan and six from Schiff. An anonymous Charter Communications employee remarked that this campaign was "buying all available airtime."[27]

Radio is also an effective communications tool for electioneering by interest groups. As with television, if the communications do not use the particular language of express advocacy, the groups do not report the expenditures to the FEC, and stations do not provide the same disclosure that they provide for campaign communications by candidates. Academics monitoring our sample of competitive contests in 2000 found the interest groups making use of radio for electioneering efforts included the

NRA, Americans for Limited Terms, U.S. Chamber of Commerce, National Federation of Independent Business (NFIB), National Education Association (NEA), League of Conservation Voters (LCV), Million Mom March PAC, Planned Parenthood, and the National Right to Life PAC. Of the 105 radio ads we recorded, only 20 ads contained the magic words.

One contest where interest groups made extensive use of radio was the Virginia Senate race in 2000. Radio ads began airing in early October, and various groups funded hundreds of ads. The Sierra Club topped the list with 234 ads, the NRA was second at 155, and the NAACP National Voter Fund aired 62 spots. Although these numbers represent only a sampling of radio stations, our research shows that interest groups outspent the candidates on the radio by a three-to-one ratio, while the parties doubled the amount interest groups spent on the radio.[28] The high numbers of ads by interest groups and parties reflects the ability of these groups to evade FECA contribution and source limits.

A sixty-second spot from the Missouri Senate race is a good example of a typical radio ad. The spot begins with Don Wainwright, owner of Wainwright Industries in St. Peters, talking about his employees' health insurance. Wainwright says he's depending on John Ashcroft to get a real patient's bill of rights. The announcer then discusses Ashcroft's record. Wainwright says that trial lawyers and their friends in Congress are blocking reforms. The announcer then says, "Senator Ashcroft is fighting for you, call him . . . to say 'keep on fighting.'" The ad sponsor for this particular ad is the Health Benefits Coalition, but the tag line was different for various airings of the commercial. The five tag lines in the St. Louis area included Business Roundtable, U.S. Chamber of Commerce, NFIB, National Association of Wholesalers-Distributors, and the National Association of Manufacturers. A similar thirty-second ad ran in the Delaware Senate race. In this spot a local businessman from southern Delaware voices his concern about health care for his workers and the ways in which Senator William Roth has worked to make this a reality. The business owner says that trial lawyers are blocking progress in Washington. An announcer then takes over to explain that Roth has been working on this and encourages voters to call him to say, "Keep on fighting." Business Roundtable paid for the ad.[29] As this example illustrates, interest groups can communicate an election message without using the magic words of express advocacy.

When we contacted cable and broadcast stations in our sample races in 1998 and 2000, we found some stations, like the CBS affiliate in Lexington, Kentucky, willing to provide complete information on the advertising purchased by political parties and groups communicating on ads of "controversial and of public importance." Other stations provided us with "ad buy data," which is the advertising purchased by candidates, parties, or groups for a specified time period. However, because stations do not always fulfill the initial commitment made at the time the advertising is purchased, the ad buy data may overestimate the actual advertising aired by a station in that time period. When stations run ads previously paid for at a later date, they "make good" on the earlier purchase by providing time at a later date.

In our 1998 studies, we purchased the campaign ad tracking data from Strategic Media Services, a media marketing and tracking firm in Alexandria, Virginia. In our 2000 studies, we purchased data from the Campaign and Media Analysis Group (CMAG). The CMAG data reinforced the findings of the data gathered by the academics from their monitoring of television and radio. There is substantial agreement between the research conducted for the Brennan Center for Justice at New York University's Law School in its *Buying Time* studies and my own research. Both projects used the CMAG data but the CSED project, as noted, gathered data in contests where CMAG did not have coverage and the CSED project included radio, telephone, mail, and other forms of interaction. Among the areas of agreement in core findings are that "political advertising by independent groups has sharply risen [in 2000] over 1998," that "the magic words test for express advocacy has no basis in the reality of political advertising," that "electioneering issue advocacy ads by groups grew dramatically from 1998 to 2000," and that "a majority of television ads sponsored by independent groups were electioneering ads." [30] The broader scope of the CSED project, including mail and radio communications, is consistent with these findings.

GROUND-WAR ELECTIONEERING. Individuals and interest groups have multiple means of communicating with voters that are not covered by BCRA or FECA. For example, mail and telephone communications are not covered, nor are Internet or newspaper communications. CSED case studies in 1998 and 2000 have found that mail and telephone communications can make up an important part of interest group campaigns.

While television and radio are the primary and most visible means noncandidate campaigns use to influence voting behavior, these campaigns also utilize mail, telephone, Internet, and interpersonal communications as elements of campaigning, which I referred to earlier as the "ground war." Our 1998 case studies documented that election advocacy grew and diversified to include more widespread use of mail, telephone, and person-to-person contacts, while still including substantial amounts of television and radio communications.[31] Just as labor unions were first to launch a large-scale broadcast campaign using issue advocacy in 1996, they were also leaders in the use of mail, telephones, personal contact, and get-out-the-vote (GOTV) efforts. Labor spent approximately $18 million on the ground war in the 1998 election and coordinated a state/national GOTV, including over 13 million targeted union members. Efforts included extensive phone calls, GOTV efforts, and rides to the voting booth on Election Day. Labor doubled the number of campaign coordinators in 1998, compared with the 1996 presidential year, and aimed these organizers at half as many targeted races. These ground-war efforts successfully mobilized voters.[32] The ground war continues to be an important part of the electioneering strategies of candidates, parties, and interest groups. BCRA provisions do not change ground-war options such as mail, telephone, and person-to-person contacts.

The BCRA leaves groups free to continue to communicate an electioneering message without disclosure or limitation through mail, telephone, personal contact, and the Internet. Ground-war tactics permit groups to do election-related work without telegraphing to the opposition or the media what they are doing.[33] Research conducted by CSED has documented substantial campaign activity through the mail and on the telephone and this activity is likely to increase should the BCRA provisions regarding electioneering advertisements via broadcast be upheld.

Mail. In our sample of competitive congressional general elections in 2000, we observed 159 interest groups (and 81 national and state party organizations) that sent out mail or mounted a telephone campaign.[34] These numbers were up substantially from 1998. Campaign mail can be very effective. To get the attention of voters, interest groups often use oversized mail or mail with attention-grabbing messages and formats.

Telephone. Phone bank activity by interest groups was a regular part of the competitive races we monitored in 1998 and 2000. Phone calls in our sample races made by outside groups were rarely neutral in tone. Several groups and both parties have found telephone contacts to be a very important electioneering tool.[35] For example, Steve Rosenthal, AFL-CIO political director, stated that labor "got an enormous response from one-on-one phone bank contacts, not from paid vendor contacts, but from union members talking to each other."[36] Other groups who told us that they used the telephone for millions of calls include National Right to Life, Christian Coalition, and the NRA.[37] This electioneering tool is still available to unions and others under the BCRA. In our sample races in 2000, we learned of 148 different telephone communication efforts by groups, parties, and candidates, and our interviews suggest that this estimate is very low.[38]

PERSONAL CONTACT AND GET-OUT-THE-VOTE. An example of a group that conducted its own GOTV effort in a 1998 congressional race was Planned Parenthood, whose members worked to help mobilize voters for Joe Hoeffel (Democratic challenger) in Pennsylvania's Thirteenth Congressional District.[39] Pro-choice groups were not the only abortion-related groups who mounted GOTV efforts. National Right to Life was active in the Michigan Eighth Congressional District in 2000.[40] Personal contact, often in the form of internal communication, was a major part of interest group electioneering in the 2000 presidential primaries. Over 25,000 union households in Iowa received AFL-CIO president John Sweeney's videotaped endorsement of Al Gore.[41]

Strategies and Techniques of Electioneering Advertisements and Election Advocacy

For the most part, the electioneering advertisements that our study monitored sidestepped disclosure and source limitation because they avoided express advocacy language or were defined as internal communications.[42] Nevertheless, these communications were nearly universally oriented toward electing or defeating specific federal candidates and have distinct characteristics demonstrating their electioneering character.

THEME AND MESSAGE. While the noncandidate campaigns are presumed to be independent of the candidates, there is remarkable congruence between the themes of the candidate campaigns and those of the interest groups and parties. There is also remarkable similarity between the themes and messages raised by the parties through their soft-money-funded ads and the interest groups through their electioneering advocacy.[43]

The similarity in theme of candidate-, party-, and group-funded ads only reinforces the point that to voters the ads are all part of one campaign. The fact that interest groups play by very different rules as to how the ads are paid for and the absence of disclosure from those interest groups do not alter the fact that their ads were clearly linked to the themes of the candidate campaign.

Advertising themes also illustrate the electioneering intent of their sponsors because often they focus on issues that are not of prime concern to the sponsor's mission. For example, an interest group doing election-eering primarily focused on the candidates arose in the New Mexico Third District in 1998. The AFL-CIO ran two television issue ad spots, spend-ing more than any other interest group, totaling $183,380. These com-mercials were shown a total of 427 times. The first commercial focused on tax cuts that were paid for by raiding the Social Security trust fund, and the second commercial focused on HMOs. Both ads had tag lines indi-cating voters should "call" their representative. But despite union funding, neither of these ads directly relates to union issues, like working condi-tions, pay raises, or employment benefits. The issue content of these ads, like most electioneering advocacy, appeared to be driven by the issue con-cerns of the campaign more than the policy focus of the interest group.

The convergence of theme and message can even go so far as to include messenger and images. Candidate campaigns sometimes pick up on the attack of the electioneering advocacy groups. In Washington's Second Congressional District in 2000, for example, the largest radio buy for any party, group, or candidate committee was made by the Building Industry Association of Washington (BIAW). The ad presented the plight of Vicki Klein, a previously anonymous homeowner whose floodplain zoning problem had been "ignored" by the Democratic candidate, Rick Larsen, and the Snohomish County Council on which he served.[44] Some of the mail from Larsen's opponent, John Koster, also featured a quote about flood regulations from "Vicki Klein, homeowner."[45] Thus groups not only followed candidate campaigns, but at times candidate campaigns adopted interest group messages.[46]

Interest groups also play defense on issues through electioneering advo-cacy, trying to diffuse the impact of issues like Social Security, prescription drug benefits, and expanded support for education. According to Dawn Laguens, Democrat Debbie Stabenow's media consultant in the 2000 Michigan Senate race, "[Chamber of Commerce] activity was significant in the Michigan Senate race, helping muddy the water on prescription drugs. Pharmaceuticals also played a major role in muddying the water."[47] Interest groups appear to be able to muddy the waters of campaigns by how they name themselves, for example, Citizens for Better Medicare, and by the assertion that they have a plan with regard to an important issue like prescription drugs.

Interest groups conducting electioneering advertisements appear to rec-ognize the importance of reinforcing candidate themes and messages even more than communicating the issues of central importance to the interest group. An example of a group attacking a candidate on an issue central to the campaign but not central to the interest group was the 1998 attack on Harry Reid's view on taxes mounted by the Foundation for Responsible Government, a group affiliated with the American Trucking Association.[48] Other examples of interest groups campaigning on issues not central to the group include National Right to Life and Americans for Tax Reform running ads against John McCain in the New Hampshire primary on campaign finance reform, not abortion or taxes.[49]

Electioneering advertisements most frequently oppose a particular candidate by raising doubts about that candidate or criticizing that candidate along some dimension, but occasionally an interest group devotes most of the time or space in the advertisement to an attack on one candidate and then quickly contrasts that with positives about the preferred candidate. This is fundamentally different from the way genuine issue advocacy works; it generally promotes a particular theme.

MASKING IDENTITY. Electioneering advertisements are often run by front groups, created at least in part to mask the identity of those interest groups funding them. Hiding behind a high-sounding name usually increases the credibility of the group and thereby its chances of influencing election outcomes. Because disclosure laws do not apply to groups avoiding the magic words of express advocacy, this strategy often escapes the attention of most voters and sometimes even the media in a state. An example of a race in which masked identity troubled editors of at least one newspaper is the 2000 Montana Senate race where Citizens for Better Medicare was active. Commenting on the inaccuracy of the CBM ads, a *Missoulian* editorial concluded that Schweitzer had been "zinged . . . by cleverly worded, but inaccurate, messages financed by a national group with a name that doesn't represent the forces behind it."[50] Another newspaper, while agreeing about the inaccuracy of CBM ads, went further in castigating CBM. The *Billings Gazette* labeled one ad a "total misrepresentation of Schweitzer's position. It had the credibility of a cockroach."[51]

An example of an interest group that not only masked its identity through an innocuous name but ran ads on a topic unrelated to the function or purpose of the group was the Foundation for Responsible Government (FRG). In 1998 FRG spent nearly $300,000.[52] Who was the Foundation for Responsible Government? The trucking industry. Upon investigation, Professor Eric Herzik of the University of Nevada–Reno found that the trucking industry was upset with Senator Harry Reid for supporting legislation that would have banned triple-trailer trucks. Rather than discuss their policy difference with Reid on triple-trailer trucks, FRG ran mostly positive ads late in the campaign, discussing the positions of Reid's opponent, John Ensign, on health care and taxes.[53]

Voters evaluate the source of political communications as well as the content. Some sources are more distrusted than others. When groups believe it is in their political interest to campaign in their own name, they do so. It is when they masquerade as "Citizens for . . ." or "Coalition opposed to. . . ." one can assume they have liability or a less effective measure if they presented their true identity. This has often been the case in ballot initiative campaigns and appears to also be true in electioneering advocacy.[54] Most voters work from the assumption that the communications are from the candidates, though in several of the races we monitored, most of the communications were not. In our focus group and web-TV survey in 2000, we demonstrated that voters could not differentiate the source of political communications (including mail), and, moreover, they assume that communications come from the candidate.[55]

The current system places an unreasonable burden on voters to ascertain who is attempting to persuade them in an election. Our focus groups and survey data from 2000 show that to voters, party and interest group electioneering ads are indistinguishable from candidate ads. Even the candidates and their campaign managers are unable to ascertain who some of the groups running ads were. In the 1998 Nevada Senate race, Mark Emerson, chief of staff for John Ensign's campaign, said, "No voter out there knows [who the interest groups are], because I didn't even know."[56] A media consultant, David Weeks, working for Ensign in this same race observed, "The clutter on television during the last few weeks of the campaign really prevented our message from getting through as clearly as we would have liked. Voters had a tough time figuring out which ads were run by the candidates, which by the parties, and which by independent groups."[57] Voters are unable to distinguish who was behind the advertisement they saw on television, heard on the radio, or saw in the mail they received. And in the CSED national survey, I found that respondents were often confused as to whether party ads were paid for by candidates or parties. More than 40 percent of the time, the respondents thought the party ads were paid for by a candidate.[58]

The task of unraveling this information is too much even for most news media outlets. Not surprisingly, the news media has a difficult time helping voters sort out who is behind the numerous issue advocacy organizations, as well as the difference between party and candidate communications.[59]

Interest groups are well aware of the difficulty of unmasking their front organizations set up to conduct electioneering. In the Connecticut Fifth

Congressional District, labor campaigned behind a group called Coalition to Make Our Voices Heard. A combination of their masked identity and labor's emphasis on ground strategies made them difficult to track. Labor "fell below the radar" of journalists, according to Matthew Daly, the political reporter who covered the Maloney/Nielsen race for the *Hartford Courant*.[60]

Voters, when asked, have consistently indicated that they would like to know who it is that is conducting electioneering. In 2000, voters in Montana faced a competitive U.S. Senate and a competitive U.S. House race. A late October Montana State University–Billings poll found that "78 percent of the survey respondents reported that it was 'very' or 'somewhat important' for them to know who 'pays for or sponsors a political ad.'"[61] Our focus group participants in 2000 had very similar views on the question of the importance of their knowing who is paying for or sponsoring an ad. More than four-fifths (81 percent) said it was very or somewhat important to know the identity of the sponsor. In the national Knowledge Networks Survey in 2000, 78 percent said the same thing.

TARGETING MEMBERS, DEMOGRAPHIC AND OTHER GROUPS. Electioneering advocacy comes in two broad categories. First, groups communicate with their members or other interested parties about their views of particular candidates generally. The NRA, a group known for targeting, communicates to its membership its views of candidates in races from state legislature through U.S. president. These communications appear in magazines provided to members as part of their affiliation with the NRA and in other means. Other membership groups do the same thing, and increasingly corporations communicate this kind of message to employees. Groups like the NRA also often both communicate with their membership and try to influence a larger group of voters likely to agree with their position. For example, in the Washington Second Congressional District, the NRA sent a "Dear Washington Hunter" mailer reaching beyond NRA members to Washington hunters.[62] The NFIB sent out an internal communication that could fold out to become a poster with the intent that store owners would publicly display them.[63]

Interest groups not only target memberships or affiliates, they also take aim at particular states with competitive U.S. Senate races or congressional districts where the outcome is in doubt. In 1998, 2000, and 2002, I conducted numerous interviews with key staff in scores of interest groups to assess where they engage in electioneering advertisements. The widely shared view of interest groups is that they campaign where their investment can make a difference, and that is almost always in competitive contests. This tendency has been reinforced by the exceedingly close margin of party control in Congress in recent years. Interest groups routinely do their own polls to determine where to spend their electioneering advocacy money. For example, before they sent mailings, the NEA conducted surveys to determine "if they could make a difference" with their spending.[64]

Interest groups and parties also note the relative cost of media markets, and when a competitive race occurs in a cheap media market, they target more there. Montana in 2000 and Nevada in 1998 provide good examples of this. Lisa Wade of the LCV said, "Montana was a cheap media market, so you got lots of value for your money."[65] One Montana newspaper even editorialized on the extent of outside advertising in the Senate race and said, "For better or worse, Montana has become a national political battleground and always will be. The reason is simple. A Senate seat can be purchased cheap in Montana."[66]

Targeting discrete voter groups within a district that are persuadable on an issue with polling and communications has also become a preferred strategy. An example of this strategy is the California Twenty-Seventh Congressional District race in 2000. NARAL used independent expenditures and perhaps other money to fund paid phone banks to identify Schiff supporters from a file of 10,000 pro-choice voters it had accumulated over years of telephone identifications. After three or four rounds of persuasive calls, NARAL identified "86 percent to 88 percent" of the file as Schiff supporters. These voters then received GOTV calls on Election Day, reminding them to vote.[67] NARAL political director Gloria Totten commented, "We consider it our role to go to people who might be predisposed to Jim Rogan . . . and take them away from him and give them to Adam Schiff."[68] Chris Mather, NARAL's deputy political director describes the strategy deployed in the Michigan Eighth Congressional District as follows, "NARAL's niche in the pro-choice movement is we do the best targeted voter contract work. We don't open a phone book." In the Eighth, there are "close to 25,000 pro-choice identified voters," and "we worked 10 percent of the voters needed to win the election."[69] NARAL also used phone canvasses to identify 35,000 to 40,000 voters to call in the Washington Second Congressional District in 2000.[70] The NARAL activities in California and Michigan may have been funded by an independent expenditure.

Groups opposed to abortion have also used targeted phone banks. Professors Don Gross and Penny Miller of the University of Kentucky monitored the 1998 Kentucky Senate race as well as the Kentucky Sixth Congressional District race in 1998 and learned of targeted phone banks paid for by Right to Life. Phone calls on the Sunday before the election went to registered African Americans before they went to church. The gist of the message was that Democrats Ernesto Scorsone and Henry Baesler are pro-abortion-on-demand, and that, as good Christians, blacks should vote for pro-life candidates Ernie Fletcher and Jim Bunning.[71]

Targeting can also be done on television and radio. Consultants can learn the types of voters who view different types of programs and aim their electioneering advertisements at that audience by advertising on those programs. The NAACP National Voter Fund ad on hate crimes in 2000, for example, was aimed at young African American males.[72] This same pattern of targeting broadcast electioneering advocacy messages happens at the congressional district level. A Sierra Club official commenting on the campaign in 2000 in Washington's Second Congressional District indicated that their anti-Koster ad ran primarily on cable during shows directed at "independent women voters aged 25–50 . . . in Snohomish and Whatcom County."[73] Records show that in late October they spent about $45,000 on cable TV in that area.[74]

An exception to this widespread practice of investing in highly competitive races is groups who pursue a single issue and ask candidates to pledge to support their position on that issue if elected. The contests in which groups like Americans for Limited Terms become involved is therefore limited to those in which one candidate has taken the pledge and the other declined. These contests are not always highly competitive.

TIMING. The timing of electioneering advocacy often suggests coordination among the political parties, candidates, and interest groups. As Ken Goldstein and Jonathan Krasno noted, the timing of ads is "related to the activity of candidates not the activity of Congress."[75] In some instances, like the Michigan Senate race, groups went in early to help keep Democrat Debbie Stabenow competitive while she replenished her campaign war chest. After Governor Mel Carnahan's death in Missouri, Democratic Party and allied groups capitalized on the tragedy and Republican-allied groups toned down their attacks.[76] After hearing about the death, the NFIB, for example, stopped the presses on a mailer that attacked Carnahan.[77]

In the contests we monitored in 1998, most interest group electioneering advocacy came in the final weeks of the campaign. In 2000, 58 percent of the interest group electioneering advocacy came in the last two weeks of the election. But as noted in contests like the New Mexico Third

Congressional District race in 1998 and Michigan Senate race in 2000, early spending by interest groups can be important.

IMPACT OF ELECTIONEERING ADVERTISEMENTS ON ELECTION OUTCOMES

While disentangling cause and effect in campaigns is never simple, CSED's experienced political scientists, who interviewed major players in the races and who know the political culture of their state or congressional district, determined that these communications often have a significant impact on elections and that they are intended to have such an impact.

Purpose of Soft Money and Electioneering Advertisements: Defeating or Electing a Candidate

The timing, content, and targeted audience of soft money and election-eering advertisements all point to the fact that they are intended to influence the outcome of particular elections. From the perspective of the voters, party and interest group electioneering ads are clearly intended to persuade voters to vote for or against a particular candidate. As noted previously, almost all soft money and interest group electioneering efforts are aimed at the most competitive races. There is strong evidence that the purpose is to defeat or elect a particular candidate.

Typically, interest groups invest electioneering advocacy money in contests in which the preferred candidate was "right" on their issue. I have also noted a strong convergence of themes between candidates, parties, and interest groups in most races. Some interest groups choose not to pursue their issue agenda so much as their candidate agenda in competitive elections. Examples of groups who have done that are environmental groups. One contest in which they had a choice between their core issues and candidates was New Mexico's Third Congressional District. In a special election held in 1997, a Green Party candidate, Carol Miller, received 17 percent of the vote.[78] In 1998 environmental groups could have backed the Green candidate whose core issues centered on the environment or they could back a major party candidate with a less environmentally focused issue agenda. Gregory Green of the LCV indicated to Lonna Rae Atkeson and Anthony C. Coveny of the University of New Mexico that what his group did for Democratic candidate Tom Udall included independent expenditures on direct mail, phone banks, person-to-person persuasion, and get-out-the-vote efforts. Its main strategy was to return the Democratic base to Udall and to reduce Green Party candidate Carol

Miller's vote.[79] Arguably, a Green Party candidate reflects the issue agenda of the LCV more than a Democratic or Republican candidate. Yet, in the New Mexico example, the LCV expressly sought to move voters from the Green Party candidate to the Democrat.

This same pattern of environmental groups more concerned with electing Democrats than advocating issues recurred in 2000. In the Michigan Eighth Congressional District, the Sierra Club pursued the same strategy the LCV used two years before in New Mexico. The Sierra Club's national executive director and president personally appeared in the Eighth District for Democrat Dianne Byrum. Dan Farough, the Sierra Club's environmental voter education campaign coordinator in the race, said bluntly, "The Green Party candidate did not figure prominently in the conversation."[80] The Sierra Club also made the same choice in the presidential race as in Michigan. As Bonnie Bucqueroux, the Green candidate in the race, said to Eric Freedman of Michigan State University, the real impact of soft money came with efforts "to demonize the Greens." She cited ads with Gloria Steinem and the Sierra Club executive director's trip to Michigan to push Gore: "It's unfortunate because it showed up some of the non-profit groups as not being as ideologically driven as they said they were. They were basically soft-money extensions of the Democratic campaign, masquerading as independent."[81]

Effectiveness of Electioneering Advertisements

Understanding how voters perceive and react to soft money and issue advocacy communications helps us address three important questions. First, do voters perceive that messages that avoid the magic words of express advocacy are different from other election-centered ads? The logic of *Buckley's* distinction between express advocacy and issue advocacy is the assumption that voters perceive issue advocacy to be different from express advocacy or candidate communications. A similar question is, do voters perceive differences between party communications and candidate communications in terms of any component that might be perceived as "party building?" Finally, what, if any, impact do these different forms of communication have in influencing how people vote?

VOTER PERCEPTIONS. With regard to voter perceptions of interest group electioneering advertisements that do not use the magic words and party soft-money-funded messages, voters in focus groups and a national survey identified the primary purpose of these ads to be electing or defeating a candidate. Indeed, in the 2000 cycle, the party soft-money and interest group issue advocacy that referred to a candidate in some way were to most voters even more about the election or defeat of specific candidates than the candidates' own communications.

Voters see clear differences between pure issue ads, which have no candidate or election referent, and electioneering ads. When asked, "What do you believe was the primary objective or purpose of this ad?" respondents in the national survey clearly distinguished between the issue ads that had an election focus and those that did not. As expected, more than two-thirds of respondents (70 and 71 percent) saw the pure issue ads as primarily about an issue. However, less than 10 percent (6 and 8 percent) of the respondents saw the electioneering ads as primarily about an issue. Instead, 80 and 81 percent of respondents said these electioneering ads were urging them to vote against a candidate."[82]

INFLUENCE ON ELECTION OUTCOMES. In terms of influencing the outcome of elections, several of the academics monitoring races with substantial party soft money or interest group electioneering advocacy believed that the noncandidate campaigning was important to the outcome of the race they monitored. Examples would include the NRA independent expenditure-funded endorsement of Democrat Ted Strickland in the Ohio Sixth Congressional District in 1998, which generally helped him with social conservatives;[83] and the support of the League of Conservation Voters, which helped Tom Udall in the New Mexico Third Congressional District in 1998 win back voters who likely supported the Green party.[84] Also, the American Medical Association PAC ran a $450,000 campaign for Republican Jon Fox in the Pennsylvania Thirteenth Congressional District. Though equal to more than a third of Fox's war chest, the ante may have been misplaced in the air rather than the ground war, leading to Fox's defeat.[85]

Party participation also clearly affected election outcomes. In the 2000 U.S. Senate race in Delaware, Joseph Pika of the University of Delaware concludes, "The story of this election hinges on the difference in party funding that dramatically favored the Democrats."[86] Pika also cites the state's most respected political journalist, Celia Cohen, as saying, "The money is critical because the Democrats were able to equalize it. . . . This is the first campaign [in which] I had not heard one candidate complain about the lack of money. The state was awash in it."[87] Another race where party money was important was in Pennsylvania's Fourth Congressional District in 2000. Christopher Jan Carman and David C. Barker of the University of Pittsburgh saw the difference in party soft-money support as determinative in that race. Carman and Barker state, "We contend that this race boiled down to the national and state party organizations' soft money support of their candidates: Hart had it; Van Horne did not."[88]

Speaking more generally, Michael Traugott of the University of Michigan concluded with regard to the Michigan Senate race that "a strong mobilization and communication effort by certain key interest groups for Stabenow may have made the difference in such a close race."[89] Traugott also specifies how groups made a difference:

> Outside group support was also critical for mobilization and GOTV efforts on Stabenow's behalf. This was especially important because the Michigan Democratic Party did not control the main political institutions in the state. Unions supplied money, paid for extensive mailings and organized GOTV drives. The NAACP and African-American churches in the Detroit area also mobilized voter turnout in Detroit and other urban areas in southeastern Michigan. And women's and pro-choice groups like EMILY's List and NARAL supported Stabenow's campaign with advertising, professional staff located to the state, and extensive mailings with their combined efforts. They provided her with the critical margin in a race decided by 1 percent of the votes cast.[90]

The closeness of the Michigan Senate race is not atypical of the contests we monitored in 1998 and 2000. Indeed, one reason why noncandidate spending is so heavily directed to these contests is that they remained competitive to the end. Groups and parties correctly perceived that these were the types of races where additional spending could make a difference. Even influencing small percentages of voters, along with the increased mobilization that has occurred with outside money, can swing such an election. Sometimes the involvement of outside groups and party soft money was enough to make a candidate competitive. This was the case in Arkansas's Fourth Congressional District in 2000, according to the campaign staff of Democratic challenger Mike Ross.[91] It was also the case in the close Nevada Senate race in 1998. The turnout drive of organized labor was decisive in an election with relatively low levels of voter participation. The academics who studied this race point to Nevada's increasingly Republican electorate, Ensign's attractive image, and a popular Republican gubernatorial candidate. They conclude that Ensign therefore might well have won without the strong efforts of the AFL-CIO.[92]

Another way to assess the impact of noncandidate communications in a competitive race is to see if the expenditures by outside groups alter the campaign dynamics. An example of a group that altered campaign dynamics in 2000 was Citizens for Better Medicare. This group, often in partnership with the Chamber of Commerce, campaigned aggressively on the prescription drug question and found candidates to respond to their ads in races like the California Twenty-Seventh Congressional District contest and Montana U.S. Senate. For example, Parke Skelton, lead campaign consultant for Democrat Adam Schiff, observed that "the prescription drug issue became much larger in this race than it would have without these [CBM] expenditures. . . . We couldn't compete with the money that was being spent on Rogan's behalf and much of our natural advantage was eroded. The expenditures turned it from an issue that we could go on the offensive with to one that we had to defend against."[93] Similarly, in the Montana Senate race, Democratic challenger Brian Schweitzer confirmed to Craig Wilson that he felt that the Citizens for Better Medicare ads placed him on the defensive and made it harder to woo voters.[94]

In some of the races we monitored, academics and the experts they interviewed believed that the campaigns had reached the "saturation" point. In such cases, there was a sense that voters started shutting out these messages.[95] And in some of our races, observers did not see the outside money as important. Examples of races in which the academics did not find electioneering advertisements or party soft-money spending to be central to the outcome of the race included the Arkansas Fourth Congressional District election in 2000 and the race in Pennsylvania's Thirteenth Congressional District in 2000.[96]

Notes

1. Allan J. Cigler, "The 1998 Kansas Third Congressional District Race," in David B. Magleby, *Outside Money: Soft Money and Issue Advocacy in the 1998 Congressional Elections* (Lanham, Md.: Rowman and Littlefield, 2000), p. 88.

2. Steven Rosenthal, AFL-CIO political director, lunchtime discussion panel at the Pew press conference, "Outside Money: Soft Money and Issue Ads in Competitive 1998 Congressional Elections," National Press Club, Washington, D.C., February 1, 1999, as cited in Magleby, *Outside Money*, p. 71.

3. Telephone interview with Tim Ryan, executive director, Citizens for Better Medicare, by David B. Magleby and Anna Nibley Baker, May 14, 2001.

4. According to the Annenberg Center, the Committee for Good Common Sense is run mostly by Republicans with insurance and business ties. See Annenberg Public Policy Center, "Issue Ads @ APPC," University of Pennsylvania (www.appcpenn.org/issueads/gindex.htm, accessed March 10, 2002).

5. Anthony Corrado, "A History of Federal Campaign Finance Law," in Anthony Corrado and others, eds., *Campaign Finance Reform: A Sourcebook* (Brookings, 1997).

6. Deborah Beck and others, "Issue Advocacy Advertising during the 1996 Campaign," and Jeffrey D. Stranger and Douglas G. Rivlin, "Issue Advocacy during the 1997–98 Election Cycle," Annenberg Public Policy Center report, cited in Magleby, *Outside Money*, p. 47.

7. Magleby, *Outside Money*, p. 47.

8. Ibid., fig. 3.1, p. 48.

9. David B. Magleby, ed., *Getting Inside the Outside Campaign* (Brigham Young University, 2001), p. 4, and David Magleby, ed., "Outside Money," *PS Online e-Symposium*, June 2001 (www.apsa.com/PS/june01/outsidemoney.cfm [accessed August 6, 2001]).

10. Linda Fowler, Constantine Spiliotes, and Lyn Vavreck, "The Role of Issue Advocacy Groups in the New Hampshire Primary"; and Bill Moore and Danielle Vinson, "The South Carolina Republican Primary," both in Magleby, "Outside Money."

11. The Sierra Club attacked Bush's environmental record early in the primary season. The National Abortion and Reproductive Rights Action League also attacked Bush early, claiming he was a threat to choice on the abortion issue. To a much lesser extent, Republican-allied groups attacked Gore. See David B. Magleby, "Outside Money in the 2000 Congressional Elections and Presidential Primaries," in Magleby, "Outside Money."

12. Telephone interview with Roy Fletcher, McCain deputy campaign manager, by David B. Magleby and Jason Beal, June 6, 2000, cited in Magleby, *Getting Inside the Outside Campaign*, p. 4.

13. Interview with Karen Ackerman, AFL-CIO, by David B. Magleby, Washington, D.C., November 9, 2000, cited in Anna Nibley Baker and David B. Magleby, "Interest Groups in the 2000 Congressional Elections," in David B. Magleby, ed., *The Other Campaign: Soft Money and Issue Advocacy in the 2000 Congressional Elections* (Lanham, Md.: Rowman and Littlefield, 2003), p. 59.

14. Telephone interview with Bill Miller, U.S. Chamber of Commerce, by David B. Magleby, November 18, 2000, cited in Baker and Magleby, "Interest Groups," p. 56.

15. Interview with Will Lutz, deputy communications director, and Gloria Totten, political director, NARAL Pro-Choice America, by David B. Magleby, Washington, D.C., December 14, 2000, cited in Baker and Magleby, "Interest Groups," p. 60.

16. Interview with Glen Caroline, National Rifle Association, by David B. Magleby, Washington, D.C., November 15, 2000, cited in Baker and Magleby, "Interest Groups," p. 60.

17. Magleby, *The Other Campaign*, pp. 229–30.

18. Lorie Slass, "Spending on Issue Ads," in *Issue Advertising in the 1999–2000 Election Cycle* (Annenberg Public Policy Center, University of Pennsylvania,

2001), p. 4 (www.appcpenn.org/political/issueads/1999-2000issueadvocacy.pdf [accessed August 6, 2001]), cited in Magleby, *The Other Campaign*, p. 4.

19. Ibid., p. 12.

20. Ibid., pp. 12–13.

21. David B. Magleby, *Dictum without Data: The Myth of Issue Advocacy and Party Building* (Center for the Study of Elections and Democracy, Brigham Young University, 2000).

22. Magleby, *The Other Campaign*, pp. 229–30.

23. Estimates of how much was spent on television in our races are unavoidably imprecise, whether relying on the ad buy data retrieved from the stations or the CMAG ad buy estimates.

24. Baker and Magleby, "Interest Groups," p. 67.

25. Patrick McGreevy, "California Elections U.S. House; High-Profile Contest Is Awash in Soft Money," *Los Angeles Times*, October 22, 2000, home edition.

26. Todd Donovan and Charles Morrow, "The 2000 Washington Second Congressional District Race," in Magleby, *The Other Campaign,* p. 218.

27. Interview with anonymous employee of Charter Communications, by Drew Linzer and David Menefee-Libey, October 5, 2000, cited in Drew Linzer and David Menefee-Libey, "The 2000 California Twenty-Seventh Congressional District Race," in David B. Magleby, ed., *Election Advocacy: Soft Money and Issue Advocacy in the 2000 Congressional Elections* (Center for the Study of Elections and Democracy, Brigham Young University, 2001), p. 134.

28. Robert Holsworth and others, "2000 Virginia Senate Race," in Magleby, *The Other Campaign,* p. 118.

29. Baker and Magleby, "Interest Groups," p. 71.

30. Craig B. Holman and Luke P. McLoughlin, *Buying Time 2000: Television Advertising in the 2000 Federal Elections* (Brennan Center for Justice, New York University School of Law, 2000), p. 15.

31. Magleby, *Outside Money.* The complete set of case studies can be found at www.byu.edu/outsidemoney/1998. See also David B. Magleby and Marianne Holt, eds., *Outside Money: Soft Money and Issue Ads in Competitive 1998 Congressional Elections* (Center for the Study of Elections and Democracy, Brigham Young University, 2001). Election issue advocacy was also a part of the 2000 presidential primaries, especially in the South Carolina Republican primary. See Magleby, *Getting Inside the Outside Campaign.*

32. Magleby, *The Other Campaign*, p. 12.

33. Magleby, *Outside Money*, p. 64.

34. Magleby, *The Other Campaign*, p. 230.

35. The Republican Leadership Council (RLC) not only delivered an attack on Steve Forbes via telephone in the 2000 primaries, but its mode of calling also tied up the Forbes campaign phone lines answering questions for people who received the RLC calls. The RLC first attacked Forbes and then asked if the person called would like to speak to the Forbes campaign. Linda L. Fowler, Constantine J. Spilliotes, and Lynn Vavreck of Dartmouth College report, "The

infuriated caller would then be patched through to the Forbes campaign." See Dal Col, interview, cited in Fowler, Spiliotes, and Vavreck, "The Role of Issue Advocacy Groups in the New Hampshire Primary," in Magleby, *Getting Inside the Outside Campaign*, p. 32.

36. Steven Rosenthal, lunchtime discussion panel at the Pew press conference, cited in Magleby, *Outside Money*, p. 69.

37. Telephone conversation with Eric Freedman by Anna Nibley Baker, September 2000, cited in Baker and Magleby, "Interest Groups," p. 63.

38. NARAL, for example, spent close to $22,000 in the Michigan Eighth Congressional District alone. Most of these calls were inhouse, but in some instances NARAL contracted with out-of-state political firms to call undecided Republicans and Independents to try to sway votes. See interview with Chris Mather, NARAL's deputy political director, by Jonathan Ladd, December 5, 2000; Adam J. Berinsky and Susan S. Lederman, "The 2000 New Jersey Twelfth Congressional District Race," in Magleby, *The Other Campaign*, p. 190.

39. Robin Kolodny and Sandra Suarez, "A Profile of the Pennsylvania Thirteenth Congressional District," in Magleby and Holt, *Outside Money*, pp. 168–70; telephone interview with Michelle Fetheringill, Planned Parenthood New Mexico president and CEO, by Lonna Rae Atkeson and Anthony C. Coveny, April 13, 1999, cited in Magleby, *Outside Money*, p. 71.

40. Telephone interview with Larry Galmish, Right to Life of Michigan PAC director, by Eric Freedman, November 13, 2000, cited in Eric Freedman and Sue Carter, "The 2000 Michigan Eighth Congressional District," in Magleby, *The Other Campaign*, pp. 176–77.

41. Arthur Sanders and David Redlawsk, "Money in the Iowa Caucuses," in Magleby, *Getting Inside the Outside Campaign*, p. 23.

42. As noted, internal communications not primarily about an election are not reported to the FEC at all. There are no limits on how much can be spent on internal communications.

43. In the general election races we monitored in 2000, abortion and health care were common themes to both parties and groups, and recurrent mail themes included education, gun control, and social security. Despite general similarities, themes differed among groups, and groups took up the causes of the parties they supported. For instance, education was a Democratic and Democratic-allied interest group theme. Taxes were the most prominent GOP theme. The economy and taxes together were common themes for both parties and Republican-allied interest groups, but taxes were not a top theme of Democratic allies and were ranked fifth behind jobs, gun control, health care, and abortion. Neither Republicans nor their interest group allies emphasized the environment, but it was a major concern for interest groups supporting Democrats. Interestingly, interest groups on both sides, more than parties, emphasized gun control.

44. Telephone interview with Elliot Sweeny, Building Industry Association of Washington Political Affairs, by Todd Donovan, November 2000, cited in Donovan and Morrow, "The 2000 Washington Second Congressional District Race,"

p. 218. Sweeny offered this as a "ballpark estimate" and stated the group spent less than $100,000.

45. Donovan and Morrow, "The 2000 Washington Second Congressional District Race," p. 218.

46. Also in 1998 in the Kansas Third Congressional District, the television ads of the AFL-CIO on social security and health care were seen by Alan Cigler of the University of Kansas as "almost lead-ins to the Moore commercials in early October. For example, one union ad invited viewers to call Snowbarger and protest the Republican stance on social security and health care; approximately fifteen minutes later a Moore commercial appeared talking about Moore's support for social security and health care choice." See Cigler, "The 1998 Kansas Third Congressional District Race," p. 86.

47. Interview with Dawn Laguens, cited in Baker and Magleby, "Interest Groups," pp. 58–59.

48. Tim Fackler, Nathalie Frensley, Eric Herzik, Ted G. Jelen, Todd Kunioka, and Michael Bowers, "The 1998 Nevada Senate Race," in Magleby, *Outside Money,* p. 125.

49. National Right to Life communicated, at least in part, through independent expenditures in 2000. Fowler and others, "The Role of Issue Advocacy Groups in the New Hampshire Primary," p. 31.

50. "Finding Your Way through the Ad Maze," *Missoulian (Mont.),* April 19, 2000, cited in Craig Wilson, "The Montana 2000 Senate and House Races," in Magleby, *The Other Campaign,* p. 142.

51. "Ads Dump Political Garbage in Montana," *Billings Gazette,* April 21, 2000, cited in Wilson, "The Montana 2000 Senate and House Races," p. 42.

52. David Barnes, *Transportation Topics,* TT Publishing, November 22, 1998, pp. 1, 27, cited in Fackler and others, "The 1998 Nevada Senate Race," p. 125.

53. Fackler and others, "1998 Nevada Senate Race," p. 125.

54. See David B. Magleby, *Direct Legislation: Voting on Ballot Propositions in the United States* (John Hopkins University Press, 1984); also Arthur Lupia, "Shortcuts versus Encyclopedias: Information and Voting Behavior in California Insurance Reform Elections," *American Political Science Review,* vol. 88 (1994), pp. 63–76.

55. Magleby, *Dictum without Data.*

56. Interview with Mark Emerson, cited in Fackler and others, "The 1998 Nevada Senate Race," p. 122.

57. Telephone interview with David Weeks, media consultant, by Ted Jelen, June 24, 1999, cited in Fackler and others, "The 1998 Nevada Senate Race," p. 114.

58. During the focus group discussions, 75 percent of focus group respondents said that candidate and party soft-money ads are indistinguishable. David B. Magleby, "The Impact of Issue Advocacy and Party Soft Money Electioneering," paper presented at the conference, "Measuring Advertising and Advertising Effectiveness: Political Advertising in the 2000 Elections," Chicago, April 18, 2001, p. 25.

59. One notable exception is Al Cross of the *Louisville Courier Journal*. Gross and Miller, "1998 Kentucky Senate and Sixth District Races," in Magleby, *Outside Money,* p. 206.

60. Interview with Matthew Daly, *Hartford Courant* political reporter, by Sandra Anglund and Clyde McKee, March 30, 1999, cited in Anglund and McKee, "The 1998 Connecticut Fifth Congressional District Race," in Magleby, *Outside Money,* p. 165.

61. Craig Wilson and Joe Floyd, co-directors, "The MSU-Billings Poll" (Montana State University at Billings, October 2000), pp. 4–8, cited in Wilson, "The Montana 2000 Senate and House Races," p. 144.

62. Magleby, *The Other Campaign*, p. 230. This mail may have been funded by an independent expenditure.

63. Interview with Sharon Wolff, National Federation of Independent Business, by David B. Magleby, Washington, D.C., November 14, 2000.

64. E-mail correspondence of Kris Hanselman, political director, Washington Education Association, to Todd Donovan, December 2000, cited in Donovan and Morrow, "The 2000 Washington Second Congressional District Race," p. 219.

65. Interview with Lisa Wade, League of Conservation Voters (LCV), by David B. Magleby, Washington, D.C., November 13, 2000, cited in Magleby, *The Other Campaign*, p. 14. LCV did independent expenditures in 2000.

66. "Burns Is a Proven Voice in D.C. for Montanans," *Missoulian (Mont.)*, November 2, 2000, cited in Wilson, "The Montana 2000 Senate and House Races," p. 137.

67. Telephone interview with Gloria Totten, NARAL political director, by Drew Linzer and David Menefee-Libey, November 17, 2000, cited in Linzer and Menefee-Libey, "The 2000 California Twenty-Seventh Congressional District Race," p. 159.

68. Ibid.

69. Telephone interview with Chris Mather, NARAL's deputy political director, by Eric Freedman, December 5, 2000, cited in Freedman and Carter, "The 2000 Michigan Eighth Congressional District Race," p. 176.

70. Telephone interview with Karen Cooper, Washington NARAL, by Todd Donovan, November 2000, cited in Donovan and Morrow, "The 2000 Washington Second Congressional District Race," p. 219.

71. Don Gross and Penny Miller, "1998 Kentucky Senate and Sixth District Races," in Magleby, *Outside Money,* pp. 201–02. These phone banks may have been an independent expenditure.

72. Interview with Mike Lux, Progressive Strategies CEO, by David B. Magleby, Washington, D.C., December 14, 2000.

73. Telephone interview with Bill Arthur, Sierra Club Northwest Seattle political director, by Todd Donovan, December 2000, cited in Donovan and Morrow, "The 2000 Washington Second Congressional District Race," p. 218.

74. Donovan and Morrow, "The 2000 Washington Second Congressional District Race," p. 218. The Sierra Club is another group that both did independent expenditures and election advocacy in 2000. Some of their activity in this district was an independent expenditure.

75. Jonathan S. Krasno and Kenneth Goldstein, "The Facts about Television Advertising and the McCain-Feingold Bill," *PS: Political Science*, vol. 35 (2002), p. 209.

76. Martha E. Kropf, Anthony Simones, E. Terrence Jones, Dale Neuman, Allison Hayes, and Maureen Gilbride Mears, "The 2000 Missouri Senate Race," in David B. Magleby, ed., *Election Advocacy*, pp. 79–80. "Six thousand [union] volunteers . . . walked the streets, delivering the message 'Don't Let the Fire Go Out! Continue the Progress Mel Carnahan Started in Missouri! STAND UP FOR WORKING FAMILIES! Vote Democratic!'"

77. Interview with Wolff, cited in Baker and Magleby, "Interest Groups," p. 58. This would have likely been an independent expenditure.

78. Keith Easthouse, "Greens Celebrate Miller's Strong Showing, Reject Spoiler Label," *Santa Fe New Mexican*, May 14, 1997, p. A1; Mark Oswald, "Redmond Stuns Serna: GOP Candidate Pulls Big Upset in Primarily Democratic District," *Santa Fe New Mexican*, May 14, 1997, p. A1, cited in Lonna Rae Atkeson and Anthony C. Coveny, "The 1998 New Mexico Third Congressional District Race," in Magleby, *Outside Money*, p. 136.

79. Gregory Green, League of Conservation Voters (LCV) Independent Expenditures campaign director, telephone interview by Lonna Rae Atkeson and Anthony C. Coveny, November 23, 1998, cited in Atkeson and Coveny, "The 1998 New Mexico Third Congressional District Race," p. 142. This was a conscious effort by the LCV.

80. Telephone interview with Dan Farough, Sierra Club environmental voter education campaign coordinator, by Eric Freedman, November 2000, cited in Freedman and Carter, "The 2000 Michigan Eighth Congressional District Race," p. 168.

81. Telephone interview with Bonnie Bucqueroux, Michigan Eighth Congressional District Green candidate, by Eric Freedman, November 13, 2000, cited in Freedman and Carter, "2000 Michigan Eighth Congressional District Race," p. 168.

82. Magleby, "The Impact of Issue Advocacy and Party Soft Money Electioneering," p. 11. More than three out of four (77 percent and 85 percent) focus group respondents saw the pure issue ads as having the primary objective or purpose of presenting an issue. Furthermore, 91 and 94 percent saw the election issue ads as primarily urging them to vote for or against a candidate. See Magleby, *Dictum without Data*, p. i.

83. DeLysa Burnier and Michael Burton, "Profile of Ohio's Sixth Congressional District," in Magleby and Holt, *Outside Money*, p. 148.

84. Telephone interview with Gregory Green, League of Conservation Voters

(LCV) Independent Expenditures campaign director, by Lonna Rae Atkeson and Anthony C. Coveny, November 23, 1998, cited in Atkeson and Coveny, "The 1998 New Mexico Third Congressional District Race," p. 142.

85. Robin Kolodny, Sandra Suarez, and Michael Rodriguez, "Profile of Pennsylvania's Thirteenth Congressional District," in Magleby and Holt, *Outside Money,* p. 168; and Magleby, *Outside Money*, p. 57. This may have been an independent expenditure.

86. Magleby, "Outside Money," *PS Online e-Symposium*, June 2001 (www.apsa.com/PS/june01/pika.cfm [accessed 24 August 2002]).

87. Ibid.

88. Christopher Jan Carman and David C. Barker, "The 2000 Pennsylvania Fourth Congressional District Race," in Magleby, *The Other Campaign,* p. 197.

89. Traugott, "The 2000 Michigan Senate Race," in Magleby, *The Other Campaign,* p. 103.

90. Ibid., p. 108. The NARAL spending was at least partly an independent expenditure.

91. Interview with Kris Schultz, Mike Ross for Congress Campaign communications director, by Bass, Kirkpatrick and Wilson, Little Rock, Arkansas, November 15, 2000, cited in Bass, Kirkpatrick, and Wilson, "The 2000 Arkansas Fourth Congressional District Race," p. 127.

92. Fackler and others, "The 1998 Nevada Senate Race," p. 127.

93. Interview with Parke Skelton, Schiff campaign consultant, by Drew Linzer and David Menefee-Libey, November 12, 2000, cited in Linzer and Menefee-Libey, "The 2000 California Twenty-Seventh Congressional District Race," p. 164, fn. 34.

94. Telephone interview with Brian Schweitzer by Craig Wilson, January 10, 2001, cited in Wilson, "The Montana 2000 Senate and House Races," p. 132.

95. Telephone interview with John Truscott, Engler aide, by Eric Freedman, December 4, 2000, cited in Freedman and Carter, "The 2000 Michigan Eighth Congressional District Race," p. 180; interview with Schultz, cited in Bass, Kirkpatrick, and Wilson, "2000 Arkansas Fourth Congressional District Race," p. 128.

96. Magleby, "Outside Money."

Electioneering Communications in Recent Elections: The Case for a New Standard

Kenneth M. Goldstein

Kenneth M. Goldstein is an associate professor of political science at the University of Wisconsin–Madison who specializes in interest groups, political advertising, and survey methodology. He was an expert witness for the defense and reported the findings of his empirical analysis of the source, content, and targeting of political advertisements in the 2000 elections. His report also provided a detailed description of the methodology on which his research was based.

In this excerpt, Goldstein details the growth of electioneering advertisements by interest groups and party committees and identifies the major sponsors of the ads broadcast in the 2000 election cycle. He argues that the current test used to determine the applicability of federal campaign finance regulations, the so-called magic words test accepted by a number of federal courts, is an ineffective means of distinguishing "genuine issue ads" from "electioneering ads" that are designed to support specific candidates. In contrast, he notes, most of the electioneering ads sponsored by parties and interest groups are aired in close proximity to an election and are concentrated in competitive electoral contests. He concludes that the reform act's criteria for distinguishing election-related ads, which include the timing and targeting of broadcast advertisements, as well as the featuring of a particular federal candidate, would encompass almost all of the electioneering ads aired in 2000 and thus be a better test for election advocacy than the magic words doctrine.

SUMMARY OF FINDINGS

The Bipartisan Campaign Reform Act's (BCRA) provisions focus on broadcast ads sponsored by parties and interest groups. The main subject of this report is the nature of interest group advertising in the 2000 contest and, more specifically, the ads and sponsors that would be directly affected by BCRA provisions relating to ads that mention or depict a candidate and are broadcast within sixty days of a general election or thirty days of a primary election for federal office. A secondary focus is the nature of advertising by political parties.

I draw primarily on a database of political television advertisements aired in the top seventy-five media markets, which serve 80 percent of the country's population. The data are compiled by the Campaign Media Analysis Group (CMAG), a commercial firm that tracks advertising for political clients. University of Wisconsin–Madison graduate assistants and I processed the CMAG data for 2000. I have used these data in a series of reports and articles to describe the source, content, and targeting of political advertising in the 2000 elections. In this report, I set forth nine principal conclusions that emerge from my study of the CMAG data:

—Advertisements sponsored by parties and interest groups made up a significant and increasing portion of political television ads broadcast in federal races over the course of the entire year, especially during the last sixty days of the 2000 election.

—The "magic words" defined in *Buckley* v. *Valeo* do not provide an effective way to identify political television ads that have the purpose or effect of supporting or opposing candidates for election to a public office.

—Interest group–financed ads that depicted or mentioned candidates for federal office were concentrated in the weeks immediately preceding the election and stopped on Election Day. Interest group ads that did not mention or picture candidates for federal office were distributed more evenly throughout the year, rising and falling with the ebb and flow of the legislative calendar.

—Interest group ads that mentioned a candidate within sixty days of the general election almost invariably targeted House or Senate candidates in hotly contested races or presidential candidates in battleground states.

—Ads that mentioned or depicted federal candidates for office differ from ads that did not mention or picture candidates in other ways, such as their content, their distribution over time, and their geographic dispersion.

—Ads that did not mention or depict a candidate are readily distinguishable from quintessential electioneering ads (such as ads run by a candidate seeking election to public office) in numerous ways, such as their content, their distribution over time, and their geographic dispersion.

—Virtually all (97.7 percent) political television ads aired during 2000 that would have been covered by BCRA were perceived by project coders as having an electioneering purpose.

—BCRA requirements would have applied to 3.1 percent of the ads broadcast by interest groups during 2000. These ads were perceived as genuine issue ads by coders.

—Broadcasting issue ads in close proximity to an election is not necessarily an effective way to inform voters about public policy issues or to generate action on such issues.

THE CAMPAIGN MEDIA ANALYSIS GROUP DATA

Until recently, the lack of comprehensive data on the content, timing, volume, and targeting of political advertising has limited what policymakers, journalists, and scholars can report about the magnitude, content, and targeting of political television ads.

A technology marketed by Competitive Media Reporting (CMR) now tracks television advertising activity in the country's major markets. The ad-tracking technology monitors the transmissions of the national networks (ABC, CBS, NBC, and Fox) as well as 42 major national cable networks (such as CNN, ESPN, and TBS). The system monitors local television advertising in the country's top seventy-five media markets (comprising approximately 80 percent of the nation's population).[1] The system's software recognizes the electronic seams between programming and advertising. When the system first detects a commercial spot's unique broadcast pattern, it downloads the ad and creates a "storyboard" of the sort described below. Analysts at CMR classify the advertisements into particular categories by product for commercial clients and by candidate or sponsor for political clients. The ads are then tagged with unique digital fingerprints. Thereafter, the system automatically recognizes and logs that particular commercial wherever and whenever it airs. The ad-tracking information is marketed to political clients by the Campaign Media Analysis Group.

In 2000, the Brennan Center for Justice at New York University purchased the CMAG data through a grant from the Pew Charitable Trusts.[2] The 2000 data were processed and coded by teams of graduate and undergraduate students working under my supervision at the University of Wisconsin–Madison.

CMAG supplied two forms of data used in this project. First, for every political ad produced, CMAG created a storyboard, that is, a complete transcript of all audio and a still capture of every fourth second of the video. Second, CMAG tracked political ads in the nation's top seventy-five media markets, as well as all ads run on the major national broadcast and cable networks. The unit of analysis in these files is an individual broadcast, or "airing," of a unique ad. For each such airing, CMAG reported on the time, length, station, show, and estimated cost. For each ad, this frequency information was then merged with the coded content from the storyboards in order to produce a single, comprehensive dataset. I have great confidence in the CMAG data in terms of tracking the airings of particular ads at particular times.

The CMAG storyboards enabled us to undertake an extensive analysis of the ads and develop a database of information concerning political television advertising. Specifically, a team of students (the coders), working under my supervision, assessed the content of each of these storyboards on a wide range of topics, such as content, tone, issues addressed, whether the ads mentioned a political candidate or provided a toll-free number to call, and so on. Multiple coders reviewed a subset of storyboards as a check on the reliability of the coding. I reviewed all ads financed by interest groups and broadcast within sixty days of a general election. I also reviewed and revised the coding where coding by the initial coders was in conflict or where I determined that an error had been made.

In addition to collecting certain specific information concerning each storyboard reviewed, the study also asked coders: "In your opinion, is the purpose of the ad to provide information about or urge action on a bill or issue, or is it to generate support or opposition for a particular candidate?" In this report, I refer to ads coded as providing information or urging action as "Genuine Issue Ads," and ads coded as generating support or opposition for a particular candidate as "Electioneering Ads."

THE SCOPE OF POLITICAL ADVERTISING

Advertising in the 2000 election was financed by three principal groups: (1) the candidates; (2) political parties; and (3) interest groups. Some interest groups formed political action committees (PACs), which are regulated under current election laws, and aired ads sponsored by these PACs. Most interest group ads, however, were not sponsored by PACs and fell outside Federal Election Campaign Act (FECA) regulation.

In the 2000 election cycle—that is, from January 1, 2000, through Election Day—the CMAG database collected 970,424 political television ad broadcasts, 838,169 of which applied to federal races financed by candidates, political parties, and interest groups at a cost of roughly $720 million. Thirty-six interest groups financed the broadcast of political television advertisements that would have fallen within BCRA's coverage. During the federal elections in 2000, interest group spending accounted for 16 percent of all political television ads broadcast at an estimated cost of $93 million; political parties paid for 27 percent at an estimated cost of $162 million; and candidates paid for 52 percent at an estimated cost of $338 million.[3] These figures, in fact, underestimate television expenditures because the CMAG estimates only cover markets serving 80 percent of the nation's population and make no attempt to measure the increased cost of advertising during the peak season of political campaigns, when the demand for television advertising time pushes up spot prices.

In the federal election of 2000, a total of 838,169 ads were broadcast, 36 percent (301,521) of which were aired in the presidential contest, 29 percent (241,497) in Senate contests, and 29 percent (240,490) in House elections.[4] In House and Senate races, a total of 481,987 ads were broadcast in 2000, an increase of 64 percent over the 293,452 aired in 1998. Interest group expenditures for political television ads increased most dramatically, rising from approximately $11 million in 1998 to an estimated $93 million in 2000.

ROLE OF INTEREST GROUPS AND POLITICAL PARTIES IN POLITICAL TELEVISION ADVERTISING

Political parties were the largest purchasers of television ads in the 2000 presidential campaign. Parties purchased 41 percent of such ads, candidates 38 percent, and interest groups 8 percent.[5] Interest groups broadcast one commercial for every five broadcast by the candidates in the presidential election of 2000. In certain states, interest group advertising rivaled that of the candidates or parties. For example, in Missouri, interest groups ran almost three-quarters as many ads as candidates, while in Washington State, interest group ads exceeded 50 percent of the candidates' ads.

As a general matter, interest group ads that would have been defined as electioneering under the BCRA formulation were even more significant in House elections, accounting for 17 percent of total House ad broadcasts during the 2000 election cycle. Parties accounted for 22 percent of total television ads run in House elections and candidates, 60.6 percent.[6]

Party expenditures on television advertising were almost exclusively devoted to promoting their candidates. Some 99.8 percent of party-financed television ads mentioned or depicted a candidate. Only 1.8 percent even mentioned the name of the party and many fewer promoted the candidate by virtue of his of her party affiliation.[7]

BCRA UNIVERSE OF INTEREST GROUP ELECTIONEERING

The CMAG database presents an informative view of the interest group–financed political television ads that are the focus of BCRA's electioneering communication regulations, that is, ads that mentioned a candidate and were broadcast within sixty days of the general election.

Thirty-five interest groups broadcast communications on television that would have been defined as electioneering by BCRA during the 2000 elections. The top ten of those interest groups, listed below, sponsored 87 percent of the total amount spent by all interest groups on such communications during the 2000 election: Citizens for Better Medicare, Chamber of Commerce, Planned Parenthood, AFL-CIO, Women Voters: A Project of EMILY's List, Americans for Job Security, Business Round Table, Handgun Control, Sierra Club, and League of Conservation Voters. The top twenty interest groups accounted for 90 percent of all monies spent on communications that would have come under the BCRA regime.

The principal sources of interest group financing for electioneering communications were for the most part readily recognizable forces in American politics. An exception is an organization unrevealingly described as Citizens for Better Medicare. Citizens for Better Medicare, which turned out to be the largest interest group financier of electioneering communications in the 2000 election, is an organization representing certain pharmaceutical manufacturers.

That would have been the BCRA universe:[8] 59,632 broadcasts financed by thirty-five interest groups at an estimated cost of $40,491,141.[9]

MAGIC WORDS TEST FAILS TO IDENTIFY POLITICAL ADVERTISEMENTS

The vast majority of political ads broadcast on television fall into one of two distinct categories. Some plainly have the main purpose of persuading citizens to vote for or against a particular candidate. Other ads have the purpose of seeking support for or urging some action on a particular policy or legislative issue.

Heretofore, the "magic words" test—derived from a footnote in the Supreme Court's 1976 decision in *Buckley* v. *Valeo*—has been the legal standard for distinguishing between the two types of ads. This test defines express advocacy (ads with an election goal) as advertisements that contain words such as "elect," "defeat," or "support." Ads that do not contain magic words are technically not election ads under this test. Is this test effective?

As candidate-sponsored ads are paid for by hard money and clearly fall within the realm of partisan electioneering, the magic words test does not apply to them. Still, precisely because all advertisements sponsored by candidates are electioneering by definition, they can provide a test for the current standard of express advocacy. If the use of magic words provided an accurate way to classify an ad, then advertisements clearly and obviously created and aired to influence elections would be expected to employ such magic words.

Of the 433,811 ads broadcast by candidates, 11.4 percent contained the magic words. Just under nine in ten (88.6 percent) of the candidate ads aired in 2000, which were unarguably examples of partisan electioneering, were technically undetected by the *Buckley* magic words test and would not have been classified as electioneering. The data from 2000 demonstrate that magic words are not an effective way of distinguishing between political ads that have the main purpose of persuading citizens to vote for or against a particular candidate and ads that have the purpose of seeking support for or urging some action on a particular policy or legislative issue.

Interest Group Television Ads within Sixty Days of an Election

The two primary criteria by which BCRA defines electioneering communications are the ads' reference to a candidate and the proximity in time of their broadcast to the election. The CMAG database provides empirical evidence of a strong positive correlation between these two BCRA criteria and consequently of their validity as a test for identifying political television advertisements with the purpose or effect of supporting or opposing a candidate for public office.

Interest group ads that mention or depict a candidate tend to be broadcast within sixty days of the election. Interest group ads that do not mention a candidate tend to be spread more evenly over the year. More specifically, 78 percent of interest group ads that mentioned a candidate for federal office were broadcast within sixty days of the election. Fully 85 percent of interest group ads mentioning a presidential candidate ran within sixty days of the general election. By contrast, only 18 percent of interest group–financed ads not mentioning a candidate were broadcast within sixty days of the election.

Similarly, the distribution over time of interest group ads mentioning candidates is closely correlated to the distribution of electioneering communications broadcast by candidates and political parties. Seventy-six percent of all interest group–sponsored ads that mentioned a House candidate were broadcast within sixty days of the House of Representatives election, as were 79 percent of candidate ads and 94 percent of political party ads. Similarly, in the Senate election, 74 percent of interest group ads that mentioned a candidate aired within sixty days of the election, as did 67 percent of candidate ads and 81 percent of political party ads.

INTEREST GROUP ADS ARE CONCENTRATED IN COMPETITIVE DISTRICTS

The CMAG database shows that interest group–financed television ads that mentioned a candidate and were broadcast within sixty days of an election were highly concentrated in states and congressional districts with competitive races. During the 2000 Senate elections, 89.2 percent of such interest group ads ran in states where the race was competitive.[10] Four states accounted for 77 percent of the ads broadcast by interest groups; political parties broadcast 65 percent of their ads in these four states. Interest group ads were particularly important in Michigan, where interest groups broadcast 22 percent of the total ads broadcast in the race.

The geographical distribution of interest group ads in Senate elections closely paralleled that of the political parties, which ran 90.6 percent of their ads in those competitive states. The same was true in House elections. During 2000, 85.3 percent of interest group–financed ads broadcast within sixty days of the election were aired in congressional districts with competitive elections. Similarly, the political parties ran 98.2 percent of their ads in those districts.

In certain key congressional districts, such as California 49 and North Carolina 8, interest groups broadcast more ads than candidates or the political parties. In twenty-two congressional districts, interest group ads exceeded the number of ads run by the political parties. Overall, interest groups aired 17 percent of all ads aired in races for the U.S. House of Representatives.

The CMAG database provides strong evidence that the interest group ads covered by BCRA are targeted at competitive electoral contests and closely parallel political party ads in their geographic distribution.

CODERS' PERCEPTIONS OF INTEREST GROUP ADS

Another useful perspective on BCRA's definition of electioneering communications emerges from the coders' assessments of the political television advertisements as being either "Genuine Issue Ads" or "Electioneering Ads." The coders were asked to classify the ads by reporting their perception of whether the purpose of an ad was to provide information about or to urge action on a bill or issue or to generate support or opposition for a particular candidate. Applying this criterion, the coders, working under my supervision, classified all political television ads broadcast by interest groups during 2000 as being either "Genuine Issue Ads" or "Electioneering Ads."[11]

The coders' perceptions provide evidence that BCRA's definition of electioneering communications accurately captures those ads that have the purpose or effect of supporting candidates for election to public office. The coders classified 97.7 percent of the 60,623 interest group–sponsored political television ads that mentioned a candidate and were broadcast within sixty days of an election as Electioneering Ads. Only six distinct ads, which were broadcast a total of 1,413 times, were classified as Genuine Issue Ads.[12]

For the year 2000 as a whole, the coders classified 33.8 percent (45,001) of interest group–sponsored political television ads as Genuine Issue Ads and 66.2 percent (88,106) as Electioneering Ads. The fact that 97.7 percent of interest group ads that would have been classified by BCRA as Electioneering Communications were coded as having the purpose of generating support or opposition for political candidates, coupled with the coders' classification of a third of all interest group–financed political television ads broadcast during 2000 as a whole as Genuine Issue Ads, is persuasive evidence that BCRA would capture political television ads that have the purpose or effect of supporting or opposing the election of electoral candidates.

Conversely, there is persuasive evidence that the BCRA definition of electioneering communications is not overbroad in the sense of applying to any meaningful number of advertisements that are perceived as Genuine Issue Ads. Using the coders' classifications, only 3.1 percent of the 45,001 Genuine Issue Ads broadcast by interest groups during the 2000 election cycle would have been covered by BCRA.[13]

SUPPORT FOR AD CLASSIFICATION AS GENUINE ISSUE ADS OR ELECTIONEERING ADS

To the extent that the coders' classifications are supported by other characteristics of the ads suggesting that the ads had the purpose or effect of supporting the election of candidates for office, these characteristics provide corroborative evidence of the validity of the coders' classifications of the ads as Electioneering Ads and of the utility of the virtually congruent BCRA definition of electioneering communications as a test for identifying these ads that have the purpose or effect of supporting a candidate.

Electioneering Ads financed by interest groups are concentrated in the two months before the election. During the first six months of 2000, interest groups broadcast 72 percent of their Genuine Issue Ads, but only 7 percent of their Electioneering Ads. During the first eight months of the year, interest groups broadcast 35,413 of 45,001, or 79 percent, of their Genuine Issue Ads, while airing only 24,773 of 88,106, or 28 percent, of their Electioneering Ads. During the three months preceding the election, interest groups broadcast 23 percent of their Genuine Issue Ads while airing 82 percent of their Electioneering Ads, 72 percent of which were broadcast within the 60 days leading up to the November 7, 2000, election day.

Interest group expenditures for Electioneering Ads in congressional races were heavily concentrated in districts where there were competitive electoral contests. Approximately 91 percent of interest group–funded Electioneering Ads in the Senate general election were spent in competitive states ($9,079,235 out of $9,941,797).[14]

The same is true of interest group expenditures directed at elections for the House of Representatives. Using sources such as the *Cook Report*, I determined that 45 House races were competitive. Interest group Electioneering Ads ran in 41 House races covered by CMAG's top seventy-five markets. Ninety-one percent of interest group Electioneering Ads aired in House races were aired in races deemed competitive by the *Cook Report*.

Political television ads coded as Electioneering Ads differed in content from those perceived as Genuine Issue Ads overwhelmingly in two aspects. First, 85 percent of Electioneering Ads mentioned a candidate; only 15 percent did not. Conversely, 94.2 percent of Genuine Issue Ads did not mention a candidate while 5.8 percent did. Second, Electioneering Ads broadcast by interest groups tend to be overwhelmingly negative in tone, while Genuine Issue Ads are not. During 2000, 60 percent of all Electioneering Ads broadcast by interest groups attacked a candidate; 2.9 percent of interest group–sponsored Genuine Issue Ads were negative in tone.

Finally, Genuine Issue Ads differed from Electioneering Ads with respect to their publication of toll-free telephone numbers: 62.4 percent of Genuine Issue Ads contained toll-free numbers; by contrast, only 13 percent of Electioneering Ads contained a toll-free number.

To summarize, the information relating to the content of the ads, their timing, and their geographic distribution strongly corroborates the coders' classification of the ads as Electioneering Ads or Genuine Issue Ads.

ISSUE-ORIENTED ADS ARE DISTINGUISHABLE
FROM QUINTESSENTIAL POLITICAL ADS

Interest group ads intended to inform the public concerning some issue, as opposed to supporting a candidate for elective office, are readily distinguishable. If we take interest group–sponsored ads that do not mention or depict a candidate as a surrogate for quintessential issue-oriented ads and compare them with ads sponsored by candidates or parties—a surrogate for quintessential electioneering ads—it becomes readily apparent that issue-oriented ads are markedly different with respect to timing, content, and coder perception.

First, 63.5 percent of candidate ads and 66 percent of political party ads ran within sixty days of an election; only 17.7 percent of group-sponsored issue-oriented ads were broadcast during that period.

Second, 45.0 percent of political party ads were negative in tone, whereas only 0.7 percent of group-sponsored issue-oriented ads were negative in tone. During the fifteen days prior to an election, negative political party ads rose to 68.4 percent of all party ads broadcast. Almost 69 percent of BCRA-regulated group ads were negative in tone. Similarly, 65 percent of group-sponsored issue-oriented ads contained a toll-free number whereas less than 1 percent of candidate or political party ads did so. Only 2.1 percent of BCRA-regulated group ads contained a toll-free number.

Finally, viewers perceived 99 percent of candidate ads and 100 percent of party ads as intending to generate support or opposition for a candidate. While 99.7 percent of BCRA-regulated group ads were perceived as supporting or opposing a candidate, none of the issue-oriented interest group ads were so perceived.

ISSUE ADS RUN NEAR AN ELECTION GET LOST
AMONG ELECTION-RELATED MESSAGES

One concern sometimes raised by those opposed to the BCRA regulations is that the restriction may harm interest groups by preventing them from advertising on their issues at a time when citizens are supposedly paying the most attention to politics. There is no reason to believe that BCRA would significantly hinder interest groups from effectively getting out their messages on public policy issues. Running genuine issue ads near an election does not increase the effectiveness of those ads; in fact, it is likely that the ads' effectiveness actually decreases.

First, while there is evidence that interest in politics and *elections* rises as Election Day approaches, there is absolutely no evidence to support the position that interest in *public policy* issues rises as well during that time.

Second, communication theory has concluded that advertising is likely to be most effective (at informing or persuading) when viewers are exposed to one-sided flows of information in isolation from other advertising.[15] The last two months before an election is the time period of the most intense political advertising activity. In 2000, for example, 538,404 political ads, or 64.2 percent of all political ads run during the year, appeared during the last two months before an election. With the flood of advertising taking place during the last two months before an election, an individual interest group's message on a public policy issue is likely to become lost.[16]

Third, in conjunction with an increased interest in politics and elections, partisan attachments also harden during the last two months of a campaign. These hardened partisan attachments make it more difficult to persuade otherwise open-minded viewers of the merits of an interest group's policy stance.[17]

In addition to being less effective at conveying their messages, issue ads run close to an election are also less cost-effective, since the price of scarce television and radio air-time is higher near an election than during the rest of the year.

Data from my study support the conclusion that interest groups themselves understand that airing Genuine Issue Ads near an election carries no special advantage, and that it makes strategic sense to spread the airing of these ads over the course of the entire year. Of ads run by interest groups that do not name any candidate—quintessential issue ads—17.7 percent ran within sixty days before a general election. This approximates the 16.4 percent of issue ads that would have run if the ads had been equally distributed throughout the year. The frequency of issue ad broadcasts exceeds an even temporal distribution only in the April-through-June time frame. Forty-five percent of all issue ads were aired then, as against an expected percentage of 25 percent if the ads were spread evenly throughout the year. This concentration of ads during April through June is a likely result of groups turning on the heat to pass or defeat bills before Congress adjourned for the summer. There is no concentration of these quintessential issue ads during the sixty days before a general election. This time— the most cluttered time for advertisements and a time with hardened partisan attachments—is probably the worst time for an interest group to educate the public on its particular issue.

NOTES

1. CMAG data do not include ads broadcast on local cable channels.

2. The Brennan Center published two reports, entitled *Buying Time: Television Advertising in the 1998 Congressional Elections* ("*Buying Time 1998*") and *Buying Time 2000: Television Advertising in the 2000 Federal Elections* ("*Buying Time 2000*"), which used databases prepared under my supervision, upon which I relied in part to prepare this report.

3. The remaining 5 percent of ads were coordinated expenditures in the presidential race, with almost $30 million spent on those advertisements. Coordinated expenditures are those in which a candidate and a party jointly pay for the cost of the advertisement.

4. The remaining 6 percent of ads were coordinated expenditures.

5. The remaining ads were coordinated expenditures.

6. The remaining 0.4 percent were financed by undetermined ad sponsors.

7. Virtually all ads contain a "tag line" that identifies the organization financing the ad, which may include the party name where appropriate.

8. That is, the BCRA universe revealed by the CMAG data, which covers television markets serving 80 percent of the nation's population. No comprehensive information is available for the balance of the markets or for ads airing on local cable stations, but from my familiarity with political advertising I would estimate that few additional organizations spent more than $10,000 on political advertising in 2000.

9. There are 60,623 ads listed as aired within sixty days mentioning a candidate. The difference between that number and the 59,632 listed is due to the existence of ads for which the interest group sponsors were unclear.

10. In determining which races were competitive, I relied on my professional judgment, as informed by various media sources such as the *Cook Report*.

11. Specifically, coders were asked whether the purpose of the ad was to "generate support or opposition for candidate," or to "provide information or urge action." Coders were also given the option of "unsure/unclear."

12. These six ads represent every unique ad ever coded as a Genuine Issue Ad by the coders of the 2000 data. In some prior publications, fewer than six ads covered by BCRA were treated as Genuine Issue ads. See, for example, Brennan Center, *Buying Time 2000*, available online at www.brennancenter.org/programs/buyingtime2000.html; and Jonathan S. Krasno and Kenneth M. Goldstein, "The Facts about Television Advertising and the McCain-Feingold Bills," *PS: Political Science*, vol. 35 (June), pp. 207–12. In those publications, certain of these six ads—particularly those that student coders disagreed on—were ultimately treated as electioneering. In fact, my own judgment is that five of these six ads were clearly intended to support or oppose the election of a candidate (the lone exception being the Feingold/Kohl Abortion Ad). However, in this report, I have chosen to take the most conservative approach and count all six as Genuine Issue Ads.

13. In fact, this percentage overstates the proportion of all Genuine Issue Ads covered by BCRA, because it does not take into account the unregulated ads run in nonelection years during a single congressional term, such as 1999.

14. I used the *Cook Report* to identify the following senatorial elections as competitive races in 2000: Delaware, Florida, Michigan, Minnesota, Missouri, Nebraska, Nevada, New Jersey, New York, Virginia, and Washington.

15. See William McGuire, "The Myth of Massive Media Impact: Savagings and Salvagings," *Public Communication and Behavior,* vol. 1 (1986), pp. 173–257; John Zaller, *The Nature and Origins of Mass Opinion* (Cambridge University Press, 1992).

16. McGuire, "The Myth of Massive Media Impact"; Zaller, *The Nature and Origins of Mass Opinion.*

17. Zaller, *The Nature and Origins of Mass Opinion.*

Issue Advocacy and the Integrity
of the Political Process

JONATHAN S. KRASNO AND FRANK SORAUF

Jonathan S. Krasno is a visiting fellow at the Institute for Social and Policy Studies at Yale University. Frank Sorauf is a Regents' emeritus professor of political science at the University of Minnesota. Both served as expert witnesses for the defense and are experts on public opinion, political parties, and campaign finance.

Their coauthored report reviews the academic empirical data on political party and interest group activity to refute the claim that soft money has had a significant effect in building stronger party organizations. In the section excerpted here, Krasno and Sorauf discuss the effect of issue advocacy advertising on the integrity of the political system. They note that the structure of the campaign finance system and the interests of the actors within it make issue advocacy an attractive option for those seeking to influence public officials. In their view, the rise of candidate-specific issue advertising has made a "mockery" of the restrictions on campaign funding under the Federal Election Campaign Act (FECA) and thus increases the risk of corruption. They specifically highlight the lack of disclosure of issue advocacy sponsors and sources of funding, since disclosure is widely regarded as an essential safeguard against corruption. Although they do not cite specific examples of corporate influence through issue advocacy, they conclude that issue advocacy advertising undermines the integrity of the electoral process and may have a corruptive effect by influencing policymakers to grant favors and access to those who sponsor such efforts.

DEFINING CORRUPTION

In our earlier discussion of soft money we argued that corruption encompassed bribery, undue influence, and the more extreme forms of privileged access. We stand by that definition here. The use of candidate-oriented issue ads for electioneering by an array of established interest groups, freshly minted "organizations," and parties in the last several election cycles has also created a broader set of problems about elections that we will address in this subsection. Our decision to place this discussion here is inspired in part by the Supreme Court's earlier concern for the "integrity of the electoral process," the controlling interest in campaign finance and related jurisprudence before *Buckley*.[1] Indeed, by previous standards—and from our own perspective as long-time students of elections—we regard the recent use of issue ads as inimical to the integrity of the electoral system and, in that respect, corrupting.

We would judge the health of the electoral system by a few simple criteria. The first is choice: elections should offer voters an alternative between two or more candidates with a reasonable chance of winning. As desirable as it would be for voters to like their choices, it is even more essential that more than one of the names on their ballot have some possibility of election. This suspense, of course, raises the stakes of voting for citizens and spurs turnout. It also provides the chief means for popular control of elected officials; legislators for whom defeat is unthinkable have much less incentive to heed or serve their constituents than officials whose careers are even slightly precarious. Obviously, practical considerations like the underlying partisanship of many jurisdictions and the popularity of many incumbents shrink the odds of truly competitive elections in most states and districts. Even taking these considerations into account, however, the number of contested races, particularly for the House of Representatives, has sunk to dangerously low levels: as of August 6, 2002, nonpartisan observers believed that just 39 House districts out of 435 were "in play" in the 2002 elections, a phenomenally small number in a redistricting year and one that left more than 90 percent of Americans living in districts written off that November.[2]

Second, we would point to the importance of citizen participation. Voting is the main form of participation, but not the only one. Citizens may also participate in politics by becoming candidates for office, an enormous but vital commitment. Scholars are largely agreed that the difficulty in recruiting candidates is a principal reason for the lack of competition in elections.[3] We should also not forget another group of participants, the shrinking percentage of Americans who volunteer on election campaigns or partisan endeavors.[4] These activists have always been a small minority of the population, but their energy and commitment are vitally important to the system. On a practical level, we know that personal face-to-face contact is the most effective way to increase voting. But our interest in volunteerism is broader, for we would argue that politics—and political careers—begin with local associations, local issues, and local organizations. Replacing that activity with a system driven by cadres of professionals, mainly in Washington, threatens to turn citizens into passive consumers of politics instead of active participants.[5]

Finally, there is accountability, a term we used earlier with reference to parties. In this case, however, we refer not just to voters' ability to hold groups of officials responsible for the actions of government, but their ability to assess individual candidates on their own actions and words. Much as we might like to see more informative and perhaps higher-minded campaigns, we know of no easily applicable standards to judge them or means to achieve them. Instead, we do insist on the simpler idea that it be relatively uncomplicated for voters to associate candidates with the ideals they actually espouse, the programs they actually propose, and the tactics they actually use. Transparency, a main goal of both FECA and the Bipartisan Campaign Reform Act (BCRA), is indispensable for informing voter choice and influencing candidates' behavior in addition to its value as a deterrent to influence peddling.

The explosion of candidate-oriented issue ads undermines all of these goals. To begin with, issue advocacy has radically escalated the financial arms race for candidates and all other participants in elections. The average spending by winning House candidates has nearly tripled over the last twenty years, with almost half of that increase coming after the first widespread use of issue ads in 1996.[6] Astonishing as the average expenditures of 2000's winners—over $850,000—may seem, this number is actually misleading because the vast majority of incumbents faced little more than token opposition. Candidates in the most competitive races averaged closer to $1.5 million.[7] Issue ads have helped drive these expenditures up by forcing candidates to consider not only what their opponents may do with hard money but also what outside groups do with soft money. Candidates have responded by raising more, spending more, and saving more; FEC reports show candidates with considerably more cash on hand following the 1998 and 2000 elections than previously.[8] And parties, given the opportunity to avoid limits on coordinated expenditures that encouraged them to allocate their resources over many states and districts, have spent most of their issue advocacy dollars on just a handful of the best-funded House and Senate candidates, further raising costs in these races.[9]

This increased spending raises the fund-raising bar for candidates and potential candidates. For individuals contemplating a run for federal office, the question that they have long been confronted with—"How much money can you raise?"—has taken on new urgency and new dimensions as the price of viability goes up and up.[10] It is obvious that the rising costs likely price some potential candidates out of the market, affecting both the nature of choices in many races (owing to the effort to recruit rich candidates able to finance their own campaigns) and its existence in others (where potentially viable candidates choose not to run).[11] For the candidates who do run, the constant attention to their fund-raising becomes another hurdle as parties and groups who run issue ads try to "target" their efforts in races where their spending might tip the balance. Thus a challenger who has raised $1 million (no longer such an impressive amount) and is a half dozen points back in the polls is seen as a less fruitful investment than one who has raised $2 million and is only three points behind, even though victory seems solidly in reach for both of them. The result is that standards of viability rise steadily, leaving fewer races that seem winnable or worth investing in. Put another way, back in August 2002, when most campaigns had barely begun to contact the public, it seemed highly unlikely that just 39 House seats were "in play" in November in the sense that victory was an all but foregone conclusion for one of the candidates.[12]

The emphasis on financial resources also leaves nonfinancial resources undervalued. One sign is that candidates with potentially strong bases of support or formidable organizational capacity are often overlooked in favor of those with healthy bank accounts. Another is something we discussed earlier in reference to party building: the failure of the parties to invest resources in their organizational structures. Their approach has been driven by demands to provide direct aid to candidates, particularly television advertisements. The result is that state and local parties have been used to move money around and to purchase advertising, not to build strong organizations, recruit activists, or engage in grassroots campaigning. Many interest groups play a similar game, focusing on advertising to the apparent exclusion of almost everything else.[13] Citizens are left as passive consumers of political campaigns conducted for their benefit by trained professionals rather than as participants in the struggle to lead the nation. Granted, technological change has played the major role in this transformation, but the growth of issue advertising has accelerated the process, leaving the grassroots to wither.

Finally, the impact of issue advocacy on accountability is unmistakably disastrous. The Annenberg Public Policy Center keeps tabs on over 100 groups (excluding parties) that sponsored issue ads in 2000. Some were familiar, but many others—Voters for Campaign Truth, Aretino Industries, Montanans for Common Sense Mining Laws, American Seniors, Inc.—were organizations about which literally nothing was publicly known, including information about their sponsors, their finances, and the extent of their activities.[14] Others, of course, turned out to be fronts for trade associations, labor unions, and even wealthy individuals, but these revelations came courtesy of reporters or, in some cases, the groups themselves. By creating organizations with names like Citizens for Better

Medicare (Pharmaceutical Research and Manufacturers Association) or American Family Voices (American Federation of State, Local and Municipal Employees), the sponsors added credibility to their appeals and offered anonymity to their donors, but these advantages were realized only by withholding information from the public.[15] By comparison with all other players in campaigns—candidates, parties, and PACs—these organizations were enigmas.

Beyond the true identities of many issue advocates, there is also their relationship to the candidates' campaigns. In many instances, the degree of synchronization between the issue advocates and the candidates' campaigns belie the notion that issue ads are truly independent. For example, candidate ads in 1998 and 2000 were overwhelmingly positive in their tone, commercials whose primary purpose was to "promote" a specific candidate. Issue ads, by contrast, were rarely positive; instead they usually concentrated on attacking the opponent or, somewhat less frequently, on drawing contrasts between pairs of candidates. Even ads that contrast candidates often have a critical edge to them, making them similar to pure attack ads. This pattern suggests a division of labor in campaigns where candidates take the high road and issue advocates are left to do the dirty work of bloodying the other side.[16] We are skeptical that viewers even noticed this division of labor, yet its existence illustrates the difficulty voters face in determining who bears responsibility for the commercials they see.

THE CORRUPTIVE POTENTIAL OF ISSUE ADVOCACY

Issue advocacy, being in part a style of advertising, presents a somewhat different set of challenges to the integrity of the electoral system than does soft money. Those challenges, however, include many of the same concerns relevant to our earlier discussion of soft money and corruption. In particular, we believe that issue advocacy also produces special avenues of legislative influence for their sponsors and funders. The structure of the campaign finance system and the interests of the players within it make issue advocacy an attractive tool for those seeking to influence public officials. In this section, we return to the same definition of corruption we used earlier in conjunction with soft money to address the corruptive potential of issue advocacy.

Our analysis begins with the secrecy surrounding issue ads. Earlier we noted the nearly complete lack of disclosure of receipts and expenditures for issue advocacy, and how it reduces citizens' ability to discern the source of many of the communications they witness during a campaign. Secrecy is one of the outstanding characteristics of issue ads, especially those financed by interest groups. As a result, we—and regulators—are hampered by a remarkable paucity of information about them. The media tracking data fill in some of the blanks, but many key factual questions remain unanswered or may be answered only after painstaking investigation. Nonetheless, the dangers of issue advocacy are plain to see.

This secrecy, by itself, creates enormous opportunities for wrongdoing, for favors to be exchanged between issue advocates and public officials. Disclosure, of course, is a main accomplishment of FECA; it was seen by its sponsors and by the Supreme Court as an essential element—along with limits on contributions to candidates—in the Congress's system to guard against various forms of corruption. In fact, disclosure has been a central feature in reforms long predating FECA and in most states, and courts across the land have repeatedly affirmed attempts to make campaigns report their financial transactions.[17] Among its various advantages, disclosure is thought to combat corruption by illuminating the dark corners in which undue influence may be exerted far from public view. The idea is that politicians eager for popularity and votes will be loath to enter into situations that cast doubt on their probity; thus the more these situations are revealed, the stronger the politician's impulse to avoid them.

One of the ironies of this litigation is that many of BCRA's opponents are otherwise champions of disclosure. A serious argument advanced, primarily by conservatives, holds that campaign financing ought to be deregulated and disclosed, since transparency alone is sufficient to ensure against corruption. We remain thoroughly skeptical about the full sweep of these claims, yet we share the same desire to shed light on the financial transactions of campaigning. The public's interest in revealing these transactions is countered by the private interest of many groups and donors to keep them secret. Thus the ability to route money to groups for candidate-oriented issue ads without disclosure has attracted an increasing amount of money to this activity. In the growing opaqueness of campaign financing, the opportunity for donors and officeholders to forge close relationships or strike deals without risk of detection increases, too.

Among the mysterious groups sponsoring issue ads or the mysterious donors funding various organizations—all without making information known to the public—the example of "Republicans for Clean Air" stands out. This group sponsored ads praising then-Governor George W. Bush and criticizing Senator John McCain before the 2000 Republican presidential primaries in three states. Eventually, after the first of these primaries

(South Carolina's) reporters uncovered that Republicans for Clean Air consisted of two brothers, Charles and Sam Wyly, long-time friends and supporters of Governor Bush. Charles Wyly, in fact, was an authorized fund-raiser for the Bush campaign.

One remarkable aspect of this situation is that the pivotal South Carolina primary came and went without voters there discovering who was responsible for these ads. At the same time, it is impossible to imagine officials of the Bush campaign were in the dark about Republicans for Clean Air. According to press estimates, the Wylys spent $25 million on their ads for Governor Bush.[18] We find it inconceivable that an expenditure of that magnitude could remain unknown to the small circle of financial leaders close to both the Bush campaign and the Wylys (including Charles Wyly himself) or the even smaller circle of Republican media consultants. When the Wylys' involvement was later uncovered during the New York primary, the news qualified as a small bombshell and led to a wave of publicity critical of the brothers and the Bush campaign, which in turn distanced itself from Republicans for Clean Air.[19] After the election, knowledge of the Wylys' activities during the primaries inspired reporters to pay particular attention to the brothers' role in advising the vice president in connection with his energy task force.[20] In sum, we have a major campaign conducted in secrecy during a key part of the 2000 Republican primary campaign, and a marked change in the level of scrutiny once its sponsors became known. Much as we applaud the ingenuity of the reporters who eventually broke the story, we strongly believe that there is a compelling governmental interest in making these facts known to all from the start. BCRA would accomplish this.

Finally, issue advocacy, like soft money, allows funds from corporate and union treasuries to return to the electoral sphere after decades of absence. The purpose of the long-standing bans on these funds is multifaceted, but we focus on their potential to corrupt. That potential is largely determined by the sheer size of the financial resources available to corporations and unions. We do not pretend that wealthy individuals like the Wylys cannot mobilize enormous sums of money, but corporate and union assets dwarf all but the largest personal fortunes. Congressional fears of the potential impact of these funds both on elections and on legislative processes were a main reason for prohibiting them. We see the dangers as no less real today, especially as the technology of campaigning has changed and the emphasis on money has increased enormously along with the willingness of many corporate and union leaders to participate in the electoral arena. For legislators to defy the wishes of Bill Gates or the executives of Microsoft is one thing; to defy Microsoft itself—should the company choose to dedicate a substantial part of its treasury to federal electioneering—remains quite another. It is difficult to point to specific examples of corporate influence felt through issue advocacy because of the newness of the phenomenon and the lack of disclosure. But, to cite one example, the potential for legislators to perceive greatly higher stakes in the lobbying they receive from the pharmaceutical industry because of the millions of corporate funds spent on candidate-oriented issue ads by Citizens for Better Medicare seems real enough.

APPEARANCES

Assessing public perceptions of candidate-oriented issue ads and their impact on public opinion is difficult because of the sheer complexity of the subject. Few people are aware of the distinction between express and issue advocacy, let alone the enormous consequences for behavior that flow from it. But because citizens are the intended audience for these ads, it is fair to ask what they think of them. The best answer to this question comes from *Dictum without Data* by Professor David Magleby. Magleby conducted a survey using interactive television to show combinations of eight different issue ads aired in 2000 to a sample of 2,035 respondents.[21] All of the ads—a pair of spots from the presidential campaigns, from the parties' national committees, and from interest groups (one favoring Bush and the other favoring Gore), as well as two "pure" issue ads that mentioned no candidates—are entirely typical of the different types of commercials that aired in 2000.[22] Respondents were shown a random selection of three of the eight ads, eliminating concerns about ordering effects. Several of their perceptions are relevant here.

When asked to assess the "*primary* objective or purpose of the ad" (emphasis in the original), at least 85 percent of respondents found that the four issue ads by parties and interest groups were intended to persuade them to vote for or (much more often) against a candidate and only as many as 11 percent thought one of these ads was concerned mainly with presenting an issue.[23] In contrast, viewers were less likely to interpret the candidates' ads as electioneering (the results ranged between 64 and 74 percent) and more likely to see them as issue-oriented (20 and 30 percent).[24] These conclusions held for both the pro-Bush and pro-Gore ads in each category. It is likely that the issue ads seemed more partisan than those sponsored by the candidates because parties and groups criticized the opposing candidate, while the Bush and Gore ads featured them speaking on camera about their plans without mentioning the other. This pattern is familiar; the overwhelming majority of candidate ads are positive in tone, while parties and groups emphasize attacks or commercials that contrast the candidates.[25] Respondents did draw an enormous distinction between these spots and the pure issue ads: at least 70 percent felt the primary objective of these latter ads was to present an issue and just 13 percent perceived any electoral purpose. In short, respondents' perceptions of the intent of the ads were remarkably accurate.

The respondents were less accurate, however, in determining who was responsible for a commercial.[26] In response to the question asking who paid for an ad, just over 60 percent of survey participants correctly attributed the candidate ads and the pure issue ads to their actual sponsors. Identification of the sponsors of the candidate-oriented issue ads was much more scattered, with most people (38 to 48 percent) assuming in each case that they came from candidates and fewest (9 to 18 percent) assuming that they were paid for by an interest group. These results, of course, suggest that the disclaimers that appear on these ads are almost completely ineffective. We applaud the section of BCRA mandating that they be made more prominent. But even if they were easier to read, we suspect that viewers would judge the ads on their underlying message, not the accompanying attribution. The confusion over sponsorship also illustrates the problem of accountability created by these advertisements, for one would need a fair amount of expertise, sharp eyes, and perhaps research skills to determine who was behind many of the commercials on television in an election year.

Ultimately, do these candidate-oriented issue ads, however confusing, appear corrupting to citizens? From our perspective there is no doubt that they do. The combination of findings above—candidate-oriented ads are seen as electioneering and they are frequently assumed to come from the candidate—show that the distinction between the actions of candidates and those of parties and interest groups is largely lost. By itself, the conflation of candidates with other, self-interested actors is disturbing and gives the appearance of impropriety. It also indicates that efforts to keep these actors separate from one another have little impact on public opinion. Citizens have the opportunity to view the results of decisions that candidates, parties, interest groups, and their legions of consultants make, but they are in no position to see how these decisions get made or whether deals are made and understandings reached. From the perspective of the nation's living rooms, most of the ads by parties and interest groups are no different from those by the candidates, nor do citizens have any reason, aside from blind faith, to assume that allies are not working in concert.

We conclude by recalling that campaign finance law is intended to increase public confidence in elections and campaigns. Yet the campaign finance system, without BCRA, asks citizens to disregard what they see, hear, and think—that the issue ads on their television sets are clearly designed to help or hurt a candidate—and believe that they are watching a rational, nonpartisan discussion of issues. No confidence can be built on a public reaction that either their senses are deceiving them or that their government is. We would argue that campaign finance law must have "integrity," so that undermining that integrity is neither good for the perception of the law nor for the government that makes it. The rise of candidate-oriented issue ads in recent elections has made a mockery of FECA, diminishing the transparency of its regime and demeaning its reasonable limits on contributions. Many Americans see those ads as no different from those run by candidates except that they are generally meaner and more aggressive. Pretending they are not campaigning generates further cynicism about the law and damages public confidence that the government has the will and means to restore its integrity.

NOTES

1. This includes two of the main precedents cited by the *Buckley* v. *Valeo,* 425 U.S. 946 (1976) court: *Burroughs* v. *United States,* 290 U.S. 534 (1934), and *Ex parte Yarbrough*, 110 U.S. 651 (1884). See Frank J. Sorauf, "Caught in a Political Thicket: The Supreme Court and Campaign Finance," *Constitutional Commentary,* vol. 3, no. 1 (1986); Frank J. Sorauf, "Politics, Experience, and the First Amendment: The Case of American Campaign Finance," *Columbia Law Review,* vol. 94, no. 2 (1994).

2. Adam Nagourney, "Economy Stirs G.O.P. Worry in House Races," *New York Times,* August 6, 2002.

3. For example, see Gary C. Jacobson and Samuel Kernell, *Strategy and Choice in Congressional Elections* (Yale University Press, 1984).

4. Robert D. Putnam, *Bowling Alone: The Collapse and Revival of American Community* (Simon & Schuster, 2000), chap. 2.

5. For a broader discussion of the larger issue, see ibid.

6. Federal Election Commission, *FEC Reports on Congressional Financial Activity for 2000* (www.fec.gov/press/051501congfinact/051501congfinact.html [May 15, 2001]).

7. www.cfinst.org/studies/vital/3-3.htm.

8. For House figures, see Federal Election Commission, *Financial Activity of General Election U.S. House of Representatives Candidates—1988–2000* (www.fec.

gov/press/051501congfinact/tables/gehouse/html [May 15, 2001]). For Senate figures, see Federal Election Commission, *Financial Activity of General Election Senate Candidates—1988–2000* (www.fec.gov/press/051501congfinact/tables/gesenate/html [May 15, 2001]).

9. This reflects the parties' effort to choose races where their involvement might tip the balance. But with parties and many interest groups all trying to do the same thing, outside involvement is concentrated in relatively few districts. Because of diminishing marginal returns, it is unclear whether this spending has any appreciable impact on the vote. See Jonathan S. Krasno, "The Electoral Impact of 'Issue Advocacy' in 1998 and 2000 House Races," in Kenneth Goldstein and Patricia Strach, eds., *The Medium and the Message* (Upper Saddle River, N.J.: Prentice-Hall, 2003).

10. On the number of challengers raising various amounts of money, see www.fec.gov/press/051501congfinact/tables/number_of_house_nonincumbents.html.

11. The fact that the number of competitive House races (including 1998 and 2000) has fallen to its lowest point in several decades during a period in which party and interest group spending on issue ads was plentiful and matched by a rise in candidate receipts suggests, contrary to the conventional wisdom, that inadequate overall funding in not a main reason for the shortage of hard-fought campaigns.

12. Adam Nagourney, "Economy Stirs G.O.P. Worry in House Races," *New York Times,* August 6, 2002.

13. The AFL-CIO, the NAACP, and the Christian Coalition are notable exceptions.

14. Annenberg Public Policy Center, Issue Advocacy Profiles, *Club for Growth* (www.appcpenn.org/issueads/gindex.htm, last modified January 2001).

15. Sometimes the benefits of a particular name are subtle. We found identical ads aired against two Republican incumbents by separate interest groups, FAIR and Coalition for the Future American Worker.

16. This situation is similar to earlier allegations that the Bush campaign of 1988 quietly encouraged Americans for Bush, an independent group, to air an ad that used Willie Horton's mug shot, allowing the campaign to disclaim any responsibility for this commercial.

17. Indeed the first precedent on campaign financing noted by the *Buckley* court, *Burroughs* v. *United States,* involved the constitutionality of disclosure requirements. See Sorauf, "Caught in a Political Thicket: The Supreme Court and Campaign Finance."

18. The $25 million figure comes from the Annenberg Public Policy Center.

19. T. Christian Miller and Janet Wilson, "Campaign 2000: McCain Blasts Pro-Bush TV Ad Campaign Financed by Texans," *Los Angeles Times,* March 4, 2000, p. A16.

20. Craig Gordon, "The Fight for Computer Associates," *Newsday,* July 2, 2001, p. A3.

21. David B. Magleby, *Dictum without Data: The Myth of Issue Advocacy and Party Building* (www.byu.edu/outsidemoney/dictum/index.html).

22. The two interest group ads were American Family Voices, which attacked Governor Bush as beholden to special interests, and the Republican Leader Coalition, which criticized Vice President Gore for his stands on Medicare and Social Security.

23. Magleby, *Dictum without Data.*

24. We discuss twin sets of numbers because two ads were shown in each category, one favorable to Bush and one to Gore.

25. Jonathan S. Krasno and Kenneth M. Goldstein, "The Facts about Television Advertising and the McCain-Feingold Bill," *PS: Political Science,* vol. 35 (June 2002), pp. 207–12.

26. All the results discussed in this paragraph are summarized in Magleby, *Dictum without Data.*

Rebuttal to the Expert Reports of Kenneth M. Goldstein and Jonathan S. Krasno and Frank J. Sorauf

James L. Gibson

James L. Gibson is the Sidney W. Souers Professor of Government at Washington University. He was the primary consultant for Senator Mitch McConnell of Kentucky and the AFL-CIO, who were among the lead plaintiffs in the case. On behalf of these plaintiffs, Gibson conducted a critique and secondary data analysis of the data proffered by Kenneth Goldstein and Jonathan Krasno. His report provides a glimpse into some of the substantive and methodological issues raised in connection with the case. This is an unedited version of his rebuttal report, the second of three reports he prepared. Gibson issued an initial report on September 30, 2002, a rebuttal report on October 7, 2002, and a supplemental report on November 5, 2002, all three of which are available online.

In my review of the original *Buying Time* reports (1998 and 2000), I drew several major conclusions about the reports, their conclusions, and the data upon which the studies were based. It is perhaps useful to begin this rebuttal with a brief restatement of these conclusions.

—As provided by Professor Goldstein, the 1998 and 2000 data bases are riddled with errors and inconsistencies and the findings of the reports cannot be replicated from the data.

—The key measures that are the focus of this litigation require highly subjective assessments and the student coders making those judgments never received any instruction on how to exercise their enormous discretion.

—The data bases are constantly being manipulated by Professor Goldstein, with many iterations of new scores being produced for the variables of primary interest in this litigation.

—Thus, the conclusions from those reports should not be accepted.

—Indeed, to the extent that the data bases are able to support any conclusions, they are that the ads under consideration in this litigation have policy matters as their primary focus and therefore to ban or regulate them would be a substantial intrusion upon the freedom of interest groups to communicate with citizens and to attempt to shape public policy.

I will focus this rebuttal to the expert reports around the question of whether my conclusions are altered by the reports or the new data analysis that underlies them. I conclude that nothing in these reports has caused me to change the conclusions I expressed in my report of 9/30/12002.[1] Since nearly all of these issues are common to both the 1998 and 2000 studies, I will generally integrate my discussion of these studies in the analysis that follows.

REPUDIATING THE RESULTS FROM
BUYING TIME 1998 AND *BUYING TIME 2000*

These new reports make plain that the authors and I agree on one basic point: The statistical analyses presented in *Buying Time 1998* and *Buying Time 2000* should not be accepted. Professor Goldstein now reports entirely new estimates of the effect of the Bipartisan Campaign Reform Act (BCRA) on "genuine issue speech,"[2] thereby repudiating the figures reported in *Buying Time 2000,* and Dr. Krasno and Professor Sorauf report new estimates for 1998 that differ from the numbers reported in *Buying Time 1998.*

The same conclusion applies to the data bases. Professor Goldstein has provided with his expert report yet another version of the 2000 data base, so presumably the earlier versions are defunct and should not be relied upon. Dr. Krasno and Professor Sorauf do not provide a newer version of the 1998 data base, but do offer calculations in the appendix that apparently render the old data base obsolete. I assume that one day these data bases will be archived and made available for use by other interested scholars, as most data bases of this sort are, and that at that point the authors will create clean, properly documented, and final versions of the data bases.[3] That day has not yet arrived.

As I have noted, the Buying Time data and studies are constantly evolving (with changes apparently being made in the codes of airings even in connection with this litigation), and with the conclusions of the authors representing targets that are always on the move. But at the same time, details about the methods employed by the studies are slowly beginning to emerge. Let us consider first the basic question of the quality of the data collected by Campaign and Media Analysis Group (CMAG).

ERRORS IN THE CMAG DATA

The data collected by CMAG deserve closer scrutiny than they have received to date. Professor Goldstein professes confidence in these data,[4] but considerable empirical evidence exists to suggest that this confidence is misplaced. The CMAG data base should be scrutinized from several vantage points:

1) Were all of the airings represented in the data base in fact aired?

2) Does the data base represent all ads aired or instead were some airings not captured by the CMAG technology?

3) Did the CMAG "analysts" accurately code the content of the ads?

4) Was CMAG in fact able to capture storyboards for every unique ad? Unfortunately, the answers to some of these questions cast very serious **doubt** on the CMAG data.

I have access to no independent information with which I can verify that the airings represented in the CMAG data base were actually broadcast, or that the information captured is in fact accurate.[5] However, Professor Goldstein has presented some evidence in his paper entitled "Measuring Exposure to Campaign Advertising" indicating that the accuracy of the information collected is certainly less than perfect (see Ridout et al. 2002).[6]

An equally serious issue is whether the data base fails to capture all ads that are broadcast. The available evidence suggests that there are some very serious omissions.

Professor Goldstein has reported that he compared the information in the CMAG data base with the actual billing records of eight television stations in five different markets (see Ridout et al. 2002). He discovered that the error rate of the CMAG data varied from 0 to 20% (see Table 2, page 28).[7] From the figures reported in Table 2, we can derive an estimate of the overall degree of accuracy of the CMAG data base.

Note first that station billing invoices appear to document more ads than found in the data base in every one of the stations examined. Thus, the CMAG data always under represent the number of airings by each of these television stations.

By how much does the data base under-represent actual broadcasts in 2000? We can derive an estimate quite simply. For instance, the 8,526 airings in the data base for WJRT apparently represent 99 percent[8] of the actual airings broadcast by WJRT. Applying the arithmetic, this means that WJRT probably broadcast 8,612 spots, and that the CMAG methodology therefore failed to capture 86 of these.[9] Applying this methodology to the figures for each of the stations, we discover that the CMAG data for these 8 stations likely missed 1,764 ads.[10] This represents a small percentage of the overall airings of these eight stations (5.04%), but when this proportion is applied to the data base as a whole, it translates into an estimate of 48,864 airings that in fact were broadcast but that were not captured by the CMAG methodology. This is a sizable number indeed. Moreover, the number is of sufficient magnitude that failure to include these airings 'in the analysis most likely biases the substantive conclusions drawn from the data base.

We do not know any of the characteristics of these 48,864 missing airings. But one might reasonably hypothesize that the clearer and more obvious the political content of an airing, the more likely it is to have been included by the CMAG analyst. Conversely, to the extent that ads did not have a clear "political purpose" that could be discerned by the CMAG analysts, the more likely they were to have been excluded from the data base by the analysts. Thus, it seems reasonable to assume that these 48,864 missing airings are not simply a random sub-set of the data, but instead tend to include a disproportionate number of "genuine issue ads."

Having addressed the "errors of omission" in the CMAG data base, I now consider the evidence on "errors of commission." In footnote 4 (page 17) of the Ridout et al. paper, the authors note an important anomaly in the CMAG data base: ". . . some advertisements . . . . were never coded in the original data set [the student codings of the ads]. This is because these ads were not political, but were nonetheless included in the data provided by CMAG." This sentence raises a host of questions about the data base, including: What criteria did CMAG employ for selecting ads to be included in the data base? How was the content of the ads (e.g., "political" versus not) coded, and by whom, according to what criteria, and with what degree of reliability? Perhaps this problem with the CMAG data accounts for some basic puzzles and discrepancies in the data base.

Finally, I return to the inability of the CMAG technology to capture text and storyboards for each unique ad. Because the technology cannot distinguish airings that are very similar but not identical, so-called cookie-cutter ads are not properly represented in the data base. The failure to capture all airings of all unique ads is a very serious limitation of the data base.

In conclusion, the CMAG data are apparently plagued by numerous errors, making reliance on these data bases for drawing conclusions about the nature of political communications in the United States extremely precarious, hazardous, and subject to error.

THE EVOLUTION OF QUESTION II

The second portion of the data bases used for these two reports was created by the student coders at Arizona State University and the University of Wisconsin. In the 2000 data set, Professor Goldstein provides yet another incarnation of the ad's scores on the all-important Question 11.[11] In the 2000 data set appended as Appendix L to his expert report, an entirely new variable can be found. This variable was not present in any of the earlier versions of the data base previously provided by either Professor Goldstein or the Brennan Center. The name and label of this variable are:

BT00_Q11 oldest available q 11 codes (older than feb version)

This variable is of considerable interest given the importance of Question 11 to the findings and conclusions of Professor Goldstein's expert report. Where it came from, what it means (the individual response codes on the variable, ranging from 0 to 99, are unlabelled),[12] how it was match/merged to this data set, and indeed whether it is in fact the "oldest available" incarnation of Q 11 all remain open questions. I assume that this variable gets closer to representing the original codes assigned to the ads by the student coders at the University of Wisconsin. I do not know if in fact some earlier version of this variable exists.[13]

Many issues surround the coding of Question 11 by the students and by Professor Goldstein. Since new information about this variable has come to light in Professor Goldstein's expert report, how this information about the ads was created deserves some additional scrutiny.

INTER-CODER RELIABILITY. In my report of 9/30/2002, I offered an analysis of both the reliability and validity of the information collected by the students. I surmised in that report that no formal test of inter-coder reliability was conducted in 1998. Nothing in the new expert reports leads me to a different conclusion about the 1998 data.

However, new information does indeed emerge about the 2000 data. In Appendix I to his expert report, Professor Goldstein offers a copy of a paper currently under review at *Political Communication.* In this paper, consideration of the reliability of the variables is presented, beginning on page 17 and extending through page 2 1. Here, the author reports an analysis of "the accuracy of the human coding" (page 17), based on a randomly selected sample of " 150 unique advertisements from the over 4,000 advertisements airing in 2000" (page 17)[14] Goldstein asserts: "As part of a larger project, we asked five undergraduate students to code the ads using our coding sheet, thus allowing us to compare our original coding with five independent assessments. We then compared each coder's results with those of the CMAG data base" (pages 17–18). Several questions about this process emerge.

One first wonders about how Professor Goldstein compared the new codings to the "original coding." Is the original coding represented in the variable "BT00_Ql1 oldest available q 11 codes (older than feb version)"? If so, why is this variable referred to as the "oldest available" incarnation of the coding rather than the "original version" of the variable? This a most troubling discrepancy, unless BT00_Q 11 purports to be the scores assigned to the ads by the students and before the various post-coding manipulations and changes by Professor Goldstein.

This "test" of the accuracy of the coding relies upon 143 advertisements (since some of the 150 selected had to be discarded due to the discrepancies in the CMAG data base). In order to establish the relevance of this test to the issues in this litigation some considerable attention must be given to this sample of 143 airings.

Consider the 2000 data base and the coding of Question 11 in the version represented by BT00_Q 11. Once four pesky airings are removed from the data base, 970,424 airings remain.[15] When aggregated by the ad identification number, this produces 3,111 unique ads (or ads found to be unique by virtue of their ad identification number, to be absolutely precise).[16] Of these airings, 2 seemed to have been coded differently at different times (i.e., for different airings) on the "earliest known" Question 11. Furthermore, the student coders assigned what are apparently missing data scores to 19 of the ads.[17] Of the remaining ads, 2,953 were said to be "electioneering" ads (promoting support or opposition for a candidate) and only 127 ads were scored as providing information or urging actions ("genuine issue ads").

This distribution on the "purpose" variable has two very important consequences. First, in statistics, we call this a "skewed" distribution since almost all of the cases are scored in a particular way (and in the sense that deviation from a 50/50 split is extreme). When a variable is highly skewed, as this one, sampling cases on this variable becomes very difficult. A randomly selected sample of 100 ads from this "population" of 3,111 would be expected to find only 4 ads (actually 4.1 ads) that were coded as issue ads. A sample of 150 ads would be expected to generate 6 issue ads; and a sample of 250 would be expected to include no more than 10 issue ads. Thus, if one took a sample of 150 ads as Professor Goldstein asserts in his paper, one would find only a tiny number of ads that were coded as having a "purpose" of providing information or urging action.[18] Since group-sponsored ads constitute less than 14% of the data base from which the sample was apparently drawn, one would expect that 21 group ads were included in the inter-coder reliability data base (and of course that a tiny number of ads would be group-sponsored issue ads).

Consequently, any conclusions about whether this sort of ad was in fact reliably coded cannot be accepted on the basis of an examination of such a small number of ads. Perhaps this reliability test provides some information about candidate and party ads, but it provides virtually no useful information about group-sponsored ads and especially the degree to which group-sponsored ads were reliably and validly coded as to the "purpose" of the ad.[19]

A second consequence of this distribution is that, for whatever reasons, the overwhelming decision of the coders was that these ads represent electioneering. Issue ads were not quite the equivalent of needles in a haystack, but they were exceedingly rare. Thus, it seems quite likely that even after coding only a few ads, the coders developed a strong expectation, implicit or explicit, that the next ad they coded would be an electioneering ad. It is very difficult to make subjective assessments of infrequently occurring events. Once a coder discerns a pattern in the responses to a subjective variable, it becomes difficult indeed for the coder to "break the habit." Especially in a circumstance in which there is an ideologically charged bias in favor of finding a particular outcome, "true" issue ads had a very heavy burden to overcome among the coders.

SUBSTANTIVE CONSIDERATION OF THE RESULTS FROM QUESTION II

As I have noted, both Professor Goldstein and Dr. Krasno/Professor Sorauf have provided in their expert reports new estimates of the percentage of "genuine" ads/airings that mention or depict candidates and that were aired within the last 60 days of an election. Notwithstanding the flaws in their data bases, it is important that we give their reports close scrutiny.

Professor Goldstein offers Table 7 (immediately following page 24) as his calculations on the 2000 data base. He concludes:

. . . . there is persuasive evidence that the BCRA definition of Electioneering Communication is not overbroad in the sense of applying to any meaningful number of advertisements that are perceived as Genuine Issue Ads. Using the coder's classifications, only 3.1 percent of the 45,001 Genuine Issue Ads broadcast by interest groups during the 2000 election cycle would have been covered by BCRA. (Pp. 26–27)

The denominator he uses for these calculations—45,001—represents the number of "genuine issue ads" broadcast in 2000. In the use of such a

Table 1. *Six Advertisements Prohibited under BCRA That Goldstein Considers "Genuine Issue Ads"*

Ad number	Media market	Name of advertisement
627	KY/CFAW	Call Northrup
1389	FAIR/IA	Latham Foreign Worker Bill
2862	UT/COC	Matheson Can't Decide Rx
1269	CBM/Rx	Plan for Seniors 60
1367	RI/RIWV	Langevin Abortion
2107	WI/NPLA	Feingold Kohl Abortion 60

denominator, Professor Goldstein is at odds with both the authors of *Buying Time* 2000 and with me. But in order to make some progress, let us put aside the denominator issue for a moment and focus on the numerator.

In his expert report, Professor Goldstein analyzes only 6 ads as "genuine issue ads" that would be prohibited under the criteria adopted in BCRA. These ads are [shown above].

These six advertisements were aired 2,123 times in 2000. It is instructive to look at the results of the three codings on Question 11 as they have evolved over the course of the different manipulations of the data set. Figure 1 reports the transformation of these variables as represented in the most recent version of the 2000 data provided by Professor Goldstein as an appendix to his expert report.

The figure makes plain that these ads/airings were transformed from being coded entirely as issue ads to being almost entirely represented as electioneering ads! I recognize that Professor Goldstein, in his expert report, has converted these six ads yet again, changing them back to issue ads as originally coded by the students. But the treatment of these ads demonstrates two important points: Coding these ads is highly subjective and reasonable people disagree about their content, and Professor Goldstein seems to have claimed the authority to manipulate the data base at will.

As noted above, Professor Goldstein identifies 6 ads in 2000 that would be adversely and unfairly affected because they are "genuine issue ads," broadcast in the last 60 days of the election, and mentioning candidates. Two of these ads (#1367 and #2107) are included in the 30 ads I focused on in my discussion of the 2000 data (see pages 62–63 in my report of 9/30/2002). It is instructive to revisit this analysis based on the new claim by Professor Goldstein that these six ads should now be identified as "genuine issue ads" in the 2000 data base.

Figure 1. *The Transformation of the Coding of Question 11*

Percent of coded issue ads

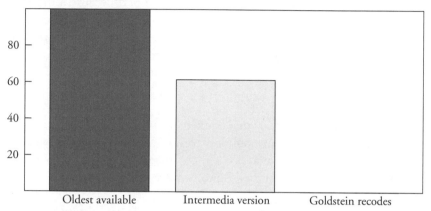

Note: The percentage for the Goldstein transformation of the variable is .4%. Number of airings = 2,123.

Putting these two samples together, we find that these 34 ads (Professor Goldstein's six plus my non-duplicative ads) were aired 15,347 times during the last 60 days of the 2000 election, according to the data base. Using the denominator from my 9/30/2002 report, these airings therefore represent 25.6 % of the 60,006 issue airings (without "magic words") within 60 days of the 2000 election and which depicted or mentioned candidates. What this demonstrates again is that Professor Goldstein's estimates of the impact of the three criteria are wholly dependent on the subjective assessments of the "purpose" of individual ads, assessments that are reasonably subject to debate.

As I noted in my report of 9/30/2002, a more reliable variable exists characterizing the content of the ads. The students were asked to code Question 27:

27. In your judgment, is the primary focus of this ad on the personal characteristics of either candidate or on policy matters?

   1. Policy matters
   2. Personal characteristics
   3. Both
   4. Neither

In my opening report of 9/30/2002, I set forth the view that the data produced by this question are of superior reliability and validity.

The coding on Question 27 is more reliable in part because it does not seem to have been subject to the post-coding manipulations inflicted on Question 11. If we consider once more the ads with the three important characteristics, we discover that the "primary focus" of 51,144 airings was on policy matters. Applying the Goldstein denominator:

$$51,144/60,623 = 84.4\%$$

This means that any policy that banned ads with these three characteristics would in fact pertain to political communications that overwhelmingly (84.4 %) had policy matters as their "primary" focus. Or to restate Professor Goldstein's conclusions 7 and 8 (page 3):

> 7. An extremely large percentage (84.4 %) of the political television ads aired during 2000 that would have been covered by BCRA were perceived by project coders as having policy matters as their primary focus.

> 8. BCRA requirements would have applied to 42.9 % of ads broadcast by interest groups during 2000 which were perceived by the coders as having policy matters as their "primary focus."[20]

COMPARING THE CHARACTERISTICS OF ADS

In Table 9 of his expert report, Professor Goldstein reports data apparently designed to demonstrate that a) "Interest Group Ads with No Candidate" differ from "Interest Group Ads Mentioning Candidate 60 Days Before General Election," and b) that the latter share some characteristics with "Ads run by Candidates" and "Political Party Ads." The first part of this analysis is indeed interesting, although to the extent that the two types of issue ads do not exhibit different characteristics, the second pail of the inquiry is not particularly revealing or relevant. Therefore, I set out to test the hypothesis that the two types of issue ads identified by Professor Goldstein in his analysis in Table 9 of his expert report are cut from different cloth.

In column 3 of this table, Professor Goldstein reports data concerning "Interest Group Ads with No Candidate" and data for "Interest Group Ads Mentioning Candidate 60 Days Before General Election." The new data set [in] his expert report allows me to approximate his analysis, but

Table 2. *Comparing Group-Sponsored Ads in the 2000 Election*

Ad characteristic	Interest group ads with no candidate (N = 55,648)	Interest group ads mentioning candidate 60 days before general election (N = 60,087)
Does the ad urge action?		
% of urging some action	72.9	65.8
Types of actions urged		
% to vote for someone	1.2	0.0
% to write, call, or tell someone to do something, or to send a message or call someone to express yourself	54.1	53.0
Information provided		
% giving telephone number (toll-free or toll)	76.6	56.8
Primary focus of the ad		
% with a primary focus on policy matters	93.3	78.8
% with either a primary focus on policy matters or a primary focus on both policy matters and personal characteristics	93.7	98.6
Issue content		
% addressing health care	28.8	39.2
% addressing Medicare	34.9	24.3

also to consider a broader range of characteristics of the airings.[21] Professor Goldstein concludes that these two types of ads are fundamentally different in character. Unfortunately, his analysis fails to report the many ways in which these two groups of ads are similar.

In Table [2], I report my analysis of the characteristics of these two types of ads by demonstrating that these ads are similar in a number of important respects. First, large majorities of both types of ads urge the viewer to take some action; for a majority of these ads, that action involves writing, calling, or telling someone to do something, or sending a message or calling someone to express yourself. Approximately none of either type of ad asks the viewer to vote for someone. A majority of both types of ads give a telephone number for viewers to call. Virtually all of both types of ads (93.7% and 98.6%) have policy matters as either their primary focus or have a primary focus on both policy matters and personal characteristics.

Interest group ads with no candidate mentioned or depicted tend to stress issues of health care more often than interest group ads mentioning a candidate and airing within 60 days of a general election, but the reverse is true in terms of the issue of Medicare. The most important conclusion I draw from analysis is that these two types of ads have quite similar attributes. This is not surprising since virtually all of them focus on policy matters.

SUMMARY OF CONCLUSIONS ABOUT PROFESSOR GOLDSTEIN'S EXPERT REPORT

Professor Goldstein's expert report continues to focus on the highly subjective coding of Question 11, ignoring his own evidence on the policy focus of the ads. As I have demonstrated in this rebuttal, ads that have policy matters as their primary focus predominate in the data set in general, as well as comprising a large majority of those ads depicting candidates and broadcast in the last 60 days of the 2000 election (and not mentioning "magic words"). Indeed, the key distinction Professor Goldstein seeks to make between ads with these characteristics and so-called genuine issue ads is not supported by the data, especially insofar as the policy foci of these ads is concerned.

THE 1998 CONCLUSIONS

In my report of 9/30/2002, I concluded the following about the 1998 data:

> Thus, by this calculation, nearly two-thirds [64.0%] of the group ads that aired within 60 days of [the] 1998 election were coded by the students as "genuine issue ads"; all of these (again in the words of the Brennan Center authors) would b "unfairly caught" by application of the criteria now set forth in BCRA.

It is necessary to determine whether the report of Dr. Krasno and Professor Sorauf affects these calculations.[22]

My calculations were based on two groups of ads. First, I accepted the 2 ads that the authors of *Buying Time 1998* treated as "genuine issue ads." To that list of 2, Dr. Krasno and Professor Sorauf have now added a third ad (named CENT/Breaux, aired two times—see page 60 and page 20 of the appendix). Second, I accepted the original coding by the students of 8 ads. These are all ads that Professor Goldstein transformed from issue ads to electioneering ads after the coders had completed their job. Were I to re-do my calculations on the basis of the 2 newly designated CENT/

Breaux airings, the figures would change insignificantly (since so few airings are involved).

Dr. Krasno and Professor Sorauf make several other important "corrections" to the original 1998 calculations and ultimately derive a numerator of 713 ads. The authors refer to these as "all pure issue ads (as rated by the coders) by groups that appeared within 60 days of the election and mentioned a candidate by name." Since they acknowledge in their description of these ads the importance of coder ratings—and incorporating the justification I presented in my report of 9/30/2002—I revert to the original student codings of the 8 ads I identified in my report, and (accepting their identification of 713 airings only for the sake of argument), calculate a new percentage as follows:

$$(713 + 2{,}405)/5{,}064 = 61.6\%$$

Again for the sake of argument, let me accept their adjusted 60-day denominator, and the percentage becomes

$$(713 + 2{,}405)/4{,}847 = 64.3\%$$

Thus, the substantive conclusions I drew in my report of 9/30/2002 remain unfazed by this new analysis.

Since my report was completed, new information has become available about the airings of these 8 ads. In particular, the "Index of AFL-CIO Issue Advertising, 1995–2001" has been produced as an Exhibit to Ms. Mitchell's declaration. This document allows me to address the problem of so-called cookie cutter ads. Two of the eight ads appear to be cookie-cutter ads (#11 and #15). According to the data base, these ads were broadcast in several different locations throughout the country. Unfortunately, however, the CMAG technology does not capture the text or images of such ads, so one cannot confirm from the storyboards that a candidate was actually mentioned (because storyboards do not exist, the name of the individual mentioned or depicted in each ad is not known and must be inferred). In their expert report, Dr. Krasno and Professor Sorauf have offered a methodology for addressing this problem.

Following the methodology of Dr. Krasno and Professor Sorauf, I have reexamined the airings of these 8 ads. In 8 instances, we do not have any verifiable information as to whether a candidate was identified. These are [shown in table 3].

For the remainder of the airings of #11I and #15, the data base is compatible with the information presented in the AFL-CIO document,

Table 3. *Eight Ads for Which Airings Were Reexamined*

Ad number	Market location
2	Washington, D.C.
1411	Greenville
11	Albuquerque
11	Birmingham
11	Kansas City
15	Albuquerque
15	Grand Rapids
15	Kansas City

and therefore I accept the data base's coding of these ads as mentioning candidates.

With this adjustment to the data, the figures are:

$$(836 + 1,736)/5,064 = 50.8\%$$

Thus, using the methods adopted by Dr. Krasno and Professor Sorauf in the appendix to their expert report, about one-half of the airings in 1998 would be, in the words of the authors, "unfairly caught" by application of the BCRA criteria, if one were to accept (as Professor Goldstein does in his analysis of the 2000 data) the coders' determinations of the purposes of the ads prior to Professor Goldstein's manipulation of the data.

For the sake of argument, let me produce one additional calculation. Let me accept the new claim of Dr. Krasno and Professor Sorauf that their portion of the numerator is 713 airings. Let me accept their denominator as 4,847. And let me accept my new calculations on the 8 student-coded ads. The new percentage therefore becomes:

$$(713 + 1,736)/4,847 = 50.5\%$$

Perhaps the only other adjustment that could be made to this figure would be to declare, as Dr. Krasno and Professor Sorauf do, contradictory evidence as missing data and exclude the airings from the calculations. Such a strategy would only serve to reduce the denominator in the above quantity, thereby increasing the percentage to some figure above 50.5%.[23] To be clear, this analysis in effect assumes that none of the ads airing in the markets for which we have no independently verifiable information actually identified a candidate in that market. Consequently, this 50.5% figure represents the statistical floor under the Krasno/Sorauf methodology;

the 64% figure cited in my report of 9/30/2002 (calculated from the data base itself) provides the ceiling.

The dispute over this percentage reflects two fundamental truths about this data set. First, the coding of the ads is highly subjective. It is difficult if not impossible to determine what the "purpose" of an ad is, and reasonable people will disagree even about categorizing the manifest content of an ad. Since errors in coding a single ad are amplified by the number of showings of that ad, the conclusions one draws from the data base are highly volatile and sensitive to errors.

Second, this data base has been subject to numerous post-coding manipulations. Not only does this undermine all of the conclusions and calculations reported in *Buying Time 1998*, but it also strongly under-mines the claim that the student coding has much to do with the figures in the "final" analysis.[24] The figures Dr. Krasno and Professor Sorauf produce are no longer a function of the student coding, but instead reflect a series of ever-changing manipulations and re-codings of the data base. Such a methodology sabotages any claim the study might make to scientific accuracy.

GROUPS COMMUNICATING WITH CITIZENS

Missing from the entire discussion of ads and airings in the expert reports submitted is any consideration of the people who consume these ads. After all, the purpose of all ads is to communicate with citizens. Fortunately, the Buying Time data sets provide some information that allows us some purchase on this important question.

The Buying Time data bases include a variable representing the "Gross Rating Points" of each airing. As described on page 6 of *Buying Time 1998:* "Gross ratings points are the sum of ratings for a particular time: if the local news is watched by ten percent of viewers with televisions, an ad run during the program represents ten gross ratings points." These points are Of Course idiosyncratic to each individual airing, and were apparently added to the data set by CMAG.

According to Dr. Krasno and Professor Sorauf, there were 713 airings in 1998 that the authors treat as "genuine issue ads," depicting a candidate and broadcast within 60 days of the election. These ads and the markets in which they were shown are listed on page 20 of their appendix. According to the data base, no Gross Ratings Points estimate is available for 6 of these airings.

Using the 1998–1999 Neilsen estimates of the number of households with television sets in the seven markets in which these ads were broadcast,[25] and using the Gross Ratings Points to estimate the number of households viewing each airing, I find that these 707 airings represent communications with a staggering number of household—30,108,857. Thus, were these ads Oust the ads accepted by Dr. Krasno and Professor Goldstein as "genuine issue ads") prohibited, over 30 million group-citizen political communications would be affected (and this figure is based on the quite conservative assumption that each household only has a single person viewing television).

WHY WOULD INTEREST GROUPS ATTEMPT TO PERSUADE CITIZENS ON POLICY MATTERS DURING THE ELECTION SEASON?

Professor Goldstein asserts in his expert report that a reasonable interest group would not air its issue ads during an electoral period. His argument is based on a couple of suppositions:

1) the ads are more expensive at this time of year

2) citizens are overwhelmed with information and will not pay attention to the ads, and

3) partisan attachments harden as the election draws near.

He cites the work of William McGuire and John Zaller. In fact the theory he cites argues in favor of exactly the opposite conclusion.

Issue advertising is an exercise in persuading citizens. Political Psychologists have long known (McGuire) that to persuade someone involves two steps. First, one must get the attention of the person one is attempting to persuade. Second, one must overcome the strength of existing attitudes if the attempt at persuasive communication is to result in attitude change. Unfortunately, these stages in the process are related to each other.

As it turns out, those with strong attitudes tend to pay attention to political communications while those with weak political attitudes tend to ignore them. This results in a paradox. Those most easily reached are least easily changed; those most easily changed are those most difficult to reach. This paradox has long bedeviled those researching processes of persuasion.

Those with strong political attitudes pay attention to politics year round, in part because the reason why they have strong attitudes in the first place is because political affairs are interesting to them. Those with weak attitudes, on the other hand, only pay attention to political affairs under the most extreme circumstances (indeed, perhaps only when there is little choice but to pay attention because the airwaves are saturated with political information). Thus, election periods open a window of opportunity to reach those citizens who are most likely to be influenced by policy advertising. During the election, those with weak and potentially alterable attitudes are paying attention to political affairs. It therefore makes sense that an interest group would attempt to influence people when in fact they are most "influencable." Just as one does not attempt to sell Christmas trees in July (because people will screen out such attempts and will not pay attention to them), interest groups will try to take advantage of the window of opportunity opened by the electoral season. Consequently, it is entirely reasonable that an interest group would attempt to reach citizens on public policy issues during any given election period.

The last point Professor Goldstein makes is that partisan attachments harden. By this logic, candidates should abandon advertising as the election approaches since these hardened attitudes are difficult to convert. In fact, that does not happen, since, as the election approaches, candidates try to reach an even greater percentage of marginal voters, who have little interest in politics, and relatively pliable issue views.

This point about susceptibility to persuasion within 60 days of an election turns out to be intimately related to the controversy concerning the most appropriate denominator to use in our calculations of the proportion of "genuine issue ads" affected by BCRA. Those who would use a denominator based on all issue ads aired in the year are implicitly making the assumption that ads aired anytime throughout the year are equally as valuable as ads aired in proximity to the election. As I have indicated, this is not so. The damage of prohibiting an ad within 60 days of an election cannot be ameliorated by allowing that ad to be broadcast at some other point throughout the year.

Thus, I conclude that there is nothing peculiar or nefarious about interest groups seeking to influence citizens on policy matters during the last 60 days of an election period.

Overall Summary of This Rebuttal

The various reports based on the 1998 and 2000 data are built upon a house of cards. As more information about the methodology becomes available—information that would ordinarily have become public were these reports subject to peer review—one sees the numerous infirmities in the data base. From the inability of CMAG to capture each unique ad (even in the limited part of the country it purports to monitor), to the subjectivity of the student coding, to the unrestrained and undocumented recoding of the data by Professor Goldstein, one comes to see that this data set and the analyses based upon it cannot be trusted.

NOTES

1. A listing of additional materials upon which I have relied is attached as Exhibit 1.

2. To assist readers in comparing my analysis with that of Goldstein/Krasno/Sorauf, I adopt some of their language (e.g., "genuine issue ads"). The use of these terms should not be taken to represent agreement with either the conceptualization or operationalization of these concepts and issues, but is instead simply a convention I adopt so as to facilitate communication.

3. While Appendix F of Professor Goldstein's report provides a document entitled "2000 Coding Sheet," this document provides information on only a tiny fraction of the variables included in the data set.

4. See Ridout, Travis N., Michael Franz, Kenneth Goldstein, and Paul Freedman. 2002. "Measuring Exposure to Campaign Advertising." Unpublished paper, June 19, 2002, at page 17.

5. In the appendix to their expert report, Dr. Krasno and Professor Sorrauf claim that the CMAG data base is incorrect in the information it depicts about the ad with the id number 13. They provide no explanation for the error in the data base. Unfortunately, the appendix is not pagenated, but this seems to be the 15th page of text in the appendix.

6. Counsel for the AFL-CIO has provided me a copy of the Declaration of Denise Mitchell, 10/4/2002. In her Declaration, Mitchell asserts that she cannot reproduce from AFLCIO records Professor Goldstein's calculations from the data base on the airings sponsored by the AFL-CIO. She notes that the CMAG data base makes two types of errors: errors of omission (failure to include ads aired by the AFL-CIO) and errors of commission (the inclusion of ads said to be aired by the AFL-CIO but that were in fact not aired). Since the AFL-CIO is the group with the second largest number of airings in the data base (well behind the Citizens for Better Medicare), any such failure to track accurately the airings of this organization would be a major indictment of the quality of the data base. See Declaration of Denise Mitchell, 10/4/2002, paragraph 64.

7. Working through the example Professor Goldstein provides in the paper is useful for understanding the meaning of the error rate. The error rate for station WJRT is .01. This means that of the 618 airings for which the station has billing records, the CMAG data base includes only 612. Thus the error rate is .0 1: ((618 − 612) / 618) = .0 1.

8. This figure is equal to 100 % minus the error rate.

9. (8,526/8,612) = .99.

10. Were I to use the more demanding standard of "Percent correct within 1 sec." the number of ads estimated to be missing or that contain serious errors would be significantly higher than the numbers I report here.

11. I will not repeat all of the objections I laid out in my report of 9/30/2002, but I do incorporate those objections into this analysis since I have not changed my views on any of the issues addressed in that report.

12. Data sets are typically documented with a "codebook" that details the meaning of each variable and each code on each variable in the data set. Moreover, to facilitate understanding and avoid analytical errors, variables are typically fully documented with labels. This variable is labeled as to its possible content (e.g., "oldest available q 11 codes (older than feb version)"), but the individual scores or codes (what we would call the "response set") are not documented. No codebook was provided with this data set, and the norm in the data set is for the variables to be entirely undocumented.

13. I have confirmed that this variable differs from the variables Q 11 and Q 11_1 as represented in the data set: cmag_2000-labeled-data-mayO2_feb0l_w-Compet.sav

14. It is not clear how this sample of 150 ads relates to the 250 ads discussed in footnote 4 of the Krasno/Goldstein PS report (published in June 2002).

15. Professor Goldstein asserts on page 8 of his report that "the CMAG database collected 970,424 political television ad broadcasts . . . Yet the data base he attaches as an appendix to his report includes 970,428 airings. I removed the four airings with a "system missing" score on the variable named COUNT. This produces a data base with a number of airings consistent with the number identified in Professor Goldstein's report.

16. It is unclear to me why Professor Goldstein refers to "4,000 advertisements airing in 2000." See Ridout, Travis N., Michael Franz, Kenneth Goldstein, and Paul Freedman. 2002. "Measuring Exposure to Campaign Advertising." Unpublished paper, June 19, 2002, at page 17.

17. I say "apparently" since the codes "98" and "99" are conventionally used as "missing data" codes. However, the scores are undocumented in the data set.

18. The situation is little improved with a sample of 250 ads, the number said by Dr. Krasno and Professor Goldstein in their PS report to be subject to intercoder reliability checks.

19. The solution to this problem is stratified random sampling. That is, the proper methodology is one in which the original ads are segregated by type on this variable—"strata"—and then sampling takes place within stratum. Of course, with so few ads coded as issue ads in the first place, one would most likely have to adopt a strategy of recoding all ads coded as having an issue purpose and a random sample of those ads coded as having an electioneering purpose. There is no indication in any of the Buying Time documents, published or unpublished, that this was the strategy employed in assessing the reliability of this variable.

20. This figure represents 48,370 divided by 112,844: ads with policy matters as their primary focus, mentioning candidates, and airing within the last 60 days of the election.

21. I cannot replicate the findings in Professor Goldstein's Table 7. Although I can identify in the new data set 55,648 ads sponsored by groups and not depicting a candidate, 2.4 % of these (not 0.0 %) in fact mention "magic words." Moreover, I find from the data set that the size of the second group of ads is 60,087, not 60,623, although my analysis does indicate that 0.0 % of these 60,087 airings mention "magic words."

22. For reasons I outline above (and in my report of 9/30/2002), I do not accept the method of calculation used in *Buying Time* 1998, and therefore I will not address the portion of the Krasno/Sorauf appendix entitled "SPREAD-SHEET: 1998 Formula" (pages 13–15, pagination I assigned to the pages). Instead, I will consider their calculations as reported in "SPREADSHEET: 2000 Formula" (pages 16–21, my pagination).

23. For instance, the data base reports that ad #2 was aired in the Washington DC market, although the storyboard mentions North Carolina Senator Faircloth. According to the Dr. Krasno and Professor Sorauf methodology, these airings could be treated as missing data and therefore excluded from both the numerator and the denominator for purposes of these calculations.

24. Indeed, I should note that the report by Dr. Krasno and Professor Sorauf may not be the final analysis, since there may ultimately be some means of resolving various missing data problems that afflict their calculations.

25. A copy of these estimates is attached as Exhibit 2.

Rebuttal to Gibson

JONATHAN S. KRASNO

Jonathan S. Krasno is a visiting fellow at the Institute for Social and Policy Studies at Yale University. Prior to serving as an expert witness for the defense in this case, he helped design and carry out the research on political advertising that led to the Buying Time *report in 1998. This research was continued in the 2000 election cycle under the direction of Kenneth Goldstein. In this selection, Krasno, who was the lead author of the 1998* Buying Time *report, responds to the methodological queries and criticisms raised by James Gibson in his expert reports for the plaintiffs.*

Professor James L. Gibson raises a series of concerns—some serious and some less so—about the 1998 and 2000 editions of *Buying Time* and the datasets from which they were derived. In this rebuttal, I address many of these issues by drawing on my experience as lead author of *Buying Time: Television Advertising in the 1998 Congressional Elections* (*Buying Time 1998*), author of the grant proposal that produced it, and author of the coding instrument used in 1998 and later adopted with little revision for 2000. I confine my remarks to Professor Gibson's discussion of *Buying Time 1998*, although they may also be relevant to his critique of the later volume.

I organize my comments into four sections. The first clarifies some confusion about the origins of *Buying Time 1998* by briefly recounting the relevant history behind it. These clarifications, I believe, relieve many of Professor Gibson's concerns. The second section takes up the purported difficulties replicating its findings, a major theme of Professor Gibson's report. The third and fourth sections address his two most serious claims in turn: that the analysis of "pure" issue ads ignores a more appropriate means to designate these ads, and that the analysis of the impact of McCain-Feingold in *Buying Time 1998* misses the relevant theoretical questions and is wrong. In both cases, a careful examination of Professor Gibson's claims reveals important errors in his reasoning and computations and shows that the original findings in *Buying Time 1998* are correct.

THE ORIGINS OF *BUYING TIME 1998*

Professor Gibson notes that the grant proposal that produced the first *Buying Time* is an advocacy document.[1] As its author, I can confirm that

that is largely true. Like many other political scientists, influenced by the commercials we had seen on television and the vast litany of complaints and comments from politicians, journalists, and judges, I had come to believe that political parties and interest groups were using the magic words test as cover to sponsor thinly veiled campaign ads masquerading as issue advocacy. What no one knew—at least not for certain—was the scope and content of candidate-oriented and "pure" issue advocacy.[2]

The *Buying Time* study was meant to supply that information, but to be authoritative it had to do so in a way that was as value-free and defensible as possible. In short, it had to be able to stand up to accusations, like Professor Gibson's, that I and others associated with the study stacked the deck to find what we were looking for. The fact that we expected certain results (and that those expectations were largely realized) loads the issue emotionally, but misses the point. Scholars rarely embark upon research without some expectations as to its results. But more than most scholars, we had a compelling reason to ensure that our results could withstand allegations of bias. Thus some of the very things that Professor Gibson questions—the presence of alternate codings of q11 in the 2000 data set, the extensive e-mail discussions about various cases and issues, the comprehensive presentation of the results from the 1998 study without commentary—could and should be viewed as part of a concerted effort to make certain that the results and data were valid and reliable.

The other imperative of the *Buying Time 1998* project was timing. To satisfy the demands of the funders and policymakers, the results of the study had to be available in the shortest possible time. The political calendar dictated that the publication date of *Buying Time 1998* be in late April 2000—approximately six months after the data were delivered. That abbreviated timetable created enormous difficulties, and Professor Gibson and others are welcome to question whether the sheer amount of analysis conducted over this short period could be entirely free of errors (see the next section). At the same time, the need to meet a short deadline explains away a number of concerns raised by Professor Gibson. These include

—The lack of text accompanying the tables in *Buying Time 1998* (pp. 4, 5).[3] The main reason was to allow readers to draw their own conclusions, but the secondary reason was more practical: lack of time.

—The role of Daniel Seltz (p. 6). Mr. Seltz organized an enormous number of tasks relevant to the preparation of *Buying Time 1998*. His myriad responsibilities did not include data analysis, and Professor Gibson's fear that he contributed findings to *Buying Time 1998* are unfounded.

—The constant consultation with Brennan Center attorneys (fn. 3). Brennan Center attorneys—along with a larger number of political scientists—were consulted in preparing the coding instrument in order to make certain that the resulting analysis addressed policy concerns and proper legal categories. There was no consultation with attorneys about the results of the analysis, both for reasons of propriety and practicality. The short time window left no opportunity to request or receive feedback on results, even if Mr. Seltz and I had wanted to consult. Indeed, it left no time to adjust the coding instrument at all once the process had begun.[4]

—The lack of peer review (pp. 4, 5). The need to release the results made the normal peer review process—which adds months and, sometimes, years to publication dates—impossible. In fact, subsequent publications by myself and by Professor Goldstein have withstood the peer review process.[5] Furthermore, peer reviewers are rarely, if ever, given the authors' data to evaluate, instead focusing on their theoretical arguments, supporting analysis, and presentation. The absence of peer review no more automatically disqualifies *Buying Time 1998* than the presence of peer review automatically guarantees the quality or accuracy of every book or article published.

—The "dataset in constant flux." The need to release results after a few short months inevitably meant that small changes to the dataset would continue even after the release of *Buying Time 1998*. This process, far from being unusual, is extremely ordinary. Virtually every provider of large datasets, from the National Election Studies to the Commerce Department, prepares versions of their data and continues to fix problems in subsequent releases. Any problems with the Campaign Media Analysis Group (CMAG) dataset arise from the sheer complexity of the enterprise, from the gradual filling in of missing data and the discovery of internal contradictions. There is no evidence at all in Professor Gibson's report that any of the changes in the successive versions of the data that he examined had more than a trivial impact on his results or on those reported in *Buying Time 1998*.

This background also sheds light on the role of Professor Goldstein, a topic that Professor Gibson raises repeatedly in his report. Professor Goldstein's responsibilities for the 1998 project included supervising the coding of the storyboards, providing additional contextual information about the ads, merging this information with the broadcast data, and advising on use of the dataset. No item on this impressive list includes any responsibility for the grant proposal or the results of the data analysis that I performed several thousand miles away. This division of labor certainly reduces, if not eliminates, any incentives Professor Goldstein could have had to tilt the results of the analysis in any direction. In fact, Professor Goldstein's prospects in academia—his chosen career—would make such behavior inimical to his interests and to the project itself. Professor Gibson's persistent questioning of Professor Goldstein's motives somehow manages to lose sight of this simple and obvious fact.

Professor Goldstein's work adding contextual information to the dataset warrants special attention. Since the coders received no formal training and were not experts on the several hundred federal candidates who appeared in 1998's advertisements, it fell to Professor Goldstein to add information about the actual race in which an ad appeared and its partisan direction.[6] Both tasks were relatively straightforward exercises that Professor Goldstein, with his knowledge of American politics, could easily accomplish. It is worth noting that Professor Goldstein's contextual coding occurred independently of the content coding, thus providing a useful way to check the accuracy of both processes. This division of labor revealed occasional inconsistencies in the 1998 dataset that resulted in some additional correction of errors.

Finally, Professor Gibson raises a slew of objections to various aspects of the CMAG data, from the fact that it covers just seventy-five media markets (that reach 75–80 percent of the public) and the accuracy of the CMAG system, to the missing video frames in the storyboards (see particularly pp. 5–6). All of these characteristics are painstakingly explained in *Buying Time 1998* and elsewhere. None strikes me as particularly serious. Indeed, it is noteworthy that Professor Gibson advances no hypotheses to show why these alleged shortcomings would affect the results. Absent any reason to think otherwise—such as an argument that the content of political advertising in the seventy-five markets covered by CMAG is systematically distinct from political advertising in other markets— none of these objections undermines the findings in *Buying Time 1998*.

REPLICATING THE RESULTS OF *BUYING TIME 1998*

Professor Gibson reports difficulty reproducing the "specific numbers" reported in *Buying Time 1998*, concluding that this "undermines tremendously any confidence one should place in the findings produced" (p. 5). Professor Gibson is certainly correct to point out that replication is a core precept of science, but he rather overstates the case by insisting on "exact" replication. By their very nature, social scientific concepts are subject to nuances of measurement and model specification that make exact replication difficult, if not impossible, in many instances. For example, Professor Gary King notes in his introduction to a large symposium on replication (to which Professor Gibson contributed an essay) in the September 1995 issue of *PS*:

> As virtually every good methodology text explains, *the only way to understand and evaluate an empirical analysis fully is to know the exact process by which the data were generated and the analysis produced.* Without adequate documentation, scholars often have trouble replicating their *own* results months later. Since sufficient information is usually lacking in political science, trying to replicate the results of others, even with their help, is often impossible. (Emphasis in original.)[7]

Professor King goes on in the next paragraph to provide examples of eighteen questions political scientists might ask when attempting to replicate one another's results.

This example suggests several problems with Professor Gibson's argument that *Buying Time 1998* violates important principles of political science and ought to be disregarded as a result. If ability to reproduce precise results is the standard, then it is clear that vast chunks of the literature must also be jettisoned. Most of all, though, Professor King's comments alert readers that replication is usually difficult to accomplish and may require time and communication with the authors of the original article. In this case—thanks to the rules of litigation—Professor Gibson had neither much time nor was he able to consult with me. If he had, I could have shared the original command files used to produce the numbers in *Buying Time 1998*.[8] In addition to these hindrances, Professor Gibson also had to work with a large and complex dataset, replete with "nuances and peculiarities" (p. 6). Nonetheless, a careful examination of Professor Gibson's attempt to reproduce various findings of *Buying Time 1998* shows him to be extraordinarily successful, a testimony both to his ability and, I think, to the dataset and the report drawn from it.

Professor Gibson's report notes three discrete instances in which he attempted to replicate specific findings in *Buying Time 1998* on page 24.[9] How close does he come to the results reported in the volume? Very close, indeed. Professor Gibson reports that the dataset includes observations from seventy-six media markets (p. 24); *Buying Time 1998* claims seventy-five.[10] Professor Gibson reports the number of airings in the dataset is 307,028 (p. 24); *Buying Time 1998* discusses 302,860. Professor Gibson reports 21,926 ads sponsored by interest groups in the dataset (p. 24);

Buying Time 1998 claims 22,151. In short, all of these numbers are virtually identical (or identical) to those in *Buying Time 1998*. More important, not only are these differences statistically insignificant in a dataset with more than 300,000 cases, but none lend themselves to different substantive interpretations. To be sure, Professor Gibson alleges numerous other discrepancies (p. 24), but these are the only examples that he provides.[11] I know from experience that much of the confusion likely results from different ways of handling missing data, the small percentage of storyboards that were missing and not coded, or the small percentage of items that were not coded.[12]

The question, of course, is whether "close" is sufficiently exact to confirm the results reported in *Buying Time 1998*. There is no doubt that in the social sciences, where laboratory replication is impossible, the prevailing standards lean heavily toward the ability to reproduce the essential nature of the results, not numbers. For example, Professor King asserts that "future scholars, with only your publication and other information you provide, ought to be able to start from the real world and arrive at the same substantive conclusions."[13] The dataset with which Professor Gibson and I have both worked is maddeningly complex, and he uses other coding items and algorithms to argue for completely different conclusions. But to the extent that he has attempted to reproduce the results of *Buying Time 1998* in his report, his efforts confirm the substantive findings contained in the volume and come tantalizingly close to confirming the exact numbers.

THE PURPOSE OF ADS (Q6) VERSUS THEIR EMPHASIS ON POLICY OR PERSONAL FACTORS (Q22)

A main thrust of Professor Gibson's comments is his contention that another item on the coding instrument, q22 in 1998, is a better indicator of "pure" issue ads than the one used in *Buying Time 1998*. If true, this is a potentially major problem, for the analysis of the Bipartisan Campaign Reform Act's (BCRA) effect in both volumes makes extensive use of a different variable, q6. Cursory examination of Professor Gibson's claims, however, reveal both conceptual and empirical problems with his argument and confirm the validity of the approach taken in *Buying Time 1998*.

The two items in question are:

—Q6: "In your opinion, is the purpose of this ad to provide information about or urge action on a bill or issue, or is it to generate support or opposition for a *particular candidate*?" (emphasis in original).

—Q22: "In your judgement, is the primary focus of this ad on the personal characteristics of either candidate or on policy matters?"

The first is a "forced-pair" item, giving coders the choice of the options in the question plus "unsure/unclear." The second asks them to choose between the options in the question, or "both" or "neither." Professor Gibson argues that the second is the superior question both for its use of the word "primary" and for giving coders a wider set of answers to choose from (p. 31–34).[14]

Putting aside this critique, the most important question about these items is whether they measure the relevant distinction between candidate-oriented and pure issue ads. The matter of whether an ad is a campaign ad or not would, on its face, seem to go to purpose of the commercial. Campaign ads are intended to help candidates win election; intention is the essence of the definition of "electioneering" and certainly the essence of the commercials that candidates air.[15] Thus one of the important pieces of supporting evidence for the validity of q6 is that coders rated 99 percent of candidate ads (and 93 percent of party ads) as generating support or opposition for a candidate (*Buying Time 1998*, p. 41).[16] My affirmative report provides a series of other results showing that issue ads rated by the coders as electioneering in their purpose were quite similar to candidate ads.[17]

Whether an ad focused primarily on personal characteristics of a candidate or on policy matters is a different issue entirely. Most important, it is not clear why the focus of an ad demarcates candidate-oriented issue ads from pure issue ads. While some observers may particularly decry the emphasis on personal characteristics in campaigns—especially in attack advertising—this style of campaigning has not, at least to my knowledge, been equated with the practice of electioneering. Indeed, political scientists routinely take the view that politicians frequently adopt and advertise policy positions in order to appeal to voters.[18] Thus there seems little reason to imagine that campaign ads are characterized by an emphasis on personal characteristics and issue ads by an emphasis on policy.

The best illustration of this point appears in *Buying Time 1998* (p. 42): coders rated 11 percent of candidate ads as focused on the personal characteristics of the candidates, 64 percent as policy-related, and the remaining 25 percent as neither or both. If one assumes, as both common sense and the FECA indicate, that candidates are wholly motivated by their desire to win election, then the problem with using q22 as Professor Gibson would use it becomes obvious: it miscategorizes at least two-thirds of candidate ads as not being electioneering. This is the same criticism that both editions of *Buying Time* level at the magic words test, that it does not work for the one group of ads whose purpose and category are already known, regardless of their language or style. Professor Gibson's approach is empirically contradicted by the data themselves.

Measuring BCRA's Impact

Professor Gibson's most serious claims involve *Buying Time 1998*'s estimate of the effect of BCRA. He makes several assertions. First, he argues that the approach taken in *Buying Time 1998* has "no theoretical meaning" (p. 38). Second, he adopts a different approach to produce estimates of BCRA's effect on pure issue ads that are orders of magnitude higher than any previous estimate. Neither his theoretical argument nor his computations withstand scrutiny.

The sponsors of BCRA acted under the assumption that there are two kinds of issue ads: candidate-oriented and pure issue ads.[19] The first are those at which the legislation is aimed, the campaign ads that attempt to pass themselves off as nonpartisan discussions of policy. The second are the ads that everyone agrees ought not be materially affected by campaign finance laws, the sincere attempts by citizens and groups to address the issues of the day using the mass media.

Given this division, two obvious questions emerge: what is BCRA's impact on candidate-oriented issue ads, and what is BCRA's impact on pure issue ads. The first goes to the effectiveness of the law, while the second asks whether it inadvertently sweeps many pure issue ads into FECA's regulatory structure. Both are obviously important questions. There is little need for a bill that does not fulfill its own intention of treating a great portion of candidate-oriented issue ads like other electioneering by candidates, parties, and groups.[20] But it is really the second question that goes to the heart of the main political and legal questions surrounding BCRA. It is widely understood that a bill that treats too many pure issue ads as campaign ads risks rejection by legislators and jurists for being an infringement on political speech. The strategy that BCRA's sponsors adopted uses both the timing of ads and their identification of federal candidates to try to minimize its impact on pure issue ads. Does this strategy work?

Buying Time 1998 addressed that question by calculating the percentage of pure issue ads affected by BCRA out of the universe of all pure issue ads that appeared in 1998.[21] In other words, this figure is the result of simple division whereby the numerator (the number of pure issue ads sponsored by interest groups that identified federal candidates and appeared in the last sixty days of the campaign) is divided by the denominator (the number of pure issue ads sponsored by interest groups that appeared in 1998).[22] Owing to the lack of time, Mr. Seltz and I did not factor in the impact of the additional thirty-day period before the primaries.[23] In my report for this litigation, I confirmed that the pre-primary period has no effect on this calculation of BCRA's effect in 1998.[24] In short, had BCRA been in effect in 1998, 6 percent of the pure issue ads aired by interest groups that year would have been subject to FECA's regulation.[25] Conversely, 94 percent of these ads would have been unaffected.

Professor Gibson raises different sorts of objections to both the numerator and denominator in *Buying Time 1998* and produces a rather dizzying array of estimates of BCRA's impact on pure issue advocacy. The effect of his discussion, whether by design or not, is to create the mistaken impression that the data lend themselves to practically any estimate of BCRA's effect, including the admittedly unacceptable notion that more than four of every ten pure issue ads would be touched by the legislation. Both of these conclusions are entirely unfounded. In fact, close examination of Professor Gibson's analysis reiterates that, with proper understanding of the data, BCRA's effect can be measured with precision and certainty, and also reveals conceptual and computational errors in Professor Gibson's calculations that enormously inflate his estimates.

The simplest way to understand this array of estimates is to separate the discussion of Professor Gibson's calculations into two parts, looking first at the dispute over the appropriate denominator before turning to the more mundane question of how to compute the numerator. Professor Gibson's criticism of the denominator of the equation used in *Buying Time 1998* is theoretical in nature, claiming that it relates to a "virtually meaningless question" (p. 39). His complaint involves the timing of the ads included, asking "Why not include ads from December 1997, or even the entire election cycle beginning in November 1996?" (p. 38). Professor Gibson is correct to suggest the universe of pure issue ads that could be affected by BCRA in 1998 includes all of these commercials that appeared between elections. In fact, my affirmative report notes that for presidents and senators the appropriate period is even longer, corresponding with the four- and six-year terms of these officials. This use of the calendar is a key component of BCRA's design to make certain that only very few pure issue ads are touched by the legislation.

The answer to Professor Gibson's question, of course, is that we had no data from 1997 or the last weeks of 1996 to include in the denominator. That does not mean that this calculation—the percentage of pure issue ads affected by BCRA—should be abandoned, but the effect of any omitted ads merits consideration. Adding missing ads from 1996 or 1997 would only increase the size of the denominator, leaving the numerator unchanged since none of these ads could have appeared near an election. This, in turn, would *decrease* the percentage of pure issue ads affected by BCRA. The figure reported in *Buying Time 1998* thus should be understood as the upper bound of BCRA's impact on pure issue advocacy. Put another way, BCRA would have affected at most 6–7 percent of pure issue ads that appeared during the 1997–98 election cycle.[26]

Professor Gibson's alternative is to use a different denominator, the number of *all* issue ads sponsored by groups that appear in the last sixty days and mention a candidate. This figure essentially comprises the universe of issue ads affected by BCRA (at least in the last sixty days) and thus consists of both pure issue ads and candidate-oriented issue ads.[27] This choice of denominators has several empirical consequences. Most important, its size varies considerably with the amount of candidate-oriented issue advertising before an election. This is particularly relevant because of the volume of candidate-oriented issue ads devoted to presidential campaigns. The result, of course, is highly unstable estimates of BCRA's impact from year to year.

The matter of which is the appropriate denominator, however, is driven by the question to be answered, not the results. Professor Gibson characterizes his choice as responding to the following question:

> I will assume that all ads aired within 60 days of an election and which depict a candidate for public office have a particular characteristic (i.e., they are engaged in electioneering). What percentage of time would this assumption result in an error in the sense that the assumed characteristic is not the same as the actual characteristic? (pp. 38–39)

Put perhaps more simply, Professor Gibson gauges the percentage of issue ads affected by BCRA in the sixty-day window that are genuine issue ads, the sort of ads BCRA is not supposed to affect.[28] This is a strikingly different question from the one answered by *Buying Time 1998*—what percentage of pure issue ads aired would be affected by BCRA?—and asked, I believe, by the legislators who considered the bill.

As the appendix to my affirmative report shows, this dispute over the appropriate denominator accounts for estimates of BCRA's impact in 1998 that range from 6.1 percent (using the formula from *Buying Time 1998*) to 14.7 percent (Professor Gibson's approach). This latter number is well short of the estimate he produces, 44.4 percent (p. 39), and smaller than the even smallest in his wide range of estimates (pp. 37–43). Indeed, Professor Gibson himself notes, "There is quite some distance between a figure of 7 percent, reported in *Buying Time 1998*, and my calculation of 44.4 percent" and asks how this has come about (p. 40). The denominator, with all of its theoretical significance, accounts for a relatively small portion of this discrepancy; the bigger part is attributable to the numerator itself.

In every calculation that Professor Gibson and I present, the numerator is the same: the number of pure issue ads aired in the final sixty days of the 1998 campaign that mentioned a federal candidate. Professor Gibson notes his preference for using q22 rather than q6 to demarcate these ads (see the preceding section), but for the sake of argument he adopts the approach used by *Buying Time 1998*. Thus, the fact that he comes up with a numerator that is four times larger than *Buying Time 1998*'s is not a matter of theoretical dispute but one of simple computation. How does one count the number of pure issue ads that mention candidates in the last 60 days?

This straightforward question is complicated by one factor: information about candidate identification was not coded and is not contained in the datasets with which either of us has worked. Coders were instructed to skip ahead thirteen questions if they rated a storyboard as providing information or urging action on a policy matter in order to avoid confusion when confronted with a series of questions about candidates. That leaves it to the analyst to consult the storyboards themselves to see if a candidate is mentioned, an easy if somewhat tedious process. This is precisely what I did when preparing *Buying Time 1998*. Apparently, coders did incorrectly complete items about candidate mentions for at least one pure issue ad—"HMO Said No"—so that all 2,808 of its airings are listed in the dataset as mentioning candidates. Knowing that there should be no data on this item for these storyboards, I never checked the dataset for this information and therefore never corrected this miscode, allowing it to survive until Professor Gibson discovered it.

This is an especially important oversight because the spot in question, "HMO Said No," is a "cookie-cutter" ad that aired in thirteen media markets. The commercial, about Senate Bill 2330, complained that "Republicans in Washington are pushing an empty HMO proposal" and urged viewers to call a named senator to vote against the bill. I quickly determined that Republican senators were running for election in 1998 in just four of the markets in which "HMO Said No" appeared and thus reached the decision to treat airings in those markets as mentioning candidates and to treat the other nine markets as airings where a candidate was not identified since no Republican senators were on the ballot. This logic was well supported by the facts at hand at the time, especially the fact that the two storyboards of the ad that we possessed each featured a Republican senator who was not a candidate in 1998, Senators Dan Coats of Indiana (retiring) and Olympia Snowe of Maine (up for reelection in 2000).[29] Information subsequently obtained in this litigation reveals that this decision rule was too generous, and that one of the ads we attributed to the numerator actually named the second Republican senator in Pennsylvania who was not up for reelection in 1998. The result, of course, lowers all estimates of BCRA's impact on pure issue ads.[30]

The miscoding of the items about candidate identification for this single storyboard is certainly a glitch in the dataset, but not a glitch that had any impact on the analysis of BCRA in *Buying Time 1998*. It does, however, have a great effect on Professor Gibson's affirmative report, for he depends heavily on this miscoding to construct his numerator. That he does so is entirely understandable in the sense that these are data in the dataset. On the other hand, Professor Gibson admits on several occasions that he is aware of this error. He writes that "ads coded in Question 6 as 'provide information or urge action' should *not* have been coded on *any of the variables indicating whether candidates were depicted or not*" (p. 29, emphasis in original), and adds an accompanying footnote that some of these storyboards nevertheless are unaccountably coded as depicting candidates (fn. 30). He refers to "various unpublished and undocumented machinations" that led only a portion of the airings of "HMO Said No" to find their way into the numerator. He hypothesizes that confusion over this ad stems from the fact that, as a cookie-cutter spot, we possessed only one version of the ad (fn. 40), apparently without noticing that this version featured an official (Senator Coats) who was not a candidate in 1998. Professor Gibson, in fact, goes so far as to argue that "it is *important* not to accept the numerator" (p. 41, emphasis in original) used in *Buying Time 1998*, claiming that it has been subject to manipulation by Professor Goldstein. His suspicions, however, do not comport with the fact that Professor Goldstein had no role whatsoever in determining which airings of "HMO Said No" mentioned candidates.

In short, Professor Gibson manages, by ignoring the contradictory statements in his own report, to compile a count of the set of pure issue ads affected by BCRA that is dominated by commercials that make no reference to federal candidates. The result is a numerator that is more than four times too large and estimates of BCRA's impact on pure issue ads that are similarly inflated. So, while Professor Gibson's estimates that using

Buying Time 1998's denominator (with his numerator) reveals that 25.7 percent of pure issue ads aired in 1998 would have been affected by BCRA, the correct number is 6.1 percent. And, while Professor Gibson claims that 44.4 percent of the ads affected by BCRA in the last sixty days are pure issues ads, the correct number is 14.7 percent (see appendix, Krasno and Sorauf). There are, to be sure, a variety of other statistics presented on pages 35 thru 43 of his report, but these figures appear to be intended to amplify his main—and mistaken—contention that 44.4 percent of the ads affected by BCRA are pure issue ads. In most cases, the interpretation and derivation of these statistics are difficult to understand, as when he divides his estimate of *Buying Time 1998*'s numerator by his preferred numerator (p. 41),[31] when he unaccountably introduces a completely new denominator (5064) reputedly related to *Buying Time 1998* (pp. 42 and 43, fn. 39), and the somewhat tendentious example on page 43 in which he manages to compute an even larger numerator.

This blizzard of computations, as I note above, creates the false impression that estimating BCRA's impact on pure issue advocacy is an exercise capable of yielding virtually any result. That is clearly wrong. There is no doubt that the underlying dataset is unwieldy and complex, but there is also no doubt that a careful and informed analyst can count the number of pure issue ads that would have been affected by BCRA and create from that count a reliable and precise estimate of the legislation's impact. That process, done correctly, shows that just a small fraction of the pure issue ads aired in 1998 would have been subject to FECA's regulation had BCRA been in effect at the time. This is the question that occupied Congress as it crafted and debated the bill, and the data show that it achieved its goal.

NOTES

1. See Gibson's full report at www.campaignlegalcenter.org for this discussion.

2. The Annenberg Public Policy Center estimated $135 million was spent on issue advertising in 1996, but this estimate does not distinguish between candidate-oriented and pure issue ads.

3. These and subsequent page numbers and footnote references refer to Gibson's longer critique, available in full at www.campaignlegalcenter.org.

4. A meeting about coding the storyboards in the late winter/early spring of 1999 led to a first draft of the coding instrument. Comments were solicited via e-mail in March; then a final version was created the following month. No changes occurred after that point. Actual coding began in late April, but results were not available until the fall, when the broadcast data were purchased.

5. See, for example, Jonathan Krasno and Kenneth Goldstein, "The Facts about Television Advertising and the McCain-Feingold Bill," *PS: Political Science,* vol. 35 (June 2002), pp. 207–12.

6. While the decision to forgo formal training has drawn some criticism from Professor Gibson (p. 10), it is likely that a training program would have caused complaints that Professor Goldstein and I were attempting to impose our standards on the coders. Given the alternatives, I felt the first course was preferable, especially since we were hoping for a (reasonably informed) ordinary viewer's impression of the ads. Limited pretesting of the coding instrument showed that training was unnecessary because coders were apparently able to understand and answer the questions without further explanation. Mr. Seltz and I coded information about the sponsor and type of ad.

7. Gary King, "Replication, Replication," *PS: Political Science,* vol. 28 (1995), p. 444.

8. I spot-checked an assortment of figures and can confirm that I am able to reproduce the precise numbers in *Buying Time 1998* when using these command files with the dataset available at the time.

9. Professor Gibson also notes the presence of two variables with similar names, WHAT and WHAT4, that do not generate identical results (p. 26). While the documentation in the version of the dataset that Professor Gibson received from Professor Goldstein provides no explanation, the CD-rom attached to my affirmative report explains that the former is the appropriate variable to use in replicating *Buying Time 1998.* WHAT4 is an interim variable created from WHAT; in the data set Professor Gibson used, it does not reflect the addition of several issue ads originally coded as missing data.

10. The question about the number of media markets in the dataset stems from the fact that Birmingham, AL, is listed both as "BIRMINGHAM" (2,955 times) and as "BIRMINGHAM-ANNIS" (86 times). The correct number of markets is seventy-five.

11. I do not count Professor Gibson's discussion of replicating *Buying Time 1998*'s calculation of BCRA's impact on pure issue ads because this analysis, as I explain here in the section "Measuring BCRA's Impact," cannot be replicated by depending solely on the machine-readable data in the dataset.

12. Furthermore, it appears that Professor Gibson worked with a slightly different version of the dataset than that used to create *Buying Time 1998.* See fn. 8.

13. King, "Replication, Replication," p. 444.

14. Professor Gibson's faith in q22 is ironic since it is clear that coders' responses to this item exhibit a great deal of positivity bias; that is, coders showed a marked tendency to characterize ads as pertaining to policy regardless of the actual topics raised in an ad. This is evident when examining the questions immediately following q22, which asked coders to list up to four themes for each ad from a list that included seven described as "personal characteristics of the candidate(s)" (like their background or integrity) and another 48 described as "policy

issues" (like social security or taxes). Even ads for which coders listed only themes related to the personal characteristics of the candidates—and no policy issues at all—still generated mixed responses on q22, with 20 percent of these commercials scored as being primarily focused on policy issues and another 12 percent coded as referring to both personal and policy issues.

15. This, of course, is one reason for a result that Professor Gibson finds suspicious, that 97.7 percent of group ads coded as electioneering mention candidates (p. 30, also p. 17). Given their goal of helping candidates, it would be surprising to discover that electioneering ads do not identify candidates. Professor Gibson expresses concern that these items are cognitively connected so that when coders see an ad mentioning someone who appears to be a candidate (they would not be able to identify specific contenders in most races) they assume that the ad must be electioneering. This theory, however, ignores the fact that candidate mentions are coded *after* the purpose of the ad, and that coders did score a number of ads that mentioned actual and apparent candidates in reasonably neutral ways as genuine issue advocacy.

16. This is particularly relevant since coders were not responsible for determining whether an ad came from a candidate, party, or group, and because the disclaimers were often difficult to read on their copies of the storyboards.

17. See Jonathan S. Krasno and Frank J. Sorauf, "Issue Advocacy and the Integrity of the Political Process," in this volume. See pages 55–58 of the original report, available at www.campaignlegalcenter.org, for additional discussion on the research results. Henceforth, this is referred to as Krasno and Sorauf.

18. For instance, see Anthony Downs, *An Economic Theory of Democracy* (Harper and Row, 1957).

19. The first are referred to as "sham" issue ads in *Buying Time 1998* and as "electioneering" issue ads in the work of Professor David Magleby. The second are called "genuine" issue ads in *Buying Time 1998*.

20. My affirmative report shows that 58 percent of candidate-oriented issue ads in 1998 and 67 percent in 2000 identified federal candidates and appeared within sixty days prior to the general election (Krasno and Sorauf, p. 60). These figures, of course, can only grow when the pre-primary period is taken into account.

21. This calculation included pure issue ads aired by parties. Parties have been removed from the analysis and several small errors have been corrected in the description of this calculation reported in the appendix to Krasno and Sorauf.

22. From this point on, I confine my discussion to issue advocacy by groups only.

23. As I note below, determining whether a pure issue ad identified a candidate requires inspection of the storyboards, not the dataset, making it much easier to consider the smaller set of pure issue ads that appeared within sixty days of the general election than the larger group that aired throughout the year.

24. No additional pure issue ads that mentioned a federal candidate appeared within thirty days of a primary, leaving both the numerator and denominator unchanged.

25. This slightly adjusted figure comes from the appendix to Krasno and Sorauf.

26. The 7 percent figure comes from *Buying Time 1998*; the 6 percent figure is the result of a careful reestimation described in the appendix to Krasno and Sorauf that takes advantage of some additional information revealed through this litigation.

27. *Buying Time 2000* takes the same approach, and the resulting estimates are discussed in Krasno and Sorauf.

28. In my affirmative report, I characterize this mainly as measure of regulatory efficiency, and a highly unstable one at that. A hypothetical example illustrates the problem. Imagine a single media market where no candidate-oriented issue ads appear (perhaps owing to a lack of competitive elections). If just a single genuine issue ad is affected by BCRA in this market, Professor Gibson's calculation would yield the result that 100 percent of the ads affected by BCRA are genuine issue ads—even if thousands of other genuine issue ads appeared during the course of the election cycle without being touched by this law. By contrast, the approach in *Buying Time 1998* would use the number of pure issue ads that appeared in that market throughout the available time period to gauge the percentage of total issue ads affected by BCRA.

29. Commercials mentioning Coats and Snowe account for nearly one-fifth of Professor Gibson's numerator.

30. For a more detailed discussion, see Krasno and Sorauf, appendix.

31. The text implies that Professor Gibson was attempting to calculate the percentage of issue ads affected by BCRA that are pure issue ads using his estimate of Buying *Time 1998*'s numerator (p. 40). He describes denominators in each calculation in nearly identical terms: the "airings that were shown within 60 days of the election and which depicted a candidate" (p. 39) and the "airings shown within 60 days of the election and depicting candidates" (p. 41). However, the two quantities—6,896 in the first case and 3,064 in the second—bear no resemblance to one another.

The National Association of Manufacturers' Advertising Helps Lobby Congress

PAUL R. HUARD

Paul Huard is the senior vice president for finance and administration of the National Association of Manufacturers (NAM) and is the association's former senior vice president for public policy and communications. He was a fact witness for the U.S. Chamber of Commerce, a plaintiff, and testified on the association's issue advertising campaigns and the need for clear coordination definitions.

To advance the interests of its members, the National Association of Manufacturers must regularly consult with members of Congress, officers of the executive branch, and others, including political party officials and current or likely candidates for election to federal office. At the same time, NAM must consult and work with a wide variety of other politically active organizations. The groups we work with range from other business associations to national labor organizations to citizen groups organized around specific policy views or objectives, depending on the issue.

NAM has on occasion run broadcast issue ads. For example, on two occasions in the late 1990s we ran ads advocating support of the president's tax proposals. In at least some of those ads we referred to the proposal as being that of the president, and that was an important element of our message.

More commonly, however, NAM supports coalitions or similar groups that have formed around an issue or group of issues and that create and broadcast advertisements as part of their legislative or policy strategy. We may well support such groups with our own funds, and we also may contact our members to urge them to support group efforts. To give one example among many, in 1996 NAM participated in a nonprofit group of business associations known as the Coalition, which was formed to broadcast ads to respond to the American Federation of Labor–Congress of Industrial Organizations' (AFL-CIO's) planned $35 million issue ad campaign. We urged our members to provide support, and they contributed about $2 million to the Coalition.

Our partners in legislative efforts can vary widely, depending on the issue. For example, our coalitions have worked with unions on issue ads on job-related issues such as drilling for oil in the Arctic National Wildlife Refuge or various Environmental Protection Agency (EPA) regulations that restrict coal mining. Similarly, through the Alliance for Worker Retirement Security, we have worked with various associations of senior Americans.

NAM does not support issue ads as an end in itself. They are used to support some legislative or policy agenda. The effort to pass or defeat legislation also necessarily involves working closely with members of Congress and their staffs, as well as with political parties and others who take positions on legislation and policy. For example, during 1996 NAM participated in the Thursday Group, which was organized by Representative Boehner (R-Ohio) to advance the legislative components of the Contract with America. That group brought together various associations that supported the Republican legislative agenda and provided a forum for information exchange and planning. Boehner also brought in key members to discuss their areas of responsibility and interest.

Members of Congress are elected to office. In selecting legislative and policy initiatives to support or oppose, they naturally must be concerned with the likely views of their constituents. Thus an important element of a legislative or policy agenda may be developing or demonstrating public support for or opposition to ideas or proposals. In some cases, it may be necessary to pursue a nationwide shift in public attitude. In other cases, what is needed is education targeting a few key districts or states. In some cases, the need is not to create a public position but to convince members of Congress that such a position already exists. NAM has supported issue ads for all of these purposes.

NAM has run issue ads at times when there was no impending election. In broad terms, however, Americans tend to have greater interest in political matters as an election approaches. At the same time, elected officials are most attuned to the views of their constituents in the preelection period. Thus, the preelection season is a critical time for issue ads. Conversely, after an election, public interest in policy fades—perhaps because of fatigue. Thus few issue ads are run following an election.

The timing of nonelection issue ads is driven by external events. For example, issue ads supporting a particular tax bill may be needed as the bill approaches a vote. If it happens that primaries or elections are imminent, they diminish the need to speak out right then.

There are many reasons that an issue ad may need to refer to the name of an elected official or candidate. Many bills are identified with particular sponsors and may be known publicly by the sponsors' names. Also, both incumbents and candidates may be prominent people whose support or opposition to a bill or policy may have important persuasive effect. Thus identifying a bill as having the support of President X or member of Congress Y may be persuasive. It also may be informative since many people understand the general political inclinations of prominent officials or candidates better than they understand the intricacies of legislative policy. Calling something a "Kennedy labor bill" tells most people a good deal. Also, if an issue ad is used to explain why a legislative position of a particular member of Congress is good for his or her district or state, the member generally must be mentioned. The same is true if the purpose of the ad is to induce viewers to contact the member and communicate a policy position.

Members of the House of Representatives must seek reelection every two years. One-third of the members of the Senate are elected every two years. Thus any organization that maintains an active federal legislative and policy program will have extensive and repeated contacts with persons who are or will be candidates. Those contacts involve legislative and policy issues of interest to the members. Not surprisingly, when those members run for reelection, those same issues may well arise as part of the campaign. If it appears that a member's support for an issue is being used against that member, it may be important to educate the voters about the merits of the issue.

We also need a clear, narrow, and objective definition of the type of speech that is subject to federal regulation. The present express advocacy standard has worked reasonably well, and it would work even better if it were definitively reaffirmed to mean just what it says—that there must be explicit words that expressly advocate the election or defeat of a clearly identified candidate. A standard that turns on whether speech "promotes" or "supports" or "attacks" or "opposes" a candidate is much too subjective and vague to work. For example, consider the statement that a candidate is a member of a trade union. Some might regard that as support and promotion while others might regard it as an attack and many might consider it a simple and neutral fact. Adding other subjective terms, such as asking whether the speech is "suggestive" of "plausible" meanings, would make matters worse.

For similar reasons, any other restrictions or requirements that might apply to NAM's involvement in issue ads must be narrowly, clearly, and objectively defined. Forcing NAM to guess the point at which a series of conversations, e-mails, and other communications amounts to the execution of a contract for future disbursements relating to a particular type of speech would be burdensome and would chill our participation in issue advocacy.

If our members were forced to choose between being publicly identified as supporters of particular issue ads and not running those ads, many would opt against the ads. This results from a wide variety of concerns. For example, a business that is subject to the jurisdiction of a particular congressional committee may be very reluctant to be known to espouse policies that the committee chair opposes. Or a unionized business may be reluctant to be seen financing positions opposed by organized labor. For this reason, in 1996, the Coalition had both public and nonpublic supporters and assured the nonpublic supporters that their identities would be guarded carefully.

My understanding is that spending for ads that are coordinated with a federal candidate, campaign, or political party may be deemed a contribution. NAM cannot lawfully make such contributions. However, NAM wants and needs to remain free to maintain extensive contacts with members of Congress and their staffs and to freely participate in issue advocacy. To permit this type of activity, it is critical for the law to provide an objective, clear, bright-line definition of coordination.

The definition of coordination must be clear, objective, and narrow enough that NAM and its representatives can deal closely and effectively with members and representatives of political parties while being confident that their conduct will not expose NAM to a colorable charge of coordination. Likewise, it must be clear and narrow enough that NAM can have reasonable confidence that other participants in coalitions or other groups that engage in issue advocacy will avoid arguable coordination.

Importantly, it is not enough to have a standard that, after years of litigation, ultimately will be held to permit what NAM does. Federal Election Commission (FEC) enforcement proceedings are very disruptive and expensive. Exposure to such proceedings tends to discourage contributors caught up in the proceeding from future support of issue advocacy. Thus it is essential for the standard to be clear and narrow enough that unfounded charges can be detected and rejected immediately.

The serious problems that can be caused by an inadequate definition of coordination are illustrated by NAM's experience with a complaint to the FEC about the 1996 activities of the Coalition. The Coalition decided from the outset that nothing smacking of coordination would occur. All members were instructed to avoid anything that might be perceived as coordination of the content, location, or frequency of ads. Yet the FEC pursued the investigation for years on the possibility that contacts with the Thursday Group or the hiring of individuals whose firms, through other individuals, represented some candidates that might have somehow influenced the Coalition's decisions. The inquiry was extremely burdensome and disruptive and, in my judgment, substantially chilled the willingness of members of the Coalition to support a similar effort in 1998. If the law had been clear that coordination required an agreement with a candidate or campaign as to the content, placement, or frequency of the ads, the FEC proceeding would not have occurred.

Why the Chamber of Commerce Runs Issue Ads

R. BRUCE JOSTEN

R. Bruce Josten is the executive vice president for governmental affairs of the U.S. Chamber of Commerce. He has held this position since 1994 and has been with the Chamber since 1974. Josten testified for the Chamber as to the organization's political activities and issue advertisements.

To advance the interests of its members, the Chamber of Commerce must and does regularly consult with members of Congress, officers of the executive branch, and others, including political party officials and current or likely candidates for election to federal office. At the same time, the Chamber must consult and work with a wide variety of politically active organizations. Depending on the issue, the groups we work with may range from other business associations to national labor organizations to citizen groups organized around specific policy views or objectives.

In building and maintaining support for the Chamber's legislative and policy agenda, we need to be able to communicate our views to the public. To that end, the Chamber regularly produces and purchases television, radio, cable, and other public communications on matters of interest to the public. Sometimes the Chamber sponsors these communications directly in its own name. For example, in 1999, the Chamber ran ads relating to "Y2K," and the Chamber's president, Tom Donohue, had delivered a series of radio talks entitled "Speaking of Business." Sometimes the Chamber contributes to groups or coalitions of like-minded organizations and persons that take responsibility for preparing and airing the communications. For example, in March 2000, the Chamber helped support ads by the American Business for Legal Immigrations. In December 2001, the Chamber supported ads by People for Common Sense Courts that urged Senator Tom Daschle to schedule a Senate vote on Eugene Scalia's nomination as solicitor of labor.

Not surprisingly, since these communications are intended to advance the Chamber's objectives, they sometimes also address issues that the Chamber has discussed with the persons and groups with which it regularly cooperates, including members of Congress, representatives of political parties, and various cooperating organizations of all types.

Because we are a democracy, many of the members of Congress with whom we work are—or will soon be—candidates for reelection. Members of the House run every two years. One-third of the Senate runs every two years. Also, there are periodic special elections. As one would expect, the policy views and political activities of such candidates are often the subject of public discussion during such campaigns.

The Chamber and many other groups with which it cooperates with respect to legislative and public policy were the subject of a complaint filed with the Federal Election Commission. It alleged that issue advertisements (advertisements that did not expressly advocate the election or defeat of a candidate) that the Chamber helped sponsor in 1996 through a group known as the Coalition were coordinated with federal candidates, campaigns, or political committees and were subject to federal campaign finance regulation and were an improper use of corporate funds. In fact, the Chamber and the Coalition had gone to great lengths to ensure that no coordination occurred, but nevertheless, they were subjected to years of intrusive, burdensome, and very expensive proceedings before the FEC dismissed the complaint. In my judgment, that experience discouraged many participants in the Coalition from further similar efforts and public communication.

For obvious reasons, members of Congress often seek to attach their names to legislation that they sponsor. These designations become how the legislation is known in public discourse. A recent and obvious example is the recent campaign finance legislation, which in various permutations was known as McCain-Feingold or Shays-Meehan.

An important reason to run issue ads in the home district or state of members of Congress can be to get the members' attention—make them think about how their constituents are likely to feel about their legislative and policy positions—and to either encourage or discourage those positions. To achieve those objectives, it often is important for an issue ad to use a member's name. Moreover, because both members and the public are most focused on political issues at election time, it is important for such ads to be run near the election.

Legislative efforts can extend for many years. At times during such an effort, it may be very important to run public advertising at the time that a committee or chamber of Congress is about to vote. But issue ads also may plan a longer-range purpose—building for the future. It may be important for such long-range ads to take advantage of recent events. For example, if a presidential or prominent legislative candidate says or does something that may be persuasive on a legislative issue, it may be important to use that event or statement in a prompt issue ad, even though no vote is impending.

The Chamber and similar groups cannot afford to be tied up in campaign finance enforcement proceedings. Such proceedings use up resources intended for other purposes and the mere threat of such proceedings discourages donor support. For those reasons, as well as because we want to obey the law and certainly do not want to risk punishment for an inadvertent error, it is critical for us to have a clear standard for identifying the type of campaign speech that is subject to federal limitation and regulation. The express advocacy standard—whether an ad contains speech that in explicit language expressly advocates the election or defeat of a clearly identified candidate—generally has proved workable.

By contrast, a standard that turns on whether speech promotes, supports, attacks, or opposes a candidate would be impossible to comply with. The terms are hopelessly vague and subjective. Also, like beauty, their meaning often lies in the eye or ear of the beholder. Adding a requirement that the speech be suggestive of no plausible meaning other than an exhortation to vote for or against a specific candidate does not cure the problem. Application of the express advocacy standard costs the Chamber substantial sums for legal advice alone. Attempting to make confident judgments as to what an ad is "suggestive" of or what meanings might be "plausible" would be impossible. We would end up paying lawyers a fortune and would still be told that to be sure of our safety we should steer far clear of arguably regulated speech.

Our experience has been that the ability to assure contributors that our contemplated advertisements will not be express advocacy and hence will not require public identifications of our contributors is vital to obtaining contributions. Contributors have a wide range of reasons for not wanting to be identified with particular issue ads. In some cases, they fear that the ads may provoke difficulties with opposing groups, such as labor. Others fear that state or federal officeholders or regulators may retaliate. A company with important legislation pending may not want to be publicly identified with a position that the relevant committee chairman strongly opposes. Thus, for example, the 1996 Coalition I mention above gave financial supporters the option of remaining anonymous, and many chose that option. Pooled financial support is essential because producing and broadcasting advertising, particularly television advertising, is very expensive.

Timing is often critical to issue ads and to political ads generally. Issue ad campaigns are often swiftly developed on the basis of informal understandings, often oral, e-mail, fax, or some combination thereof. There are false starts, reversals, and new directions. Plans change depending on funding availability. Initial commitments may be modest, but they can escalate quickly, and the annual amounts ultimately spent can reach millions of dollars.

In such an environment, a requirement that a public report be filed within twenty-four hours of each time the Chamber or its agents execute a contract that requires disbursements aggregating more than $10,000 in a calendar year for any speech that might be considered an "electioneering communication" would be a serious burden, as would any requirement that all contributors of more than $1,000 be publicly identified.

I understand that the new law includes a requirement that broadcast licensees collect and make public disclosure of requests to purchase broadcast time for communications that relate to "any political matter of national importance," including but not limited to communications concerning a federal candidate, a federal election, or "a national legislative issue of national importance." These standards are exceptionally vague. To the extent that licensees genuinely seek to comply, they likely will interpret these standards very broadly. This will lead to premature disclosures of possible ads that will never be run and will require extensive and burdensome reporting to the licensees.

Moreover, for the above standard to be applied, it appears that the content of the ad would have to be disclosed at the time the request to purchase broadcast time was made. In my experience, it is not unusual to change the content of an ad immediately before broadcast. If such changes were permitted freely, then the advance disclosure requirement could be circumvented by initially specifying an ad that would not have reportable content and making a switch at the last minute. If such changes were not permitted freely then the ability to adjust speech to circumstances would be seriously impaired and reportable speech would be chilled because of the associated reporting burdens.

How the Reform Act Adversely Affects the Associated Builders and Contractors

Edward L. Monroe

Edward L. Monroe is the director of political affairs for the Associated Builders and Contractors (ABC). He is also the treasurer of the ABC Political Action Committee and testified for the ABC on the organization's election-related activities and contributions. The ABC is a plaintiff in the McConnell v. FEC *suit.*

The Associated Builders and Contractors, Inc., is a Maryland nonprofit corporation funded primarily by membership dues. It is a national trade association representing more than 23,000 contractors and related firms in the construction industry. Its members include both unionized and nonunion employers and share the philosophy that construction work should be awarded and performed on the basis of merit, regardless of labor affiliation. Representatives of ABC meet with officeholders, candidates, political party officials, and their respective staffs to encourage their support of legislation that advances our goals. In addition, it has paid for broadcast communications that referred to clearly identified candidates for federal office and that aired within sixty days of a general election and within thirty days of a primary election.

ABC often engages in political communications, including broadcast ads, that seek to protect merit-based employers from legislative initiatives or regulatory proposals that would restrict market opportunities for these. Such an initiative might seek to prevent firms from bidding on government contracts or government-funded contracts unless the bidding firm hires union members or uses restrictive union work rules. Such initiatives often originate with or have the vigorous support of labor unions or labor organizations.

Initiatives of interest or concern to ABC members arise or are actively contested within sixty days of a general election or within thirty days of a primary election. If ABC and coalitions in which it participates could not run ads that mention officials of the executive branch, members of Congress, or candidates for federal office, it would be much more difficult to use broadcast advertising to educate or motivate the public to take action we believe appropriate in the circumstances. Proponents of such initiatives could time them within such regulated windows with the express purpose of suppressing effective communications that might marshal opposition to the proposals.

The Associated Builders and Contractors, Inc., will be injured by the Bipartisan Campaign Reform Act (BCRA). The injury arises in circumstances in which a request is made for broadcast time and a judgment must be made as to whether the content of the contemplated communication must be disclosed under vague and overbroad standards. This will have chilling effects. The injury also arises in circumstances in which the request to purchase broadcast time is made in advance of the actual purchase. The result will be that plans and strategies are disclosed, flexibility is impaired, and messages may be confused or obscured. The injury also arises whenever the burden of complying with the complex reporting requirements is incurred, either directly or via an agent.

Effective communication by ABC and its members would be inhibited if the companies contributing money to support ads or similar communications were required to disclose their names in public filings. Once, we disclosed the names of our contributors in an edition of an ABC publication, and some of those companies soon suffered substantial vandalism. They were of the view that this vandalism was a result of labor union member efforts to intimidate firms that publicly opposed union policies and that they were targeted because of public disclosure of their donations. Since then, ABC has felt constrained to not disclose the names of contributors. We are very concerned by any statute or regulation that would compel such disclosure.

A requirement that a public report be filed within twenty-four hours of each time ABC or its agents execute a contract that requires disbursements aggregating more than $10,000 in a calendar year for any speech that might be considered an "electioneering communication" would be a serious burden, as would any requirement that all contributors of more than $1,000 be publicly identified. Such disclosures could definitely reduce the number of companies willing to make contributions for political ads owing to reasonable fears of violent retaliation. It would also require difficult judgments as to when complex informal exchanges in various media amount to an executed agreement as well as to the likely level of future disbursements.

I understand that the reform act includes a requirement that broadcast licensees collect and make public disclosures of requests to purchase broadcast time for communications that relate to "any political matter of national importance," including but not limited to communications concerning a federal candidate, a federal election, or "a national legislative issue of national importance." These standards are exceptionally vague and will require extensive and burdensome reporting to the licensees.

The defendants in this proceeding have argued that ads run near the time of an election are evidence that the intent is to advocate the election of one candidate or another. However, there are other, more valid, explanations for the timing of our advertising. One is that serious legislative initiatives or regulatory proposals often are considered near the time of elections. It is clear that members of the public are generally more receptive to and engaged in considering government policy ideas and issues as elections near. If that is the time when people will listen, then that is the time to speak. And once an election occurs, there seems to be a period of fatigue during which political matters are of less interest, making issue ads then less effective.

In addition, it must be noted that ABC's speech timing often is reactive. If ABC's policy adversaries—for example labor unions and their supporting organizations—launch a disinformation campaign that threatens our members' interests or attacks officials that support policies favored by ABC, then ABC frequently will respond with information intended to provide a basis for the public's having a correct understanding of the matter addressed by our adversary. In such circumstances, the timing of our speech is selected largely by our adversary.

All that being said, there certainly have been instances where issues of importance to ABC members have also become important in an election. Issues are, presumably, the basis for choosing a candidate. When people learn about the issues of importance to ABC, they may decide to vote in a certain way. We are concerned with the issues, seeking to educate the public about a variety of issues that are important to our members, and, we believe, the general public. If people choose to vote on the basis of the information we provide about the issues, that is not the goal of our communications. In some elections, public attitudes developed in response to our advertisements may have influenced the outcome. But from ABC's point of view, it is clear that what comes first is the issue. We seek broad acceptance of our policy positions. Other impacts are categorically of less interest to us. If ABC seeks to influence an election, it uses the highly regulated resources of our political action committee.

The Associated Builders and Contractors, Inc., is concerned about the chilling effects of the coordination provisions in the reform act. A coordination investigation, or the threat of one, could inhibit activities in which we have participated in the past. For example, on a wide variety of legislative matters, representatives of ABC meet with elected officers and

their staff to explore legislative and policy matters relevant to the construction community. These meetings necessarily encompass discussions
on relevant political considerations. Under the pre-BCRA standards of
coordination, we could have some (though not complete) confidence that
such contacts would not be formally disclosed to the FEC so long as there
was no "agreement or formal collaboration" with respect to advertisements
by ABC. Also, we could have some confidence that allies could follow
clear standards to avoid conduct that might support a collaboration
charge. As a result of the relatively clear pre-BCRA standard, despite frequent contacts with elected officers and staffs, ABC could engage in issue
advertisements and coordinate speech with allied groups without serious
concern that it would be deemed coordination to a candidate, campaign,
or political party. The BCRA, however, imposes a much more uncertain
standard for judging coordination. As a result, either we will have to be
considerably more limited in our contacts with elected officers and staffs,
or we must eschew spending on issue advertisements with content that has
any arguable relevance to earlier contacts. Similarly, we will have to be far
more cautious in funding issue speech with allies whose conduct in dealing with elected officers and staffs are not in ABC's control and that might
give rise to a coordination charge. We also will be more constrained in our
choice of creative talent and similar personnel because of the risk that,
under the new vague standards, vendor conduct may be deemed coordination. This testimony does not imply that the pre-BCRA standard was
sufficiently clear, but the new standard is much less clear in ways that pose
serious difficulties.

A Practitioner Looks at How Issue Groups Select and Target Federal Candidates

ROCKY PENNINGTON

Rocky Pennington is a Republican political consultant and the owner and president of three Florida companies specializing in political fund-raising, direct mail, campaign consulting, and political advertising in state and federal elections. He was a fact witness for the defense. His statement focuses on the ways in which interest groups select candidates for targeted issue advocacy campaigns.

Some interest groups conduct what amounts to a vetting process to decide if they will help a particular federal or state candidate. These groups often do a lot of screening before deciding to commit resources. Many make the candidates fill out lengthy questionnaires and then bring them in and essentially grill them about their positions on specific issues. Some groups, such as Associated Industries, actually videotape the interview so they can have it to show the candidate if they're successful and the issue comes up in the legislature, to remind them of what their position should be. Many groups have gotten pretty sophisticated and aggressive about trying to pin down elected officials on what their vote's going to be ahead of time.

If an interest group does decide to assist a candidate, it's usually helpful in the campaign, and even more helpful if you have good communications with the group, and can persuade them to do things that you feel are more productive. Interest groups can help in different ways. They can raise funds from their members, and in federal races, this may take the form of raising federal funds (hard money) and bundling the checks, then delivering them all together. They can produce and run TV and radio ads using hard money on independent expenditures, or nonfederal funds (soft money) to run electioneering that avoids express advocacy. They can create direct mail plans, conduct mass or targeted mailings, and buy billboards and print ads. They can set up phone banks or push polling to create positive impressions of a candidate or negative impressions of the opponent. Just before the election, they can make get-out-the-vote calls to help a candidate or vote suppression calls to tell voters something bad about the opponent. In addition to trying to elect candidates, these groups are often trying to create appreciation or even obligation on the part of successful candidates. And candidates usually do appreciate this kind of help even when they deny it publicly, which they usually do.

Party and interest groups' attack ads can help candidates in many ways. In addition to getting out a negative message about the opponent, they allow candidates to conserve their limited resources and focus on getting out a positive message about themselves. At the same time, the candidate can disavow the negative ads, saying—with a wink—"I didn't know anything about it and I condemn these ads." I think this now happens in virtually every campaign. Very few politicians would stand up and say, "I think it's great, keep it up." Of course, occasionally the approach these groups take is off base, and in those cases the ads may not be that helpful. But usually the ads are helpful and candidates appreciate them.

How Issue Ads Are Designed to Target Federal Candidates without "Express Advocacy"

Douglas L. Bailey

Douglas L. Bailey is a Republican political consultant and founder of Bailey, Deardourff & Associates. His clients have included President Gerald Ford's 1976 campaign, political parties, and interest groups. Bailey was a fact witness for the defense and addressed the ways in which political consultants select the language and content of political advertisements.

In the modern world of thirty-second political advertisements, it is rarely advisable to use such clumsy words as "vote for" or "vote against." If I am designing an ad and want the conclusion to be the number 20, I would use the ad to count from 1 to 19. I would lead the viewer to think 20, but I would never say it. All advertising professionals understand that the most effective advertising leads the viewer to his or her own conclusion without forcing it down their throat. This is especially true of political advertising because people are generally very skeptical of claims made by or about politicians.

Contrary to what many people would like to believe, it is well known among campaign consultants that the "swing voters" who regularly determine the outcome of elections usually vote on candidate personalities rather than issues. Regardless of the substantive topic of any particular ad, one of the single most important messages that a political ad can convey is the underlying sentiment that a candidate has value similar to or different from the target viewers of the ad. A campaign commercial is most effective if the candidate is perceived as likeable to the citizens relaxing in their living rooms, and if the viewers feel comfortable that the candidate shares their values. Often, the substantive issue is merely the vehicle used to demonstrate personal qualities.

The notion that ads intended to influence an election can easily be separated from those that are not based upon the mere presence or absence of particular words or phrases such as "vote for" is at best a historical anachronism. When I first entered this business, and up through the mid-1980s, we were regularly able to purchase five-minute slots of airtime. In a five-minute spot, I could introduce a candidate, bring the viewer to a comfort level with the candidate, cover a few different substantive issues, and, at the end, have the candidate make a direct appeal for a vote. In this bygone era, it made sense for a candidate to appeal directly for votes using words such as "vote for," "support," or "cast your ballot" on the basis of a more full or substantive story told in a five-minute time period. By contrast, in a thirty-second ad, there is not enough time to make a positive direct sale.

In addition to the work we did for candidates at Bailey, Deardourff and Associates, we also made political ads for political parties and issue groups. When we were creating true issue ads (for example, for ballot initiatives or more general issues such as handgun control), and when we were creating true party-building ads, it was never necessary for us to reference specific candidates for federal office in order to create effective ads. For instance, we created a series of ads opposing a gambling referendum in Florida that made no reference to any candidates. We were successful in conveying our message, and the referendum failed 2 to 1.

Similarly, issue organizations can design true issue ads without ever mentioning specific candidates for federal office. In my decades of experience in national politics, nearly all of the ads that I have seen that both mention specific candidates and are run in the days immediately preceding the election were clearly designed to influence elections. From a media consultant's perspective, there would be no reason to run such ads if your desire was not to have an impact on an election. This is true not only in the 60 days immediately prior to an election but probably also in the 90 or 120 days beforehand.

When I had a client who wanted to run a true issue ad to change or bolster public attitudes on an issue, I would recommend avoiding the time period when the airwaves are saturated with electioneering ads. Such pure issue ads would likely get drowned out by the din of election-related ads. Moreover, any ads that mention specific candidates that are aired during the height of an election season are almost certain to be perceived by the public as electioneering.

Few political advertisements go onto television without being subject to rigorous polling, word testing, and focus groups. This is big business, and a lot of money goes into pre- and post-development analysis. The political parties and issue groups that run so-called issue ads in the fall of an even-numbered year know exactly what they are doing. I certainly don't think that it is inappropriate for these organizations to sponsor broadcast ads that talk about issues and include positive or negative comments about particular candidates; I just wouldn't call them issue ads. They are designed to influence elections and should be recognized as such.

A Consultant's View on How Issue Ads
Shaped a Congressional Election

TERRY S. BECKETT

Terry S. Beckett is a retired Democratic political consultant and has worked in campaigns since 1976. Beckett was a consultant to Linda Chapin's 2000 campaign for Florida's Eighth Congressional District. Beckett was a fact witness for the defense. His statement addresses the interest group and political party activity in Chapin's race.

Interest groups were an important factor in the 2000 congressional election in Florida's Eighth District. Many interest groups offered to provide campaign support, telling us all about what they would do for us if Linda Chapin would pledge to vote a certain way on their issues. You can send them your position, and they may come back and say, "This isn't worded the way we like it worded." They want you on record saying it the way they want before they will provide the money. We lost some money that way in the 2000 race because we didn't like those kinds of commitments. One group wanted Ms. Chapin to pledge to take a certain position on partial birth abortion before they would agree to provide assistance, as I recall, in the form of direct mail. Ms. Chapin is pro-choice, and we gave them a written statement of her position, but they came back saying, we want to change it. It was very important to them. Ms. Chapin declined, and they really put a lot of pressure on her, but she still declined. I am proud of her for doing so. This group did not help us in the campaign. Mr. Ric Keller (Ms. Chapin's opponent) received assistance from the Club for Growth and the National Rifle Association (NRA). I understand that the NRA did events for Mr. Keller, including at least one at his campaign headquarters. In addition, interest groups ran electioneering ads for Ms. Chapin and her opponents.

Through my experience in political campaigns, including overseeing the creation and running of television ads for Ms. Chapin in her federal and county races, I am familiar with political campaign advertising. I am aware of the idea that particular "magic words" might be required in order for an advertisement to influence an election. However, no particular words of advocacy are needed in order for an ad to influence the outcome of an election. No list of such words could be complete; if you list 50, savvy political actors will find 100 more. Many so-called issue ads run by parties and interest groups just before an election attack a candidate and end by supposedly urging the viewer to "tell" or "ask" the candidate to stop being that way. These ads are almost never really about issues. They are almost always election ads, designed to affect the election result, and many do affect the election result. You can see this most clearly in the ones that amount to personal attacks or that criticize a candidate on several unrelated issues. In fact, in my experience, candidates tend to shy away from such negative attack ads because there would be political repercussions for them. But entities like the Democratic Congressional Campaign Committee (DCCC) and the Club for Growth do not have such constraints. According to my observations, the candidate ads in the 2000 congressional race, which were financed with federal funds (hard money), were actually more about issues than the supposed issue ads run by political parties and interest groups, which I understand were financed at least in part with nonfederal funds (soft money).

Television and radio electioneering advertising by political parties and interest groups played an important role in the 2000 congressional election in Florida's Eighth District. Political parties on both sides of the campaign ran so-called issue ads that were financed partly with soft money but clearly directed at influencing the outcome of the election. The DCCC ran television advertising through the state party in order to take advantage of the more favorable hard-money/soft-money allocation ratios enjoyed by state parties. Typically, the DCCC sends money to the state party, and the state party buys the airtime. Six of these state party ads, which as I recall were run in the two months prior to the general election, praise Ms. Chapin or criticize Mr. Keller or Mr. Bill Sublette and were clearly designed to help Ms. Chapin's election prospects. One ad, ("FL/Chapin Record"), features video footage of Ms. Chapin speaking with some senior citizens in a pharmacy. That footage was originally shot by our campaign's media consultant and later purchased by the DCCC. We did not coordinate our activities with the DCCC but did give permission for the sale of this footage—with the understanding that we could not use the footage ourselves once the sale took place—and we were not surprised that the footage later turned up in a DCCC ad run by the state party.

I support the restrictions in the new reform act on the use of soft money to affect federal elections. My observations in recent election cycles lead me to conclude that political campaigns have become more and more about the money of private interests—both the unrestricted money those interests use to influence election results by making soft-money donations to political parties or running so-called issue ads, and also the additional money many of those interests hope to make by doing so. These private interests are concerned with who they can install in public office and how they can influence that officeholder so that he or she feels obligated to them, so they can influence policy and make more money. Of course candidates often appreciate the help that these interests groups can provide, such as running attack ads for which the candidate has no responsibility. If some outside third party runs attack ads, a candidate can distance him- or herself from them, and the message gets across to the voters without the candidate getting dirtied. Ms. Chapin was uncomfortable with the role of the interest groups that used soft money to influence the 2000 race, and she challenged the Republicans to call off the outside groups on both sides but was rebuffed. And if the interest groups are coming in on behalf of the other guy but not you, then you're in trouble. In my opinion, Mr. Keller could not have beaten experienced, better-known politicians like Mr. Sublette or Ms. Chapin without the support of the Club for Growth and other special interest groups. Mr. Keller was virtually unknown and had no real record in the community—but he was able to find a powerful Washington group to help him, and he is now in Congress.

PART III
Public Opinion and Corruption

259
EVIDENCE FROM PUBLIC OPINION RESEARCH

297
DONOR PERSPECTIVES

317
OFFICEHOLDER PERSPECTIVES

330
PARTY CHAIR PERSPECTIVES

A note about the evidence on corruption presented in this section: with the exception of experts on public opinion, the challengers to the Bipartisan Campaign Reform Act did not present witnesses who argued that the current campaign finance system is *not* corrupt. Instead, the challengers argued in court that evidence of corruption is "anecdotal" and relatively minor and does not justify what they characterized as the "extreme anti-corruption measures of BCRA."

As a result, the testimony excerpted in this chapter by political donors, federal officeholders, and national party officials, with the exception of a brief statement by Senator Mitch McConnell, comes solely from supporters of the reform act, who were the only witnesses to directly address the corrupting aspects of the soft-money system.

Public Attitudes toward Campaign Finance Practice and Reform

ROBERT Y. SHAPIRO

Robert Y. Shapiro is chair and professor of the Department of Political Science at Columbia University. He has written and taught extensively on survey research and public opinion. He was an expert witness for the defense in this litigation.

Shapiro's full report summarizes relevant scholarly studies and public opinion data on campaign finance practices and reform proposals based on many surveys conducted over the past decade. This excerpt presents what he considers are the major findings supported by the evidence from these sources. The public, he argues, is troubled by the role of money in the political process, associates large campaign contributions with special interest influence and corruption, opposes large unregulated contributions to political parties, and supports the Bipartisan Campaign Reform Act (BCRA) reforms of the campaign finance system.

OVERVIEW

The analysis and summary here focus on public opinion data based on responses to surveys that were fielded since 1990 (except for trend data that go back a bit further). The full data assembled include responses to questions that were asked in surveys since the 1940s. The findings from those earlier questions are similar, but for purposes of brevity they are not included nor discussed here.

To what extent has the public seen the need to reform the campaign finance system to limit the influence of money in the political process?
For well more than a decade, the public has continued to see the need to limit the political influence of money. The political science literature on public opinion toward political reform shows that large majorities of Americans, as a general matter, see the need for limits on the amount of

money candidates for federal elective office can raise, contribute, and ultimately spend on their campaigns.[1]

Regarding the general need for campaign finance reform, solid majorities of the public have been somewhat or very dissatisfied with the campaign finance laws governing the way political parties and candidates raise money, particularly as they hear news about questionable political fund-raising. The public has seen these problems in fund-raising as occurring in most or all campaigns, and it has perceived that they have occurred more often, or have otherwise been worse, than in the past.

The public has consistently responded that the campaign finance system needs major or complete overhaul. Large majorities of the public, when asked, have supported the idea of reform and new campaign finance laws to deal with this problem; they have also supported stricter laws controlling campaign fund-raising. When polls ask directly about the need for stricter new laws in contrast to increased enforcement of existing laws, the need for stricter laws receives more support.

Critics of reform have emphasized how the public does not see campaign reform as a high-priority problem. The evidence they cite, however, is completely misleading. We report data that these critics consistently ignore. First and foremost, when asked directly about campaign finance reform in different ways, majorities or sizeable percentages of the American public have been concerned about this issue and have considered it a high and even top priority, consistent with the troubles the public has seen in campaign fund-raising. When compared with other issues that compete for government and public attention, it is understandable that the issue has not normally been seen in the same way as pressing economic problems, crises in health care and retirement income, crime, war, terrorism, and other international crises. Campaign finance has been more salient when campaign finance problems and scandal have been given the kind of attention by political leaders and the news media that these other issues have regularly been given. In light of this, the large percentages of the public (often majorities, depending on the survey question wording and context) who have reported that campaign finance reform is an important issue is striking.

Last, notwithstanding the public's ongoing cynicism and lack of confidence toward many aspects of political life,[2] substantial percentages of the public have thought that campaign finance reforms can be effective, can reduce the influence of money in politics at least somewhat, can make the public more optimistic about government, and would be good for democracy.

Has the public seen politics and politicians consumed and harmed by fund-raising?

The public is troubled by particular developments that have occurred as the result of contemporary campaign fund-raising. The public has seen more money raised than in the past, and it has seen these contributions as having too much influence. Americans have perceived that elections have been for sale and that there would be more progress in solving national problems if the role of money were reduced. The public has seen the scrambling for political funds that elected officials engage in as taking time away from important government activity; further, the public has seen officials as having to spend too much time on fund-raising and has indicated that this is a problem. An additional—and major—problem that the public has perceived in the political system is that potentially good leaders have been discouraged from running for office by the need to raise large amounts of money.

To what degree has the public perceived corruption in politics connected to the influence of money and large campaign donations?

The public is troubled by the problem of corruption in politics generally. The data show that a substantial proportion of the public has perceived corruption in the political system, and that we have been losing ground. Political leaders, in particular, have been seen as a major part of the problem. In a study by Louis Harris and Associates in 1990, large majorities saw large political contributors and fund-raising in campaigns as a major source of corruption. The data also show that the public has perceived pressures on companies to contribute to campaigns as a major cause of corruption. A more recent survey reveals that fully 77 percent of the public in 2001 have seen the way in which candidates raised money as unethical if not fully corrupt, with 31 percent viewing it as corrupt.

To what extent has the public associated campaign donations with the general political influence of "special interests" and political contributions?

[The data] show that the public has been concerned with contributions from special interest groups and has placed a high priority on reform that limits the influence they have through campaign contributions. The public has overwhelmingly seen elected officials as more likely to represent special interests than the public interest and that this influence has increased: specifically, the public has perceived more influence of special interests, and especially special interest money, than in the past.

Moreover, the public has connected this influence to political contributions: the public has seen a major problem in elected officials seeking and receiving such contributions while making decisions about issues of concern to those giving money. Specifically, that influence has been associated with government officials paying attention to campaign contributors as they make decisions on important issues, and in the end the public has perceived that elected officials in Washington are influenced more by pressures from major, large campaign contributors than by the best interest of the country. What is especially striking is the vast majority of the public—consistently more than 70 percent, according to the data—who have thought that government officials make or change policy decisions as a direct result of major campaign contributions. It is not surprising, then, that in considering possible campaign finance reform, the public has seen protecting the government from the excessive influences of campaign contributors as more important than allowing individuals to support parties and candidates financially. Other data show, further, the extent to which the public has seen campaign contributors as having too much influence over public officials to whom they contribute, and how the public has seen questionable fund-raising influencing the country's domestic and foreign policy.

What have been the public's perceptions and opinions toward substantial political donations in the form of soft-money contributions to political parties?
The public has opposed large unregulated soft-money contributions to political parties. [The data] show that the public has been troubled by large soft-money donations and sees this situation as requiring an important change in the campaign finance system. Large majorities of the public have disapproved of unlimited soft-money contributions to political parties overall, including funds that are spent on political advertisements. (The public similarly disapproves of individuals and organizations spending large sums of money on political advertising and would limit such spending.) The data show that there has been majority or better support for a ban on soft-money contributions to political parties. Support is even greater when the public has been asked about limiting, not fully prohibiting, such contributions. Among those favoring limiting soft-money contributions to parties, half or more "strongly" favor it. This opposition to soft money is consistent regardless of whether the donations are given by individuals or corporations or labor unions.

*How greatly was the public troubled by the political influence that could
be associated with campaign contributions, in particular high-profile cases
such as Enron, party fund-raising during the Clinton and Gore election
campaigns, and other such behavior?*

The public was troubled by the apparent connection between political
donations and political influence, in particular high-profile cases such as
Enron and contributions to the Democratic Party during the Clinton and
Gore presidential campaigns. The Enron scandal and allegations against
Clinton, Gore, and the Democratic Party were widely publicized, and the
public was polled on its opinions about these issues. The public has been
troubled by the behavior of both parties.

In the Enron case, the survey data show that the public indirectly
linked the ability of the company and its executives to get away with their
misbehavior to campaign contributions. The reported results show that
the public thought it was at least somewhat likely that Enron received
favorable treatment from the Clinton administration as a result of its history of campaign contributions. The public was also suspicious, though
a bit more divided, about the extent to which Enron's Republican Party
and campaign contributions kept the Bush administration from acting
effectively to protect the company's employees and investors. One party
was not blamed noticeably more than the other, but rather, the public
overwhelmingly saw this as a problem of interest group and corporate
donors' general access to and influence on politicians and policymakers
of both parties.

The public clearly saw Democratic Party and campaign fund-raising
involving Al Gore and Bill Clinton in this way, and pollsters asked the
public numerous questions about this from the 1996 election through the
2000 election. The tables present some illustrations of the survey data
regarding Gore and the Democratic Party. The public was troubled by
what transpired, and pluralities or majorities saw the behavior of Gore and
the party as unethical or inappropriate. This behavior, again, was not seen
as peculiar to Gore and the Democrats but as the behavior of politicians
and parties generally. At the time of the 1996 election, the public was
divided, in a Gallup poll regarding the ethics of the Democratic Party,
when it came to raising campaign money from political contributors—
and the percentage perceiving the Democratic Party as "very unethical"
was more than twice that seeing the party as "very ethical." In early 1997
there was substantial public concern regarding Republicans offering
potential donors special access to members of Congress.

In the case of Bill Clinton's behavior as president, [the data] show the public's dissatisfaction with Clinton's involvement in Democratic Party fund-raising from the White House. There were widely publicized stories of activities involving the use of the White House itself. Again, the public saw this as typical of presidents and both parties generally. And, again, this raised questions about the extent to which political leaders gave special access and favorable treatment to campaign contributors, and whether this produced changes in government policy. The public, in the case of Clinton, was suspicious that it did.

In the case of the 1996 election, questions arose about efforts by Chinese interests to contribute to the Democratic Party, and these raised concerns about the parties turning a blind eye and accepting (illegal) foreign contributions because they get lost in the chase for unlimited soft-money contributions. [The data] show that a large percentage of the public thought that Chinese officials tried to funnel money to the Democratic Party to influence the outcome of the election.

Further, the public was also concerned about donations to the Democratic Party from sources in Indonesia, and this concern extended to foreign interests generally. This, too, was an issue that the public thought applied to both political parties and to politics generally, and the public opposed allowing such donations.

To what extent has the public been concerned about campaign fund-raising involving business and corporations in general, as well as labor unions?

The data reported show that the public has been bothered by political campaigns soliciting donations from companies that do business with the government or are regulated by Congress. The public has supported limiting such contributions in House and Senate elections. When asked about contributions from private corporations or labor unions, the public has widely agreed (and a majority "strongly") that government should be able to put restrictions on the amount of money that corporations and unions may contribute to an election campaign.

When the public has been asked about unions alone, the results are similar to those for the campaign donations of companies. Furthermore, a large majority of the public has disagreed with the use of union dues to support parties and political candidates without individual members' permission; it has supported requiring that unions get such permission.

Has the American public supported the Bipartisan Campaign Reform Act and its predecessor bills?

Given the data presented above, it is not surprising that the public has supported the enactment of the reforms in the new campaign finance law that restricts soft-money contributions to the political parties. The data are based on responses to polls conducted since January 1, 2001, including the period of the Senate debate regarding the Bipartisan Campaign Reform Act. The data show, overall, that the public has consistently favored the reform bills and that the public wanted President Bush to sign the new legislation into law once Congress had passed it.

NOTES

1. Greg M. Shaw and Amy S. Ragland, "The Polls—Trends: Political Reform," *Public Opinion Quarterly,* vol. 64, no. 2 (Summer 2000), pp. 207–08. On public opinion toward political reform in general, see also David Magleby and Kelly Patterson, "The Polls—Poll Trends: Congressional Reform," *Public Opinion Quarterly,* vol. 58, no. 3 (Fall 1994), pp. 419–27; and Kelly Patterson and David Magleby, "The Polls—Poll Trends: Public Support for Congress," *Public Opinion Quarterly,* vol. 56, no. 4 (Winter 1992), pp. 539–51.

2. On public cynicism, see John R. Hibbing and Elizabeth Theiss-Morse, *Congress as Public Enemy* (Cambridge University Press, 1995); John R. Hibbing and Elizabeth Theiss-Morse, eds., *What Is It about Government that Americans Dislike?* (Cambridge University Press, 2001); and Seymour Martin Lipset and William Schneider, *The Confidence Gap: Business, Labor, and Government in the Public Mind* (Johns Hopkins University Press, 1987).

Public Views of Party Soft Money

Mark Mellman and Richard Wirthlin

Mark Mellman is chief executive officer of the Mellman Group, a polling and consulting firm. He has worked with scores of Democratic candidates, public interest organizations, and corporations. Richard Wirthlin is chairman of the board of Wirthlin Worldwide, a strategic opinion research firm that has conducted nearly 2,000 national public opinion polls over the last decade. He served as President Ronald Reagan's strategist and pollster. Mellman and Wirthlin were principal investigators for a public opinion survey commissioned by the defendants.

The full report presents the findings of a new survey of public attitudes toward party soft money. This excerpt summarizes its major conclusions. Mellman and Wirthlin argue that the American public believes that large contributions to political parties (that is, soft money) improperly influence and skew policy decisions by public officials in Washington. Moreover, they assert, the public also believes that the amount of time federal officials spend raising money for their parties compromises their ability to do the public's business.

Overview

This study demonstrates that large political contributions to parties are seen by the public to have a significant and detrimental influence on the American political system and the actions of elected representatives of the federal government. Our principal finding is that the American public believes:

—The views of large contributors to parties improperly influence policy and are given undue weight in determining policy outcomes.

Another significant conclusion is that the American public believes:

—The amount of time federal officials spend raising money for their parties compromises their ability to do the public's business properly.

The strength of these findings is also important to note. In this study, we saw an unusually high number—70 percent or more—of similar responses when it came to questions regarding the impact of large contributions to political parties. In public opinion research it is uncommon to have 70 percent or more of the public see an issue the same way. When they do, it indicates an unusually strong agreement on that issue. In addition, we asked most core questions in more than one way, to ensure that responses were not an artifact of question design or wording.

266

A significant majority of Americans believe that those who make large contributions to political parties have a major impact on the decisions made by elected federal officials. Indeed, many believe the views of these big contributors sometimes carry more weight than do the views of constituents or the best interests of the country

Over three in four Americans (77 percent) believe that big contributions to political parties have a great deal of impact (55 percent) or some impact (23 percent) on decisions made by the federal government. Just (6 percent) think that big contributions do not have much or any impact.

Nearly eight in ten Americans believe that members of Congress decide how to vote based upon what big contributors to their political party want, at least sometimes. Almost half of Americans (45 percent) believe that this happens often. In contrast, only a quarter of Americans believe members of Congress often decide how to vote based on what they think is best for the country (25 percent) or what the majority of people in their district want (24 percent).

When the views of big contributors to political parties run contrary to the views of constituents or to what is best for the country, most Americans believe that the will of contributors takes precedence. Specifically, nearly three-quarters (71 percent) think that members of Congress sometimes decide how to vote on an issue based on what big contributors to their political party want, even if it is not what most people in their district want, or even if it is not what they think is best for the country (71 percent).

A large majority (84 percent) think that members of Congress will be more likely to listen to those who give money to their political party in response to their solicitation for large donations.

In addition, over two-thirds of Americans (68 percent) think that big contributors to political parties sometimes block decisions by the federal government that could improve people's everyday lives.

About four in five Americans think a member of Congress would be likely to give special consideration to the opinion of an individual, issue group, corporation, or labor union who donated $50,000 or more to his or her political party (81 percent) or who paid for $50,000 or more worth of political ads on radio or TV (80 percent). By contrast, only about one in four Americans (24 percent) thinks that a member of Congress is likely to give the opinion of someone like them special consideration. Americans see very little difference between the influence of a soft-money donation to a political party and the funding of political ads on television and radio.

Twenty-seven percent believe that members of Congress will do the right thing no matter who has given money to their political party. Similarly, just one in three Americans (34 percent) believes that the government can be trusted to make fair decisions when so much big money is involved. About one-third of Americans (31 percent) think that large political contributions to political parties have little influence on the decisions made in Washington, D.C.

Even when presented with positive statements using powerful symbols, majorities do not accept that large contributions to political parties may be necessary or beneficial
Half (50 percent) of Americans reject the view that individuals and/or groups should be free to give as much money to political parties as they want. Less than half (46 percent) accept this position.

About half of Americans (49 percent) feel it is important for individuals, issue groups, corporations and labor unions to have the freedom to express their views by making large political contributions. Slightly less (44 percent) disagree.

In considering the responses for the two questions above, it is important to keep in mind the power of the words "free" or "freedom." In general, Americans are more likely to agree with any statement that includes these words compared with a similar statement without them.

Forty-six percent of Americans believe that their views are not represented in Washington, D.C., by some of the groups that make large contributions to political parties, while 41 percent believe that their views are represented by some of these groups. Americans are evenly split (47-47 percent) on whether they think political parties need these large contributions to effectively communicate their positions and ideas to voters.

More than one-quarter (28 percent) say that the large sums of money raised by political parties result in worse candidates, and very few (6 percent) say they result in better candidates. Over one-third of Americans (37 percent) say that the large sums of money raised by political parties do not make any difference to the types of candidates who run for political office.

The public believes that when members of Congress ask for large political contributions to their parties, it leads to improper influence and compromises their ability to do their jobs, and they become beholden to contributors. Therefore, it is not surprising that most Americans believe that members of Congress should not be allowed to ask for large political contributions for their parties
Seventy-one percent of Americans agree that members of Congress spend so much time raising large campaign contributions for their political

parties that it interferes with their ability to do their jobs properly. Only 22 percent disagree with this. When presented with a slightly different wording, the majority of Americans (55 percent) think that when members of Congress spend time raising large political contributions on behalf of their parties, it interferes with their ability to do their jobs properly. Only about one in five Americans (19 percent) thinks that members of Congress have enough time to raise large political contributions without it interfering with their ability to do their jobs properly.

The majority of Americans (58 percent) think that members of Congress should not be allowed to ask for large contributions from individuals, corporations, and labor unions to fund their political parties' activities, while only 36 percent of Americans believe they should be allowed to do so. However, a slim majority of Americans believe that members of Congress learn about issues from various people while they ask for large political contributions for their parties. Over half of Americans (54 percent) believe that members of Congress learn about issues from a broad range of people while asking for political contributions. Over one-third (37 percent) do not believe this to be the case.

Most Americans want to know who is behind political advertisements
Three in five Americans (61 percent) want to know who is paying for political advertisements, while about one in four (24 percent) says it does not matter.

CONCLUSION

These results demonstrate that the American public believes that the views of large contributors to parties improperly influence and skew policy decisions by government officials in Washington. Further, the American public believes the amount of time federal officials spend raising money for their parties compromises their ability to do the public's business properly.

The Reform Act Will Not Reduce the Appearance of Corruption in American Politics

Whitfield Ayres

Whitfield Ayres is the president of Ayres, McHenry & Associates, a national public affairs and public opinion firm that has worked for many prominent Republican candidates. He is a former professor of political science at the University of South Carolina. Ayres was retained by the Republican National Committee as an expert witness for the plaintiffs.

Ayres prepared two reports. The first was based on a secondary analysis of public opinion data from the Roper Center, the Gallup Organization, the Pew Center, and NBC/Wall Street Journal. The second, in the form of a rebuttal to the declarations of Mellman and Wirthlin and of Shapiro, reports on a new survey designed to question the findings of the Mellman-Wirthlin survey. This excerpt contains the major conclusions of both the original declaration and the rebuttal report.

The thrust of Ayres's reports is that the new campaign finance law is unlikely to reduce the appearance of corruption in American politics. He reaches this conclusion initially by drawing on a theory of public opinion in American democracy and by reviewing survey data on campaign finance. He argues that public opinion about campaign finance is shallow and poorly informed, campaign finance reform is a low priority in the public mind, previous changes in campaign finance have had no impact on trust in government, and few people believe the Bipartisan Campaign Reform Act (BCRA) will reduce the power of special interests in American government.

Ayres also conducted a new survey to determine whether the public makes any distinction between large, unregulated soft-money contributions to parties and the new hard-money limits to parties included in BCRA. He finds that the public makes no such distinction. Asking the Mellman-Wirthlin questions based on soft money substituting the hard-money limits of BCRA yields almost exactly the same results as the Mellman-Wirthlin survey. This finding, Ayres asserts, reinforces the conclusion that BCRA will not reduce the appearance of corruption in American politics.

I have reviewed data on campaign finance from the Roper Center for Public Opinion Research, one of the most widely respected repositories of publicly available public opinion data; the Poll Track database, compiled by the *National Journal;* an extensive online repository of data published in the

Hotline; as well as historical data available from the Gallup Organization, the Pew Research Center at Princeton University, and NBC/*Wall Street Journal* polls. The data do not support the contention that the Bipartisan Campaign Reform Act will reduce the appearance of corruption in American politics.

In American democracy, public opinion sets the range of acceptable policy alternatives that policymakers can consider, much like a stream bed controls the width and direction of a stream. Within the range of acceptable alternatives, or within the banks of the stream, elites and public officials determine the particular policy.[1]

On a few issues the range of acceptable policy alternatives—the width of the stream—is very narrow. On these issues public opinion is deep and well informed. The essence of the public's view is: "I have heard a lot about it, I've thought about it, and I've reached a pretty firm conclusion about it." Examples of these issues are abortion in a strongly religious conservative district, the impeachment debate surrounding President Clinton, and whether the U.S. should respond militarily to the terrorist attacks of September 11, 2001.

On the vast majority of issues the range of acceptable policy alternatives is very wide, and on these issues public opinion is shallow and poorly informed. The essence of the public's view is: "I really don't know what you are talking about, but if you'll ask me a question, I'll give you an answer so I won't seem ignorant." When pollsters ask questions on this type of issue they are more likely to create rather than measure public opinion. Examples of these types of issues are American foreign policy toward Uzbekistan, the role of the International Monetary Fund in Central America, and changes in campaign finance regulations.

Substantial evidence supports the contention that public opinion about campaign finance regulations is shallow and poorly informed
The public is not aware of campaign finance regulations, such as the distinction between hard and soft money. Nor has the public identified a particular campaign practice (such as issue advertisements) or a particular campaign finance practice (such as paying for issue advertisements partly with soft money) as a source of corruption. Indeed, the public is not even aware of practices that are currently illegal: only 4 percent know, for example, that corporations are not allowed to contribute directly to the presidential and congressional candidates' campaigns.[2] According to this Princeton study, which is largely sympathetic to campaign finance reform, "Most Americans know little or nothing about the details of campaign finance. . . . Less than one percent of respondents chose the right answer to all five (campaign finance regulation) questions."

Consequently, any effort to demonstrate that public opinion regarding corruption in the political process will be altered by changes in campaign finance regulations is inherently suspect. If the public knows nothing about campaign finance regulations as they currently exist, then changing those regulations through the reform act cannot possibly affect the public's view of corruption in the political system. While public opinion data can be generated on the changes—just as they can on any issue—those data will be so dependent on the information provided and the wording of the question that the poll is far more likely to create public opinion than to measure it.

As opposed to public opinion about campaign finance laws and regulations, the public does have more stable views about the important issues facing the country, and campaign finance consistently falls at or near the bottom of the list. Indeed, a concerted effort must be made to find a national public policy issue that the American public cares less about than campaign finance reform
For example, in January of 2002, near the height of the reform act debate, an ABC News/*Washington Post* survey found that only 40 percent of Americans placed "reforming election campaign finance laws" as a high or the highest priority for President Bush and Congress. That placed campaign finance reform dead last on the list, behind "handling the U.S. campaign against terrorism" (90 percent high or highest priority), "improving the economy" (89 percent), "improving education and the schools" (83 percent), "protecting Social Security" (80 percent), "handling national defense and the military budget" (79 percent), "improving the health care system" (78 percent), "keeping the federal budget balanced" (69 percent), "helping the elderly pay for prescription drugs" (68 percent), and "protecting the environment" (59 percent). Not only does campaign finance reform rank tenth out of ten issues tested, it ranks a distant tenth. The gap between the ninth and tenth issues—19 percentage points—was greater than the gap between any two other consecutive issues.[3]

The low priority of campaign finance reform has been consistent over time. In 1997, one national survey showed that not a single respondent out of 1,017 named campaign finance reform as the problem he or she was most concerned about.[4]

Because campaign finance regulation is such a low priority in the public mind, previous changes in campaign finance laws appear to have had no impact whatsoever on trust in government
The "trust in government" question tracked by the University of Michigan Survey Research Center and now asked by the Gallup Organization is the longest running, identically worded measure of governmental trust in

America, with data going back forty-four years. Trust in government was declining as the first Federal Election Campaign Act (FECA) was passed in 1971, and continued to do so after its enactment. Trust plunged during the Watergate scandal of 1973–74, and the FECA amendments passed in 1974 did nothing to arrest the slide. It was not until Ronald Reagan's election in 1980 that trust began to improve. Trust began to decline again during the early 1990s and reached its nadir in 1994, when disgust with Congress led to a sea change in party control. Trust began to climb again during the remainder of the 1990s and the first two years of the new century, during the period of increasing criticism of political action committees and soft money that led to passage of the Bipartisan Campaign Reform Act. Indeed, before passage of BCRA trust in government rose to its highest level in three decades. If governmental trust were affected by campaign finance regulations, trust would not have increased at precisely the time when the spotlight was focused on campaign finance but Congress seemed unable to pass reform legislation. Trust in government appears to be completely unaffected by campaign finance regulations, but rather, driven by other factors that Americans actually care about, like the state of the economy and the war against terrorism.

Despite the upward trend in trust in government, a majority of Americans remain dissatisfied with their government, but concern about the role of money in politics is not the primary source of that dissatisfaction
A 1997 Pew Research Center survey probed the source of Americans' dissatisfaction with their government. At that time, 40 percent were satisfied and 57 percent dissatisfied with their government. When those who were dissatisfied were asked for their reasons, 48 percent of respondents mentioned some aspect of poor governmental performance, like gridlock or politicians not keeping promises, 21 percent said some aspect of the budget, such as wastefulness or high taxes. Only 9 percent mentioned some aspect of sleaze, the politics of the system itself, or a tendency toward corruption.[5] Since the specific issue of campaign finance is some subset of this latter category, it is clear that campaign financing is at best a minor reason for dissatisfaction with the way government works.

Just as past campaign finance reform efforts had no effect on trust in government, BCRA is unlikely to reduce the appearance of corruption in American politics, because few people are aware of the act, and once informed, they do not believe it will work
After the U.S. Senate first passed the reform act in 2001, the Pew Research Center asked Americans, "Do you happen to know whether the Senate

passed the McCain-Feingold campaign finance reform bill, or did they vote it down?" Only 21 percent said the Senate passed the bill, 15 percent thought the Senate voted it down, and nearly two-thirds—64 percent— admitted that they did not know.[6] In other words, only one out of five adult Americans could even guess the correct answer shortly after the first Senate passage of the act.

After being informed of the law, from three-fifths to two-thirds of Americans do not believe it will have the intended result. For the past four years, the Gallup Organization has asked, "Some people say major changes to the laws governing campaign finance could succeed in reducing the power of special interests in Washington. Other people say no matter what new laws are passed, special interests will always find a way to maintain their power in Washington. Which comes closer to your view?" In March of 1998, Americans said special interests would maintain their power, by a margin of 63 to 31 percent. By October of 2000 that margin had grown to 64 to 28 percent. And by February of 2002, shortly before BCRA became law, the margin had grown to 67 to 28 percent.[7] In other words, overwhelming majorities of Americans think the reform act will have no effect on the power of special interests in American government. Given this level of cynicism about the role of special interests, changing campaign finance regulations through the act will not reduce the perception of undue influence by special interests on American politics.

The Wirthlin-Mellman Survey

Richard Wirthlin and Mark Mellman conducted a national survey of American adults to assess public opinion about large contributions to political parties. Their principal finding is that the public "believes the views of large contributors to parties improperly influence policy and are given undue weight in determining policy outcomes." This survey drives home the point in my original declaration that the Bipartisan Campaign Reform Act will not reduce the appearance of corruption in American politics.

On October 1–3, 2002, our firm conducted a follow-up survey to the Wirthlin-Mellman survey that replicated their methodology. We tested the perception of the new hard-money limits for contributions to political parties included in the BCRA. In addition, we re-asked several of the key questions from the Wirthlin-Mellman survey, substituting the new hard-money limits for contributions to political parties included in BCRA for the phrase "big contributors" or "large contributors," the phrasing used in the Wirthlin-Mellman survey. We found that:

—Americans overwhelmingly believe that the BCRA annual contribution limit to political parties of $25,000 per person is viewed as a "large" contribution. Sixty-six percent think that an individual who gave $25,000 to a political party in one year would be making a large contribution, 22 percent think the individual would be making a medium contribution, and only 10 percent think the individual would be making a small contribution.

—Americans overwhelmingly believe that the BCRA contribution limit to political parties of $50,000 per person over a two-year election cycle is viewed as a "large" contribution. Seventy percent think that an individual who gave $50,000 to a political party during a two-year election cycle would be making a large contribution, 21 percent think the individual would be making a medium contribution, and only 7 percent think the individual would be making a small contribution.

—Americans overwhelmingly believe that the BCRA annual contribution limit to political parties of $50,000 for a married couple is viewed as a "large" contribution. Seventy-nine percent think that a married couple who gave $50,000 to a political party in one year would be making a large contribution, 15 percent think they would be making a medium contribution, and only 4 percent think they would be making a small contribution.

—Americans overwhelmingly believe that the BCRA contribution limit to political parties of $100,000 for a married couple over a two-year election cycle is viewed as a "large" contribution. Eighty-eight percent think that a married couple who gave $100,000 to a political party during a two-year election cycle would be making a large contribution, 9 percent think they would be making a medium contribution, and only 2 percent think they would be making a small contribution.

—Not surprisingly, given the view of most Americans that contributions to political parties allowed under BCRA are "large," re-asking the Wirthlin-Mellman questions with the BCRA limits yields almost exactly the same conclusions as found in the Wirthlin-Mellman survey.

The Wirthlin-Mellman survey found that 71 percent of Americans think that members of Congress sometimes decide how to vote on an issue based on what big contributors to their political party want, even if it is not what most people in their districts want. Our survey found that 71 percent of Americans think that members of Congress sometimes decide how to vote on an issue based on what people who give $25,000 per year to their political party want, even if it is not what most people in their districts want.

The Wirthlin-Mellman survey asked, "If an individual, issue group, corporation, or labor union donated $50,000 or more to the political party of a member of Congress, how likely would a member of Congress be to give the contributor's opinion special consideration because of the contribution?" They found that 81 percent thought it likely that the member of Congress would give special consideration to that opinion—41 percent very likely, and 41 percent somewhat likely. We asked, "If an individual donated 25,000 dollars to the political party of a member of Congress, how likely would a member of Congress be to give the contributor's opinion special consideration because of the contribution?" We found that 81 percent thought it likely that the member of Congress would give special consideration to that opinion—41 percent very likely, and 40 percent somewhat likely.

In other words, every conclusion that the Wirthlin-Mellman report reached about "large" or "big" contributions and contributors applies with equal force to the new hard-money limits in BCRA. Wirthlin and Mellman note in their report that "in public opinion research, it is uncommon to have 70 percent or more of the public see an issue the same way. When they do, it indicates an unusually strong agreement on that issue." I agree. The American public shares an unusually strong agreement that the contribution limits to political parties adopted in BCRA are large contributions, and they view those large contributions in precisely the ways the Wirthlin-Mellman survey so effectively discerned. Consequently their survey reinforces the conclusion that BCRA will not reduce the appearance of corruption in American politics.

OTHER EXPERT REPORTS

Other expert witnesses have produced impressive reviews of public attitudes toward the current campaign finance system. They demonstrate effectively that the public has a skeptical, indeed cynical, view about the role of money in politics. They address a number of questions regarding public perception about various reform proposals. But they offer no persuasive evidence on *the* critical public opinion question in this case: will the Bipartisan Campaign Reform Act, as written, reduce the appearance of corruption in American politics?

These experts point to surveys that purport to demonstrate popular support for specific campaign finance reforms. For example, Robert Shapiro points to majority support for a ban on soft-money contributions to political parties. But, as demonstrated in my original declaration, the public has no clue about the distinction between soft- and hard-money contributions. And, as demonstrated in our survey discussed above, the public views the BCRA hard-money contribution limits to political parties as large contributions, with presumably all the nefarious effects attributed to any large contribution. What is driving these public perceptions is not soft money versus hard money, or regulated money versus unregulated money, but money itself. But BCRA actually raises the hard-money contribution limits to individual candidates and sets limits to hard-money contributions to political parties at a level that the public overwhelmingly views as large. Therefore BCRA, as written, will not reduce the appearance of corruption in American politics.

Rebuttal to Ayres

ROBERT Y. SHAPIRO

In this response to the original Ayres declaration, Shapiro asserts that the public has real, not artificially constructed, opinions about campaign finance, that inferences about future behavior and outcomes based on current responses to survey questions are highly speculative, and that the failure to find connections between opinions toward campaign finance and trust in government result from the absence of appropriate multivariate analyses.

I have reviewed the expert report of Whitfield Ayres. I find that it contains serious flaws in reasoning and conclusions that are not supported by his data. In preparation of my original expert report, I studied many hundreds of survey questions and presented more than 200 tables of survey results. By contrast, Mr. Ayres selectively cited a total of eight polls.

In this rebuttal report, I take issue with three major claims he makes in his report based on polling analysis that is highly problematic. First, Ayres claims that he can predict future public perceptions and actual political behavior based upon past polling data. Ayres asserts that public opinion regarding corruption in the political process will not be affected by changes in campaign finance regulation. In contrast to this claim, however, it is a basic and fundamental rule of survey research that responses to survey questions about behavior and outcomes in the relatively distant future do not accurately measure anything about actual future behavior and outcomes. Any such inferences from these data are purely speculative.

Second, Ayres claims that opinion surveys cannot provide meaningful measures of public opinion toward campaign finance because the public does not really care and its knowledge is "shallow." To the contrary, opinion surveys can and do explore meaningful opinions about current circumstances and issues regarding campaign finance, and the public does indeed care about the issue.

Third, Ayres claims that changes in campaign finance laws and the public's concern about the role of money in politics have had no impact on trust in and satisfaction with government. His conclusion on this point is improperly based on careless reasoning. Understanding the effect of opinions toward campaign finance on trust in government requires a multivariate analysis, not the very simplistic analysis of two variables that Ayres offers.

1. Responses to survey questions about behavior and outcomes in the relatively distant future do not accurately measure anything about actual future behavior and outcomes; any such inferences from these data are speculative
Data from opinion surveys can only be validly and reliably used to examine and understand current and, at best, short-term behavior and outcomes. Survey data cannot be used effectively to measure behavior in the distant past or future.[8] Questions that ask survey respondents to recall their past opinion, voting, or other political behavior are fraught with problems having to do with the accuracy or selectivity of people's memories. While individuals can offer predictions of future circumstances and behavior, these are only *projections and opinions;* their actual future opinions and behavior may change as circumstances change, new information becomes available, and so forth. For example, in predicting election outcomes, survey researchers would not use polling data from a year, or even several months, before an election, to predict which candidates or parties will win. Such polls only tend to estimate who would win the election *if* the election were held that day.[9] When new facts or events intervene and circumstances are likely to change, decisional inputs are altered and hypothetical future questions become useless.

Ayres asks to what extent public opinion data show that the Bipartisan Campaign Reform Act will solve the problem of the appearance of corruption. Polling data cannot answer this question: the survey questions he cites ask about *hypothetical* future actions. In doing this he is engaging in an exercise of complete *speculation* for which survey data cannot validly and reliably be used. Current public opinion data cannot measure to what extent the act will reduce the appearance of corruption. The public's future perceptions of corruption will depend, in part, on how the act is implemented, how political actors respond to the provisions and implementation of the act, and how potential political contributors react to those responses.

Ayres cites survey data that show that only a modest percentage of the public has thought that changes in campaign finance laws will reduce the power of special interests in national politics. I, too, have included data that similarly show the public's uncertainty and skepticism about the effect of campaign reform. However, the only way that public opinion research can gauge the future effectiveness of the act is to wait until after the act is implemented, and after the public is able to see the effects of campaign finance reform. Then, and only then, will public opinion polling be capable of measuring whether the American public perceives less corruption in politics due to the reform.

Nevertheless, looking at the full body of data, as opposed to the few surveys that Ayres selectively cites, the data overall suggest that the public—more than 50 percent in some cases—has been more optimistic about campaign finance reform than what Ayres would lead one to believe. To quote again from my report: "substantial percentages of the public have thought that campaign finance reforms can be effective, can reduce the influence of money in politics at least somewhat, can make the public more optimistic about government, and would be good for democracy." Even though Americans are skeptical about what the results will be, they have considered the problems with campaign finance so pressing that they have supported reforms and want to give the reform effort a chance to mitigate, if not eliminate, corruption and thereby improve the political process.

In reviewing Ayres's assertions, it must also be noted that the term "corruption" should be more broadly construed than the limited definition of "dollars for political favors" that Ayres uses. Even though Ayres assumes a limited definition of the term corruption, he nonetheless admits that "surveys that use the words 'corrupt' or 'corruption' in their questions rarely define the term at all. . . ." With respect to campaign donations, political influence, and democratic processes, the public equates corruption with a disruption of democratic norms—that is, that politics has moved outside the normal bounds of democratic or representative processes. In democracies, elected officials are expected to make policy decisions that are influenced either by the wants of the constituents who have elected them, by the officials' own good judgment—the personal quality that may have motivated voters to elect them, or by a combination of constituent influence and the leaders' judgment.[10] Any outside influences that bypass or thwart these influences contribute to perceptions of corruption of the political process.

2. Opinion surveys can explore meaningful opinions about current circumstances and issues

Ayres questions whether the public is capable of rendering a sufficiently informed opinion about campaign finance reform to warrant consideration in the policymaking process. As an initial matter, it is worth noting that the policymaking process is done. While Ayres's observations may have been relevant to agenda setting in Congress, that debate has concluded and the act has passed.

Certainly, it would be good for democratic politics if the public at large knew all the details of every political issue as it formed its opinions on the problems of the day, but such a level of knowledge is simply not realistic. Substantial research has shown, however, that the public does not need detailed information to develop and adhere to opinions on particular issues.

For example, in the political debate about whether the United States should invade Iraq, the public is quite capable of having strong opinions even though individuals do not know the details of Iraq's ethnic composition, its borders with neighbors, the size of the Iraqi military, and the implications of these for American geopolitical strategy and military tactics. This was also the case for public opinion concerning the impeachment debate surrounding President Clinton—which Ayres cites as an example of deep and well-informed public opinion. The public did not support removing President Clinton from office, and it reached this opinion without needing guidance from political leaders on both sides.[11] Moreover, the public was not deeply knowledgeable about all the legal standards for impeachment, the history and meaning of "high crimes and misdemeanors," the procedural details in the House and Senate, and the facts of the Paula Jones suit. Even during this national spectacle, public opinion was not as focused on the details as Ayres would imply.

According to substantial research, the public bases its opinions on many considerations.[12] Public opinion is influenced by the public's values, especially those concerning fairness, individualism, and equality, as well as by its perceptions and responses to threat.[13] What also matters is what individuals believe is morally acceptable or unacceptable, as this relates to religious or other deeply held beliefs. The public is also influenced by other predispositions, including the extent to which people might adhere to an ideology, or the extent to which it connects its opinions on new issues with other issues toward which it already holds opinions.[14] In forming and altering its opinions, the public uses any pieces of information that it receives that can be used as shortcuts to knowledge (known in the academic literature as heuristics) about particular issues.[15] These include information that members of the public receive from normal day-to-day news reports and from interactions with friends, associates, and family members.[16] Often most important is information that becomes more visible and widely accessible as issues are debated and as political leaders emphasize the choices of policies that are available and which ones they support.[17]

In the case of campaign finance reform, the data in my original report show that the public has been troubled by the campaign finance system overall and the particular problems that it sees with the role of money in politics. These are hardly opinions created by the wordings of survey questions, as Ayres claims. The issues related to money in the political system are familiar and real, in contrast to issues like American policy toward Uzbekistan. Comparing American foreign policy toward Uzbekistan to American campaign finance is simply disingenuous. Survey respondents can and do say that they don't know or have no opinion in response to the survey questions examined. This occurs both when response options such as "don't know" and "no opinion" are offered explicitly in survey questions and when they are not. The public does not need detailed knowledge about all political contributors, the amounts of their donations, the nuances of existing campaign finance regulations, and the extent to which these regulations are enforced in order to form strong opinions toward campaign finance. The public can easily understand how political donations can lead to political access and influence—how political parties and politicians will pay attention to those who give money to the parties. The public has long questioned the motivations of and responded with distrust toward labor unions, corporations, special interests more generally, and the government itself.[18] The public is especially troubled and animated by these problems when they become blatantly visible in widely publicized incidents and scandals such as those involving Enron and the large soft-money donations to the Democratic Party and the roles played by the Clinton administration, President Bill Clinton, and Vice President Al Gore.

In contrast to Ayres's claim that campaign finance has not been a salient issue, the data show that the public does in fact care deeply about campaign finance. He is incorrect in claiming that the public does have more stable views about the important issues facing the country. Research on the dynamics of what the public sees as the nation's most important problem has shown that these perceptions are highly changeable: they vary depending on what problems are most prominent on the political agenda and most visibly covered by the media. Campaign finance has not ranked highly in responses to the open-ended "most important problem" questions because the issue has not received the same amount of attention from prominent political figures and news coverage as some other issues, such as education and Social Security.[19]

That the public does not automatically cite campaign finance as the nation's single most important problem does not mean the issue is unimportant. The federal government deals with *many issues* on an ongoing basis, so campaign finance need not be ranked in the top ten for it to be considered a pressing problem that warrants direct and substantial governmental attention. While Ayres correctly observes that the issue does not command the same high level of priority as problems such as fighting terrorism or dealing with the national economy, when the public is asked directly about campaign finance, it says it is an important issue. The 40 percent saying that campaign finance deserves "high or highest" priority is a significant percentage. Moreover, the percentage of the public who assign priority to campaign finance has been higher at different times and when the survey questions used are worded differently.

Majorities of the public have consistently responded that they favor the new campaign finance reform legislation. This is apparent in the extensive data that Ayres does not cite. These data show that the public has had *real* opinions on what its members have seen as an important national issue.

3. Understanding the effect of opinions toward campaign finance on trust in government requires a multivariate analysis, not the simplistic analysis of two variables that Ayres offers

Ayres's observations that previous changes in campaign finance laws have had no impact on trust in government and that the role of money in politics has not been a primary source of Americans' dissatisfaction with their government is misleading. In making these claims, he does not directly address the question of the connection between campaign donations and the public's perception of corruption in politics. Ayres cites the lack of a statistical correlation between campaign finance and trust in government as evidence for the lack of a causal effect of campaign reform on trust and satisfaction with government. However, trust and satisfaction with government, as he acknowledges, have been affected by other factors, like the economy and other indicators of the government's effective performance. To make statistical inferences about causation requires taking into account multiple factors simultaneously, through multivariate statistical analysis. Ayres would have to control for, and thereby exclude, the effects of these substantial other factors, such as foreign military engagements and peaks and troughs in the economy, before reaching his conclusions. Ayres makes no such attempt.

NOTES

1. See V. O. Key Jr., *Public Opinion and American Democracy* (Knopf, 1961).

2. Princeton Survey Research Associates, *Money and Politics Survey* (April 1997).

3. See ABC News/*Washington Post* Survey, January 24–27, 2002.

4. *Tarrance Group Survey,* May 27–29, 1997.

5. See Pew Research Center, 1997.

6. See Pew Research Center, April 18–22, 2001.

7. See Gallup Polls, March 20–22, 1998; October 6–9, 2000; February 8–10, 2002.

8. See, for example, Robert S. Erikson and Kent L. Tedin, "The 1928–1936 Partisan Realignment: The Case for the Conversion Hypothesis," *American Political Science Review,* vol. 75 (1981), pp. 951–62; Frederick Mosteller and others, *The Pre-Election Polls of 1948: Report to the Committee on Analysis of Pre-Election Polls and Forecasts,* Bulletin 60 (New York: Social Science Research Council, 1949); and the relevant literatures they cite.

9. See Mosteller and others, *The Pre-Election Polls of 1948.*

10. See John C. Wahlke and others, *The Legislative System* (Wiley, 1962).

11. See John R. Zaller, "Monica Lewinsky's Contribution to Political Science," *PS: Political Science and Politics,* vol. 31 (1998), pp. 182–89.

12. See John R. Zaller, *The Nature and Origins of Mass Opinion* (Cambridge University Press, 1992).

13. See Benjamin I. Page and Robert Y. Shapiro, *The Rational Public* (University of Chicago Press, 1992).

14. See Zaller, *The Nature and Origins of Mass Opinion*; Paul M. Sniderman, Richard A. Brody, and Philip E. Tetlock, *Reasoning and Choice* (Cambridge University Press, 1991).

15. See Samuel L. Popkin, *The Reasoning Voter* (University of Chicago Press, 1991); and Sniderman, Brody, and Tetlock, *Reasoning and Choice.*

16. See Popkin, *The Reasoning Voter*; and Page and Shapiro, *The Rational Public.*

17. See V. O. Key Jr., *The Responsible Electorate* (Harvard University Press, 1966); Key, *Public Opinion and American Democracy*; Zaller, *The Nature and Origins of Mass Opinion*; and Page and Shapiro, *The Rational Public.*

18. See Seymour Martin Lipset and William Schneider, *The Confidence Gap: Business, Labor, and Government in the Public Mind* (Johns Hopkins University Press, 1987).

19. See Shanto Iyengar and Donald R. Kinder, *News That Matters* (University of Chicago Press, 1987).

Campaign Contributions, the Appearance of Corruption, and Trust in Government

David M. Primo

David M. Primo is assistant professor of political science at the University of Rochester. He specializes in American politics, political economy, and political institutions. Primo was an expert witness for plaintiffs represented by the Southeastern Legal Foundation, a public interest law firm, and its co-counsel Kenneth W. Starr of Kirkland & Ellis, who also represented Senator Mitch McConnell in the case.

Primo's report is a rebuttal to the claims of a number of defendants' experts about the linkages among campaign finance law, the appearance of corruption, and trust in government. In this excerpt, he marshals data on public trust in government and on campaign fund-raising and expenditures to demonstrate that no such linkages exist. Trust in government has not declined with the increases in soft money and the growing dependence of elected officials on large donors. In fact, Primo observes, trust in government rose at the very time when soft-money contributions were skyrocketing and the parties were becoming more dependent on these large donations.

I. DEFENDANTS' THEORIES REGARDING CORRUPTION AND CONFIDENCE

Defendants' experts make assertions regarding the links among the appearance of corruption, campaign finance law, and Americans' confidence in their government. These are empirical claims that can be analyzed if phrased precisely and if terms are well defined. This requires informal statements to be cast as hypotheses, with precise causal relationships stated.

Following are three interrelated claims about how campaign finance affects government institutions. These are intended to represent defendants' experts' views as presented in various reports. As support, note "Intervenors' Responses to Republican National Committee's Second Set of Interrogatories to Defendants," page 7, which states, "Intervenors contend that the proliferation of soft money leads to actual corruption, the appearance of corruption, and the potential for corruption. . . . The prevalence of soft money in the campaign finance system has increased citizens' cynicism, their sense of disenfranchisement, and their perception that their voices, actions, and contributions make little difference in the political process. . . ." See also the reports of Robert Shapiro and Jonathan Krasno and Frank Sorauf.[1]

—*Hypothesis 1:* Campaign contributions and soft money lead to the appearance of corruption, which has a deleterious effect on confidence in government institutions.

—*Hypothesis 2:* Confidence in government institutions is inversely related to campaign contributions and soft money.

—*Hypothesis 3:* Confidence in government institutions is inversely related to the dependence of elected officials on large donors.

Hypothesis 1 implies that there is a causal link between campaign contributions, the appearance of corruption, and confidence in government institutions. This link can be represented as follows:

$$\text{contributions} \longrightarrow \text{appearance of corruption} \longrightarrow$$
$$\text{confidence in government.}$$

Hypotheses 2 and 3 state that confidence in government institutions moves in the opposite direction to political contributions, and that confidence erodes as elected officials become more dependent on "big" donors.

Defendants' expert Robert Shapiro states, "Assuming that Congress enacted this [soft money] ban to decrease the appearance of corruption, it is important to discern whether the current campaign finance system . . . does or does not create an appearance of corruption."[2] Shapiro argues that it does. There is evidence against this claim. For example, in a 1997 Center for Responsive Politics poll on campaign finance, fewer than 10 percent of individuals attributed their dissatisfaction with government to the campaign finance system.

Regardless of whether contributions produce an appearance of corruption, however, the downstream relationship is the central concern. The key question is whether any appearance of corruption caused by campaign finance law translates into lower confidence in democracy or less trust in government. Therefore, we can take hypothesis 1 as a *maintained hypothesis* that is assumed for the purposes of further examination of related claims. In other words, the analysis proceeds *as if* campaign finance creates an appearance of corruption. The key relationships lie in hypotheses 2 and 3, which link the appearance of corruption caused by contributions to less confidence in government. If the evidence fails to support hypotheses 2 and 3, then logic dictates that any "appearance of corruption" caused by campaign contributions cannot be affecting American democracy. Since it is via this "appearance of corruption" that campaign contributions are claimed to harm confidence, the argument for weighting this over First Amendment concerns is obviated.

Thus far the discussion has focused mostly on the *appearance of corruption,* but, of course, it also of interest to see how overt instances of corruption are dealt with by the American electoral process. This report will explore the view that the political process is to a large degree "self-regulating," precisely because of the relatively open system of elections we have in the United States. Scandals come to light because of the incentives created by the electoral process.

2. Analysis

The standard measure of confidence in government comes from the University of Michigan's National Election Studies (NES), which has asked the following question during its biannual nationwide surveys: "How much of the time do you think you can trust the government in Washington to do what is right—just about always, most of the time, or only some of the time?" "Trust" is usually defined as answering just about always or most of the time (see figure 1 for complete survey responses). The over time trend is fairly clear. Whereas in the early 1960s a sizable number of Americans trusted the government to *always* do the right thing, that figure took a hit during the Vietnam era and flat-lined after Watergate. Those who trusted the government to do the right thing most of the time dropped as well. These figures cut across party and demographic lines.[3] There are other questions in the NES that ask about satisfaction with government or whether an individual believes he can influence the political process. However, the trust question gets directly at the issue of confidence and is the one that can most plausibly be linked with corruption or the appearance thereof.

Tying aggregate trust data to one-time, specific events, such as Watergate or Vietnam, in a precise, statistical way is difficult. However, the trends in the data suggest that the late 1960s and 1970s represented a sea change in how *all* Americans viewed the government. This era was, of course, one of great tumult in the international and domestic arenas, and government missteps almost surely contributed to the erosion of confidence in government.

Total congressional campaign spending is used as a measure for analyzing hypothesis 2 because this series provides the most complete and reliable data. To analyze the dependence of contributors on large donors, I employ two variables based on soft-money receipts. Caps on hard-money

Figure 1. *Trust in Government, 1964–2000*

Percent response

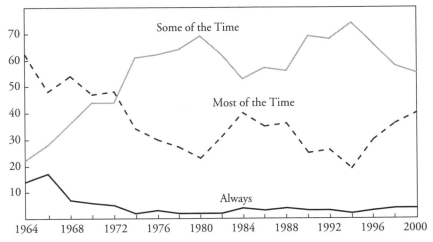

Source: University of Michigan, National Election Studies, various years.

a. The question asks, "How much of the time do you think you can trust the government in Washington to do what is right—just about always, most of the time or only some of the time?"

contributions are so low that a corresponding measure for these types of donations would not be a useful analytical tool.

To measure how dependent parties are on soft-money *relative to* hard-money contributions, which tend to be lower, I calculate the percentage of overall contributions to the major parties that came from soft money in the 1990s, when soft money was increasingly used as a tool for fund-raising. The results suggest that both parties became more dependent on such contributions during the 1990s.

To establish that soft-money contributions are concentrated among large donations, I calculate the percentage of total soft-money receipts in the 1997–98 and 1999–2000 election cycles that are based on donations of at least $100,000 by organizations, including individuals closely affiliated with the organizations. (This uses the proreform Center for Responsive Politics' cutoff of $100,000 and its data for contributions.) In 1997–98 there were 452 organizations that fit this criterion, and they contributed over 50 percent of total soft-money receipts to the parties. In 1999–2000, that number was 526, and they generated approximately 40 percent of soft-money revenues. Nearly identical results are obtained if Democrats and Republicans are considered separately. Large donors therefore do contribute a large and significant share of total soft-money contributions. This does not imply, however, that soft money is inherently corrupting or a negative influence on democracy. The analogy can be made to so-called concentration indices utilized by economists to measure the concentration of market power in an industry. Without context, one cannot know whether high concentration is automatically a negative. As demonstrated below, this strengthens the argument that contributions have little effect on trust in government, rather than weakens it.

When the trust data are combined with the spending and fund-raising data, it becomes clear that trust in government and campaign finance are not linked in the way reformers assert. Figures 2 and 3 show the trust measure overlaid with congressional campaign spending as well as the dependence figure. From these figures, it is not possible to argue that campaign finance could be *harming* trust in government. In fact, for congressional campaign spending, the correlation coefficient between trust and spending is approximately .25.[4] This moderately strong relationship is *positive*. This is also seen in the soft-money figures. At the very time when soft-money contributions were skyrocketing and the dependence of the parties on these contributions was increasing, trust in government was similarly rising. Statistically one cannot observe two series moving in the same direction and assert that one is causing the other. So these data do not imply that campaign spending increases confidence in government. But they strongly refute the hypothesis that spending is driving a *decrease* in trust at the macro level.

This trend holds if data for another question are analyzed. The NES asks, "Would you say the government is pretty much run by a few big interests looking out for themselves or that it is run for the benefit of all the people?" Since the question was first asked in 1964, there has been a steady decline in the percent of respondents who believe that government is run for the benefit of all the people. However, there is a *positive correlation,* yet again, between campaign spending and the percent of respondents who believe that government is run for the benefit of all the people. This finding is supported by individual-level research conducted by political scientists John J. Coleman and Paul F. Manna, who study the 1994 and 1996 U.S. House elections and find that campaign spending "neither enhances nor erodes trust and efficacy in politics or attention and interest in campaigns."[5]

In his report Derek Cressman writes, "In 1999, only 29 percent of Americans trusted the government to do the right thing, according to a poll by the Center for Excellence in Government. The same survey found

Figure 2. *Trust in Government and Campaign Spending*

Percent trust   Real congressional campaign spending (millions)

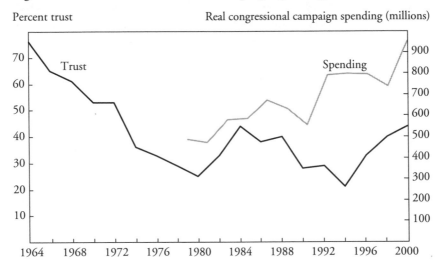

Source: Spending data are from the Federal Elections Commission; for trust data, see figure 1.

a. Trust is defined as answering all of the time or most of the time to the question in figure 1, note a. Spending is real congressional campaign spending.

Figure 3. *Trust in Government and Soft Money*

Percent response

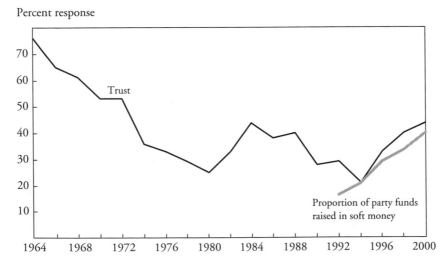

Source: See figure 2.

that 63 percent of respondents feel that government serves the special interests, while only 25 percent said it serves the public interest. Just 39 percent said that they believed our current government meets Abraham Lincoln's goal of government of, by, and for the people, while 54 percent said we do not have a government of, by, and for the people. . . . The feeling of disenfranchisement is a significant reason for declining rates of voter participation and a barrier to citizens getting involved in federal elections through volunteering or making small contributions. This then exacerbates the undue influence of large donors on the process."[6]

This argument looks at a snapshot in time (a 1999 poll) to make a *temporal* argument, which does not allow for accurate inferences. For instance, suppose that trust in government did not change in the last two decades and was at a low level, but that turnout had declined over the same time period. Then it could not be possible that trust in government influenced turnout at the aggregate level. Valid temporal arguments cannot be made by looking at only the final data point in a time series.

Krasno and Sorauf are implicitly using the same approach when they write, "Many of them believe that moneyed interests—whether corporations or trade associations or unions or wealthy individuals—use their cozy relationships with policymakers to exert special influence over government. A majority of Americans, for instance, agree with survey statements such as 'government is pretty much run by a few big interests looking out for themselves.'"[7] This was just as true in 1970 as it is now.

In addition, Krasno and Sorauf state, "We think it likely that campaign financing—particularly the huge gifts of soft money given to the parties, with the resulting skepticism it breeds—is among the developments undermining public opinion in these areas. That means, of course, that banning soft money will not restore public confidence to its highest levels. No single piece of legislation could. But by removing an *obvious* irritant, it is a step in the right direction."[8] These claims are directly contradicted by the empirical evidence just presented.

One reason for the trust-related findings is that Americans are simply uninterested in the issue of campaign finance. Shapiro argues, "Critics of reform have emphasized how the public does not see campaign finance reform as a high priority. The evidence they cite, however, is completely misleading. . . . First and foremost, when asked directly about campaign finance reform in different ways, majorities or sizable percentages of the American public have been concerned about this issue and have even considered it a high or even top priority, consistent with the trouble the public has seen in campaign fund-raising."[9] Shapiro's evidence, however, uses the least appropriate of the various questions that can be used to assess issue importance.

There are generally three ways to ascertain an issue's priority vis-à-vis other policy areas. Polling questions that ask citizens to prioritize a predetermined list of issues typically find that campaign finance is at or near the bottom of the list. These questions are usually phrased as follows: "Of the following issues, which is the most important for government to address?" and are accompanied by a handful of possible responses. The issue fares even worse in so-called open-ended questions, where citizens select the issue without prompting. One commonly asked version of this type of question is, "What do you think are the two most important issues for the government to address?" Here, campaign finance is typically of primary importance to 1 to 2 percent of the public.

Campaign finance is sometimes viewed as a high priority when asked with a poorly framed question that simply asks people whether they believe an issue should be the highest, a high, a medium, or a low priority for government. This query does not require individuals to face the reality that agenda space is scarce. At any point there are innumerable issues for policymakers to consider, but reality dictates that only a limited number can be considered. Because citizens are not forced to choose between issues, there is no way to know what it means to say that an issue should be a high priority. Prioritization implies competition for a limited resource. The first two types of questions build in agenda scarcity. The latter fails to.

Shapiro's data utilize only the last of these methods, completely ignoring the other two, and does not offer consistent support for the hypothesis that campaign finance matters to Americans. For example, a March 19, 2001, Gallup poll found that 41 percent of Americans did not believe that Congress and the president should take time to address campaign finance reform. Therefore, even when considering the most favorable (as well as the least appropriate) evidence, the claim that Americans view campaign finance as a priority is not supported systematically.

Shapiro states that "campaign finance has been more salient when campaign finance problems and scandals have been given the kind of attention by political leaders and the news media that these other issues have been regularly given."[10] However, in 2000 alone—when the issue of campaign finance was receiving extensive attention due to Senator John McCain's campaign for the presidency—the following polls asking open-ended questions found campaign finance to be a priority of on average 1 to 2 percent of the public: the Harris poll, October 19, 2000, September 8,

2000, July 13, 2000, June 8, 2000, and January 6, 2000; Fox News Opinion Dynamics poll, August 9, 2000, May 10, 2000, January 26, 2000; the ABC News/*Washington Post* poll, February 3, 2000, January 13, 2000.

Similarly, Enron is now a household name, and even after all the attention Enron received and the links that were made between Enron and the need for campaign finance reform, a January 2002 Harris poll found that 1 percent of the public mentioned campaign finance as a policy priority. In an extensive search on the Lexis-Nexis database of polling questions (which draws from the Roper database), I was unable to find any evidence that more than 1 to 3 percent of those polled responded with campaign finance reform in the open-ended response questions.[11] The Harris poll question about the two most important issues for government to address has similarly not registered higher than a 3 percent response for campaign finance in January 1993, February 1994, February 1995, April 1996, May 1997, January 1998, February 1999, August 2000, September 2000, February 2001, June 2001, July 2001, August 2001, and October 2001.[12]

Shapiro argues, "When compared with other issues that compete for government and public attention, it is understandable that the issue has not normally been seen the same way as pressing economic problems, crises in health care and retirement income, crime, and war, terrorism, and other international crises." In response, there are two key points to remember. First, campaign finance is consistently at the bottom of priorities, even when the issue is receiving extensive press attention, contrary to Shapiro's claims. Second, unlike an issue such as homelessness, the public's views on campaign finance are in many ways the raison d'etre of reform. Public sentiment surrounding the issue is viewed as the reason why reform is important. The public's continued indifference to the issue is therefore an extremely important finding.

Shapiro argues that "notwithstanding the public's ongoing cynicism and lack of confidence toward many aspects of political life, substantial percentages of the public have thought that campaign finance reforms can be effective, can reduce the influence of money in politics at least somewhat, can make the public more optimistic about government, and would be good for democracy."[13] Data can be found to support both sides of all of these claims, but as an analysis by the National Association of Business Political Action Committee (NABPAC) has suggested, the key is how the questions are asked.

For example, a March 2001 Gallup poll cited by Shapiro asked, "In general, if new campaign finance reform legislation were passed, do you think it would make our democratic form of government work—much better than it does now, just a little better, about the same, just a little worse, or much worse than it does now?" Fifty-nine percent answered "much better" or a "little better," with 32 percent believing nothing would change, and fewer than 10 percent arguing that things would get worse.

In a February 2002 poll conducted during debates over new campaign finance legislation, CBS News asked, "The House of Representatives recently passed campaign finance reform legislation, which would prohibit or limit various types of campaign contributions. If this legislation passes the Senate, do you think as a result that big business will have less influence on government, or will things go on much as they did before?" Nearly two-thirds (61 percent) responded with the latter. Similar results are cited by Shapiro in his data.

Data from a 1996 NABPAC poll shows similar results. This suggests that Americans believe that campaign finance laws could *in theory* lead to a better government, but at the same time that laws passed by Congress will do little or nothing to change the functioning of the political system. Therefore, not only do Americans view campaign finance as a low policy priority, they have little faith that new laws passed by Congress will change government. So the justification for the Bipartisan Campaign Reform Act—that the public wants the reform and it will improve citizen-government relations—is unsupported by the data. Americans are concerned about issues other than the "appearance of corruption" allegedly caused by campaign finance, and they do not believe that new campaign finance laws enacted by the Congress will improve the functioning of democracy.

While not interested in campaign finance, Americans are sensitive to scandal and corruption and respond through the electoral process. Further, elected officials who desire to remain in office know and anticipate this. Voters respond to actual events and scandals, not vague "appearances." The central idea is that the public responds to actual corruption and events to form its views of American government, with elections being a method of "self-correction" within the democratic process. Elected officials are acutely aware of the self-correcting tendencies of American elections. For instance, political scientists Timothy Groseclose and Keith Krehbiel show that the number of bad checks an elected official wrote during the House banking scandal was inversely related to whether he or she sought reelection or retired.[14] D. Roderick Kiewiet and Langche Zeng show that scandals make elected officials much less likely to run for reelection, and guarantees that they will not seek *higher* office.[15] Susan Welch and John R. Hibbing find that from 1982 to 1990, about 35 percent of the scandal-afflicted retired, resigned, or failed to win reelection. And of those who were successful, their electoral margins suffered.[16]

There are therefore two effects of scandals: First, they cause elected officials to change their behavior, by resigning or not seeking reelection. Second, those who decide to run face reduced electoral margins and sometimes defeat. This further suggests that voters weigh the allegations alongside the performance of the member when casting a ballot. When the "appearance of corruption" gets manifested in an actual scandal, there are consequences. Thus built in to the electoral process is a check against corruption. Perhaps this is why trust in government is unaffected by contributions—the money itself does no harm. In addition, political actors are aware that scandal harms elected officials, so there is an incentive for challengers and opponents to bring allegations to the fore. Many view this as evidence of the unseemly nature of politics, but rather, it is the epitome of democratic rule.

NOTES

1. Robert Shapiro, in part 3 of this volume; Jonathan Krasno and Frank Sorauf, in part 1.

2. Shapiro, in part 3 of this volume.

3. See John R. Alford, "We're All in This Together: The Decline of Trust in Government, 1958–1996," in John R. Hibbing and Elizabeth Theiss-Morse, eds., *What Is It about Government That Americans Dislike?* (Cambridge University Press, 2001).

4. Correlation coefficients range from −1 to 1. The closer to 1 the correlation coefficient is, the stronger the positive relationship; the closer to −1, the stronger the negative relationship. The closer to 0, the weaker the relationship.

5. John J. Coleman and Paul F. Manna, "Congressional Campaign Spending and the Quality of Democracy," *Journal of Politics*, vol. 62, no. 3 (2000), p. 757.

6. Derek Cressman, Declaration and Expert Report in *Victoria Jackson Gray Adams, et al. v. Federal Election Commission*, U.S. District Court for the District of Columbia, September 20, 2002. Available at www.camlc.org/attachment.html/ Cressman%2C+Derek.pdf?id=103.

7. Krasno and Sorauf, in part 1 of this volume.

8. Ibid., emphasis added.

9. Shapiro, in part 3 of this volume.

10. Ibid.

11. See David M. Primo, "Campaign Finance and Public Opinion: Reformers versus Reality," *The Independent Review*, vol. 7, no. 2 (Fall 2002), pp. 207–19.

12. Humphrey Taylor, "The Harris Poll #5: The President's Very High Ratings Continue to Slip Slightly as the Economy Increases in Importance," January 25, 2002.

13. Shapiro, in part 3 of this volume.

14. Timothy Groseclose and Keith Krehbiel, "Golden Parachutes, Rubber Checks, and Strategic Retirements from the 102d House," *American Journal of Political Science*, vol. 38, no. 1 (February 1994), pp. 75–99.

15. D. Roderick Kiewiet and Langche Zeng, "An Analysis of Congressional Career Decisions, 1947–1986," *American Political Science Review*, vol. 87, no. 4 (December, 1993), pp. 928–41.

16. Susan Welch and John R. Hibbing, "The Effects of Charges of Corruption on Voting Behavior in Congressional Elections, 1982–1990," *Journal of Politics*, vol. 59, no. 1 (February 1997), pp. 226–39.

Large Contributions Provide Unequal Access

ROBERT ROZEN

Robert Rozen is a lobbyist for corporations, individuals, and trade associations at Ernst & Young. Rosen testified for the defense regarding his experience advising clients on soft-money contributions and on the substantive benefits of contributing soft money to political parties. He argues that large contributions result in special, unequal access for donors.

I know of organizations who believe that to be treated seriously in Washington, and by that I mean to be a player and to have access, you need to give soft money. As a result, many organizations give soft money. While some soft money is given for ideological purposes, companies and trade associations working on public policy for the most part give to pursue their economic interests. In some cases, they might limit their contributions to one political party. More often, they give to both. They give soft money because they believe it helps establish better contacts with members of Congress and gets doors opened to meet with members. There is no question that money creates the relationships. Companies with interests before particular committees need to have access to the chairman of that committee and go to events where the chairman will be. Even if that chairman is not the type of member who will tie the contribution and legislative goals together, donors cannot be sure, so they play it safe and make soft-money contributions. The large contributions enable donors to establish relationships, which increases the chances they will be successful with their public policy agendas. Compared to the amounts that companies spend as a whole, large political contributions are worthwhile because of the potential benefit to the companies' bottom line.

When organizations give greater amounts of money through soft-money contributions, they get better access to members. While hard-money contributions also provide some access, the larger soft-money contributions get them significantly greater access; and of course, soft-money contributions built around sporting events, such as the Super Bowl or the Kentucky Derby, where they might spend a week with the member, are even more useful. At events that contributors are entitled to attend as a result of their contributions, some contributors will subtly or not so subtly discuss a legislative issue in which they have an interest. Contributors also use events to establish relationships, and then take advantage of the access by later calling the member about a legislative issue or coming back and seeing the member in his or her office. Obviously from the member's perspective, it is hard to turn down a request for a meeting after you have just spent a weekend with a contributor whose company just gave a large contribution to your political party.

From the perspective of the donor, the difference between hard and soft money is just the amount of money that you are allowed to give. Once an organization's political action committee (PAC) has given the hard-money limit, it is simply a matter of how much more the organization wants to give. From a donor's perspective, what account the money goes into or how it is used is not important. When it actually comes time to make out the check, you just make it out to whatever account the party or member indicates. A member or an agent will raise the money and someone will eventually tell you whether the money should go to a soft-money leadership PAC, a national party committee, or a state party. Corporations and trade associations, including the ones I am familiar with, are not usually giving to help the Republican Party or the Democratic Party. The original purpose of allowing the national parties to have soft money was to let them raise money to be used on state elections and general party building. It would be the height of naivety to think that donors have motives consistent with that purpose. Donors to the national parties understand that if a federal officeholder is raising soft money—supposedly "nonfederal" money—they are raising it for federal uses, namely to help that member or other federal candidates in their elections. Many donors giving $100,000, $200,000, even $1 million, are doing so because it is a bigger favor than a smaller hard-money contribution would be. That donation helps a donor get close to the person who is making decisions that affect your company or your industry. That is the reason most economic interests give soft money—not because they want to help state candidates, and rarely because they want the party to succeed.

Even though soft-money contributions often go to political parties, the money is given so that the contributors can be close to, and recognized by, members, presidents, and administration officials. Members, not party staffers or party chairs, raise much of the large soft-money contributions. Party chairs do not have that much power because the Democratic National Committee (DNC) and the Republican National Committee (RNC) by themselves do not have power to do anything. People do not give to be close to the party chairs. The members of Congress and the president are the heart of the national parties. The elected officials are the ones who are really raising the money, either directly or through their agents.

The soft-money system has allowed big money from private interests to get into the federal election system. The system works in a very pernicious way that undermines public trust. As I mentioned in my earlier declaration, campaign finance reform was one of the issues that I handled while working for Senator Mitchell. The Democratic Senatorial Campaign Committee (DSCC) did not raise and spend soft money while Senator Mitchell was majority leader, because he thought it appeared improper. I have also seen the system at work through my job as a lobbyist over the last seven years. Although there are nominal limits on what individuals and PACs can contribute to federal candidates, that law has now become a fiction because of the soft-money contributions that candidates have been able to raise through their political parties. The general public does not even begin to understand the degree to which moneyed private interests are able to influence public policy through their campaign contributions. The effect of $15,000 or $20,000 contributions on some members that I discussed is even more true with respect to larger, $100,000 or $500,000, contributions. As I noted, based on human relationships, members are grateful to people who want to help them and naturally want to be responsive to them. When people have tried to help an elected representative in the more substantial ways permitted through soft-money contributions, a member is even more grateful to them, and naturally more responsive.

Corporate America Contributes
Soft Money under Pressure

GERALD GREENWALD

Gerald Greenwald is chairman emeritus of United Airlines, having served as chief executive officer and chairman from 1994 to 2000. He testified as a fact witness for the defense. Greenwald's statement addressed the pressure political parties and officeholders place on corporations to make large soft-money donations and on the consequences of not contributing. He argues that soft money is often given by corporations only under pressure and harms business as well as government.

The fact is that the people who raise large soft-money contributions from business corporations and labor unions are often sitting members of Congress that consider matters affecting the financial health or operations of the organizations being solicited. Often, the members who solicit large corporate contributions sit on committees that directly affect the corporation's business. Similarly, these members' actions affect issues of interest to labor unions. Congressional committees regularly consider matters that importantly affect both business and labor in regulated and unregulated industries—from tax legislation to trade legislation to industry deregulation to environmental legislation, to list just a few examples.

When sitting members solicit large corporate and union contributions, the leaders of these organizations feel intense pressure to contribute, because experience has taught that the consequences of failing to contribute (or failing to contribute enough) may be very negative. Business and labor leaders believe, based on their experience, that disappointed members and their party colleagues may shun or disfavor them because they have not contributed. Equally, these leaders fear that if they refuse to contribute (enough), competing interests that contribute generously will have an advantage in gaining access to and influencing key congressional leaders on matters of importance to the company or union.

The other side of the coin is that labor and business leaders are regularly advised—and their experience directly confirms—that organizations that make large soft-money donations to political parties do in fact get preferred access to government officials. Access runs the gamut from attendance at events where they have opportunities to present points of view informally to lawmakers to direct, private meetings in an official's office to discuss pending legislation or a government regulation that affects the company or union.

If an organization is solicited by a party official rather than an elected official, the effect is the same. Companies and unions know that party officials inform elected officials about who has given significant amounts; and party officials often promise access to elected officials to those who agree to contribute large amounts of corporate or union money.

In these ways, the soft-money loophole over the past two decades has created a deeply cynical environment of real and perceived corruption that traps American government, business, and labor unions.

This debilitating and demoralizing environment damages government and business alike. It goes without saying that maintaining governmental integrity is critically important to our democracy and our citizens' faith in their government. It is also important for Americans to have faith in the integrity of their business institutions and labor unions. The recent spate of deplorable corporate scandals has broadly demoralized America, and this is having widespread and adverse political and economic consequences. It is not good for America when American citizens believe their business leaders are corrupt, and one element of that regrettably widespread perception is the appearance that business buys government decisions by making large political contributions.

Public policy decisions should be made, and should appear to all to be made, on the basis of the public interest—not on which corporation or labor union can give the most money to the political party in power. Even the appearance of this type of corruption weakens public confidence in governmental as well as business and labor institutions.

Large Contributions Are Given
to Influence Legislation

ROBERT W. HICKMOTT

Robert W. Hickmott is senior vice president at a governmental affairs firm and has worked for the Democratic National Committee (DNC) and the Democratic Senatorial Campaign Committee (DSCC). Hickmott is a political contributor, as well as an adviser to other political contributors, and testified for the defense regarding fund-raising for the Democratic Party and his experience as a contributor and lobbyist. He testified that soft-money contributions are often tied to specific legislation.

When I was at the Democratic Senatorial Campaign Committee in 1991–92, the DSCC rarely raised or spent soft money, in fact, we frequently turned away offers of corporate money. Our legal counsel at the DSCC was very strict about what soft money could be used for, and there was also a sense among senators at that time that soft money was somehow tainted. The DSCC's aversion to soft money went back at least to 1985–86, when senator George Mitchell was chair of the DSCC. To the extent that the DSCC spent soft money in 1991–92, it was for infrastructure, convention expenses, and an occasional state party donation that the DSCC would make at the request of one of the other national party committees. I know that the DSCC's practice subsequently changed to both raise and spend soft money, and in my view that came about in part because the Democratic senators recognized that they were getting their clocks cleaned by the Republicans as a result of the soft money the Republicans were raising and spending.

I believe that parties can function effectively without soft money so long as they, and other players in the political process (such as groups that run "issue ads"), play by essentially the same set of rules. The DSCC rarely used soft money when I worked there, and we managed fine. The bottom line for the DSCC was to win Senate seats—and we were successful without using soft money.

As both a contributor to candidates and parties and a lobbyist who advises clients about political spending, I am personally aware of the fund-raising practices of federal candidates. Once you have helped a federal candidate by contributing hard money to a candidate's campaign, you are sometimes asked to do more for the candidate by making hard- and/or soft-money donations to the national party committees, the relevant state party (assuming it can accept corporate contributions), or an outside group planning on doing an independent expenditure or issue advertisement to help the candidate's campaign. These types of requests typically come from staff at the national party committees, the campaign staff of the candidate, the candidate's fund-raising staff, or former staff members of the candidate's congressional office, but they also sometimes comes from a member of Congress or his or her chief of staff (calling from somewhere other than a government office). Regardless of the precise person who makes the request, these solicitations almost always involve an incumbent member of Congress rather than a challenger. As a result, there are multiple avenues for a person or group with financial resources to assist a federal candidate financially in his or her election effort, with both hard and soft money.

I also know that corporations, labor unions, and individuals make soft-money contributions to national political parties and federal candidate political action committees, including joint fund-raising committees, to influence the legislative process for their business purposes. Soft-money contributions help donors influence the outcome of a race, curry favor with a specific candidate, curry favor with the congressional leadership, and curry favor with the chairs of the national party committees. Large soft-money donations are a way to build relationships and friendships and pursue the donor's business agendas. In fact, when one of my clients is going to make a donation to a federal candidate or party (hard or soft money), I advise them on the manner in which they should contribute. I tell them not to just send the check to the party committee, where it will be collected by a young staff member. Instead, I tell my clients that they should personally give the money to a member of Congress, who then can give the money to the party committee chair, who will in turn make sure that the check reaches the young staff member. That way, the donor, with one check, gets "chits" with a member of Congress and a party chair.

As a lobbyist and a contributor during a federal election year, I receive faxes, e-mails, and telephone calls frequently from members of Congress, fund-raising and campaign staff, party committees, and fellow lobbyists. The frequency of these requests increases as the general election draws nearer. Although many of these requests are for hard-money contributions, I sometimes also receive requests for soft money. The soft-money requests typically involve an event of some sort, such as the Warner/ Nickles Golf Tournament, where a soft-money contribution of $10,000 or more allows you to play golf with those senators and some of their

Republican colleagues. Another example is the Nantucket weekend organized by the DSCC—one of its premiere events. At the Nantucket weekend (which costs either $50,000 or $100,000), a donor can meet with a large number of Democratic senators in the course of one weekend. As the general election draws nearer, I also receive requests from the same types of people for soft money to fund issue ads or for get-out-the-vote efforts. As of August 2002, I was receiving at least twelve fund-raising requests per day, and including those requests addressed to my partners, these solicitations constitute about half of the total amount of phone calls and faxes our office receives.

I also have clients who seek advice about how to spend soft money. Typically, I look at their business interests, try to determine with which members they should maintain relationships, and then find out from the campaign staff of those members whether their candidate will take soft money. In some cases they do—through a state political party or leadership or joint fund-raising political committee—and in some cases they do not. It frequently is not particularly important to the donor precisely what the money is going to be used for—if a member of Congress or member of his or her campaign staff is telling you that he or she needs money for the state party, you assume the member is going to benefit.

Elected Officials Often Used to Obtain
Large Donations for the Parties

WADE RANDLETT

Wade Randlett is the chief executive officer of Dashboard Technology, an Internet technology consulting firm. Prior to Randlett's tenure with Dashboard, he served as a fund-raiser and political consultant in Northern California. He testifies on his experience raising and donating money to political parties, which included frequent requests from officeholders for donations. Randlett was a fact witness for the defense.

I have been involved in political fund-raising long enough to remember when soft money had little value to federal candidates. Ten years ago, a senator might call a potential donor and the donor would say something like, "I would love to write you a check, I'm a big fan of yours, but I'm federally maxed, so I can't do it. If you like, I could write a soft-money check to your state party." And the senator might say, "Don't bother. The soft money just doesn't do me any good."

However, in recent election cycles, *members* and national committees have asked soft-money donors to write soft-money checks to state and national parties in order to assist federal campaigns. Most soft-money donors do not ask and do not care why the money is going to a particular state party, a party with which they may have no connection. What matters is that the donor has done what the *member* asked.

Information about what soft-money donors have given travels among the members in different ways. Obviously, the member who solicited the money knows. Members also know who is involved with the various major donor events that they attend, such as retreats, meetings, and conference calls. And there is communication among members about who has made soft-money donations and at what level they have given, and this is widely known and understood by the members and their staffs.

As a donor with business goals, if you want to enhance your chances of getting your issues paid attention to and favorably reviewed by members of Congress, bipartisanship is the right way to go. Giving lots of soft money to both sides is the right way to go from the most pragmatic perspective.

Conversely, if you're giving a lot of soft money to one side, the other side knows. For many economically oriented donors, there is a risk in giving to only one side, because the other side may read through Federal

Election Commission (FEC) reports [that detail party donations] and have staff or a friendly lobbyist call and indicate that someone with interests before a certain committee has had their contributions to the other side noticed. They will get a message that basically asks: "Are you sure you want to be giving only to one side? Don't you want to have friends on both sides of the aisle?" If your interests are subject to anger from the other side of the aisle, you need to fear that you may suffer a penalty if you do not give. First of all, it is hard to get attention for your issue if you are not giving. Then, once you have decided to play the money game, you have to worry about being imbalanced, especially if there is bipartisan control or influence in Washington, which there usually is. In fact, during the 1990s it became more and more acceptable to call someone, saying you saw the donor gave to one candidate, so the donor should also give to the opponent. Referring to someone's financial activity in the political arena used to be clearly off limits, and now it is increasingly common.

Soft-money donors and fund-raisers definitely get a special level of access, visibility, and appreciation from members that is not available to smaller hard-money donors, much less the average person. Even someone who wrote twenty-five $1,000 hard-money checks but no soft money is going to get much less attention and appreciation than someone who wrote one large soft-money check.

The raising and spending of soft money in recent election cycles has distorted the federal political system and the commercial marketplace. Many soft-money donations are made in order to advance specific legislative agendas, and they do produce at least appreciation on the part of powerful federal officeholders. Based on my observations, much of the business community believes that the federal campaign financing system is broken and needs to be fixed. People in business look for a reasonable, rational system and a level playing field. The current soft-money-oriented system does not meet that standard. At the same time, many members of the business community recognize that if they want to influence what happens in Washington, they have to play the soft-money game. They are caught in an arms race that is accelerating, but many feel they cannot afford to leave or speak out against it.

Soft-money fund-raising also takes a lot less time and effort than hard-money fund-raising. Like anyone else, politicians have only twenty-four hours in a day. As it has become increasingly valuable for officeholders to spend time with people who are writing huge checks, they have allocated more of their time to that. They now have less time to devote to other things that are part of their jobs, such as talking to their constituents.

It would be absurd to claim that the soft-money ban will result in all the same soft-money donors banding together to finance independent expenditures and that all this money will still have the exact same bad effect it has today. Most of these donations are made because they are solicited. The number of people sitting around trying to figure out how to spend a million dollars in electoral politics, getting advice from interest group or national party committee staff on how to do it, is very, very small. The core transaction is an elected official talking to an individual who may write a soft-money check in order to receive positive attention for an issue. When you take that act out of the equation, a great deal of the inappropriate influence leaves the system.

Why I Participate in a Corrupt System

PETER L. BUTTENWIESER

Peter L. Buttenwieser is involved in philanthropy and is a top soft-money contributor to the Democratic Party and affiliated organizations. Buttenwieser was a fact witness for the defense and testified as to his experience. He discusses the excesses he has seen in previous cycles and his reasons for contributing to political parties. He also addresses why he resists asking for favors in exchange for his donations, and why he supports the soft-money ban.

Since the early 1990s, I have engaged in significant political activity, working with and financially supporting a variety of individuals and organizations. From the 1992 election cycle through the 2002 cycle, I have donated millions of dollars to Democratic candidates and political committees and progressive political organizations. All of these donations have been made from personal funds.

From the 1996 election cycle through the 2002 cycle, I estimate that I have donated over $2.8 million in nonfederal funds (soft money) to national committees of the Democratic Party, including over $1.2 million in the 2000 election cycle. Also from the 1996 election cycle through the current cycle, I estimate that my wife and I have contributed approximately $100,000 per cycle in federal funds (hard money) to federal candidate committees and other federal political committees not affiliated with political parties. During this same period I have also hosted many hard-money fund-raising events for federal candidates in Philadelphia.

At the national committee level, although I have given substantial amounts to the Democratic National Committee (DNC) and the Democratic Congressional Campaign Committee (DCCC), I have focused on the Democratic Senatorial Campaign Committee (DSCC). I have a special interest in the U.S. Senate because I believe having a high-quality Senate really does make a difference in a way the country works. I also have a particular interest in assisting female candidates, as I believe they confront barriers not faced by their male counterparts.

In the 2000 and 2002 election cycles, in addition to making what I call "straight" soft-money donations directed to the DSCC, I have donated soft money to the joint fund-raising committees of a number of U.S. Senate candidates whom I strongly support and who were or are in close races. I estimate that I donated approximately $250,000 in soft money to these joint fund-raising committees in the 2000 cycle, and over $250,000 in soft money in the 2002 cycle. In my experience, the joint fund-raising committees are typically formed by the Senate candidate's authorized committee and the DSCC. My soft-money donations to these joint committees generally occur in connection with requests from the Senate candidates for their campaigns. Sometimes I have given soft money to the joint committees in response to requests from the DSCC.

In the 2000 election cycle, I focused my joint fund-raising donations on the committees formed to assist several Senate campaigns. I believe I gave approximately $100,000 each to the joint fund-raising committees of Debbie Stabenow in Michigan and Governor Mel Carnahan (later Jean Carnahan) in Missouri. I also donated to a joint fund-raising committee to assist the campaign of Tom Carper in Delaware.

I took an active role in the 2000 Carnahan Senate campaign in Missouri. I attended a private meeting with Governor Carnahan and a group of Missouri supporters in early 2000. The meeting was about the importance to the campaign of raising $1 million (including the $100,000 from me) for the joint fund-raising committee in order to respond to attacks that were expected from Governor Carnahan's opponent. I was not intimately involved in how the money would be spent, but I had confidence that it would be spent appropriately to help with the campaign.

I also took an active role in the 2000 Stabenow Senate campaign in Michigan. In mid-2000, I met with Debbie Stabenow in Michigan and, as I recall, agreed with her campaign's finance committee that I would pledge $50,000 to her joint committee if they would raise $500,000 to match it by the end of the week. They succeeded in raising the money.

In the 2002 election cycle, I estimate that I assisted perhaps ten Democratic Senate candidates through soft-money donations to joint fund-raising committees. I donated $100,000 to Senator Carnahan's joint fund-raising committee, Missouri Senate 2002, and I believe $50,000 each to joint committees assisting Chellie Pingree in Maine, Jeanne Shaheen in New Hampshire, and Senator Robert Torricelli in New Jersey.

In the 2002 cycle, I also took an active role in more Senate campaigns than I did in the 2000 cycle. In addition to assisting Senator Carnahan's 2002 campaign, I worked intensively to help four challenger campaigns: the Pingree campaign in Maine, the Shaheen campaign in New Hampshire, the Pryor campaign in Arkansas, and the Bradbury campaign in Oregon. I attended meetings focused on the financial side of the campaign in each of those four states, and I donated soft money to each of the affiliated joint committees.

I attended a huge fund-raising dinner at the Art Center in Newark, New Jersey, to benefit Senator Torricelli's 2002 campaign. Senator Jon Corzine was the host, and former president Bill Clinton attended. I donated $50,000 to New Jersey Senate 2002, Senator Torricelli's joint committee, and I understand they raised about $3 million that night.

As someone who has given hard money and soft money and been intimately involved in fund-raising and campaigning for many years, I see little difference between hard money and soft money beyond the source and amount limitation on hard-money contributions. National and state political parties use soft money to influence federal elections.

I have also given a significant amount, perhaps half a million dollars, to state political parties and state candidates over the last few election cycles, including $100,000 to former DNC chair Ed Rendell in connection with the race for governor of Pennsylvania in 2002. Federal candidates have often asked me to donate to state parties rather than joint committees, when they feel that's where they need some extra help in their campaigns. I have given significant amounts to the state parties in South Dakota and North Dakota, because all the senators representing those states are good friends and I know that it is difficult to raise large sums in those states. The DSCC has also requested that I provide assistance to state parties.

In the 2000 election cycle, I gave a substantial amount of soft money to the Democratic coordinated campaign in Pennsylvania in order to assist former vice president Al Gore in the presidential race, principally because I was concerned that he might lose the state. I had confidence in this effort because although the money went to the state party, the coordinated campaign there was run by very able Gore people. I also helped this coordinated campaign with staffing, fund-raising, and ensuring a sufficient flow of money from the DNC.

I estimate that, over the last decade, I have given roughly $2 million to interest groups engaged in political activity, including nonprofit corporations. I believe that I have given over $1 million to EMILY's List from the 1996 election cycle through the 2002 cycle, and I have given far smaller amounts to the NARAL Pro-Choice America (NARAL), Public Campaign, and the Brady Campaign/Brady Center, on whose board I have served. I also give to groups that engage in grassroots voter education and get-out-the-vote activities, including the voter fund of the National Association for the Advancement of Colored People, the 21st Century Democrats, and the Southwest Voter Registration Education Project. I believe this kind of field work can have important effects on political campaigns.

I decide which of these groups to give to primarily on my own, though I have also discussed with DSCC personnel which groups are effective at grassroots activities.

I have been approached by interest groups, such as NARAL and the League of Conservation Voters, with appeals for large donations to be used for broadcast advertisements that will help federal candidates whom the groups know I support. Groups like these know of my interest in the Senate, and they can be opportunistic in saying things like, "We think we can get Bill Bradbury elected in Oregon," or in talking about how they are going to go in and really help Debbie Stabenow. Of course, this kind of approach could be very appealing to someone like me, who puts a lot of work into the campaigns of such candidates. However, I am wary of such candidate-specific appeals from interest groups, and in general I do not respond favorably.

In early 2002, I did donate $50,000 to one "527" organization [a political organization not registered with the Federal Election Commission and not subject to limitations], Daschle Democrats, which I understand ran broadcast ads in South Dakota supporting Senator Daschle in response to the intense attacks that had been made on him. I was willing to do this because I felt that the attacks were hurting Senator Daschle, and Senator Tim Johnson's reelection campaign as well.

I donate to political committees in order to help the campaigns of candidates who, if elected, will pursue progressive policies that are important to me. I think some other major donors share my motives. However, based on my experience, there are still other major donors who may care about electing candidates who will pursue progressive policies but who are also anxious to advance their own business agendas. I am fortunate not to have to carry that kind of baggage.

There is no question that those who, like me, make large soft-money donations receive special access to powerful federal officeholders on the basis of the donations. I am close to a number of senators and see them on a very consistent basis. I regard the former majority leader, Senator Daschle, as a close friend. I understand that the unusual access I have correlates to the millions of dollars I have given to political party committees, and I do not delude myself into feeling otherwise. Not many people can give soft money on that scale, and it naturally limits the number of those with that level of access.

I am aware that some soft-money donors, such as some corporations, give substantial amounts to both major political parties. Based on my observations, they typically do this because they have a business agenda

and they want to hedge their bets to ensure they get access to officeholders on the issues that are important to them. This occurs at the national
and state levels.

Business corporations are not the only ones who attempt to use access
derived from large soft-money donations. For example, on one occasion
Senator Joe Biden came and spoke to a nonprofit group with which I have
been involved to some extent. At this event, one thing Senator Biden said
to those in attendance was, basically, "One of the reasons it's easy to deal
with Peter Buttenwieser, and I'm happy to be here, is that he's one of the
few people in this process who never asks for anything." Roughly six
months later, this same group pressured me in a very blunt way to give
them the access to Senator Biden that would be needed to pursue an issue
in which they had an intense interest. I have no doubt that I could have
assisted this group, but I chose not to do so.

Events, meetings, and briefings held for soft-money donors provide
opportunities for the donors to hear speeches and engage in policy discussions with federal officeholders. There is also a certain amount of pol-
iticking and lobbying at these events. This is true particularly in the side
discussions, in which donors can approach officeholders and discuss their
issues. In my experience, DNC events have tended to be more scripted,
less intimate, and less attractive to me than DSCC gatherings, although
on several occasions I attended small, private DNC gatherings featuring
President Clinton speaking at length on issues like international finance,
which were fascinating. I tend to favor smaller events. Most donor events
are fairly structured, to include a lot of stroking to make you feel like
you're a "big deal" guy, and a pitch for money, unless it is a donor main-
tenance event, at which existing donors are merely wined and dined and
generally made to feel important. At national party donor events you can
often tell who is the largest donor, because that is typically the person who
sits next to the president.

I am briefed on campaign matters several times a year at the DSCC and
at the DCCC. I have also had perhaps thirty individual meetings with senators since the 1996 cycle, and I may see them on the campaign trail or
speak with them on the phone. This is how I have gotten to be friends
with a number of them.

During the 1996 election cycle, I came to feel that something was not
right in much of the high-level Democratic Party fund-raising that was
going on relevant to the presidential race. As a result, I made a conscious
decision to avoid certain kinds of major donor events and perks that I was
being offered and some people I knew were receiving, such as stays in the

Lincoln Bedroom, rides on Air Force One, and so forth. For instance, I decided not to go to the White House. This was before the press began to report on these things in any detail. My feeling of discomfort increased as the election neared and it became clear that the president was going to stay in power and that there was a lot he could do for many people.

One example of the problems related to this activity is a well-known incident from June 1996 involving me and Terry McAuliffe, who was at that time a high-level fund-raiser for the DNC, and who I think has done some terrific things. One day Terry called me and said that he knew I must be thinking about doing something more for the DNC before the end of the year. He knew I did not care for big events, but he said there was to be an intimate luncheon with the president for eight people at the White House the following week. Terry basically told me that if I gave $50,000 by the end of the year, he could get me into that lunch. I was offended. I declined, and not long afterwards I wrote him a letter saying I thought this was a quid pro quo thing and that I really hated that kind of thing.

In about March 1996, this incident involving Terry and me hit the press in Philadelphia and became well known. When it did, Terry said that my account was not accurate, but the press investigation confirmed much of it. As it happens, two of the people who did attend this White House luncheon were representatives from an Indian tribe in Oklahoma, who I understand were seeking executive action on some economic issue that was important to the tribe. These representatives had apparently been told that if the tribe donated $100,000, they would have the chance to make their case to the president at this luncheon, which they did. However, I gather that although they managed to have, in a sense, a quid pro quo lunch, they did not ultimately get what they wanted. When this became public, I believe also around March 1997, it created another scandal. I was even more glad that I had not attended the luncheon. I took the trouble to pursue this issue, and to deal with the press, because I felt that this was just the kind of excess that was hurting our political system during that time period and that it was a relatively small example of a much larger problem.

Large soft-money donations can create at least the appearance of influence on federal policymaking, and in my view, can actually influence federal policy. I had particular concerns about soft-money-based influence in the mid-1990s in connection with fund-raising related to the presidential campaign. But there have also been more recent examples. One was the situation involving the pardon of Marc Rich in early 2001, which in my view was a glaring case of giving soft money, getting access, and having influence. Of course, this problem exists in the Republican Party as well as the Democratic Party, and another recent example is the access and apparent influence of Kenneth Lay and Enron on energy issues.

As for myself, by having access but not asking for anything, I feel that I have been able to have an influence in a general and constructive way. Although I believe I could have influenced federal officeholders in ways that could have specifically benefited me or my family, I have resisted doing so.

In my view, the kind of soft-money fund-raising described above harms the nation's political system because it simply takes so much of our federal officeholders' time. Many of the members of Congress I know are required to raise primarily soft money with the great majority of their free time, particularly Senator Daschle. Sometimes campaign committee leaders are on the road almost every weekend, hosting events for major donors in different parts of the nation, and I know of one who I believe absolutely exhausted himself in this process.

I strongly support limitations on the use of soft money to influence federal elections, such as the ban on soft-money raising and spending by the national party committees. This is so even though I have been, in a sense, a beneficiary of the special access that large soft-money donations can purchase. I feel that if the biggest donations are removed from the system, the worst kind of special access and potential for improper influence will decrease significantly.

How My Soft-Money Contributions Have Helped Elect Good Federal Candidates

STEVEN T. KIRSCH

Steven T. Kirsch is the chief executive officer of Propel Software Corporation. Mr. Kirsch has also been deeply involved in philanthropic and political endeavors and is a major soft-money contributor to the Democratic national party committees and federal candidates. He testified for the defense regarding his experience as a major donor.

In the 2000 election cycle, I made over $4 million in political donations. This included substantial soft- and hard-money contributions to the Democratic National Committee. It also included over $2 million in soft-money donations to Democratic state party committees, including six-figure donations to the Michigan, Missouri, New Mexico, Pennsylvania, Nevada, Florida, and Iowa Democratic parties. In addition, I made large donations to interest groups, including six-figure donations to NARAL Pro-Choice America, People for the American Way, and Campaign for a Progressive Future. I also made large independent expenditures for print and Internet banner ads in key swing states, opposing the election of George W. Bush.

The national party committees and the federal candidates who raise money for them prefer that major donors first "max out" in hard-money contributions the legal limits before making soft-money donations. For example, once a federal candidate understands that a donor has maxed out, there will often be a request that the donor make soft-money donations to a national party committee, as has been suggested when I have been in that situation. The committee receiving such a soft-money donation understands that it has been raised by or for a particular federal candidate, and this affects how much the committee spends on behalf of that candidate. I have discussed with national party committees the spending of such soft money to benefit federal candidates.

In the 2000 election cycle, I considered information from different sources in order to determine how best to spend money to promote the election of then vice president Al Gore. I learned that there were certain key swing states where money could make a big difference, states where you could actually help change the outcome. The national Democratic Party played an important role in my decision to donate soft money to state parties in this cycle, recommending that I donate funds to specific state parties just before the election. They said, essentially, if you want to help us out with the presidential election, these particular state parties are hurting, they need money for get-out-the-vote and other last-minute campaign activities.

The national Democratic Party also played an important role in my decisions to donate soft money to certain interest groups in the 2000 election. The party recommended that I donate to certain groups that were running effective ads in the effort to elect Vice President Gore, such as NARAL. The assumption was that the funds would be used for television ads or some other activity that would make a difference in the presidential election. I did not know specifically how the money would be spent, but it was pretty clear that these groups wanted Bush to be defeated. So I expected that they would not pull punches in using the money.

Today, soft-money donors can get special access and influence public policy on the basis of their donations. I feel that their donations can help them obtain policy results that are not in the best interests of the nation. Lawmakers who are supposed to represent the long-term interests of their constituents often act in a manner that is contrary to those interests, and a big part of that is the influence obtained by special interests through large soft-money donations.

Policy discussion with federal officials occurs at major donor events sponsored by political parties. I have attended many such events. They typically involve speeches, question and answer sessions, and group policy discussions, but there is also time to talk to members individually about substantive issues. For example, at a recent event I was able to speak with a senator representing a state other than California, and we had a short conversation about how our respective staffers were working together on a particular issue.

I receive no financial benefit from my donations. Propel is an Internet startup company that does not need special policy favors, but even if the company could benefit from favors, I would never ask for such favors on its behalf. I do know members of Congress and talk with them about policy issues, but my interest is in broad national issues such as education, energy policy, fuel cell vehicles, and other matters that I believe are important to the overall well-being of the nation and the economy, issues in which I have no particular financial interest.

My purpose in making political donations is to counter the impact of tens of millions of dollars that are funneled into conservative campaigns and causes. In essence, I try to level the playing field to allow progressive candidates and causes to have their voices heard.

How the Senate Was Corrupted by Soft Money

PAUL SIMON

*Paul Simon was a U.S. senator from Illinois from 1985 to 1997 and repre-
sented the Twenty-Fourth Congressional District of Illinois from 1975 to
1985. Simon testified as a defense fact witness as to his view of the soft-money
system and the access and favors given to large contributors. He provides a
first-hand insider's look at corruption in the U.S. Senate.*

It is not unusual for large contributors to seek legislative favors in
exchange for their contributions. A good example of that which stands out
in my mind because it was so stark and recent occurred on the next-to-last
day of the 1995–96 legislative session. Federal Express wanted to amend
a bill being considered by a conference committee to shift coverage of
their truck drivers from the National Labor Relations Act to the Railway
Act, which includes airlines, pilots, and railroads. This was clearly of benefit to Federal Express, which, according to published reports, had contributed $1.4 million in the last two-year cycle to incumbent members of
Congress and almost $1 million in soft money to the political parties.

I opposed this in the Democratic Caucus and argued that even if it was
good legislation, it should not be approved without holding a hearing, and
that we should not cave in to special interests. One of my senior colleagues
got up and said, "I'm tired of Paul always talking about special interests;
we've got to pay attention to who is buttering our bread." I will never forget that. This was a clear example of donors getting their way not on the
merits of the legislation, but just because they had been big contributors.
I do not think there is any question that this is the reason it passed.

Giving to party committees also helps a donor gain access to members.
While I realize some argue donors do not buy favors, they buy access, that
access is the abuse and it affects all of us. If I got to a Chicago hotel at mid-
night, when I was in the Senate, and there were twenty phone calls waiting for me, nineteen of them names I did not recognize and the twentieth
someone I recognized as a $1,000 donor to my campaigns, that is the one
person I would call. You feel a sense of gratitude for their support. This is
even more true with the prevalence of much larger donations, even if those

donations go to party committees. Because few people can afford to give over $20,000 or $25,000 to a party committee, the people who can will receive substantially better access to elected federal leaders than people who can only afford smaller contributions or cannot afford to make any contributions. When you increase the amount that people are allowed to give, or let people give without limit to the parties, you increase the danger of unfair access. People who are unemployed or cannot pay their hospital bills do not have the same access.

The fact that big donors have access gives them a huge leg up in the process. In a very real sense, we are going through the old fight between Thomas Jefferson and Alexander Hamilton: should propertied interests have preference in what goes on in government? And our answer, with our present system of financing campaigns, is yes, people with money are going to be given greater influence because their names are going to be recognized. They are going to have greater access than those who did not contribute. The soft-money system is the most egregious part of the abuse of political contributions resulting in preferred access.

Consequences of Members Soliciting Soft Money

Warren Rudman

Warren Rudman was a U.S. senator for New Hampshire from 1980 to 1992. Rudman testified for the defense as to his view of the corrupting role of money in politics. He provides a realist's inside perspective on the corrupting role of large political contributions to party committees.

No one should have any idyllic illusions about the role of money in politics. By and large, the business world, including corporations and unions, gives money to political parties for a combination of two reasons: they believe that large contributions to a party (or in some cases, to both major parties) will enable them to gain privileged access to and special influence over elected and appointed government officials so they can affect government decisions in Washington that affect their interests; and they believe that if they decline solicitations for such contributions, elected and appointed officials will ignore their views, or worse, that competing business interests who do make large contributions to the party in question will have an advantage in influencing legislation or other government decisions. The same is true in the preponderance of cases where wealthy individuals give $50,000, $100,000, $250,000, or even more to political parties in soft-money donations.

Nor should anyone have illusions about the solicitation side of the process. Much of the soft money raised for political parties is raised by elected officials—sitting members of the Senate and the House of Representatives. For example, the members of the National Republican Senatorial Committee (NRSC)—as well as the members of the Democratic Senatorial Campaign Committee (DSCC)—who raise large amounts of money are all sitting senators. These and other elected officials solicit large sums of money from businesses, unions, and wealthy individuals who have legislative matters pending before the Senate and the House. And make no mistake about it, elected officials who raise money for their party committees know exactly why most corporations, unions, and wealthy individuals contribute large sums of money to the party: they know it is exactly for the reasons outlined in the previous paragraph.

Special interests that give large amounts of soft money to political parties do in fact achieve their objectives. They do get special access. Sitting members have limited amounts of time, but they make time available in their schedules to meet with representatives of business and unions and wealthy individuals who give large sums to their parties. These are not idle chit-chats about the philosophy of democracy. In these meetings these special interests, often accompanied by lobbyists, press elected officials—senators who either raised money from the special interest in question or who benefit directly or indirectly from their contributions to the senator's party—to adopt their position on a matter of interest to them. Senators are pressed by their benefactors to introduce legislation, to amend legislation, to block legislation, and to vote on legislation in a certain way. No one says, "We gave money so you should do this to help us." No one needs to say it—it is perfectly understood by all participants in every such meeting.

Individuals on both sides of the table recognize that larger donations effectively "purchase" greater benefits for donors. Larger donors receive greater access to elected officials. Some large donors will ask for help with personal causes, such as immigration matters, tax reform, or political appointments. Others attend meetings with elected officials in order to voice their company's or industry's concerns with particular legislation and to affect the outcome of the legislation. These are not the requests or expectations of an average taxpayer. Elected officials may not intend to be affected by such access, but the fact is that they receive a disproportionate amount of input and advice from larger, more wealthy contributors. This can skew their judgment. Equally important, the assumption that more money buys more influence gravely affects the public perception of the political process.

I understand that those who opposed passage of the Bipartisan Campaign Reform Act, and now challenge its constitutionality in court, dare elected officials to point to specific instances of quid pro quo corruption. I think this misses the point altogether. What I described in the preceding paragraphs is inherently, endemically, and hopelessly corrupting. You can't swim in the ocean without getting wet; you can't be part of this system without getting dirty.

I understand that some people say that contributions to political parties from corporations, unions, and wealthy individuals of $50,000 or more are not inherently corrupting because they are not given directly to a candidate's campaign committee. This is utter nonsense. The party's involvement does not sterilize the system. Elected officials often raise this money for their parties, sometimes pursuant to fund-raising goals party leaders set for them. When party officials raise the money, they offer access to elected officials in return. Elected officials know exactly who the big party contributors are. The parties use soft money to help federal candidates get elected by running so-called issue ads funded with soft money in closely contested federal races. The parties also help federal candidates get elected in other ways.

A Cosponsor's Perspective: Why I Don't Raise Soft Money for the Party

CHRISTOPHER SHAYS

Christopher Shays is a member of the U.S. House of Representatives for the Fourth Congressional District of Connecticut. Shays was a principal cosponsor of the Bipartisan Campaign Reform Act (BCRA) with Rep. Marty Meehan (D-Mass.) and in McConnell v. FEC *he testified as to his view of the corrupting effects of soft money on the political process. He details the adverse ways soft money affects the workings of the House of Representatives.*

Part of my motivation for reforming our campaign finance system came from responses by my constituents to surveys my congressional office sent out in 1997 and in 1999. The results of both surveys indicated that over 82 percent of my constituents believe that our "democracy is threatened by the influence of unlimited campaign contributions by individuals, corporations, labor unions, and other interest groups." I agree wholeheartedly.

My personal experience includes instances when procedural maneuvers were used to prevent votes on legislative issues because of the special interests of major soft-money donors and their influence over the national political parties and congressional campaign committees. I believe, based on my time in the House, that the legislative process is skewed and influenced by the desires of soft-money donors to the national political parties and congressional campaign committees.

Soft-money donations, particularly corporate and union donations, buy access and thereby make it easier for large donors to get their points across to influential members of Congress. The donors of large amounts of soft money to the national parties are well known to the leadership and to many other members of Congress. The access to elected officials that large donors receive goes far beyond an average citizen's opportunity to be heard.

The large soft-money contributions most members of Congress raise to meet their committee chairmanship or ranking member obligations come from the corporations and unions that are regulated by those very committees. This is one of the reasons that I do not raise soft money, although I do engage in raising hard money for my party to fulfill my duties as a party member. Not only do I believe that corporate and union money is not appropriate under 1907 and 1947 legislation, I believe that the process of asking for large amounts of soft money from entities Congress regulates leads to an obvious conflict of interest and the appearance of corruption.

Like my constituents, I strongly feel that soft money has had a detrimental effect on our democracy and on the health of political parties. When I was first a candidate for federal office in the late 1980s, I understood the strength of the Republican Party to be in its grassroots efforts, which were designed to raise smaller contributions and mobilize volunteer efforts. I believe that those kinds of activities are good for the parties and for our democracy in a way that raising funds from corporations, unions, and wealthy individuals could never be. Although opponents of the reform act assert that it will cause damage to the political parties, I personally believe that the parties were stronger and more vital when I first ran for Congress, in 1987. The rise of soft money since 1987 has made the parties dependent on soft-money donations and made them dangerously weak.

Congress Is Mired in Corrupt Soft Money

JOHN MCCAIN

John S. McCain has been a U.S. senator from Arizona since 1986. Prior to joining the Senate, he was a U.S representative for four years. McCain is a defendant in this case. He testified as to his view of the corrupting influence of soft money in the Senate and the special access and favors given to large soft-money donors. He cites specific instances where soft money changed the course of legislation.

Opponents of reform frequently ask reform proponents to cite examples of "quid pro quo" corruption. I believe, based on my experience, that elected officials do act in particular ways to assist large soft-money donors and that this skews and shapes the legislative process. As Representative Eric Fingerhut has noted: "The public will often look for the grand-slam example of the influence of these interests. But rarely will you find it. But you can find a million singles . . . regulatory change, banking committee legislation (to cite a committee that I served on). . . . Think of the committee and you can think of the interest group or the company that will have an interest. . . ."[1] This statement accurately reflects my experience.

At a minimum, large soft-money donations purchase an opportunity for the donors to make their case to elected officials, including the president and congressional leaders, in a way average citizens cannot. Many legislators have been in situations where they would rather fit in an appointment with a soft-money contributor than risk losing his or her donation to the party. Legislators of both parties often know who the party's large soft-money contributors are, particularly those legislators who have solicited soft money. Members of Congress interact with donors at frequent fund-raising dinners, weekend retreats, cocktail parties, and briefing sessions held exclusively for large donors to the party. Donors or their lobbyists often inform a particular senator that they have made a large donation. When someone makes a significant soft-money donation as a result of a member's solicitation and then calls the member a month later and wants to meet, it is very difficult to say no, and few do say no.

The parties encourage members of Congress to raise large amounts of soft money to benefit their own and others' reelection. At one recent caucus meeting, a member of Congress was praised for raising $1.3 million for the party. James Greenwood, a Republican congressman from Pennsylvania, recently told the *New York Times* that House leaders consider soft-money fund-raising prowess in assigning chairmanships and other sought-after jobs. He stated, "I cringe at the notion that the would-be chairs of these committees are engaging in a mad dash to gather as much soft money as possible, then thinking about the potential obligations incurred by asking for and receiving these six-plus-figure contributions from the very entities being regulated by these committees." I share Greenwood's concerns. Congressional leaders also use soft money to enforce party discipline and loyalty to their views. At times, when members seek to support legislation their congressional leaders oppose, they are threatened with the prospect that their leaders will withhold soft money being spent on their behalf.

In June 1998 it was widely reported that during the Senate's consideration of a bill entitled the National Tobacco Policy and Youth Smoking Reduction Act (S. 1415), U.S. Senator Mitch McConnell, then head of the National Republican Senatorial Committee (NRSC), talked at a Republican senators' policy lunch about political advertising by major tobacco manufacturers. In a complaint it filed on June 19, 1998, with the Federal Election Commission, the Campaign for Tobacco-Free Kids characterized Senator McConnell's communications as follows: "Based upon reports that have been widely published in the news media, only hours before Republican Senators were due to vote for or against cloture on S. 1415, Senator Mitch McConnell informed his colleagues in a closed door meeting that if they voted to kill the tobacco bill, the major tobacco manufacturers were promising to mount a television ad campaign to support those who voted against the bill."[2] I was present at the meeting and this is an accurate report of what Senator McConnell said. This episode graphically indicates that corporate soft money is widely used to influence legislative votes.

Several years ago, Congress passed legislation purportedly deregulating the telecommunications industry in order to encourage competition and lower costs to the consumers. The Senate Commerce Committee, on which I serve, held hearings on the issue. Every industry that would be affected was heard from, and while their interests varied, they had two things in common: first, they hoped to gain entry into their competitors' business while keeping competitors out of theirs; and second, they were generous donors to members of the committee and to the political parties, having given tens of millions of hard- and soft-money contributions during the time the bill was being developed. During consideration of the bill in the committee, on the Senate floor, and in the conference committee, members of Congress who were involved in crafting the legislation were inundated with requests for meetings by soft-money contributors—and many members met with these contributors. While the halls and offices of Congress were overrun with representatives of telecommunications interests that had contributed soft money, the public interest had few lobbyists and no campaign contributions to protect it. The legislation that was finally adopted by Congress reflected the effects of soft-money contributions on the political process. The process was essentially hijacked by large soft-money contributors and their lobbyists. The legislation, which dealt with issues of interest to big-money donors, was poorly conceived and filled with internal inconsistencies designed to appease these competing donors rather than to serve the public interest. Regardless of whether the interested donors received a quid pro quo for their donation, the entire process was skewed by these large contributions and there was clearly an appearance of improper influence.

The recent debate over the expensing of stock options provides another example. When the Senate recently considered the Sarbanes-Oxley corporate governance bill, I attempted to modify the bill to require companies to account for stock options by expensing them on their income statements—a proposal that has considerable support among preeminent economists and businessmen, including Alan Greenspan and Warren Buffett. High-tech executives who have donated generously to both the Democratic and Republican parties in recent years opposed the expensing proposal, and it was reported that it was they who succeeded in defeating it. According to newspaper accounts, Silicon Valley venture capitalist John Doerr, who has given $619,000 to the Democratic Party since 1999, spoke by phone to the Senate Democratic leadership and urged them to oppose my stock options proposal. The Senate Democratic leadership then used a parliamentary procedural device to block a vote on it. Again, the legislative process was, or at least appeared to be, adversely and unfairly influenced by large soft-money contributions, demonstrating that large contributors often influence or are perceived to influence not only what goes into a bill, but also what stays out.

In yet another example from this past year, a bill recently passed by the Senate to get generic drugs to market faster stalled in the House, reportedly because of pressure exercised by the White House and the Republican House leadership. According to the Congressional Budget Office, the bill could save consumers about $60 billion over the next ten years. Not surprisingly, the pharmaceutical industry—which opposes the bill—has reportedly vastly increased its campaign contributions in order to stall the legislation's passage. While the bill was pending, the NRSC and the

National Republican Congressional Committee (NRCC) held a large gala fundraiser to raise almost $30 million in largely soft-money contributions, a substantial portion from pharmaceutical companies. According to newspaper reports, among the largest contributors to the gala were Glaxo-SmithKline ($250,000), PhRMA ($250,000), Pfizer ($100,000), Eli Lilly ($50,000), Bayer ($50,000), and Merck ($50,000). While their large and timely contributions do not prove a quid prod quo, once again, the appearance that large soft-money contributors have disproportionate influence is overwhelming.

NOTES

1. Martin Schram, *Speaking Freely* (Washington, D.C.: Center for Responsive Politics 1995), p. 93.

2. The Campaign for Tobacco-Free Kids' complaint and accompanying press release are available at www.commondreams.org/pressreleases/June98/06298c.htm.

Parties Support Members Who Fund-Raise

DALE BUMPERS

Dale Bumpers was a U.S. senator from Arkansas from 1975 to 1999. Prior to that, he was the governor of Arkansas. Bumpers testified for the defense that members of Congress expect party money they raise to be spent on their own reelection campaigns, thereby tying "nonfederal" donations to specific federal elections.

Members who raise money for the Democratic Senatorial Campaign Committee (DSCC) expect some of the money to come directly back to them. Part of this unwritten but not unspoken rule is that if you do not raise a certain amount of money for the DSCC, you are not going to get any back. The DSCC does not give a candidate the maximum allowed unless he or she has raised at least a certain amount for the DSCC. The last time I ran, I remember that the DSCC promised to give every candidate a minimal amount of money regardless of whether he or she did any fund-raising for the DSCC. To get more than the minimum, however, you had to raise money for the DSCC. For example, if I had helped the DSCC raise the maximum amount it could legally expend on my behalf, I certainly would have expected the maximum to come back to me.

For members, there would not be any real difference if the funds they solicited were for themselves, for the Democratic National Committee, or the DSCC, or if they were hard- or soft-money donations. Members and donors understand that donations to the party committees help members.

Soft money gives big corporations and the very wealthy an inordinate advantage over others in the legislative process. If these corporations or individuals have given $100,000 to either or both parties, their chances of securing a change in legislation in Congress is exponentially increased. Often, donors seek legislative changes so that they or their business can reap large financial gains.

Corruption Is Not an Issue in American Politics

MITCH MCCONNELL

Mitch McConnell has been a U.S. senator for the Commonwealth of Kentucky since 1984. In his testimony he addresses his experience as a party fundraiser at the local, state, and national levels. In this excerpt of his declaration, McConnell states that there is no appearance of corruption in politics. He asserts that he has never known a member of Congress to have altered a vote because of a contribution and that he is generally unaware of the contributions made by individuals with whom he meets.

During my eighteen years in the U.S. Senate, I have met thousands of Americans with whom I have shaken hands, posed for photographs, answered questions, and discussed legislative issues. The overwhelming majority of these meetings have been with people who are not contributors to the Republican Party at the national, state, or local levels. In fact, I am typically unaware of the contribution history of individuals with whom I meet. Additionally, I have fewer meetings with soft-money contributors to the Republican Party than meetings with noncontributors, and these meetings are typically larger and less conducive to a discussion of legislative issues than most of my meetings in a given week.

During my eighteen years in the U.S. Senate, I have never witnessed any colleague who changed his vote or took any official action as a result of either a federal contribution or a nonfederal donation to a political party at the national, state, or local levels.

Parties Undermined by Soft Money

DONALD FOWLER

Donald Fowler served as chairman of the Democratic National Committee (DNC) from 1995 to 1997. Prior to that, he served as chairman of the South Carolina Democratic Party. Fowler testified for the defense as to his fundraising responsibilities at the DNC and on his view of the corrupting effects of large soft-money contributions and his belief that contributions should be limited to a modest amount. He believes that soft money can harm political parties and that it is spent by state parties to influence federal elections.

Party and government officials participate in raising large contributions from interests that have matters pending before the executive offices, the Congress, and other government agencies. Party officials, who are not themselves elected officials, offer to large-money donors opportunities to meet with senior government officials. Donors use these opportunities— White House and congressional meetings—to press their views on matters pending before the government. This process undermines our democratic process and creates a lack of confidence in its fairness on the part of average citizens.

I do not fault party officials for playing this role, so long as it is legal. Indeed, I believe that party officials have a responsibility to provide linkage between party members, the people, and their government. Party officials should do this for small and large contributors and those who do not contribute at all. As long as the system permits big-money contributors, however, they will inevitably have a disproportionate advantage. I recognize this as a fact. The solution is to change the party and campaign finance system to eliminate, or at least reduce, the extra influence of contributors of large sums of money. I do believe and insist, however, that party officials have a duty and responsibility to provide linkage between the people and the government.

Soft money does not necessarily strengthen political parties. Both major parties use aggressive techniques in raising large sums of money because they feel that they are locked in an "arms race" with one another. Neither believes it can afford to fall behind the other, for fear of being outspent and losing key federal and state elections. This intense focus on raising larger and larger amounts from relatively few special interest sources does not make for stronger or better parties. This is particularly true for Democrats, because we are the party of average Americans, while most wealthy individuals and special interest groups tend to favor Republican politicians. Raising more money in smaller amounts from a larger number of people would certainly strengthen the Democratic Party by providing us with a stronger base of active citizens.

National parties can perform important functions without large soft- or hard-money contributors. Large soft-money contributions are a relatively recent phenomenon, yet the parties were vibrant, functional, and effective prior to the advent of gross soft-money contributions. They can continue to be effective without soft money.

As noted, I served as chairman of the South Carolina Democratic Party. Based on that experience, I know firsthand that various activities, such as get-out-the-vote campaigns, voter identification efforts, voter registration drives, and advertisements that mention federal as well as state candidates, have the effect of promoting candidates for federal office as well as candidates for state office. Soft money mixed with hard money gives parties expanded capabilities. Eliminating soft money, however, does not mean that these joint efforts will have to be eliminated. They will have to be done more efficiently with lower overall expenditures with the assistance of local, grassroots volunteers.

In conclusion, contributions of large sums of money to parties and campaigns undermine the integrity of the political process, create inequities in the system, and produce a privileged class of political actors. Sound public policy dictates that these large contributions be eliminated from the American political system.

Parties Weakened by Appearance of Corruption

WILLIAM E. BROCK

William E. Brock was a U.S. senator from Tennessee from 1971 to 1976 and represented the Third Congressional District of Tennessee from 1963 to 1970. He also served as chairman of the Republican National Committee (RNC) from 1977 to 1981. Brock testified as a fact witness for the defense on his view of the corrupting influence of soft money on the political process and on the negative impact soft money has on the system. He believes the Republican Party, and the entire political process, has been harmed by large soft-money donations.

In 1994 I ran for the Senate in Maryland. One conclusion drawn from this experience was that the enormous growth of soft money in the past decade had allowed both parties to substitute those funds for the more arduous task of grassroots organizing, thereby inflating costs and devaluing personal participation. Political parties, the essential "connection" between citizens and their government, were weakened. In effect the parties increasingly became conduits for single-interest influence rather than for the development of broadly based representative government.

Large contributions—of $50,000, of $100,000, of $250,000—made to political parties by corporations, labor unions, and wealthy individuals have an enormously negative impact in at least the two following ways: First, these contributions compromise our elected officials. When elected officials solicit these contributions from interests, who almost always have matters pending before the Congress, these elected officials become at least psychologically beholden to those who contribute. It is inevitable and unavoidable. The contributors, for their part, feel they have a "call" on these officials. Corporations, unions, and wealthy individuals give these large amounts of money to political parties so they can improve their access to and influence over elected party members. Elected officials who raise soft money know this.

Second, the appearance of corruption is corrosive and is undermining our democracy. The reliance of the major parties on large soft-money donations does not in fact strengthen the parties, it weakens them. The focus on raising and spending soft money to affect federal elections divorces both the national and the state parties from their roots. The money by and large is not used for "party building." To the contrary, the parties by and large use the money to help elect federal candidates—in the presidential campaigns and in close Senate and House elections. Far from reinvigorating the parties, soft money has simply strengthened certain candidates and a few large donors, while distracting parties from traditional and important grassroots work.

I warmly agree with those who say that political parties perform extremely important functions in our democracy. Based on my experience, however, I disagree with those who say soft money is necessary to build parties. Parties ably performed their unique functions in our political system before they became awash in soft money. And they can again perform those functions—indeed, they can perform them better and with more integrity—without reliance on soft money.

It does no good to close the soft-money loophole at the national level but then allow state and local parties to use money from corporations, unions, and wealthy individuals in ways that affect federal elections. State and local parties use soft money to help elect federal candidates both by organizing voter registration and get-out-the-vote drives that help candidates at all levels of the ticket, and by using soft and hard money to run "issue ads" that affect federal elections. Therefore, for soft-money reforms to be truly effective, it is vitally important to require the use of hard money at the state level to pay for activities that affect federal elections.